Hotels and Highways

Stanford Studies in Middle Eastern and Islamic Societies and Cultures

Hotels and Highways

The Construction of Modernization Theory in Cold War Turkey

Begüm Adalet

Stanford University Press

Stanford, California

Stanford University Press
Stanford, California

Printed in the United States of America on acid-free, archival-quality paper

Library of Congress Cataloging-in-Publication Data

Names: Adalet, Begüm, author.
Title: Hotels and highways : the construction of modernization theory in Cold War Turkey /Adalet, Begüm.
Description: Stanford, California : Stanford University Press, 2018. | Series: Stanford studies in Middle Eastern and Islamic societies and cultures | Includes bibliographical references and index.
Identifiers: LCCN 2017053164 (print) | LCCN 2017058123 (ebook) | ISBN 9781503605558 (e-book) | ISBN 9781503604292 (cloth : alk. paper) | ISBN 9781503605541 (pbk. : alk. paper)
Subjects: LCSH: Economic development—Turkey—History—20th century. | Economic assistance, American—Turkey—History—20th century. | Turkey—Economic conditions—20th century. | Social change—Turkey—History—20th century. | Turkey—Relations—United States. | United States—Relations—Turkey. | Social sciences—United States—Philosophy—History—20th century.
Classification: LCC HC492 (ebook) | LCC HC492 .A354 2018 (print) | DDC 338.9561—dc23
LC record available at https://lccn.loc.gov/2017053164

Cover design: Preston Thomas
Cover photo: Intercity bus. Courtesy of the Archives of the General Directorate of Highways, Ankara, Turkey.
Typeset by Motto Publishing Services in 11/13.5 Adobe Garamond Pro

For my parents,
Melike and Çetin

Contents

Acknowledgments

THIS IS A BOOK about the construction of political theories in material spaces and particular encounters. Its ideas and concepts were also formed in specific sites and in conversation with many friends, colleagues, and interlocutors, all of whom I owe a debt of gratitude.

I want to begin by thanking three people whose advice and guidance were essential for the development of this project as well as for my own intellectual interests: Anne Norton, who has always been supportive and encouraging; Tim Mitchell, whose suggestions have been indispensable for framing the book; and Bob Vitalis, who is an intellectual inspiration and possibly the most generous person I know.

The research for this project was funded by the School of Arts and Sciences and the Political Science Department at the University of Pennsylvania as well as by the Mellon/ACLS Dissertation Completion Fellowship. I would like to thank the staff at the National Archives at College Park, the Seeley G. Mudd Manuscript Library at Princeton University, the Institute Archives and Special Collections at MIT, the Rare Book and Manuscript Library and the Avery Architectural and Fine Arts Library at Columbia University, the Grand National Assembly Archives and the National Library of Turkey in Ankara, and the Beyazıt State Library in Istanbul. I am especially grateful to Gülçin Manka and Figen Aydoğdu at the General Directorate of Highways in Ankara, Mark Young at the Hospitality Industry Archives in Houston, and, above all, Marina Rustow, who kindly put me in touch with Margrit Wreschner-Rustow, my gracious host in New York City. During these research trips, I also benefited from the generosity of Stella Kyriakopoulos, Sonal Shah, and Julian di Giovanni.

I had the opportunity to present parts of my research at conferences at the University of Chicago and Columbia University as well as at the Political Theory Workshop at Cornell University and the annual meetings of the Social Science History Association, the Middle East Studies Association, and the Western Political Science Association. During these conferences, I received excellent feedback from Evren Savcı, Emmanuelle Saada, Selim Karlıtekin, Timothy Vasko, Jill Frank, Alex Livingston, Nazlı Konya, Tom Pepinsky, Vijay Phulwani, Mehmet Ekinci, Onur Özgöde, and Sarah el-Kazaz. At the University of Pennsylvania, I also benefited from conversations with Jon Argaman, Osman Balkan, Guzman Castro, Willie Gin, Jeff Green, Ian Hartshorn, Nancy Hirschmann, Murad Idris, Shehab Ismail, Aniruddha Jairam, Matt Levendusky, Ian Lustick, Brendan O'Leary, Thea Riofrancos, Sid Rothstein, Rudra Sil, Stephan Stohler, and Meredith Wooten. Namita Dharia and Nick Smith read and commented on the introduction of the manuscript at a critical early stage, and I am grateful for their input. I was lucky to spend a formative year at Ithaca College and would especially like to thank Naeem Inayatullah for his support for my writing.

In 2015, I was fortunate to have my book discussed at the Junior Scholar Book Development workshop, held by the Project on Middle East Political Science and the Mamdouha S. Bobst Center for Peace and Justice at Princeton University. I would like to thank Reşat Kasaba, Lisa Wedeen, and Jillian Schwedler for their careful reading of the entire manuscript; Melani Cammett, Amaney Jamal, Gregory Starrett, and Mark Tessler for their helpful suggestions; and Marc Lynch and Lauren Baker for organizing the workshop. I also presented chapter 5 at the Center for the United States and the Cold War, based at New York University's Tamiment Library and Robert F. Wagner Labor Archives, where I received insightful comments from Mary Nolan and Rossen Djagalov. I am especially grateful to the participants of the Infrastructures in/of the Middle East Working Group: Nasser Abourahme, Julia Elyachar, Gökçe Günel, Arang Keshavarzian, Laleh Khalili, Leopold Lambert, Brian Larkin, Mandana Limbert, Jared McCormick, Joanne Nucho, and Helga Tawil-Souri. Chapter 4 would not have been the same without those two days of stimulating conversation in 2016.

I completed this book at the Hagop Kevorkian Center for Near Eastern Studies at New York University. The project has been immensely improved by the interdisciplinary conversations that "Kevo" fosters. I am especially grateful to my brilliant and stimulating colleagues, Helga Tawil-Souri, Joanne Nucho, and Marc Michael. I also benefited from the generosity of Zach Lockman and Sara Pursley, who cast discerning historians' eyes on parts of the manuscript, and Arang Keshavarzian, who asked the most challenging and eye-opening questions about political economy. Leslie Peirce gave me the opportunity to present portions of the book at the Ottoman Studies Lecture Series, where I received critical feedback from Aslı Iğsız and Sibel Erol. I am grateful to all of them for showing me new ways of thinking and for the support and friendship they have shown. I am also indebted to the resourceful and delightful Greta Scharnweber, Tandi Singh, Diana Shin, and Josh Anderson, who together helped make the Kevorkian Center such a vibrant community. Gabriel Young, Moné Makkawi, and Olga Verlato provided crucial research assistance, and I am gratified to see them continue their graduate studies.

I am forever indebted to Anand Vaidya for reading and insightfully commenting on different versions of the book and for never giving up on me. As I finished writing the book in New York, I very much appreciated the opportunity of enjoying the city with him, Jyothi Natarajan, Chelsea Schafer, Vanessa Hamer, Keerthi Potluri, and Benjamin Williams these past two years. I am grateful to Richard Bensel for his sharp feedback and encouragement of the manuscript and for helping me make a new home in Ithaca. At Stanford University Press, I would like to thank Kate Wahl for exceptional editorial assistance and Leah Pennywark, Emily Smith, and Gretchen Otto for their work on this book.

Last, I would like to thank my family who have supported me and cheered me on in so many ways over the years: Cormac McGowan; Sehran, Emre, and Kerem Özer; Jennifer Tate; the Adalet family, especially my uncle Kamil and my late grandmother Zahide; and Rob, Kate, Chris, Justin, Mary-Alma, and Martina Bateman. My sister, Müge, and my parents, Melike and Çetin Adalet, inspire me with their fortitude and love. They have encouraged my writing from an early age, and I can only hope the book is worth all the years we have spent apart. I could not have written any of it without the ceaseless energy and devotion of David Bateman, my partner-in-crime, my editor, my liver.

The last phase of my writing took place against the backdrop of the ruthless witch hunt against the Academics for Peace in Turkey, some of whose invaluable work is cited in these pages. I dedicate the book to them and to my parents.

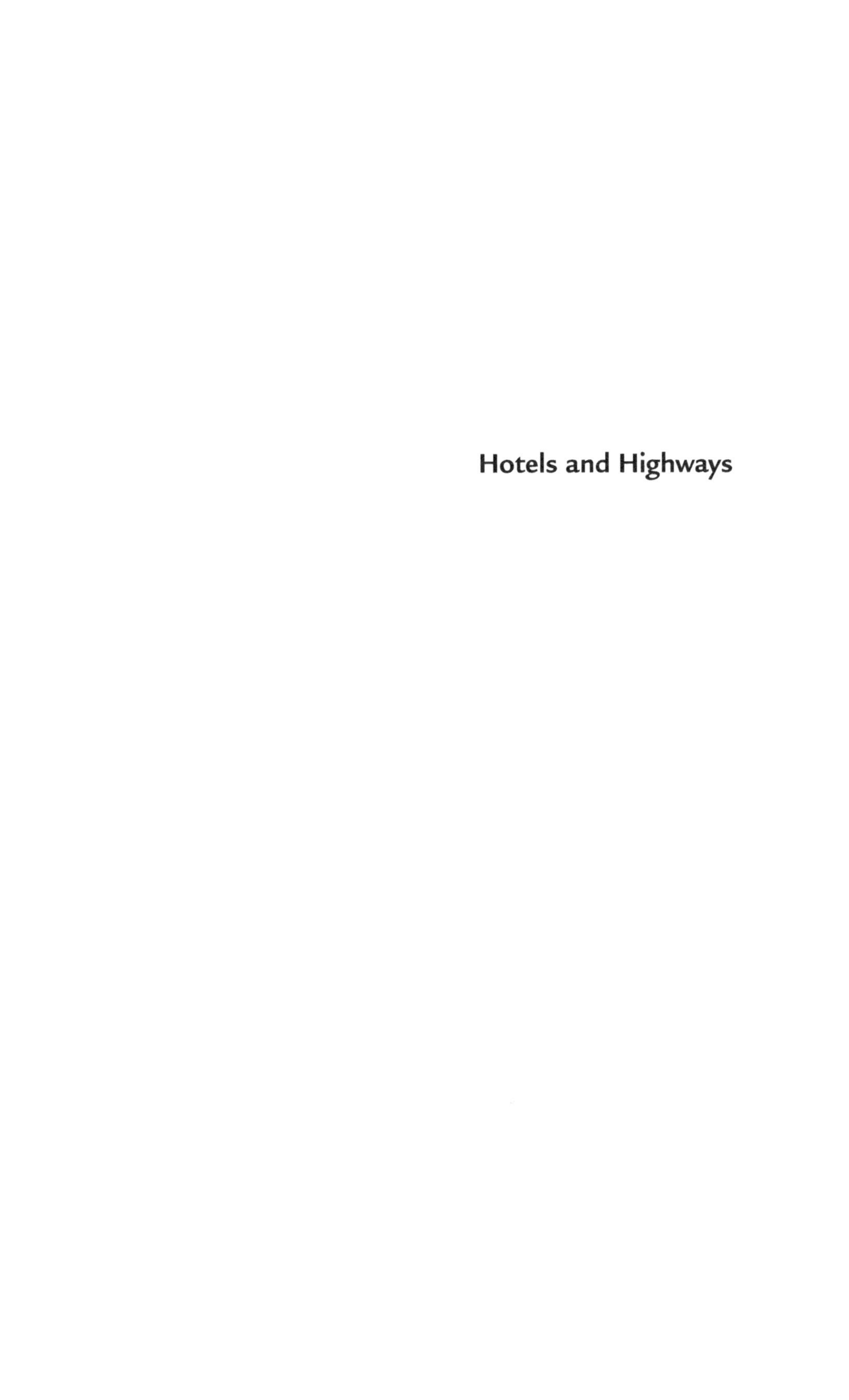

Hotels and Highways

Introduction

IN JUNE 1955, Conrad Hilton delivered a speech marking the grand opening of the Hilton Hotel in Istanbul. His remarks situated the new building—its construction, location, and architectural form—within a broader narrative of Turkey's political trajectory and its contemporary geopolitical importance. The mogul drew a line of continuity between the Ottoman Empire and the Republic of Turkey, and he praised their shared, "deep and very sound mistrust" of Russia, the "great northern neighbor," just as company publications hyperbolically advertised the Istanbul Hilton as located "ten miles from the Iron Curtain."[1] The hotel, as Hilton and company envisioned it, was to be a strategic deployment in a broader ideological conflict with the Soviet Union, a conflict that was nonetheless fought out in material terms.

Speaking to the Rotary Club of Los Angeles the following year, Hilton explained that he saw his franchises as an effort to match the "Communist sprawl" at its own game, albeit in a "friendly, industrial way."[2] Proximity to the Iron Curtain motivated the chain's outreach to Istanbul, Baghdad, and Berlin, while Cairo held "the key to Africa and the Middle East," Japan to Asia, and India to the "great 'neutral' bloc." West Berlin and Spain, meanwhile, were helping to "close the pincers over Europe." Each hotel in his international chain, Hilton insisted, was to be a "first-hand laboratory" where local and foreign tourists "may inspect America and its ways at their leisure," a site where the attitudes and psyches of locals deciding between conflicting visions of modernity could be directly manipulated and where new worldviews could be cultivated by the architects and entrepreneurs drafted into the service of American capitalist modernity.[3]

The early phases of the Cold War presented seemingly boundless opportunities for American entrepreneurs, experts, and policy makers to construct laboratories of the type envisioned by Hilton. It was in the global periphery, particularly on the terrain of developmental thought and practice, that some of the most important battles of the Cold War were fought.[4] A seminal weapon in the American intellectual arsenal was modernization theory, which prevailed in both academic and policy circles and upheld a singular, evolutionary path towards development. Scholars and experts modeled the trajectory towards modernization after the American vision of economic growth, and they presumed that it would entail such turning points as urbanization, the rise of mass media, and increasing rates of literacy. But while they assumed that development along the lines of this model was inevitable, they paradoxically believed that this model was also one that had to be induced. Between Truman's interpellation of "underdeveloped areas" in his 1949 speech announcing the Point Four program and Kennedy's declaration of the 1960s as the "Development Decade," foundations, private corporations, and foreign aid and technical assistance programs collaborated to showcase the boons of American modernization across the newly minted Third World.[5] Their projects were to aid the containment of the Soviet Union and provide the formula for winning hearts and minds on the global periphery.

The Hilton enterprise envisioned Turkey on the front lines of the Cold War, evident in the country's belonging to NATO, fighting in the Korean War, and hosting of American military bases and nuclear missiles along its northern and southern coasts. The Turkish government, in turn, participated fully in giving itself a vital location in this military and geopolitical cartography, frequently citing Soviet demands for free access to the Bosphorus in its requests for American economic, technical, and military assistance. The United States readily obliged over the years, as Truman Doctrine and Marshall Plan funds enabled agricultural mechanization and the extension of a highway network across Turkey.[6] These programs also jump-started the country's tourism industry, providing, among other things, the funding for Hilton's hotel and its showcase of capitalist enterprise. These tangible transformations in Turkey's material and social landscape, along with the country's program of economic and political liberalization between 1945 and 1960, captured the imagination of social scientists, such as Daniel Lerner and Dankwart Rustow, as they grappled with problems of modernization, inspiring a vision of Turkey as a model to be emulated, a case to be explained, and a laboratory in which to experiment.[7]

Hotels and Highways examines how Turkey served as both the template on which modernization theory was based and the object on which it was enacted. As an early participant in the American aid regime, Turkey was an important site that enabled the simultaneous construction and validation of postwar developmental thought and practice. It was a venue for fact-gathering, theory development, and experimentation but one that could also paradoxically serve as a ready-made model for the world, especially for its neighbors across the Middle East. The tensions and contradictions between these roles were manifested in the contentious and uncertain interactions between American and local actors and practices, even as they were glossed over by modernization theory's triumphant certainties. These encounters lay bare the political implications of developmental laboratories, which were material and tangible sites that also served rhetorical and social functions, sanctioning certain ideas and practices of modernization and expertise while disavowing others.

Recent intellectual histories have astutely underscored the central role that social scientific knowledge played in the ideological battles of the Cold War.[8] Even sophisticated works that examine local instantiations of modernization theory, however, reduce it to an intangible discourse or "narrative strategy," depicting it as a lens that guides or frames developmental projects.[9] In many of these accounts, academics convene at Social Science Research Council conferences in Dobbs Ferry, at the MIT Center for International Studies in Cambridge, or at the Rand Corporation in Santa Monica. Their theories are then passed on to officials in Washington, shipped abroad, and tested and implemented on the ground. If defects are found in overseas projects, scholars and experts reassemble to appraise their theoretical model, smooth out its edges, and perfect the prototype. Ironically, such narratives can reproduce the core assumption of the modernization theorists themselves, reinstating the West as the center of knowledge production.

Rather than emanating from the West and migrating to their venues of application, social scientific theories are themselves produced in particular but often uncertain encounters between actors engaged in transnational intellectual and policy networks. Put differently, theories do not hover above and independent from their destinations but rather are manufactured in material spaces where they can be worked out, refined, and given more definite form. Products of knowledge do not emerge out of secluded, disembodied scholarly practice; they are more akin to artifacts, whose fabrication requires the active construction of political alliances and material networks that they can inhabit and traverse. In these settings, the otherwise "abundant, complex, and heterogeneous" elements of the world are translated into "simpler objects that [researchers] can manipulate at leisure."[10] Researchers grow in size and strength relative to their objects of study, which are scaled down and simplified. But through the very acts of manipulation, simplification, and material fabrication, knowledge practices generate new realities and subjectivities on the ground, foreclosing some political possibilities while opening up novel sites of struggle.

The manufacturing of modernization theory rested on the construction and manipulation of architectural and infrastructural spaces. Experts built laboratories where they could scale down problems of geopolitics and development to a manageable size and where they could test and cultivate modern subjectivities. They identified the capacity for empathy, mobility, and hospitality as the primary indices of development, and they constructed microcosms where these attitudes could be measured but also incubated. In Turkey, the corresponding sites of theory construction included survey research, highways, and tourism landmarks such as the Istanbul Hilton Hotel, each of which is the subject of a chapter of this book. The survey interview was not only a method to measure modernization but also a site for its enactment; roads were not simply means to integrate the national economy but venues where subjects could develop "modern" relationships to machinery, time, and mobility; and hotels would not simply consolidate the tourism industry but refine the desired traits of impersonal and anonymous hospitality. Although these microcosms were intended to help the United States prevail in a Cold War fought over alternative models of development and expertise, they were offset by the resilience of recipient subjects as well as anxieties and hesitations on the part of practitioners. The confident modernity that Hilton and others hoped to project across the Third World concealed a persistent uncertainty, a nagging doubt, sometimes more explicit, sometimes less, that the project of shrinking the world to the manageable scale necessary for it to be successfully manipulated was a hopeless task.

The Turkish Model of Modernization

Hilton publications imagined Istanbul within striking distance of the Iron Curtain and spoke with authority about the politics, history, and aspirations of Turkey, noting that it "formerly was the focal point of all the Middle East" and was now becoming "definitely a European country, . . . making great strides in developing its economy and social structure close to Western thinking."[11] The postwar consolidation of American hegemony rested on the active construction of a geography of development, and especially of an "underdeveloped world," as regions and countries were assigned specific roles and levels of achievement in the global political economy. In this mapping, Turkey was given—and Turkish officials and policy makers actively sought out—an important role. As a country consciously opting for a pro-Western orientation, as evidenced through its membership in the International Monetary Fund, the International Bank for Reconstruction and Development (the precursor to the World Bank), and regional defense agreements, such as the Baghdad Pact, Turkey presented a special opportunity for its Western allies and an ostensible prototype for its Middle Eastern neighbors alike.[12]

This was an opportunity that both Turkish and American policy makers sought to seize. In 1948, Turkey was included in the Marshall Plan, despite the fact that the country had entered World War II at the last possible moment, after having earlier signed a nonaggression pact with Nazi Germany and having refused British entreaties to join the Allies. European Recovery Program funds brought agricultural machinery and extended a highway network across the country; these projects were included within the Marshall Plan's program of Americanizing the organization of production and consumption patterns across Western Europe.[13] The Plan, as many historians have argued, was not simply an extension of American aid to devastated European countries but also a deliberate program of forestalling and defusing calls for a more assertive redistribution of wealth that might include social guarantees for national health care, full employment, universal education, and subsidized housing.[14] American policy makers discouraged projects that might be seen as moving too far from market-oriented development, while they promoted an economic reconstruction program that produced "not the high standard of living in itself, but rather the technologies, procedures, and information about how to achieve 'a little bit more well-being.'"[15]

In Turkey, the Marshall Plan–funded highway network largely superseded a proposed land reform bill of 1945, intended to eliminate landlessness among the peasantry by redistributing the properties of absentee landlords to the tenants and sharecroppers who worked on them.[16] Rather than implement land reform, as had been done in Japan, postwar American assistance allocated agricultural machinery and built highways, which ultimately benefited large landowners. The transfer of highway equipment and expertise also prefigured Truman's 1949 Point Four Program and its goal to "help the free peoples of the world, through their own efforts, to produce more food, more clothing, more materials for housing, and more mechanical power to lighten their burdens."[17] Programs like the highway initiative helped crystallize the postwar role of development in the relationship between the United States and the global periphery. Technical knowhow would henceforth manage the "difference between extraordinary levels of affluence for some and modest levels of living for the majority of the world, rather than [offering] the effective means of addressing those differences."[18] In the words of Paul Hoffman, who oversaw the Marshall Plan between his term as the president of the Studebaker Company and the first administrator of the United Nations Development Programme, European recovery had provided a training ground for American policy makers, who "developed the essential instruments of a successful policy in the arena of world politics."[19]

Turkey's role in the creation of this postwar world order went beyond its role as an early laboratory of development. It proved to be a staunch ally of the Western bloc over the years, joining the British embargo of nationalized Iranian oil in 1952; voting against Algerian demands in the United Nations in 1954; supporting Britain, France, and Israel during the Suez Crisis in 1956; nearly declaring war on Syria in 1957; and allowing the United States to use its bases during the intervention in Lebanon in 1958.[20] Outside of the Middle East, Turkey's alignment with the Western bloc included its defense of European and American interests at the Asian-African Conference in Bandung in 1955; its participation, at the behest of the United States, was grudging at best, not least because North American observers repeatedly referred to it as a "meeting of the colored races," a status from which Turkish statesmen believed they were exempt.[21] For Western policy makers, Turkey could be deployed as a disciplinary force at the margins of the metropole. For academics and experts, it could also be evoked as a model to be emulated across the same margins.

Turkey's status as a prototypical case in the postwar social scientific imaginary was in part a legacy of the Ottoman and Kemalist reforms that characterized its landscape. During the Tanzimat period (1839–76), the struggling empire undertook centralization, bureaucratization, and the establishment of new schools, while the reign of Abdulhamid II (1876–1909) saw an attempt to embark on a modernization project that was explicitly modeled after Germany. After the establishment of the Republic in 1923, subsequent Turkish state-building projects mirrored these earlier attempts, now identifying modernization with Enlightenment-style secularism and the imposition of political and social reform in a top-down fashion. The bureaucratic elite, led by Kemal Ataturk, the self-appointed father of all Turks, implemented changes in the script, scales, calendar, and education system, breaking with Islamic code in favor of the Swiss-inspired Civil Code of 1926. Over the subsequent decades, the principle of secularism would be enforced by the state, proliferated by "Kemalist" devotees, and protected under the aegis of the army in its self-designated role as the sentinel of laïcité.

The configuration of Turkey as a model for modernization theory drew on these legacies. But it crystallized in 1950 with the implementation of the country's first multiparty elections, leading to a decade of government by the Democrat Party (DP) under Adnan Menderes between 1950 and 1960. Ataturk's Republican People's Party, now led by Ismet Inönü, waited its turn in opposition. The DP, backed by small merchants, urban petty bourgeoisie, and commercial farmers, had a populist appeal from its conception in 1946, exemplified in its support for the expansion of religious liberties, private enterprise, and foreign investment.[22] During his government, Menderes was in basic agreement with the recommendations of American advisors, who denounced railway-led industrialization projects and encouraged agricultural mechanization and the extension of a highway network.[23]

Seemingly a success story of simultaneous economic and political liberalization, Turkey thus surfaced at once as a "model ally" and the archetype of modernization theory for Cold Warriors in the United States. Still, its labeling as a model for its Middle Eastern neighbors was hardly an innocent discovery. It was just as much an effort to discredit the ways in which these neighbors had already embarked on their own political and economic trajectories, drawing on a plethora of alternative modernizing ideologies that were available across the region, such as pan-Arabism, political Islam, and socialism, among others.[24] American scholars, policy makers, and pundits rediscovered Turkey as a putative regional template in the aftermath of the Arab uprisings of 2011; in doing so, they effaced the history and political effects of previous American theories and projects. The Turkish model was equally attractive for those who prescribed "moderation" for Islamist parties and those who sought the continuation of neoliberal policies in post-Mubarak Egypt.[25] The enthusiasts of the template were silent about Prime Minister Recep Tayyip Erdoğan's escalating persecution of leftist, primarily Kurdish activists, journalists, and students during the same period and about the highly unequal effects of his neoliberalization program, which resulted in high rates of unemployment and workplace deaths.[26] The government's heavy-handed response to the 2013 Gezi Park protests and the 2016 military coup attempt have once again led political scientists to use the country as a test case for their theories of "competitive authoritarianism," but neither these reversals nor these erasures are new to the discipline's record of engagement with Turkey.[27]

When Cold War modernization theorists and policy makers praised Turkey's seeming pliability as an ally, they treated its postwar transition to multiparty politics as consistent with earlier reform projects. In doing so, they knowingly concealed its undemocratic manifestations.[28] Among the forgotten facts of Turkey's political history was its ambivalent status during the interwar period and many of its elites' sympathies for Nazi Germany.[29] Also unmentioned were the ferocious nationalism of the "reformist" state, which deemed indispensable the creation of a unified and homogeneous Turkish, Muslim, yet laic bourgeoisie. The measures taken in this direction were the expulsion of Greek communities and the massacre of Armenians and Alevi Kurds in the early twentieth century as well as the establishment of Varlık Vergisi, a capital tax targeting non-Muslims between November 1942 and March 1944, and the government-sanctioned anti-Greek pogroms of 1955.[30] Social scientists' subsequent condoning of the 1960 military coup, which led to the overthrow and hanging of Menderes and three cabinet members, was also consistent with the contradictions and amnesias of Cold War modernization.[31] The persistent erasure of such episodes from narratives of the "successful" Turkish model is a testament to the simultaneously material and ideological work undertaken by modernization theory.

Modernization Theory in Action

Following the recent applications of science and technology studies to the social sciences, we can trace the demanding work that is entailed in the crafting of knowledge claims and their material effects.[32] Social scientific theories and attendant methodologies not only measure, encode, or describe but also engender the phenomena they seek to explain, such as the economy, objectivity, probability, public opinion, madness, or the "modern fact."[33] Modernizers brought with them a positivist orientation towards the construction of knowledge: they assumed that the world existed out there, independent of themselves, as a collection of facts to be apprehended and investigated.[34] Knowing this world rendered it controllable—an urgency which ran counter to their insistence on objectivity but a sign that they remained "within the basic trope of modernity."[35] They described the changes they observed as modernization, and by labeling it as such, they contributed to the transformation of their objects of inquiry.

In acting upon and bringing order to the material and social landscape, the modernizers collected and calculated information that otherwise existed separately. The construction of developmental thought was predicated on the mobilization of an array of material equipment, such as Voice of America–funded questionnaires, Ford Foundation–funded maps, and meticulously kept reports about Marshall Plan allocations—"technologies of distance" that tallied, arranged, and organized that which they claimed to merely represent.[36] Such documents facilitated attempts to gather information about the locals and to render that data mobile, stable, and combinable in the name of universal knowledge.[37] They delineated particular places, practices, and individuals as modern while labeling others as backward and provincial. Survey respondents who were too timid to articulate their opinions were coded as traditional subjects. Delays in reports to Marshall Plan headquarters marked the local experts as indolent at the same time that their zest for large-scale developmental projects was seen as a testament to their impatience; such outlooks proved too slow and too hasty, alternately, for the temporal and behavioral comportments associated with modernization. Just as experts' maps assigned regions of the country to designated grades within a developmental scheme, local interlocutors were ascribed a location in a developmental hierarchy premised on the achievement of modern subjectivity.

The set of claims rallied by modernization theorists not only pertained to the developmental trajectory of Turkey but also generated a series of assumptions about modern psyches and postures. The different laboratory experiments were intended to occasion the enactment of modern subjectivities, on either side of the Atlantic, including those who conducted social scientific surveys and those who responded to them, those who were responsible for the allocation of road-building machinery and those who were to learn the maintenance of the machines, and those who designed the hotels and those who were to inhabit them within conventions of hospitality. Recipients of roads, hotels, and surveys were to cultivate mobility in physical and imaginary terms: if they could not literally undertake travel, they should be able to psychically accommodate the vision of self-chosen, voluntary movement. The modern self was expected to travel, imagine, and imagine travel. Modern subjects were also to know how to travel *well*, to wait in line for public transportation, and to lodge in aesthetically appealing, hygienic, and comfortable facilities. Ease of travel would occasion the emergence of new conceptions of time measurement and encourage territorial unification, an important concern to local politicians grappling with the assimilation of Kurdish populations. But given the unequal distribution of machines and roads and their use in managing the movement of unruly subjects, their ostensibly universalizing modernity in fact operated through class differentiations and ethnic hierarchies.

If the American model of development was to appear universally attainable, experts had to create the conditions for its replication across the world. Modernization theory was packaged as abstract and singular, as though it could be unmoored from the local networks, material arrangements, and political histories that enabled its production and dissemination. This erasure of the materiality of knowledge production should be thought of as an "accomplishment"; in John Law's terms, it was one that secured the coherence of concepts such as modernization into given items.[38] But we can try to dislodge the certitude of that accomplishment by unraveling the image of a "Great Divide between the universal knowledge of the Westerners and the local knowledge of everyone else," by weaving back together the strands that have heretofore separated.[39]

Local Passage Points

The diverse array of travelers embroiled in the weaving of modernization theory included survey researchers, diplomats, businessmen, engineers, and architects—all itinerants within transnational circuits of intellectual and imperial production. Although these figures seemingly agreed on the premises of their theories and projects, they furtively contested their specificities. Their travels testify to the porosity of the boundaries between the foreign and the domestic, a recurring revelation found in transnational histories of US–Middle East relations.[40] Recent histories of international development have also looked "beyond the metropolitan centers of the West" in order to show how projects on the ground "shape the ideas from which they emerged."[41] David Engerman, Nathan Citino, Nicole Sackley, and others have recovered the ways in which local practices and regional ideologies have been constitutive of development.[42] I engage with this work to show that the making of modernization theory was by no means a unidirectional process, precisely because of a material necessity to enroll and translate the interests of Turkish scholars and policy makers.[43] Intermediary figures positioned themselves as "obligatory passage points" through which flows of information and knowledge traversed the Atlantic.[44] The characters whose itineraries are traced in the following chapters were such passage points; they include social scientists Dankwart Rustow, Kemal Karpat, Nermin Abadan, and Frederick Frey as well as technical experts such as Vecdi Diker, Harold Hilts, Gordon Bunshaft, and Sedad Hakkı Eldem. They all had to be rallied in order for modernization theory to gain traction.

The otherwise obscure role of such intermediary figures can be illustrated with the example of Mahmut Makal, who was a rural schoolteacher educated in the Kemalist Village Institutes. The Institutes were founded in 1940 with the aim to modernize the peasantry and to propagate Kemalism across rural areas.[45] Makal's account of his experiences across Anatolia, ranging from social norms and food shortages to timekeeping practices he observed, captured the imagination of American and European social scientists, who nonetheless counseled caution to his Western audiences. They drew on Makal's writings to distill the elements of earlier, especially Kemalist projects of modernization, and they expurgated parts that were not to their liking. In his preface to the annotated English edition, historian Lewis Thomas suggested that Makal's "rationalist and liberal assumptions will make it all too easy for European readers to fall with him into the fallacy that we must set to work to shed light in this darkness, to fill the vacuum of ignorance with the blessings of modern knowledge."[46] Thomas's wary position was in line with the editorial interjections offered by anthropologist Paul Stirling. Where Makal proclaimed that "a woman's voice is taboo" in villages, Stirling interposed in a footnote that "as often, the author exaggerates." In response to Makal's observation that "there is no aspect of village life so confused as that of marriage," Stirling reprimanded: "The confusion exists largely in the author's mind, and results from applying a Western ideal of marriage, itself altered by his own deeper attitudes."[47]

Portions of Makal's text that detracted from the vision of the Turkish model of modernization were excised, written away as the aspirations of an individual who benefited from "modern education" and reacted to his own village as a "citizen of twentieth-century Western civilization."[48] Makal thus confirmed the self-fashioning of western scholars as sympathetic observers, more willing to "understand" their objects of inquiry. The assignation of biased, convoluted thinking to this particular mediator enabled the modernizers' own claim to objectivity. Makal figured prominently in debates about new directions not only in the Turkish social sciences but also in the work of American scholars of Turkey and modernization, such as Walter Weiker, Frank Tachau, Richard Robinson, and Herbert Hyman.[49] Sociologist Daniel Lerner used the popularity of Makal's book as both fodder and material proof for his own categories of tradition and modernization: "That there now exists in Turkey a market of over 50,000 people able to buy the book . . . is a datum which suggests that economic participation via cash, and psychocultural participation via literacy, have grown together in significant measure."[50] The fact that his later text—*The Fable of Development*, which chastised the shortcomings of the Turkish government's developmental projects—remains untranslated is indicative of the simultaneous enrollment and erasure of obligatory passage points.[51]

Local interlocutors—docile collaborators, silent skeptics, and unruly resistors alike—were active, if fickle, participants in the crafting of modernization theory. Their involvement and resistance were necessarily curtailed by an imbalanced political context marked by US aid and geopolitical ascendance. But as we will see in chapters 1 and 2, members of the political science faculty at Ankara University were not the subservient recipients of recent developments in American social science: they adapted its categories and methodologies, and they remade their premises. The engineers and architects who are the subjects of chapters 3 through 5 were the target of modernizing schemes in methods of record keeping, roadbuilding, and time management. Yet vernacular practices of expertise and competing visions of development persisted, leading to moments of "disconnect and mistranslation" that were constitutive of modernization across its sites of articulation and instantiation.[52] Finally, the recipients of academic and infrastructural projects, such as survey respondents, university students, and rural populations, remained recalcitrant, attesting to the resignification and redeployment of modernization's temporalities and associated spatial practices. Theories of modernization and attendant developmental projects were not only selectively appropriated and indigenized but produced in the very details of encounters and ultimately used in unforeseen and at times contradictory ways.

Derailments and Hesitations

Modernizing schemes could be offset by unintended consequences, such as material misuse and self-reflexive practitioners. Such roadblocks exemplify the contingencies that were entailed in the construction and implementation of social scientific theories, which proceed through the work of multiple actors and material mediators, themselves capable of doing more (and less) than their users anticipate. Developmental techniques and visions produce signs, subjects, and material objects that are capable of reworking the inevitabilities their creators imagined.

The Marshall Plan–funded highway network is illustrative of the manifold interpretive strategies that were corralled in developmental projects. Roads were engraved in accounts of modernization, which equipped transportation and attendant correlates, such as urbanization and communication, with explanatory prowess. Rather than functioning as a mere conduit for modernization theory, however, the highway network is best understood as a site where it was crafted and imbued with multiple meanings. Postwar highways were identified and tasked with political-economic integration, and they also built on residues of colonial and nation-building missions.[53] Ottoman, European, and Kemalist legacies of reform were piled on top of one another, and a new modernization was stacked on in the Cold War; republican depictions of civilizing railroads bled into their replacements by liberalizing highways, at the same time as roads continued to facilitate the ongoing interior colonial project in Kurdish-populated areas of the country. Debates about state-led development, public works, and private enterprise were also scaled down to the level of roadbuilding machinery, while American experts contested German understandings of civil engineering and bureaucracy they found to be too managerial and dismissive of manual labor.[54]

These negotiations were derailed even as they succeeded, as beneficiaries of roads would use them to leave their villages in inappropriate vehicles, such as tractors requisitioned for weekend trips into the city, much to the chagrin of social scientists and policy makers. Rural populations also began to use their newfound mobility to migrate to cities in unprecedented numbers, joining the ranks of the urban working classes. This was especially worrying given that efforts to discourage working-class consciousness and discredit alternative visions of development, such as land reform, had failed to deliver.[55] The unforeseen usage of roads can be viewed as a testament to the "self-defeating" components of infrastructural projects, the "inherent instability or volatility of the material."[56] Roads were marked by translation strategies on the part of their recipients as well as that of competing governmental agencies; in the process, their normative and positive content was contested and worked over by experts and laypeople alike.

Although critics such as Arturo Escobar have done significant work to chronicle the forms of knowledge, institutions, and technological factors that constitute developmental discourse, they overlook the ways in which that discourse may well spawn subjectivities that escape a "top-down, ethnocentric, and technocratic" approach that otherwise aims to "exclude people."[57] The disempowerment and depoliticization of local populations are taken at face value in such analyses, whereby national governments and international agencies collaborate and succeed in their allocation of developmental resources as technical, politically neutral, and benevolent solutions to those in need. Most accounts portray developmental experts as conceited, self-assured, and successful at concealing the interventionist nature of their work. Even studies that foreground the unintended consequences of developmental plans present them as "instrumental" in the exertion and intensification of this depoliticizing effect.[58] I call attention instead to the fragilities and anxieties that mark expert thinking and practice throughout this book.

The actors involved in the construction and implementation of modernization theory may at first appear to resemble James Scott's conceited high modernists, who were "uncritical, unskeptical, and thus unscientifically optimistic about the possibilities for the comprehensive planning of human settlement and production."[59] These agents were indeed invested in "covering up" the true meaning of their work, not unlike those involved in the USAID developmental schemes in Egypt, as Timothy Mitchell recounts.[60] While Mitchell insists that a degree of "self-deception" was central to the constitution of development as a discourse of rational planning, his narrative assigns more certitude and coherence to social scientific thinking and attendant expert practices than the record shows existed.[61] I suggest that instead we follow Tania Li in examining how attempts to render politically contentious issues technical are best seen as a "project, not a secure accomplishment."[62]

The modernization theorists were expected to present themselves as empathetic yet disinterested researchers, but they were often mortified at their own lack of knowledge about their objects of study. The technical experts were to utilize modern techniques in engineering, record keeping, and punctuality but were deeply troubled by incompatibilities in design and building techniques. Although Conrad Hilton believed that the Cold War could be staged and won in the lobby of his international hotel, his employees, contractors, and congressional allies did not always agree with him, and they did not share his confidence in the battle he was fighting. Their performances were precarious and apprehensive, resulting in the untethering of modern selves and belying the claim that "the modernizers not only brought the solution, they were the solution; for the standards by which progress was to be measured mirrored their understanding of themselves."[63] The experts' self-understanding was not exclusively motivated by self-deception or insidious depoliticization but incorporated what Ann Stoler has called "epistemic uncertainty," revealing provisional "truth-claims" at best, in lieu of durable "regimes of truth."[64]

The vagaries of expertise are inscribed in its often neglected affective components as well as its political and technical dimensions. The heterogeneity of interests on the part of US officials and their Turkish counterparts suggests a vision of expertise that exceeds the monolithic, disembodied, and calculating portraits we are accustomed to encountering in the literature. Failures, mistranslations, and uncertainties are intrinsic to expert knowledge and practice, yet their concealment need not secure the consolidation of expert authority. Rather, expertise is not only crafted through material and local sites of encounters but also beset by risk and uncertainty as well as anxieties and hesitations on the part of its practitioners. Misunderstandings and gaps in knowledge do not stem exclusively from the hubris of the planners but are the very condition for expert knowledge and practice.

Encounters of the Archival Kind

The assemblage of the epistemic and political order that comprised modernization theory was predicated on an array of artifacts, instruments, traveling experts, and local knowledge practices. Encounters within this semiotic universe often took textual and documentary form, the primary expression of which I was able to observe in a variety of archival settings. The organization and circulation of documents as well as their authorship (and ownership) were crucial to contesting visions of authority, expertise, and modernization.[65] Much like the other material mediators of concern to this project, archival documents were also laden with a multiplicity of meanings rather than serving as the venue for a singular interpretative exercise. Their contingency was discernible in their storage in different locations, their varying aesthetics and audience, and their materiality, which exceeded the signs inscribed on them and the meanings they were supposed to communicate.

The compilation of files in different archival sites revealed that which was deemed worthy of preservation. Their categorization reflected and facilitated the registers of truth through which experts approached their domains of study. Official memoranda and reports were crafted with multiple audiences in mind, as though they were already situated to become the property of all, or at least of the researcher with the correct kind of permit and identification. Yet some collections, such as the records at the Turkish General Directorate of Highways, were presented to me with personal anecdotes about the hindrances interfering with archival efforts: the available documents were partial, salvaged from a trip to the Pulp and Paper Industry Foundation to be recycled along with others. This particular story about gaps in record keeping readily mapped onto the dictates of the modernizers—missing paperwork was a seeming placeholder for truncated development that was manifest in material as well as conceptual terms.

A crucial research site holding the private papers of Dankwart Rustow, a modernization theorist central to this narrative, was not a designated venue of storage at all. It was in this setting, perhaps fittingly, that the affective, tentative dimensions of expertise became clear to me. Dusty folders were marked, arranged, and catalogued with a logic of their own, neither alphabetically nor chronologically; yet they were effortless to navigate once I became familiar with the dozens of drawers and boxes lying around. Those who opened up their homes, offices, and, at times, rather sterile institutional archives were equally hospitable; at the Middle East Technical University, however, "spoiled" documents were denied to me, causing me to abandon a direction of inquiry. No matter how orderly their display, archival documents were also liable to surprise. They could be misplaced, lost, or recycled, evading openness to access and legibility.

Archival materials thus mirrored the frailties of the projects they chronicled. As material sites of enactment, they deflected and distorted, rather than commanded, the display of coherent subjectivities. Self-reflexivity surfaced, if episodically, in the correspondences among the experts—an interminable yet productive breach between epistemic and political anxieties or the consternation involved in building a paradigm, a hotel, a road, or an empire. Unintended consequences of the archival record included filled-out questionnaires that had been excised from a particular published account. These surveys imbued the respondents with embodied voices and strategies of resistance, one of the few instances in which the institutional record was not able to efface the recipients of developmental projects. Often, archives exercised hegemony in their positions as selective repositories, troubled and troubling; yet they remained pregnant with the possibility of dialogical encounter with the material.[66] Excavating the parochialism of modernization through its archival inscription allows us to reconceive of its histories and futures, both of which are opened up through mutual glances and the relentless remaking of selves, theories, and artifacts over the course of their travels.

Outline of the Book

The remainder of the book shows the ways in which developmental thought and practice were not imposed in a unidirectional or homogenous fashion in Turkey. As the country became a so-called model for the Middle East and a laboratory of development, the interactions of American theorists and practitioners with their Turkish colleagues shaped their ideas and projects about modernization. Although they encouraged the enactment of certain tenets of modernity (empathy, mobility, hospitality) in specific sites (survey research, highways, hotels), the negotiations and disagreements between social scientists, government practitioners, and private sector capitalists were constitutive features of development.

One figure whose life trajectory contained within it many of the contradictions of modernization theory was political scientist and Middle East specialist Dankwart Rustow. Chapter 1 traces the emergence of modernization theory and its Turkish archetype in the postwar period, drawing on my research in Rustow's published work and private papers. His engagements with various institutions, such as the Committee on Comparative Politics of the Social Science Research Council, the Council on Foreign Relations, and the political science faculty at Ankara University reveal his status as a seminal but hesitant participant in the laboratization of Turkey in academic and policy circles. His travels between these institutions underscore the anxieties of those who benefited from the circuits of funding that joined academic centers, governmental agencies, and private foundations. The reservations of his Turkish and American colleagues came to inform Rustow's increasingly critical attitude towards modernization theory, thus attesting to his precarious position as a self-conscious contributor to its construction in Turkey. Thus, modernization theory was not simply an academic endeavor and policy prescription designed in the United States and then applied to the Third World but also an intellectual and political project that was, from its inception, in contentious dialogue with its object of development.

Chapter 2 focuses on the role of survey research as a fragile experiment that was nonetheless central to the enactment of modernization theory. I primarily explore the private papers and writings of sociologist Daniel Lerner as well as other studies his work inspired throughout the 1950s and 1960s. Many of these surveys attempted to gauge levels of modernization across Turkey during this period and were funded by organizations as diverse as the Mutual Security Agency, the Turkish State Planning Organization, the Ford Foundation, and the Voice of America, among others. I argue that these studies, which were conducted to measure and record the attitudes of peasants, students, and administrators, were also efforts to *create* modern subjects: the survey setting was in fact designed to produce the forms of subjectivity and interpersonal relations articulated and idealized by modernization theory. But the dissemination of survey methodology and attendant theories of modernization were derailed by skeptical respondents and disorderly interviewer behavior. Surveys, it seems, often outstripped the intentions of their coders, sponsors, and creators.

Modernization theory was not an internally consistent formulation. Rustow's historically informed analysis of political development and Lerner's behavioral research into what he called the communications revolution were at odds with each other. If Rustow exemplifies modernization theorists' doubts and discomforts, Lerner's survey research aimed to conceal those uncertainties. Lerner believed that surveys could help enact empathy, which he defined as "psychic mobility" and which he explicitly linked to the capacity for physical mobility. This capacity is the subject of chapters 3 and 4, with a focus on a particular medium for its cultivation: the construction of a highway network across the country.

Chapter 3 examines the flow of aid money and expertise between the United States and Turkey by looking at the American-funded and -planned Turkish highway network in the immediate aftermath of World War II. Like surveys, engineers' offices and training programs became microcosms for testing and implementing theories of private versus public sector developmentalism. I show how the arrival of American aid, experts, and machinery was expected to instigate modernization in administrative and mechanical terms by acquainting the new highway organization and its civil engineers with rational methods of record keeping, time management, and machine maintenance. From that perspective, a highway engineering program in Ankara was intended to become a center for training engineers and bureaucrats across the Middle East. Yet this project was short-lived, and interactions between American and Turkish organizations were marked by contestation. The location of highways, the employment of contractors, and the labeling of road-building equipment were material sites where the agencies competed over the management of the Turkish economy and staked out their claims to authority and visibility.

Chapter 4 describes the modernizing, civilizing, and democratizing tasks assigned to the highways that were constructed during this period as well as the unexpected consequences and unforeseen usages of those highways. I draw on parliamentary debates, newspaper articles, and engineering journals to show how the highway program displaced plans for land reform as the primary vision of development. Social scientists, experts, and officials on both sides of the Atlantic construed the provision of roads to the Turkish countryside as a "civilizational necessity," one that would enhance economic development, education, and access to an open society. The proponents of the program believed that roads would grant access to otherwise remote corners of the nation, especially areas populated by Kurdish minorities, and that highways would shrink distances between different parts of the country, thus allowing its subjects to participate in a shared national space and economy. Although the beneficiaries were expected to imagine themselves as part of a unified nation consisting of modern subjects, the impact of roads, maps, and buses often exceeded the intentions and expectations of their providers. Modernist visions of the highway system providing a path to a prosperous and open future were thus frustrated by material roadblocks and the misuse of vehicles and equipment, opening the very category of the modern up to contestation, appropriation, and redefinition.

Modernizers hoped that, in addition to their colonial and civilizational functions, roads would imbue the peasantry with a penchant for leisure activities, such as taking vacations. Chapter 5 builds on this theme with a focus on the efforts to develop a tourism industry in Turkey in the immediate aftermath of World War II and a focus especially on the design and construction of the Istanbul Hilton Hotel. The hotel was financed by the Turkish Pension Fund and by the Economic Cooperation Administration (ECA), which was responsible for administering the Marshall Plan. The actors involved in the creation of the hotel alternately framed it as a bulwark against the threatening march of Communism, a turning point in the consolidation of the tourism industry, and the signifier of a hospitable mindset, an attitude considered to be a necessary corollary to modernization. I begin with an overview of the different meanings attributed to the hotel, set against the backdrop of the purported alignment of interests between the Hilton Corporation, the Turkish government, and the ECA, all of whom sought support for tourism promotion instead of direct foreign aid from Congress. Rather than serving as a medium for the top-down imposition of an Americanized modernity, however, the hotel was contentious from the outset in terms of its style, funding, and site as well as of the various meanings it was expected to communicate: local architects and politicians protested the hotel's role in the proliferation of the corporate International Style, the incursion of foreign capital, and the expropriation of a public park overlooking the Bosphorus. Their criticisms also took place in the context of ongoing entwinements between urban redevelopment and dispossession, further revealing the local, material, and political components of modernization.

Anthropologists, sociologists, and historians have begun coming to terms with the convoluted imbrication of their research projects with empire and grand schemes of development.[67] Political scientists, however, for the most part continue to insist on the inevitability of their involvement with developmental, humanitarian, or counterinsurgency projects despite longstanding evidence of their own uncertainties and apprehensions about such work.[68] *Hotels and Highways* uncovers the material history and political effects of a particular moment of social scientific knowledge production in a context marked by unequal power relations. By tracing the crafting and application of modernization theory as central components of both American Cold War policy and domestic politics in Turkey, I cast light on what historians of science have labeled the entanglements of "problems of knowledge" with "problems of the political order."[69]

1

Beastly Politics

Dankwart Rustow and the Turkish Model of Modernization

> Since comparative government stakes its claims wider than heretofore, we can no longer permit the existence of white spots on our map of the world, of areas of knowledge unexplored or neglected either in terms of political geography or out of self-restraint. . . . Comparative government, conceived as a total science, must see to it that such tangible gaps are filled at the earliest opportunity.
>
> —Karl Loewenstein, "Report on the Research Panel on Comparative Government"

> The political scientist who insists that the world is his oyster is likely to suffer a bad case of indigestion.
>
> —Dankwart Rustow, "Modernization and Comparative Politics: Prospects in Research and Theory"

POLITICAL SCIENTIST Dankwart A. Rustow of Princeton University spent the 1958–1959 academic year in Turkey, during which time he delivered a lecture to the political science faculty of Ankara University about recent developments in the study of comparative government in the United States. In his speech, Rustow exulted the turn away from the previous "ethnocentrism" of his discipline but also noted the difficulties awaiting field researchers, such as problems of language, insufficient statistical data, changing political systems, and foreign cultural settings. Despite the predicaments beleaguering the study of comparative politics, Rustow did not hesitate to carve out the crucial role that Turkey would play in its reconfiguration; thanks to the legacy of Kemalist reforms, he said, the country's experience with westernization preceded that of its counterparts in the recently developing world, and "it is for this reason that at this moment when comparative government is being extended to the whole world, research in the political and historical system of the Republic of Turkey is exceptionally significant."[1] Given the conditions for the emergence of a "worldwide science," Rustow added, "Turkish citizens of the political science profession," rather than foreign scholars, should contribute to its practice in this country, whose transformation would then cast light on processes of westernization elsewhere.

Although Rustow's audience was receptive to his narrative of Turkish exceptionalism, one issue remained in dispute during the roundtable discussion that followed: his assertion that comparison in political science could be viewed as akin to the laboratory experience in the natural sciences. In his summary of the discussion, Bahri Savcı, professor of law and political science, reiterated Rustow's contention that the aim of comparative politics was to "investigate the institutions of nations with different variables, and thus arrive at a law, a theory that is applicable to all," but he added that "some participants in the conference pointed out the dangers of arriving at 'laws' in this scientific area that does not have the laboratory experience. . . . In the end, it was concluded that the actual aim is the search for 'trends,' rather than laws."[2] Although Rustow proposed Turkey as one site of fact gathering for the laboratory of comparative politics, his scientific certitude was undercut by the skepticism of his audience, who were designated as the subjects of this new approach and its future practitioners alike.

This brief encounter between Rustow and the Turkish social scientists was emblematic of the stakes involved in the production and dissemination of knowledge pertaining to nonwestern areas in the postwar years. The Cold War presented an important context for "discipline-defining mythologies," that is, revisionist accounts about the origins of political science.[3] During this period, scholars reformulated their work in terms of political exigencies, national security, and international development, and they tried to distance themselves from previous social scientific engagements with projects of racial uplift and imperialism. As students of comparative politics struggled to rewrite their disciplinary histories and to abandon what they reenvisioned as their foregoing "parochialism," their ostensibly newfound interest in particular locales was propelled by their search for "law-like regularities."[4] In the words of one practitioner, their goal was "to advance, in the form of rather bold and unqualified statements, generalized models of the political process common in non-Western societies."[5] As Rustow's speech suggested, social scientists traveling to their research sites believed that their task entailed procuring data and propagating the methods and theories being crafted in an emergent comparative laboratory. This conceptual exercise rested on behavioralist presuppositions and involved a rational and systematic foray into the meaning and content of social change, now defined as modernization. Even though the social scientific laboratory was seemingly situated in the ideal realm, coordinates of the local and the material were retained within it, given its position as a reflection and reversal of the world. The claims to scientific abstraction and universalism crisscrossed with the demands for personal familiarization with "exceptional" research sites, whose specific conditions resulted in detours and roadblocks in the itineraries of "traveling theories."[6]

One site for fashioning modernization theory was Turkey, which researchers cast as a model that would help elucidate *and* instigate development across the Middle East. Deemed to be at once "exceptional" and "significant" by self-proclaimed specialists, Turkey was treated as both a site of fact gathering for comparative politics and the telos of modernization processes elsewhere, thereby displaying a split character and temporality as an object of inquiry and intervention alike. Yet the dissemination of modernization theory and its axioms was derailed by the ambivalence of local collaborators and the hesitations of those undertaking social scientific work in the United States. The teleological narrative so central to visions of modernization was undermined in its own trajectory: inasmuch as its proponents hoped to present modernization theory as the highest stage of the social sciences, its instantiations in specific locales belied its claims to universality and inevitability.[7]

The study of foreign locales through the lens of modernization theory was by no means a unidirectional process, given the necessity to enroll and translate the interests of the Turkish scholars and policy makers who actively participated in the negotiation and assembly of these traveling theories. It is for this reason that intermediary figures such as Dankwart Rustow positioned themselves as "obligatory passage points" through which flows of information and knowledge traversed the Atlantic.[8] These intermediary figures were furnished with the task of translating the particular into the abstract and the universal, but their work was offset by instances of profound ambivalence, deficient knowledge of the field, and circuitous movement at best. Rustow surfaces as an erratic itinerant in this narrative—a latter-day dragoman who contributed to the efforts to extrapolate from the Turkish example to the rest of the Middle East.

This chapter begins by contextualizing the emergence of modernization theory and its Turkish archetype in the postwar period. I then turn to the work of Dankwart Rustow and his participation in Turkey's laboratization in academic and policy circles. Rustow's travels between various institutions, such as the Committee on Comparative Politics (CCP) of the Social Science Research Council (SSRC) and the Council on Foreign Relations (CFR), underscore the entwined nature of the conduct of American social science and policy production. Rustow's familiarity with the Turkish case led him to reproduce the predilection of these circles for top-down reform and elite-led development. But his conversations with incredulous Turkish and American colleagues also came to inform his increasingly critical attitude towards their theories and methods. Historians of Cold War modernization have sketched compelling portraits of dissenters and cynics but have often situated them at the margins of mainstream conversations.[9] This chapter focuses on Rustow as an uncertain translator between Turkish and American social scientists, thus recovering both the local elements of modernization theory and instances of doubt and hesitation that were central to its construction.

Amnesiac Histories

In the first issue of *Items*, SSRC's official publication, Pendleton Herring, who served as the president of the council between 1948 and 1968, argued that social science's loyalty "to the scientific method" made it "entitled to be called a science no matter whether its data are atoms or voters." Herring praised the vision of a "social science technician" who was equipped with "dealing with social forces, . . . an individual who has been professionally trained to apply to practical situations the facts, generalizations, principles, rules, laws, or formulae uncovered by social science research." The responsibility of the technician was to offer objectively analytical thought, to "diminish wishful thinking and substitute factual analysis for special pleading," and to use "social data for the cure of social ills as doctors use scientific data to cure bodily ills."[10]

The triumphalism of such narratives has led to depictions of "Cold War social science" as a novel site for the promotion of scholarship as social engineering. The figure of the social-science technician was in fact celebrated well before the Cold War, with scholars lending their expertise to the challenges of imperial administration and civilizational uplift during westward expansion and overseas ventures into the Philippines, Puerto Rico, and elsewhere.[11] During the interwar years, major foundations continued to envision "social inquiry as a means of social change."[12] World War II initiated a substantial scholarly relocation towards government research centers, such as the Office of War Information and the Office of Strategic Services, which was the precursor to the Central Intelligence Agency (CIA). These institutions were the wartime abode of many social scientists, among them Gabriel Almond, Daniel Lerner, Ithiel de Sola Pool, and Edward Shils.[13] The "Cold War" framework allowed for the justification of particular modes of inquiry into the decolonizing world, such as psychological warfare, propaganda, and counterinsurgency research. In this new episode of the relationship between political power and political science, the turn towards area studies abetted the creation of a "sovereign structure of universal knowledge," as Tim Mitchell puts it, which was "itself part of the project of a globalized American modernity to which the Cold War also belonged."[14]

The end of World War II also brought with it the possibility of rewriting the history and mission of comparative politics. Political scientist Karl Loewenstein, for instance, credited the war for the end of the "tedious and stagnating routine" of comparative government and insisted on the need for an "intimate knowledge" of the political institutions and attitudes of wartime enemies and potential allies alike; comparative government was to "assume the character of a 'total' science [so that it could] serve as a conscious instrument of social engineering."[15] In his case, the call of total science entailed signing up for The Emergency Advisory Committee for Political Defense and leading a campaign of mass incarceration against leftists in the name of "militant democracy" across Latin America.[16] Loewenstein, along with such fellow German émigrés as Sigmund Neumann and Dankwart Rustow, was also responsible for the proliferation of accounts hailing the "new interest in the politics of Asia, of the Near East, and of Africa for the first time."[17] Such proclamations erased the history of social scientific entanglements with imperialism and global capitalism and with local and internationalist struggles against both.[18] They paved the way for a new alignment between processes of knowledge production and the attempted diffusion of that knowledge to foreign locales.

An important product of the stated need to blend ventures in social engineering and social science in the postwar period was modernization theory. This theory was informed by the structural functionalism of Talcott Parsons and Edward Shils, and it held that development could be read as a process endowing society with a distinct adaptive capacity.[19] The sociologists' evolutionary lexicon was one legacy of neo-Lamarckian ideas rehearsed in *The Journal of Race Development*, the precursor to *Foreign Affairs*, at the turn of the century.[20] The assumption of a teleological, linear path towards progress was heavily rooted in racialized theories of social evolution and understood the United States to be the yardstick of development.[21] Modernization theory postulated a singular process of transition from traditional to modern societies, incorporating such turning points as the rise of mass media, urbanization, rates of literacy, and industrialization. Throughout the 1960s, these sweeping transformations were depicted through tropes of preconceived stages and replicable processes of social mobilization.[22] Such theories would give license not only to interventionist projects over the years but also to practitioners' belief that postwar political science was "pressing into strange lands and experimenting with exotic concepts," adopting comparison as "the very essence of the scientific method."[23]

The dissemination of modernization theory was facilitated by academic exchange programs and research agendas determined by Carnegie and Rockefeller as well as by the Ford Foundation, which maintained close links with the CIA.[24] The Ford-funded CCP of the SSRC was crucial in the promulgation of the theory, which had a policy relevance that culminated in the tenure in the Kennedy administration of such figures as Walt Whitman Rostow and Lucian Pye of the MIT Center for International Studies.[25] The consolidation of area and language studies also found federal support from the National Defense Education Act (1958), spurred by the launch of Sputnik I the year before. Research agendas set by these institutions were aligned with US initiatives to promote "development" through the extension of technical aid and know-how abroad, ranging from President Truman's Point Four Program (1949) and Eisenhower's International Cooperation Administration (1955) to Kennedy's US Agency for International Development and Alliance for Progress (1961). Such initiatives were means to consolidate a "brave new world—a liberal internationalist era" with the help of academic research centers that were to contribute to the production of area-specific knowledge and developmental projects alike.[26]

In this context, political scientists such as Gabriel Almond insisted on the need to "take advantage of several 'laboratory' situations which [emerged] particularly in non-Western areas," spanning Nigeria, Mexico, Indonesia, Afghanistan, and others.[27] Turkey's treatment as a laboratory involved its presentation as a model to its Middle Eastern neighbors because of its "exceptional significance." Other self-proclaimed specialists construed it as significantly exceptional—a site whose "unique" history of authoritarian reform resisted repetition elsewhere, despite similarities in geographic location or a shared political history. The postwar social scientific interest in Turkey drew on the infatuation with the legacy of Ottoman and Kemalist reform but also coincided with the country's transition to multiparty politics, when Ismet Inönü of the Republican People's Party abolished the war-era titles of national chief and permanent chairman and allowed the creation of the Democrat Party under Adnan Menderes in 1946.[28] But the period between 1946 and 1950 also saw the destruction of leftist printing presses, the banning of briefly tolerated socialist parties and trade unions, and an academic purge at Ankara University. Such incidents, along with Menderes's own authoritarian turn (exemplified in arrests of journalists and students), the government-sanctioned anti-Greek pogroms of 1955, and the 1960 coup that led to Menderes's downfall, were either justified or ignored by modernization theorists over the years. The reversals in the political trajectory of Turkey account for the shifts between its depiction as a model and an exception, attesting to the fragility of laboratory endeavors in the social sciences as well as to the contingencies entailed in the intellectual trajectory of practitioners, such as Dankwart Rustow.

Beastly Politics

In an autobiographical essay aptly titled "Connections," Rustow lays out the foundations for his pivotal role in Middle Eastern studies as contingent on three "accidents." The first was the move of his father, the renowned economist Alexander Rüstow, from Berlin to Istanbul in 1933 as part of Ataturk's plan to reenvision Darülfünun as Istanbul University. The second accident was that Dankwart Rustow's studies in Germany were interrupted by World War II, prompting him to follow his father to Istanbul in 1938 at the age of fourteen. There, he audited classes at the Faculty of Law, majored in Arabic and Persian, and minored in Italian and comparative literature at the Faculty of Letters at Istanbul University.

He also received a baccalaureate from Lycee de Galatasaray as an "external candidate" in 1944. After the war, Rustow relocated to the United States, embarked on his undergraduate studies at Queens College, and later received a PhD in political science from Yale University in 1951. On the completion of his dissertation, which examined Swedish party politics, Rustow took a job at Oglethorpe University in Atlanta. It was here that "the third and decisive accident occurred," a meeting with his former teacher Klauss Knorr, who informed him of a new program in Near East studies at Princeton, which Rustow joined the following year.[29]

In his account of the various acquaintances he made in Middle Eastern studies and political science, Rustow also explains his first encounter with the study of politics through a glimpse of Carl Joachim Friedrich's *Constitutional Government and Politics* on his father's bookshelf:

> For it was in Friedrich's book that I first came across the technical term "political science." Its German equivalent of *Staatswissenschaft* (or "science of state") had a repulsively authoritarian ring—but the term "political science" to me sounded exciting, indeed fascinating. My earliest political memories had been when, early in 1933, I returned home from the third grade to find Hitler's Gestapo on their hands and knees searching through the attic of our home in suburban Berlin—and later my father's announcement that, because of the political changes in Germany, he had to go off to Turkey. In short, I had come to think of politics as a wild beast that chased your family from its home country. But if there was such a thing as political *science*, then the beast could be tamed with the power of reason! There was no question that this was what I must study once I managed to go to the United States.[30]

Rustow's conviction in reason led him to envision politics as a brute that could be domesticated, perhaps reduced in size in a sterile, scientific setting. The United States seemed to provide the site and equipment for this experiment, but Rustow could not foresee the circulatory, accidental events that would impel his career forward. It was war that drove the Rustows out of Europe, and it was in Turkey, the ostensibly neutral third party, that they would wait it out, unlike his American colleagues, such as Gabriel Almond and Daniel Lerner, who spent the war in governmental agencies. The urge to tame, apprehend, and discipline politics as an object of study would take Rustow across the Atlantic and cause him to part ways with his father, who returned to Heidelberg to participate in the reconstruction of Germany.[31] Once in the United States, Rustow was thrust into the midst of the efforts to reenvision the *science* of politics—

a process that would take him back to Turkey repeatedly through the following decades. Rustow's travels, first by accident and later by choice, would consolidate his role in forging transnational circuits of knowledge on both sides of the Atlantic.

During his time at Princeton, Rustow also served as secretary for the Committee on the Near and Middle East, cosponsored by the SSRC and the American Council of Learned Societies (ACLS), a role that is indicative of his role as a passage point between area studies and social science during this period. He wrote the Near East section in Gabriel Almond and James Coleman's *Politics of Developing Areas*, coedited a volume comparing Turkey and Japan in the *Political Development* series of the CCP of the SSRC, and contributed profusely to the committee's various publications, writing about leadership, the military, religion, and political parties in Turkey.[32] It is no wonder, then, that Rustow often gets treated as "one of the founders of the modernization school of thought," even in the memorial essay that was published in *Comparative Politics* after his death.[33] Rustow served as that journal's editor in chief between 1979 and 1995, and he provided its logo: a sketch of the world, harkening back to his previous work as a cartographer during his doctoral studies and demonstrating the significance of scaling in the social scientific laboratory. In recent intellectual histories of modernization theory, too, Rustow is either relegated to the background or depicted as an unswerving Cold Warrior because of his involvement with the CFR.[34]

Despite his seeming complicity with this brand of developmental thought, however, the forgotten fragments of Rustow's prolific corpus reveal his vacillations between contesting visions of modernization. His involvement with the emergence of modernization theory took place during early research trips to Turkey (1953–1954, 1958–1959). Rustow remained skeptical of linear accounts of change, proposing at each turn "amalgamate patterns" that encompassed modernity and tradition.[35] He insisted that in phrases like *modernization* and *underdeveloped countries*, he detected "a parochial value judgment by which we posit our culture as the most advanced and also an implicit statement (which ought to be demonstrated rather than assumed) that 'modernization' is inevitable and a mere matter of time."[36] Propelled to situate himself as an obligatory passage point between social scientists and policy makers in Turkey and the United States, Rustow participated in efforts to construct the laboratory of comparative politics, providing requisite "raw data" from the field for this "total science." Yet each encounter over the course of this itinerary seems to have reshaped his thinking, leading him to question both the behavioralist assumptions of his colleagues and the "models" they posited in the service of the alignment of knowledge practices and Cold War politics.

Modern de Tocquevilles

Rustow's first research trip to Turkey took place during the 1953–1954 academic year under the auspices of the Rockefeller-funded Department of Near Eastern Studies at Princeton University.[37] The purpose of the project (which was never published) was to examine political change through a study of the composition of the elite, the processes of state building, and pressure groups and the press in Turkey.[38] Rustow intended the study to be a comparative overview of the political goals and ideologies of the Young Turks, the Kemalists, and the "present democrats"; the overview would provide a critique of narratives of Turkish modernization that otherwise identified the beginning of that process as late as 1920 or 1923. This work would propose, instead, continuity along the axis of Ottoman-Turkish reforms—a framework that exemplified his (and others') various writings on Turkey throughout the following decades.[39]

Although Rustow's year-long stay in Turkey prevented him from attending the seminal first meeting of the SSRC's CCP on February 19, 1954, his correspondence with Gabriel Almond, the chairman of that committee, reveals that he was thoroughly involved with their work.[40] Rustow regretted his absence from preliminary meetings, but Almond, a graduate of the Office of War Information and a frequent government consultant for intelligence and psychological warfare institutions, reassured his Princeton colleague: "If you need some vision of a payoff to sustain your spirits in the difficult days of fieldwork and library work in Turkey, may I say that you will be so far ahead of the great majority of the profession when you come back that in retrospect these costs and sacrifices will appear to have been of great value."[41] Almond's veneration of field experience was in keeping with the valorization by later CCP publications of "research time abroad" as a "precious commodity."[42]

Following that first meeting, Almond kept his colleague abreast of the recent discussions about the research agenda at the CCP, which was "trying to give birth to itself and thus far [had] labored mightily but without much result."[43] The participants of the committee believed that the problems peculiar to nonwestern areas called for a different research strategy, given difficulties in the comparison of its political processes with those of Europe and the United States. Almond consulted Rustow about what that strategy ought to entail: "For example, should a de Tocqueville kind of survey precede more specialized and intensive studies? If so, what intellectual equipment and research techniques should the modern de Tocqueville command? And what advice would you give to such modern de Tocquevilles as to how to proceed in making such surveys?" Almond's summoning of de Tocqueville, a foreigner whose survey of the American landscape once professed the necessity for a "new political science," is telling; as members of the CCP turned their gaze to nonwestern areas, they, too, would proffer all-encompassing theories that hinged on an exploitation of their status as strangers.[44] Given this portrayal of Tocqueville as the archetypal intellectual traveler, Rustow's contributions from the field would prove seminal to the makings of the new "new political science."

Soon after this initial inquiry, Almond enclosed a memorandum he sent to Guy Pauker, Lucian Pye, and George McT. Kahin regarding the suggested terms of reference for the Conference on Research Strategy for non-Western Areas, which Rustow was also slotted to attend after his return from Turkey. Almond emphasized that non-Western areas could be considered a "single field of investigation" and identified commonalities in the persistence of traditional political systems, exposure to change, and contact with the West.[45] Research in these areas, Almond explained, would attempt to "develop a body of knowledge on the basis of which predictions can be made as to how these mixed traditional and rational systems will develop" and to discern developmental patterns that would ease assimilation and adaptation "to the western rational pattern with the least dislocation and instability." The purpose of social research, in other words, was not merely to provide projections about the areas under study but also to manipulate and interfere in their future trajectories.

In his response to Almond, Rustow suggested that they compare different areas, such as the Near East and Latin America, on the basis of recurrent changes between military dictatorship and periods of parliamentary government.[46] Later, Rustow would commend what he labeled the "current reorientation in comparative politics" as a "logical stage of growth and development," noting that current events, which used to "reinforce our parochialism . . . now impel us to greater universality."[47] Rustow's reading of westernization as an irresistible force led him to conceive of the comparative method itself as a means to facilitate the generation of universal knowledge. "Not long ago Western man ruled the world," he declared. "Now he studies it."[48] Rustow's insistence on a temporal break between the rule and study of the world harkens back to his quest for "taming the beast of politics with the power of reason." But the statement also offers, perhaps unwittingly, an equivalence between colonial and epistemic practices. Examining the world in the laboratory setting offered different ways of managing and governing it for modernization theorists; subsequent CCP publications suggest that they were quite invested in the interventionist implications of their research.

Odious Comparisons

Rustow's interest in cross-regional comparison led to his contribution to the influential volume edited by Gabriel Almond and James Coleman, *The Politics of the Developing Areas*, which by most accounts allowed modernization theory to attain paradigmatic status within political science.[49] This work not only championed the structural-functional approach to comparative politics but also devised a new "conceptual vocabulary," one that would replace states with political systems, powers with functions, roles with offices, and structures with institutions, thereby constituting a "major step forward in the nature of political science as science."[50] All political systems were presumed to be mixed ones, ostensibly blurring the otherwise strict differentiation between modernity and tradition. Still, the volume's functionalist vocabulary, which included terms such as *interest articulation and aggregation* and *rule application and adjudication*, rested on a developmental scheme that privileged the Anglo-American and continental European models Almond discussed elsewhere.[51] Almond's introduction to the volume emphasized the need to "master the model of the modern" and the exigency of "practical policy motives." In this effort to extend "the boundaries of the universe of comparative politics and include in it the 'uncouth' and exotic systems of the areas outside Western Europe," he explained, field research would prove indispensable for the universal claims of "political science as science."[52]

This aspiration towards scientific universalism by means of extrapolating from local knowledge, however, was undercut by epistemic anxieties, as can be evinced in the communications between the contributors of this volume.[53] Rustow, who was responsible for the section on the Near East, for instance, was hesitant about his "ignorance about details" regarding the region. He wrote to James Coleman that "quite honestly and strictly between you and me and the bedpost, I could not name a single newspaper in Afghanistan, Libya, the Sudan or Saudi Arabia. I wouldn't be too sure whether there are any at all in Yemen. . . . Hence it hardly seems cricket for me to indicate boldly that political functions are performed by the press in these various countries."[54] Coleman, who was responsible for crafting the conclusion to the volume, seemingly shared Rustow's concerns regarding the gaps of knowledge about the areas under scrutiny and communicated as much in the various memoranda he dispatched to the contributors to the volume:

> Indeed, the results revealed in striking fashion the near hopelessness of trying to integrate the efforts of a group of collaborators who never really worked together long enough to develop a really systematic common framework mutually understood. As Gay [Almond] once remarked, we should really have had six months together, and we might have come up with something very significant. I would go a step further, drawing on Dan [Rustow], and say that before that sixth-month meeting we each should spend ten years in the field. In any event, the results were not at all comparable, and I must confess that I exercised considerable license in interpreting entries to try and achieve comparability.[55]

When researchers reconvened in the aftermath of their dithering and tottering in the field, they were supposed to assemble social scientific models that confirmed the superiority of the western developmental path. Yet their collaborative endeavor was derailed by problems of classification, revealing the fragility of attempts at comparison and data collection. Although exercises of codification aimed to flatten out differences, instances of incompatibility lingered as a testament to the arduous labor endemic to knowledge production and its subsequent concealment. Despite Almond's encouragement of extrapolation from the western model, problems of operationalization, categorization, and definition persisted for the technicians of the comparative laboratory.

The assignment of various countries to types of political systems (competitive, semicompetitive, or authoritarian) proved particularly daunting for the contributors. The rapid changes in the regions of interest was one reason why Rustow marked his own matrix "not for publication," citing "considerable pangs of conscience" when it came to placing the countries within the "democratic, semiauthoritarian, [or] traditional static" slots:

Somehow I always have in the back of my mind the Afghan aristocrat studying for his PhD at Harvard who will one day buttonhole me and say: "What's the idea calling us 'static' and bestowing the honorific of 'moving' on Saudi Arabia, which has a far more hidebound government than ours?"[56]

For Rustow, the prospect of the ungainly encounter with Afghan nobility was a further testament to the fact that "our categories are too saddled with value connotations, even if we say they are analytical."[57]

Coleman's memoranda to the contributors suggest that other participants shared Rustow's reservations. Myron Weiner noted that he put Pakistan, "after much soul searching, into the mixed-mixed category," only to find the establishment of martial law that led to its movement to the authoritarian-mixed box. He asked, "But can I be certain what box she will be in when this book is published?"[58] Lucian Pye, otherwise a sentinel of modernization theory and the author of a CIA-funded study of Malayan guerrillas, wrote:

I am afraid that I am a bit disturbed about having to put things down in such a brutal fashion. . . . Actually I am far more tough minded towards the hypersensitive peoples of Southeast Asia than most people who try to work with them, and I fully believe in calling things as one sees them. But there is something to the point that comparison is odious, and I am not sure that we accomplish much by saying who is more and who is less democratic, unless we relate it to something else.[59]

Comparative work was supposed to be the product of unswerving dedication to data collection and the observance of social and literary norms of behavior and thinking, such as objectivity. Although the practice of "political science as science" called for certitude in attempts at prediction and classification, however, the specter of the nonwest, whether it was the hypersensitive peoples of Southeast Asia or Rustow's imaginary Afghan aristocrat, called into question the validity of universalistic claims, further imperiling the coveted analogy with scientific research.

Despite the authors' reluctance, Coleman attempted to "create order out of our chaotic universe of systems" and included the matrices in his conclusion to the volume, whereby each developing country was compared with its "model" for emulation, namely the parliamentary system of the western country with which they had the most contact. Although

Coleman acknowledged some of the contentions that informed the writing process, he concluded that the authors' account relied on "functional profiles constructed from existing knowledge, however inadequate the latter may be."[60]

It might be tempting to dismiss the preceding correspondence as necessary, perhaps inevitable, wrinkles in knowledge production that get sorted and flattened out over time. But negotiations and standstills were constitutive of the process of naming, comparing, and classifying that enabled the construction of modernization theory. Tables of regime types or charts showing the correlation between average levels of economic and political development were ways of arranging data that allowed the social scientists to scale down and present not just the world that they observed and knew about (at least to the best of their ability) but also the actual world that they wanted to create. The certitude with which they displayed their data concealed their doubts and uncertainties not only about the research they were undertaking but also about how that research was impelled by their investment in "modernizing" the lives of those they were studying. In other words, when the researchers codified their data into compact form, they erased any trace of their own entanglements with what they came to call political and economic development. But their scholarly anxiety remained prevalent at each stage and was mirrored in the hesitations of their local interlocutors, whose collaboration was crucial for the assemblage and dissemination of modernization theory.

Modernization Theory in Turkey

In a retrospective account of his engagement with *The Politics of the Developing Areas*, Rustow conceded that he adopted the functional-structural terminology begrudgingly: "Instead, I would have much preferred to stay with plain English and with the political role of groups that had been the SSRC Committee's original focus. But in the crucial discussions among the contributors to the Almond-Coleman volume, I remained the only dissident, and rather than quit the fascinating project, I did my best to analyze Near Eastern politics according to those seven 'functional' dimensions."[61] Although Rustow was wary of the committee's categories, he did not fail to employ them, citing a high degree of modernization under indigenous auspices for Turkey and no levels of westernization at all in Yemen and Afghanistan. All other Near Eastern countries fell under a mix of foreign and indigenous initiatives. At the end of his chapter, however, Rustow parted way with the volume's evolutionary language and suggested that "even if at some future stage politics, society, and culture throughout the Near East should have become thoroughly modernized, there is no reason why this should make the countries of the region into replicas of any western country or of each other—any more than Norway is a replica of France, or Canada of Austria."[62]

Rustow's misgivings about the replicability of a western model of modernity seem to have been informed by an unpublished essay in which he reviewed recent works written on Turkey during the mid-1950s:

> In reading about the forced cultural changes of the Kemalist period we still are likely to encounter statements to the effect that "Turkish script and vocabulary had been modernized to keep pace with the world" (Bisbee), and in the last few years we have almost grown used to hearing all nonindustrial areas condescendingly referred to as "underdeveloped countries." It is above all the fatuous notion that social progress is automatic and unilinear of which we must beware in studying the problems of culture change in non-Western countries. . . . The "world" did not progress from the Arabic to the Latin script or from a highly literary and eclectic language to an artificially archaizing idiom. The present condition of the countries that are in the process of Westernization does not closely resemble any particular stage in our own historical development, and their striving towards such patterns of social organization as representative government and capitalism, which telescopes centuries into a few decades, does not follow the path we ourselves pursued in the past. Nor will these countries, once Westernization has run its course, be exact replicas of a Western country any more than Western countries are of one another.[63]

The passage indicates that Rustow recognized the shortcomings of teleological accounts of development and that he was apprehensive of worldwide generalizations presuming that the knowledge of the western past would cast light on the future of "underdeveloped" countries. Regardless of these hesitations, he continued to study Turkey as a site of fact gathering for the production of social scientific knowledge.

In line with studies that treated Turkey as the model and laboratory of modernization, Rustow co-edited, with Japan scholar Robert Ward, the only country-specific volume to come out of the Political Development Series of the CCP. Other collections in the series splintered areas of research into their parts, such as political functions and interest groups or mass media, the school, and the bureaucracy, as a way to reassemble archetypes of development.[64] The ordering of data, after multiple stages of filtering and winnowing, was a conceptual activity, involving efforts in classification and typification, but it was also an exercise in social engineering. The shared themes of the series' policy-oriented analyses were their anti-Communist outlook and basic mistrust of the masses who the authors believed had to be managed by a responsible elite.[65]

The motivating rationale behind the CCP volume on Turkey and Japan was also explicitly interventionist, as Almond explained in his preface to the volume. He wrote, "How can we 'invest' most effectively in the 'growth' of particular institutions in order to produce the political outcomes which we prefer?"[66] A roster of Turkey and Japan scholars convened in Dobbs Ferry, New York, between September 10 and 14, 1962, in order to grapple with this question, and Rustow asked some of the social scientists he had lectured at Ankara University in 1959 to participate.[67] The minutes of the Dobbs Ferry meetings reveal the contentious nature of their cross-disciplinary endeavor. The participants disagreed about the components of modernization (secularism, democracy, and economic development) as well as about the factors that may or may not induce it (an active military, civil bureaucracy, education, or mass media). Questions of borrowing and imitation and of the pace and timing of modernization were discussed at length. Although Japan and Turkey scholars emphasized the continuity of reform in both settings, dating back their analyses to the Meiji and Ottoman periods respectively, they failed, for the most part, to arrive at a consensus about comparable periods of modernization.[68]

In their concluding meeting, seminar participants agreed with Rustow's suggestion that differences between Turkey and Japan stemmed from "givens" at the start of modernization (such as insularity or the availability of traditional institutions to "hold onto") and the subsequent choices made about the means of modernization. Although Rustow and Ward defined modernization in accordance with the central tenets of the Political Development Series ("a marked increase in geographic and social mobility, a spread of secular, scientific, and technical education, a transition from ascribed to achieved status, an increase in material standards of living"), they were hesitant to propose anything more than a "chronicle of uniqueness" given the futility of seeking a "shared substratum of experience" or a unilinear evolution from traditional to modern societies in these two settings. Thus, in their conclusion, the editors gestured at alternative models of development, such as the Russian Communist, Chinese Communist, Brazilian, and Japanese ones.[69]

On his return to Turkey, one participant of the conference, historian Halil İnalcık, reported the findings of the group, especially the conclusion "that modernism and traditionalism carry a value judgment and that they differ from society to society, from period to period."[70] In his serial and popular account of the conference in the daily *Milliyet,* Kemal Karpat celebrated the two countries' military-led modernization, presenting as consensus what had in fact been a point of dispute.[71] A notable review of the book was written by Niyazi Berkes, who studied sociology at the University of Chicago in the 1930s and was among the faculty members forced to resign from Ankara University during a red scare in the 1940s.[72] In his review of the book, Berkes, whose contributions to the modernization literature took an increasingly critical turn throughout the 1970s, expressed his disappointment with the comparative thrust of the edited volume. He wrote, "Ostensibly, their purpose would be to compare notes so that, eventually, the major factors operating positively and negatively upon the modernization of the non-Western societies would be identified, analyzed, and turned to effect in the processes of modernization itself."[73] Such comparison, Berkes thought, was lacking in the various articles of the volume, aside from the contributions by the editors themselves.

Berkes's skeptical appraisal resonated with the reception of various CCP publications among members of the political science faculty of Ankara University. Nermin Abadan, otherwise a proponent of public opinion and survey research, objected to the claims of scientific certitude, noting that "subjectively speaking, the behavioralist school is an exciting innovation for many young social scientists. . . . But this has led many young social scientists to assume that they are at the service of science, entering the mood of the scientist who is observing a successful experiment at the laboratory."[74] In an article that drew on the theoretical foundations of the Almond and Coleman volume, Yavuz Abadan applied their functionalist terminology to examine the prospects of democracy in the Middle East. He cautioned, however, that "excessiveness can always lead to false conclusions in such generalizations" and that "one cannot seek the determinism of the physical sciences and mathematical certitude in the social and political sciences."[75] Şerif Mardin, whose *Genesis of Young Ottoman Thought* was widely influential in modernization theory circles and who later criticized his own attachment to behavioralism, similarly objected to the findings of *Politics of Developing Areas*, particularly the chapter by Rustow for "failing to make use of the analytical opportunities yielded by this concept and missing the opportunity for a comparative study of Middle Eastern systems."[76] Finally, sociologist Özer Ozankaya wrote a master's thesis at Syracuse University comparing development in Turkey and Japan and published it in the political science journal of Ankara University, whose faculty he joined thereafter. Ozankaya reiterated the assumptions of the modernization template and espoused the inevitability of cultural change, confirming the conclusions of the Ward and Rustow volume, which he cited frequently ("We see that the Turkey of the 1960s is not even at the level of Japan in the 1920s"). Still, he argued that his use of the two cases to test the "reliability" of W. W. Rostow's stages of economic growth disproved the economist's hypothesis.[77]

These disparate and immediate reactions to the most recent publications in the modernization literature exemplify the intricacies involved in their reception in Turkish social scientific circles. At once apprehensive of scientific methodology and underwhelmed with the comparative nature of this work, these scholars willingly yielded the Turkish site for further examination. Although the historical nature of the work of such figures as Mardin and İnalcık would prove influential for scholars across the Atlantic, the writings of Ozankaya and the Abadans reveal the consistently partial adoption—indeed, the translation—of the main categories and methodologies being crafted in the laboratory of modernization theory.

An additional venue for Ankara political scientists and their American interlocutors' discussions about development was the journal *Forum*, which was published between 1954 and 1970. Throughout the 1950s, *Forum* functioned as an important platform for airing criticism of the Democrat Party and for efforts to reconcile the tenets of Kemalism with liberalism, which was defined as a combination of tolerance, freedom of thought, and Keynesian economics. The journal published not just the writings of the faculty members and translated articles from the *New York Times* and the *Economist* but also commissioned pieces from modernization theorists who studied Turkey, such as Rustow and MIT's Frederick Frey.[78]

Elite-led development, an important theme across CCP's Political Development Series, was a concern shared by *Forum* writers. In the same year that Rustow lectured about new directions in comparative politics to Ankara faculty, Mümtaz Soysal wrote about the university's own new curriculum, which included introductory courses in public opinion, political parties, and comparative government in the hopes of teaching the "democratic lifestyle" to their students, who historically went on to take bureaucratic positions. The role of intellectuals in a "democratic order" was much debated, with Kemal Karpat calling on sociologists to assist modernization through objective, scientific analysis. On the question of rural development, Karpat insisted that the state implement regional policies by training personnel, *kalkınma memurları* (civil servants of development), who then had to convince villagers that they were the ones who came up with the policies in the first place.[79] Rustow was in agreement with many of *Forum*'s conclusions, among them an exoneration of Turkey's single-party rule as a form of "limited democracy."[80] His long-standing—and in some cases, considerably intimate—interactions with these colleagues are a further testament to his efforts to enroll them in the crafting of modernization theory.

The Turkish Model

After Rustow's departure from Princeton in 1960, he became professor of international social forces at Columbia University. He returned to Turkey during this time, in April 1965, to discuss the Columbia Political Science Project. While there, he met with Ankara University's Aydın Yalçın, Mümtaz Soysal, and Şerif Mardin to discuss the possibility of an academic exchange program between the two departments.[81] The proposal was backed by Andrew Cordier, the dean of the School of International Affairs, and John Badeau, the director of the Near and Middle Eastern Institute at Columbia University, as well as by Kemal Karpat, then of New York University.

Karpat, who was an avid proponent of modernization theory and its applications to Turkey, became one of Rustow's most committed collaborators over the years.[82] The two scholars shared a history as double refugees in Turkey and the United States. Karpat, who was a migrant from Romania, also described the state as a beast, as a "dragon that should be combated not through class struggle but real democracy."[83] Rustow and Karpat submitted a series of proposals to Columbia University in the mid-1960s in an attempt to rekindle what they perceived to be a decline of American scholarly interest in Turkey. Upholding Turkey's singularity in its "deliberate program of modernization," they suggested that "research on Turkey in many ways can serve as a pilot project for comparative research on other developing countries." The presence at Columbia of other Middle East scholars, such as J. C. Hurewitz, Charles Issawi, and Herbert Hyman, seemingly made that university the ideal venue for building a program of social science research on Turkey "as a key example of a developing country."[84]

In an undated proposal for a center for Turkish studies, Rustow and Karpat lamented the increasing scholarly interest in "Arab nations" (presumably in the context of the rise of Nasser and Arab nationalism), which came at the expense of recognizing Turkey's "services to worldwide modernization":

> Turkey as the first Muslim state to embark on secular modernization, then on a parliamentary experiment, remains a path setting model for other developing Muslim states. The aloofness of Turkey from other Muslim states, due to her foreign policy, seems to have dimmed her prospects of remaining a model. In reality, however, liberal intellectuals from Iran, Pakistan, and the Arab countries follow closely the developments in Turkey partly as a possible policy alternative, and partly (if the Turkish democratic experiment fails) as a vindication for their present regimes.[85]

The seemingly imperceptible shift between positing Turkey as a model for the sake of knowledge production and for purposes of policy implementation elsewhere is noteworthy. Conceived as a privileged site of theory *and* practice, Turkey as a model offered lessons from its past and present for the future of "developing Muslim states." As a prototype of modernization, the Turkish landscape emerged as at once a representation on a smaller scale ("little America") in an (un)specified time to come ("in thirty years, . . . in the near future") and an archetype whose emulation was predicated on what it already was.[86] This double-fold temporality was articulated in light of the sites and sights associated with one's positioning: facing America ("what the Middle East seeks to become"), Turkey, viewed from the West, was expected to orient itself towards its Middle Eastern counterparts, participating in the drive to be seen as a template ("the area's bright model of modernization").[87] If Turkey's future was a projection of its past trajectory, multiple stages of abstraction attended its crafting as a model; its history presented "raw data" for the crafting of modernization theory, which was then repackaged and reexported to the rest of the region. The content of that model, however, was unstable at best, because it was subject to redefinition by experts and policy makers.

The Turkish Exception

In 1952, during a Council on Foreign Relations (CFR) meeting on American policy in the Middle East, historian Lewis Thomas of Princeton University declared Turkey a "natural" for the United States. Thomas's speech relied on tropes that exemplified writings on Turkey at that time, including the valorization of Ataturk despite "some" authoritarian tendencies ("He used an iron hand but for the good of the nation") and the idealization of the legacy of Tanzimat-era Ottoman reforms. He argued, however, that Turkey's successful past of modernization and its present status as a "natural" ally did not necessarily ensure its emergence as a leader in the Middle East: "Our use of the Turks in the Middle East Command was extremely awkward. All we succeeded in doing was to stir Arab-Turkish friction. It should be noted that the fact that the Turks are Muslims does not mean that they love the Arabs. It is much the same as our regard for the Mexicans." Noting Turkey's emergence as "one of Israel's best customers," Thomas added that "the Arabs think of Turkey as a sort of 'White man's nigger.'"[88]

Thomas's cautionary (if unseemly) analogies did not deter other participants from asking whether the Turkish experience could be replicated—a question that continued to preoccupy CFR meetings throughout the following decade. Six years later, for instance, John Badeau wondered whether the country was a "leader in beneficial change or a deviationist" and whether it lacked appeal in the region because the Turkish attitude was too secular."[89] The following year, Ankara political scientist and *Forum* editor Aydın Yalçın told a Council audience that Turkey's "richer history of institutions" meant that its democratic experience could not be repeated elsewhere in the region.[90]

In 1952, when Thomas ardently declared Turkey to be "a natural ally" of the United States, George McGhee, US ambassador to Turkey (1951–1953), took a three-day-long train ride across the country with President Celal Bayar. During that trip, McGhee explained to Bayar what he envisioned to be Turkey's role in the Middle East by way of reference to the Good Neighbor Policy in Latin America:

> I pointed out that whereas these states had previously distrusted and felt jealous of the United States, we had now developed a very sincere cooperation through the inter-American system in military, economic, political and social matters. I sug-

gested to the President that Turkey might well in her own interest pursue such a Good Neighbor Policy in the Middle East. Turkey was the natural leader of the Middle East because of her historical position, military strength, political stability, economic development, and membership in NATO.

The next morning, McGhee explained in his report, Bayar revealed that he had thought over the matter and agreed that the region had been neglected for too long in Turkish foreign policy. The ambassador then counseled the initiation of a program akin to the Point Four Policy, saying, "It need not entail much money—it could be started by granting spaces in Turkish civil and military schools for students from the other Middle East countries, and sending professors and training missions to those countries." It would be easier, McGhee continued, for Turkey to "teach these countries than it was for us, or the Western Europeans. The gap between them and us was too great. Our country dazzled and confused them since they had little hope of ever achieving our standards. Turkey, however, provided a much more comparable environment—one that these countries could hope to emulate."[91] This paternalistic narrative would lead US- and UN-sponsored research centers and universities to be set up in Ankara in order to train administrators, architects, and engineers for the region. But like the defense agreements, these institutions, such as the Institute of Public Administration for Turkey and the Middle East (TODAIE, 1952) and the Middle East Technical University (METU, 1956), did not end up having broad regional appeal. Still, McGhee's praise for Turkey's "centuries-long hatred of Russia" and for its status as a "true political democracy" and as a potential model of development continued throughout the years.[92]

George McGhee was a State Department recruit from the oil industry who described himself as "one of the first Cold Warriors," acted as assistant secretary of state for the Near East, South Asia, and Africa, and served as coordinator of aid to Greece and Turkey in 1947.[93] Although McGhee later claimed that "we didn't intervene as much internally in Turkey as we did in Greece," his achievements included securing petroleum legislation in Ankara similar to the deal he had brokered for Aramco in Saudi Arabia.[94] As Nathan Citino has shown, McGhee and his collaborators' valorization of Ottoman reforms "validated a Turco-centric regional strategy" that imposed an "ethno-geographic distinction between modern Turks and backward Arabs" and helped deflect alternative plans for regional development, such as an equitable distribution of oil-company profits.[95] But American assessments and recommendations for Turkey's political and economic trajectory were also erratic during these decades, reinforcing undemocratic and unequal policies within the country.

In 1957, for instance, a CFR meeting took Turkey as a case study for "human factors in economic development," with the participation of McGhee, Rustow, Lerner, and Richard Robinson, among others. Edwin Cohn, who became a prominent figure in Turkey's planning circles in the 1960s, prepared the background papers, which identified problems such as fatalism, a short time horizon, submission to authority, and inability to cooperate as the culprits for the persistence of traditional patterns in the country. Cohn called into question the Menderes government's commitment to private enterprise, and he criticized its decision to extend credit to rural sectors in response to unfavorable weather conditions and slowing international demand at the end of the Korean War.[96] Cohn's censure reflected American recommendations after 1954, which sought to encourage the development of the industrial sector through private and foreign investment and to curb Menderes's populist policies.[97] The critics did not acknowledge the abandonment of an earlier plan for land reform and the uneven distribution of agricultural subsidies and machinery in the Kurdish-populated eastern parts of the country, which were legacies of the Marshall Plan. In 1955, the onset of a severe balance-of-payments crisis led to the ultimatum that American aid would continue only under the conditions of a return to statist measures of control.[98] Menderes initially paid no heed to the foreign economists and international agencies, but then he begrudgingly began a de facto shift to import substitution industrialization (ISI) practices. Menderes's dispute with American experts and his increasingly authoritarian measures against students and the press were followed by the military coup of 1960. Conversations at the Council reflected the reversal in Turkey's political trajectory and now praised its experience with "military modernization" rather than its position as a beacon of democracy.

The Council continued its dissection of the military in the Middle East over the years, with Rustow, along with Manfred Halpern and Charles Issawi, also attending such meetings. J. C. Hurewitz prepared a series of background papers for one such group, arguing that "the intrusion of Middle East soldiers into politics has altered the pace of modernization, at times hastening it and at others slowing it down." Throughout the meetings, the participants discussed the advantages of military-led modernization, such as its production of charismatic leadership and the establishment of countrywide control. Although he pointed out the differences in times and setting, Hurewitz praised both Nasser's and Ataturk's dedication to projects of modernization and wondered "whether Egypt was indeed following the Turkish pattern, but with a time lag of thirty years."[99] Rustow commended the (alleged) civilianization of Ataturk and his retinue on entry into politics ("a trend that the United States might be eager to encourage"), but he objected to the generalization of the Turkish model: "We cannot assume every army represents the wave of the future. Modernization is a deceptive term subject to many interpretations." He added that the trajectory of military modernization had been volatile, since "not all types of armies at all times have been an asset to modernization in Turkey."[100]

The roots of Rustow's skepticism about the generalizability of the Turkish experience can be traced back to his participation in the conference on political development in Turkey and Japan, which took place the year before the CFR meeting on military modernization. In addition to his role as organizer, Rustow was responsible for the chapter on the military, where some participants objected to the designation of the army as the uncontested vanguard of modernization.[101] In a more public instance of engagement with Turkey's military experience, Rustow wrote a letter to the editor of the *New York Times* a mere three weeks before the 1960 coup and called on "every American concerned about the future of democracy" to show sympathy and support for the Turkish students who protested the martial laws, the editors who were jailed, and the professors whose tenure was curtailed by the administration—a reference to the government's refusal to approve Yalçın's promotion to full professor. Although Rustow stopped short of calling for interference, he argued that American prestige was at stake, given that the United States had trained and equipped the army that enforced Menderes's curfew.[102] But at a CFR meeting that took place three years later, Rustow praised the same military that had staged the coup, which was meant "to reverse the headlong drift towards authoritarianism that had developed under Menderes." This exoneration of the coup was consistent with the writings of Turkey scholars at the time.[103] Throughout the 1970s and 1980s, a period that saw two more military coups, Rustow continued to praise the Turkish military for assuming "power for a strictly limited period, relinquishing it as soon as law and order were restored and democratic institutions strengthened."[104]

The Council's fascination with military modernizers was in agreement with both the Kennedy administration's interest in revolutionary nationalists and the belief of the CCP Political Development Series that democracy in the developing world should be limited at best.[105] In fact, American experts and policy makers had a long history of alternating between labeling countries as democratic or despotic and as examples of modernization or deviations from the norm depending on their status as allies or enemies.[106] In analyses of Turkey, the constant variable was the army, praised either as a democratizing force that quickly left the political stage in the aftermath of coups d'état or as a reliable source of development and stability that periodically intervened in order to offset the volatile manifestations of social and political change. Participants in academic and official dialogues did question the plausibility of lawlike generalizations, but when they tried to tame the "beast of politics" through the force of reason, they continued to resort to normative claims about order and predictability. By the end of the 1960s, however, Rustow surfaced as an increasingly skeptical mediator between the production of theory and policy.

A Bad Case of Indigestion

Between 1961 and 1963, Rustow served as a senior staff member at the Brookings Institution, where he participated in a study program on political development as a key issue in "emerging countries." The result was *A World of Nations,* published in 1967 as Rustow's most comprehensive account of modernization, which he depicted as the "rapidly widening control over nature through closer cooperation among men." Parting ways with his earlier skepticism of the "value connotations" of that phrase, he argued that "society as a whole cannot engage in modernization without accepting its ingredients as beneficial or its totality as inevitable," but he added that the student of modernization need not concur in either of these judgments."[107]

Taking up questions of rhythm, speed, and timing that were addressed at the conference on Turkey and Japan, Rustow outlined various developmental models, depending on the sequence of equality, identity, and authority formation in a diverse array of settings. His description also included an assault on the work of fellow modernization theorists, such as Karl Deutsch, W. W. Rostow, Lucian Pye, and Daniel Lerner:

> They have sought the requisites of democracy in literacy or in affluence. They have traced the ambivalent attitudes of Burmese officials to crises of personal identity. They have ascribed the Middle Easterner's response to newspapers and radio programs to his capacity for empathy or his familiarity with city life. They have attributed economic growth to changing methods of toilet training. Heedless of all that Lenin, Nkrumah, and others have preached about the primacy of politics, they have relegated politics to the position of dependent variable. No one will mourn the sterile legalism of Wilson's days; but today's generation of scholars has been in danger of throwing the political baby out with the institutional bathwater, of letting their interdisciplinary enthusiasm carry them to the point of self-effacement as political scientists.[108]

In his attempt to recuperate the study of politics, Rustow objected to "any unilinear theory of 'stages of political growth': It is as if Darwin had expected amoeba, in five successive stages of growth, to evolve into a fern, an elephant, a sequoia, and a dinosaur."[109] His objection to the singular path of modernization also took into account the input from his colleagues at Ankara University a decade ago: "The attempt to forecast future developments in all societies in terms of a single evolutionary 'law' precludes any realistic insight into the diversity of human conditions."[110]

The following year, Rustow continued his assessment of modernization theory in the first issue of *Comparative Politics.* Although he believed that parts of this vast literature could be salvaged given its promising analysis of change, he thought that it had not lived up to the promise of overcoming the previous parochialism inflecting political science—an attempt he had extolled during the previous decade. One culprit for the failed delivery of this promise was the functionalism and "awkward neologisms" sullying the work of Almond and his disciples: "Almond laudably sent Western students of politics off to study the non-West, but regrettably he sent them off with a conceptual baggage far more distinctively Western than he realized. A less ambitious set of categories and one derived more closely from the non-Western data might well have guarded against such neoparochialism in disguise."[111]

Rustow's disillusionment with the science of comparison culminated in his disclosure of its unintended consequences. He had attempted to fold otherwise-neglected areas into its domain of study, but comparative politics had reversed and, in the process, had doubly exacerbated the problem of parochialism, which now resurfaced in excessive terms—hence Rustow's insinuation that Almond was one political scientist inclined to view the world as his oyster, with the likely result of a "bad case of indigestion." Rustow no longer had unequivocal praise for those who scaled down the beast of politics to a manageable size or viewed the world as an oyster available for comparison. Scholarly indigestion manifested itself in "functional abstractions" and "worldwide generalizations," especially in area studies, which presumed "geographic proximity" to produce comparability between "Turkey and Yemen, Thailand and Indonesia, Haiti and Argentina," and in the growing literature on the role of the military in politics, which expected that "Ataturk in Turkey, Stroessner in Paraguay, Chiang in China, Nkrumah in Ghana, and Peron in Argentina should all be playing similar political roles."[112]

In addition to the publication of this appraisal of modernization theory, the year 1968 also saw Rustow get arrested along with students during protests at Columbia University. A thousand demonstrators occupied five buildings on campus, criticizing the university's imperialism in Harlem and abroad, given its affiliation with the Institute for Defense Analyses, known for its counterinsurgency studies in Vietnam.[113] Rustow's arrest came less out of identification with the students' grievances and more out of his objection to the way the police were handling the protestors, and it was his attempt to interpose himself between what he called "hostile forces" that swept him into the van along with the students.[114] Still, he left Columbia for CUNY the next year, where he held the post of professor of political science and sociology until the time of his death in 1996. It is no wonder, then, that his increasingly mordant critique of the Behavioral Revolution opens with a panoramic view of the situation at home:

> There is a great deal of soul-searching in the social sciences these days. Should the sociologist, political scientist or economist remain objective, detached and above the political battles of the day? Or does he have an obligation to apply his knowledge to the urgent problems of his society? If so, should he play the role of a social engineer improving the workings of the government and strengthening the established order? Or should he be a gadfly, social critic or activist championing such causes as the peace movement and the fight for racial equality? Is objectivity possible, or is it merely a timid pose, a hypocritical form of conservatism?

Over the course of this essay, published in 1971 in the *American Scholar*, Rustow faults the fifty-year-long reign of positivism and behaviorism in the social sciences with the display of a "hypocritical form of conservatism" under the pretense of claims to objectivity. Unlike the natural scientists they aspire to resemble, social scientists yearning for "discovery" cannot remain insulated from their audience and subject matter—that is, "society." Joining the ranks of his peers at Ankara University a decade later, Rustow demurred to the validity of laboratory aspirations within the social sciences: "The astronomer peering at his stars, the biologist raising a culture of bacteria, the chemist testing the composition of his molecules, in fact, any outside observer may meaningfully search for immutable, value-free laws. But the social scientist is an observer from inside society, and within those confines his task becomes both more modest and more difficult."[115]

Rustow now believed that ethical neutrality was a posture at best, since the social scientist "is always a *participant* observer":

> "Value freedom" in his conclusions puts [the behaviorist] back ashore as a passive supporter of the wealthy and the powerful because, whereas others might have to be shown how, it is they who dispose of the most effective means of application. . . . The human qualities of social science cannot be exorcised, only grossly distorted—and one of the worst distortions is the ease with which the "value-free" scholar can become a brain-for-hire to the wealthy and the powerful.[116]

Although Rustow's indictment of the "behaviorist" may indicate a gesture of self-absolution, he did not hesitate to implicate himself in the apparent practice of "value freedom" in the service of the alignment between knowledge, power, and capital.

Children Devoured

In 1971, Rustow encouraged Benjamin Smith, a young political scientist from SUNY Cortland to undertake an "intellectual history of the Committee on Comparative Politics and the Princeton group [as a microcosm of a larger pattern revealing how major approaches and ideas are generated and disseminated, including as a key part their preliminary institutional setting]."[117] Rustow not only wrote a letter of recommendation for Smith but also offered his personal papers relating to the activities of that group for Smith's work. Rustow noted that this would be the first full-fledged study of the Council, whose operations and influence in shaping the Behavioral Revolution had hitherto remained underanalyzed. The contours of Smith's project were considerably altered after his conversation with Rustow, who persuaded him to "discover the role of SSRC in what is said to be an institutional network within which US policy processes create and select their expertise and channel resources for the formation of new areas of expertness, as well as fund specific studies. . . . When science serves through institutions which are structurally tied to the interests of class, then an entire reassessment is justified." Smith's initial findings were presented at a conference of the American Political Science Association, at which he explained that his study of the committee topics, expenditures, revenues, and affiliations of grant and fellowship recipients of the SSRC revealed that "the organization has been by and large supportive of the governing class."[118] During the same conference, Rustow sat for a roundtable discussion along with Samuel Huntington, Lucian Pye, and Bernard E. Brown.[119] The session was titled "Comparative Political Studies: Did the SSRC-Sponsored Revolution Devour Its Own Children?," bringing the analogy of beastly politics back home.

Rustow's interest in Turkey continued over the years, as he took it as one of his cases in his influential conceptualization of democratic transitions.[120] He also penned a CFR publication, *Turkey, America's Forgotten Ally*, a text regressive in its rendition of Turkey as a crucial yet neglected actor at the brink of the Cold War.[121] Such a belatedly wistful glance towards the partnership of the past was yet another indication that the expeditions of this particular traveler had failed to yield the lawlike generalities that once promised to deliver the social sciences from its foregoing parochialism. His return, late in his career, to the translation of poetry, from English to German to Turkish and back, is suggestive of the liminal nature of his standing between the various institutions, social scientists, and policy makers he encountered over the course of his travels between Turkey and the United States. Although he was drawn to the latter given the allure of its social scientific reasoning, Rustow's abiding bonds with an increasingly unruly field attested to the futility of scientific aspirations and scholarly detachment alike.

Even when contemplated as a singular, natural ally whose specific legacy of reform resisted replication elsewhere, Turkey's developmental trajectory was concocted as a template in the accounts of scholars and policy makers alike. The narrative of unremitting encounters with the

West, dating back to the Tanzimat era, was widely shared in the circles of the SSRC CCP and the CFR. The making of modernization theory and the role of Turkey within its contours—as a particular venue for crafting and testing laboratory initiatives—were mutually intertwined. Rustow's familiarity with the Turkish case enabled him to contribute to the pathologies of the theory, such as its valorization of military modernization, elite-led development, and top-down reform. But these interactions also allowed him to grow skeptical of the universalistic claims of modernization theory, its erasure of particularities, and its disavowal of value judgments and political commitments that he came to see as endemic to knowledge production. That Rustow was in disagreement with the more behavioral strands of modernization theory should not come as a surprise, given recent accounts of occasional cynics within that body of thought. Rather than the obdurate, conceited Cold Warrior we are accustomed to encountering in intellectual histories, however, this chapter has shown that even the most poised social scientists were in fact splintered selves and frequently diffident commentators. Acknowledging Rustow's role as an incredulous passage point between Turkish and American social scientists reveals both the local components that went into the making of the theory and moments of internal dissent and uncertainty. Those tensions are also central to understanding how problems of knowledge are fundamentally entwined with problems of the political order, as attested by Rustow's own vacillations between wholesale complicity with universalistic social science and a self-reflexive condemnation of its use in the service of "the wealthy and the powerful."

2

Questions of Modernization
Empathy and Survey Research

One might even speculate that *ordinary* men, at least, in some degree, have become more enlightened and scientific in their approach to social problems and their understanding of their fellow men as a result of surveys being widely disseminated in newspapers, mass magazines, and on nationwide television. They have become less parochial, more knowledgeable about their fellows and the variety of beliefs and the reasons for the differences, and more cognizant of the wider and varied moral standards by which they might guide their own conduct.

—Herbert Hyman, "The Sample Survey"

This writer was on one occasion informed with some vehemence by a Central American Minister of Justice that a questionnaire is an instrument of propaganda. "It is printed and it circulates," were his words.

—Frank Bonilla, "Survey Techniques"

AT THE NATIONAL LIBRARY in Ankara, which strives to collect copies of all published work in Turkey, sit two sample survey reports that were conducted on Turkish students in 1959. The first was a study undertaken by political scientist Frederick Frey, then of MIT, in collaboration with the staff at the Test and Research Bureau of the Turkish Board of Education and Discipline as a means to discern the values that high-school students assigned to occupational groups. Attached to this report is a replica of the instructions that were circulated to the sampled high schools along with the mail questionnaires.[1] The instruction sheet appears proverbial—indeed, pedestrian—for those accustomed to the design and dictates of the appropriate questionnaire setting. In a context in which the imperatives of survey research were not altogether familiar, however, the writers of these instructions took special care to explicate the premises (and promises) of this particular mode of inquiry. They insisted on the value of asking questions directly and the necessity of practicing candor in the students' articulation of their own opinions. Although their opinions were unlikely to find verbatim counterparts among the orderly questionnaire boxes, open to inscription with *X*'s, the instructions insisted that proximity was preferable to the silence whose latent multivalence was likely to interfere with the classificatory thrust of survey research.

The second survey, conducted by Nermin Abadan of the political science faculty at Ankara University, inquired about the spare-time activities of university students in three different faculties.[2] Abadan's survey enclosed an exhaustive description of the precautions taken for anonymity as a means to allay the students' suspicions and anxieties, which might otherwise obfuscate the findings of scrupulous research conducted in a "scientific manner." In the more credibly anonymous setting of the National Library, a patron had scribbled in the bound and otherwise vacant copy of the questionnaire his or her own answer to the question, "Where do you live?" Although the range of options was constricted ("with one's parents, friends, or spouse"), the appurtenant respondent drew in his or her own box (in compliance with survey etiquette) and wrote "under the bridge." Despite detailed safeguards against negligent behavior, it seems, omissions and substitutions remained part and parcel of the survey landscape long after its intended function had been fulfilled.

The coding system of both surveys drew on a cascade of similar studies that Turkish and American social scientists conducted throughout the 1950s and 1960s, targeting students and current and future administrators as well as the masses of peasants residing in the country.[3] Surveys inquiring about value orientation and behavioral patterns accompanied the interest in Turkey as an object of inquiry and model of modernization in the American social sciences. The demands and funding for these surveys came from organizations as diverse as the Mutual Security Agency (MSA), the Turkish State Planning Organization, the Ford Foundation, and the Voice of America (VOA), among others. The coding of the data, the preparation of IBM punch cards, the training of the research team, and the crafting of reports, in turn, took place in various institutions on both sides of the Atlantic, such as MIT and Columbia and Ankara Universities, intimating the circuitous nature of the survey itinerary.

An examination of the intellectual, political, and representational life of the sample survey reveals an alignment between the ideal subject of modernization theory and the respondent who was presumed to be familiar with the conditions of the survey setting: impersonal relationships, the promise of anonymity, and the capacity for having and voicing opinions regarding otherwise improbable situations. Deemed to be technologies central to the routinization of modernization theory, interviews invoked particular kinds of social interactions and required a series of attitudinal and linguistic adjustments on the part of the survey researcher and respondent alike. In that sense, studies conducted to measure and record the attitudes of peasants, students, and administrators were intended to be performative; the interviews were designed to occasion the forms of subjectivity and interpersonal relations articulated and idealized by modernization theory.

Despite researchers' interest in the very activity of survey taking as a modernizing edifice, instances of evasion and refusals to answer using the predesignated categories prevailed, attesting to the capacity for each survey to outstrip the intentions of its coders, sponsors, and creators. The surveys' ability to generate modern subjectivities was undercut by the respondents' challenges to the meanings and contexts that were presupposed by the interviewers. The social scientists' reporting on the content and formal aspects of the interview, however, erased the participants' manipulation of interactional frames and thereby contributed to the crystallization of survey research as both a tool and an indicator of modernization across its sites of implementation. Rather than assign certitude to the interpellation of modernized survey participants, then, this chapter traces the hesitations, apprehensions, and reinterpretations that were endemic to the travels and instantiations of survey methodology. The questionnaires and their specific stipulations surface, in this reading, as documents of a different order, as artifacts of knowledge practices that nonetheless remain "textual entities...[overflowing] their makers."[4]

The chapter's first section contextualizes the increasing affinity between survey methodology and modernization theory in the postwar United States and chronicles the problems associated with research in "modernizing" settings and the remedies proposed to overcome such hindrances. Thereafter, I offer a detailed examination of sociologist Daniel Lerner's work in Turkey, since his theory of modernization viewed respondent behavior itself as a decisive signifier of modernity. Lerner's role as a Cold Warrior in the "development theory" of communications research provides the background for his seeming awareness of the necessity of staging modernization through the interactional aspects of survey research. Although Lerner's work is increasingly credited as foundational for modernization theory, I highlight his simultaneous engagement with and erasure of local and material conditions in Turkey.[5] I then inspect a series of surveys undertaken by Herbert Hyman, Frederick Frey, Arif Payaslıoğlu, and Nermin Abadan during their time at Ankara University. These projects explicitly followed Lerner's lead in the conduct of attitude research, but at the same time they remade some of its central categories and are revealing instances of how translation nonetheless contributed to the consolidation of modernization theory along the survey trail. I conclude by examining the resilience of recipients—local social scientists, unruly respondents, and recalcitrant interviewers—to underscore both the attempted enactments of this particular laboratory of modernization and its unintended consequences.

A Most American Thing?

The lineage of survey methodology in the United States can be traced back to turn-of-the-century social surveys, the mail and voting polls popularized by the *Literary Digest* in the 1920s and, subsequently, the large-scale sample surveys undertaken by George Gallup and Elmo Roper during the 1930s. Surveys continued to be associated with market and media research, and they failed to gain prestige in academic circles until the onset of World War II initiated a scholarly relocation towards governmental research. It was at wartime centers such as the Surveys Division of the Office of War Information, the Division of Program Surveys of the US Department of Agriculture, and the Research Branch of the War Department that the affinity between the social sciences and survey research began to crystallize. Under the leadership of Rensis Likert, Samuel Stouffer, and Paul Lazarsfeld, these institutions evolved into the Survey Research Center at the University of Michigan, the National Opinion Research Center (NORC) at the University of Chicago, and the Bureau of Applied Social Research (BASR) at Columbia University, despite initial resistance from the host universities to formal integration. In 1945, the Social Science Research Council (SSRC) and the National Research Council established a Joint Committee on the Measurement of Opinion, Attitudes, and Consumer Wants, further bolstering the scholarly reputation of survey methodology.[6]

As we saw in the previous chapter, the alleged need to move away from the foregoing "parochialism" of American social scientific endeavors occasioned the celebration of a "new breed of social scientist," for whom there was to be "no land too remote, no village too ordinary or too primitive, no governmental process too imposing or too esoteric" for the study of postwar modernization.[7] The expansion in the regional application of social scientific scholarship intimated both a blurring of interdisciplinary boundaries under the purview of area studies and a reorientation in the objects of inquiry, approaches, and methods employed by each field.[8] Political scientists, for instance, followed the lead of their peers in social psychology and sociology, who were exploring the tailored fit between personality scales and the aptitudes of survey research.[9] Survey methods, which were already being employed to discern voting behavior and public opinion at home, could be rendered compatible with the overseas tasks assigned to the "new breed of social scientist." Among these tasks were contributions "to the endeavor to modernize the lives of the people in developing countries."[10] Given their roots in reformist Progressive-Era studies and their postwar employment in channeling psychological warfare into mass-communications research through government monies, surveys were to aid the conscious, at times covert, efforts to uplift and modernize non-Western areas.[11] The prowess of the methodology, as one researcher put it, stemmed from its utility in not merely capturing and measuring processes of change but *inducing* them: it was the widespread dissemination of surveys that led "*ordinary* men" to appear "more enlightened and scientific in their approach to social problems."[12]

The replicable, orderly, and standardized nature of survey research rendered it apposite for the task of measuring, coding, and recording of social change. Survey methodology was rich with the attractions of "medium-range" analysis for those concerned with the study of modernization in particular.[13] Longitudinal or panel studies enabled trend analysis over long periods of time, suggesting that once a survey was conducted that targeted a particular sample of students, rural populations, or the elite, that data could be compared with a new set of findings three, five, or even ten years down the line. This would make it easier to capture processes of change for the social scientist "seeking general principles—even laws—of political modernization."[14]

This optimism regarding the seeming fit between the needs of modernization theory and survey methodology was exceeded only by the enthusiasm for the modernity of the technique itself. The expansion of the focus of research from national samples to cross-national or cross-cultural surveys seemed to proceed along an inexorable path, one researcher noted—a move along "what might imperialistically be termed the *manifest destiny* of survey research in an extensive sense."[15] Surveys, by gathering results more "tangible and practical" than the "abstract and theoretical" knowledge yielded by other methods, helped "promote the scientific study of politics by forcing improvements in the rigor of research procedures, the quality of measures, and the techniques for certifying facts."[16] Practitioners' sanguine faith in the technological and scientific merits of survey research, however, was ultimately undermined by their own reservations about the applicability of survey methodology to foreign locales. Skepticism regarding transportability surfaced in relation to a purported equivalence between the "modernity" of the technique and the "modernity" of settings amenable to being surveyed. If surveys proved capable of serving the "cause of social change," it was not clear whether their application elsewhere necessitated some degree of change having already taken place since the method was "essentially a technique for the study of the 'alphabetized,' mobile, individualistic and market-oriented societies of the West."[17] For those who employed the survey method in non-Western areas, it remained an approximation at best since it appeared to be "better adapted" to "modern society."[18]

Such reservations are a testament to the obstacles that stood in the way of "the scientific imperialist eager to expand the realm of survey research," as a Turkish-American survey team put it.[19] Frequently cited among the hindrances beleaguering the field researcher were problems in the standardization of procedures and questionnaires as well as the shortage of local facilities, trained native interviewers, and IBM equipment; and unreliable census records that triggered sampling errors and incomplete maps that led to difficulties in locating respondents. The single most trying predicament, though, appeared to be of the attitudinal sort: the persistence of "evasion, courtesy, fear, silence and outright lying" in respondent behavior demanded various measures for "verbosity, sophistication, credulity, conformity, extremism in responses, [and] inability to differentiate, among other things."[20] Researchers attributed such unruly behavior to an overall lack of familiarity with the conditions of the survey, but it also provided fruitful ground for further reflections on the mindset of local respondents and assertions of difference along cultural lines.

In 1958, a special issue of the *Public Opinion Quarterly* was devoted to the problems of attitude research in the modernizing non-West, addressing areas as diverse as Indonesia, Iran, Uruguay and Chile, Turkey, and "Africa South of the Sahara." In his editorial introduction to the issue, Daniel Lerner noted the affinity between survey research and "participant societies," which he equated with modern societies, and presented the opinion holder as akin to the "cash customer and the voter."[21] Susanne and Lloyd Rudolph described the problems they encountered during survey research in India and questioned the presuppositions of their method, noting the "flaws in the assumption that most people hold opinions on a broad range of issues and are capable of articulating them." If the respondents they encountered were not acquainted with the premise of opinion holding and articulation, they also seemed unfamiliar with the method itself. As the Rudolphs put it, "The scholar engaged in survey research who presents himself to the American housewife can do so with considerable confidence of a friendly and understanding reception. . . . But the interviewer who faces an illiterate *Harijan* woman in village India is not likely to rouse any familiar images or ideas."[22] The image of the ubiquitous pollster at home was frequently evoked as evidence of American respondents' exceptional amenability to being surveyed.

Elsewhere, Sidney Verba noted the specific characteristics of American society that made survey research an effective technique in that setting, such as specific and impersonal relationships, an inquisitive mindset, the ease with which respondents spoke to strangers, and a "greater understanding of scientific inquiry; greater comprehension of an 'opinion'; . . . greater ability to imagine oneself in hypothetical situations; and so forth and so forth."[23] Political scientist Frank Bonilla argued that research abroad was beset not only by the absence of respondents with sufficient "social skills and intellectual capacities" but also by the interviewer's reception as a "total stranger."[24] In this account, the interviewer emerges as an unsolicited guest who nevertheless finds in himself the prerogative to set the dictates of the conversation. His demands appear exacting, his questions "embarrassing, gratuitously aggressive, or even dangerous," and his very presence a nuisance at best. Such interviews could be viewed more fruitfully as "sticky engagements," indicative of "the awkward, unequal, unstable, and creative qualities of interconnection across difference."[25]

Those who employed the survey method abroad believed that it seemed more suited to the American setting that fostered and perfected it, given ambivalence in language, hitches in research design, and seeming hostility to interviewers encountered elsewhere. The question remained: if the task of the survey researcher was to measure and record attitudinal patterns, to what extent should respondent behavior vis-à-vis the interview setting be figured into various indices of modernization? For Daniel Lerner, opinion holding itself could be factored into the analysis as a variable, thereby facilitating a reading of silences in the interview setting not as "the loss of data, but [itself] an important datum."[26]

Spelling Modernity

In May 1963, the Committee on Comparative Politics (CCP) of the SSRC held a conference in New York on "Survey Research in Developing Areas." During that meeting, Lerner enumerated the methodological and administrative requirements of survey research, such as comparability and replicability, and noted that it was particularly suited to the task of understanding *and* explaining the modernization process, which "is (or should be) relatively geography-free and even culture-free in its principal components."[27] Citing his own experience with the Middle East surveys conducted by BASR at Columbia University, Lerner insisted that it was the opportunity to test the "ideal types" against data from seven countries that "made it possible for us . . . to move from a theoretically-derived typology to empirically-determined generalizations—i.e., from what is merely plausible to what is highly probable." Lerner shared Gabriel Almond's belief that attitudinal research would help generate a universally applicable, scientifically sound model of modernization, and both scholars had also worked for the Psychological Strategy Board during the Truman Administration.[28] In fact, as Christopher Simpson points out, Lerner was a fixture in Cold War communications research, and he "either wrote, edited, or contributed to virtually every major collection of essays on psychological warfare published from 1945 to 1980."[29]

Eight years before his SSRC lecture, Lerner co-wrote an article with David Riesman and divulged the origins of the Middle East survey data:

> In the fall of 1950, three hundred long, exploratory interviews were conducted in Turkey by native interviewers trained by a researcher from Columbia University's Bureau of Applied Social Research. The respondents were selected to overrepre-

sent listeners and potential listeners to the Voice of America; thus, three men were interviewed for every woman, urbanites were over-chosen, as were upper income groups. . . . The interest of the Voice of America, which financed the original field-work and extensive analysis, in securing some feed-back from its broadcasts turned out to provide a record, as fascinating as it is complex, of a country in which old prisons of the self are in process of being shattered, while the existence of new prisons, products of liberations, is dimly recognized.[30]

Over the course of its journey between different institutions, the Middle East survey was thoroughly steeped in expectations and obligations. The study was motivated in part by State Department concerns about "Soviet jamming of Voice of America radio signals," and the original questionnaires aimed to assess the direct influence that mass media could have on Middle Eastern audiences.[31] Lerner was explicit about his concern that while "Middle Easterners more than ever want the modern package," they nonetheless "reject the label 'made in U.S.A.' (or, for that matter, 'made in USSR')."[32] He thus placed the countries under examination on a developmental spectrum, which reflected strategic interests and alliances in the region. Lerner's categorization contrasted the "modernizing" tendencies of pro-Western Turkey and Lebanon with the subversive elements of Nasserite Egypt and Mossadegh's Iran. The performative aspirations of survey methodology came to reflect its origins in and compatibility with psychological warfare and propaganda work. The travels of the VOA survey—conceived in one setting, conducted in another by trained native interviewers, and coded and (re)analyzed according to different research agendas—also reflected the changes *and* consistencies in the theoretical and methodological inclinations of Lerner, acquired during his tenures at various research institutions.

Born in Brooklyn in 1917 to Russian émigré parents, Lerner studied English literature at NYU until serving as the Chief editor of the Intelligence Branch of the US Army's Psychological Warfare Division during World War II. His participation in survey studies that attempted to measure the effect of Allied propaganda on military and civilian populations in Germany would make him a suitable match for the Middle East study, whose "central rationale" was "psychological warfare."[33] Lerner was asked to analyze the VOA data on his arrival in 1951 at BASR, which was then under the direction of Paul Lazarsfeld.[34] Although Lerner was one of the several rapporteurs who analyzed the data for VOA, he was responsible for the sections on Turkey from the outset.[35] The answers to the survey were initially to be coded according to Lazarsfeld's theory of the two-step flow model of communication. But by the time Lerner had moved to MIT as professor of sociology and a member of the senior research staff at the Center for International Studies (CENIS) in 1953, it was agreed that the data would be recoded in accordance with an opinion-range index reflecting Lerner's three-fold typology of modern, transitional, and traditional societies.[36] The Center, itself notoriously sponsored by the CIA, thus financed the reanalysis of the data as well as follow-up fieldwork in 1954. The latter included Lerner's trip to Balgat, Ankara, which inspired his arresting depiction, to be discussed in this chapter, of the Grocer and the Chief as "the symbolic protagonists of the drama of modernization."[37]

Lerner's early ruminations on the Turkey data came to inform his conceptualization of modernization, which appeared to be correlated with "socioeconomic status, urban residence, and media exposure" as well as with the capacity for "ego identification" or "introjection," which "teaches us to know the roles of others and how to assume them on appropriate occasions."[38] Although the surveys were to gather verifiable data about non-western respondents, they relied on the subjects' ability to generate a myriad of fictions. For Lerner, the prerequisite for modernity was a "great characterological transformation," traced through the psychic mobility of the individual and his or her acquisition of emphatic skills that "spell modernity." This tautological formulation held that the encounter between the actual self and the hypothetical self (be it the interviewer or the head of a radio station) was at once the condition and signifier of a modern mindset. Lerner thus constructed an "empathy index," for which he relied on a series of projective questions, ranging from the ability to imagine oneself as the editor of a newspaper, in charge of a radio station, or the head of a government to the ability to imagine oneself living in a different country from one's own. His index assigned 0's, 1's, and in rare cases, 2's ("chooses non-adjacent country in which one could live if not in native country") to the responses, at the expense of the rather detailed reasons provided by the respondents when prompted in the open-ended question-and-answer setting to imagine themselves assigned to improbable tasks or dwelling in foreign settings.[39]

Even though these responses were lost in the reported form of condensed scores and continuums that provided an "opinion range," their presentation in numerical form testified to the character of the survey setting itself as an experiment in modernization. After all, Lerner's very understanding of modernization, conceived as the ability to imagine oneself outside the self and explicitly defined through the operationalization of an empathy index, suggested the inextricable link between the research method and that which it sought to explain. "The manner in which persons perceive the interview situation," Lerner insisted, "is a datum on their readiness and competence to participate personally in essentially impersonal social enterprises."[40] He thus believed that failure to abide by the interactional prerequisites of the survey indicated an inability to partake of the modern or empathetic mindset, since "the very nature of the interview requires a certain ability to identify with others."[41] The surveys were conducted not merely to measure or describe but also to occasion the performance of the very categories—modern, transitional, and traditional—that they sought to explain. The crafting of these typologies rested on a series of omissions and misreadings that allowed Lerner to identify the capacity for empathy (or lack thereof) as indicative of different attitudes, mindsets, and, indeed, "national characteristics" in different settings.

In a series of elite interviews he conducted in Europe shortly after the Middle East project, for example, Lerner found that the "French respondents were most troubled by projective questions—showing themselves *not unable but unwilling* to empathize on questions of public policy."[42] If the French found the "role-playing" questions frivolous or silly, it was at best a testament to their opinionated predispositions since "there is a vast psychic difference between the illiterate and untutored traditionalism of Middle Eastern peasant and the traditionalism which prevails among the contemporary elite of France. The Frenchman has acquired his traditionalism as an intellectual discipline and an explicit psychic code. . . . Whereas the Arab peasant usually has no sense of possible alternatives to his traditional ways but simply 'does what comes naturally,' the Frenchman has a very sophisticated rationale for his conduct."[43] Lerner delineates two distinct mindsets in this passage: although the aversion of both sets of respondents to the hypothetical questions elicit their labeling as traditional, the category itself remains variable, if not fraught, in its application across disparate contexts. Thus, even though Lerner was aware of the imperative to devise and stage the categories of modernization theory, his assignation of different populations under its labels nonetheless relied on preconceptions that came at the expense of the particularities and nuances that otherwise characterized the interview setting.

Lerner's differential reading suggests that the survey method does more than report its findings; it expects—indeed, *demands* at every turn—that the interviewee also transport him- or herself out of the "traditional" environment (be it a coffeehouse or the subject's own house) and be placed instead in the modern, sterile, "impersonal" setting of the interview. The imperative to answer questions, to hold and articulate opinions in a predesignated manner, is an implicit corollary of participation in that setting. In his evaluation of the Turkey data, Lerner insists that it is the traditional Turkish subjects, not yet sufficiently exposed to mass media or cultivated in the ways of the modern participant style, who find the question-and-answer situation "deadly earnest" and "can more easily imagine destroying the self than making the effort to project it beyond the familiar world into the strange."[44] Unaccustomed to the norms and rules dictated and regulated by the survey setting, these traditional Turks remain improper interview subjects. Their inability to imagine themselves in an alien context, in turn, tarnishes their modernity score, gauged strictly in quantitative terms. The survey aims to interpellate its respondent and subject matter; its claim to representation—necessarily condensed, seemingly disciplinary—is simultaneously a claim to its own legitimacy. Foreign to its locale of application, the survey demands answers that will have to be rendered proper to its object of inquiry. By the interactional standards of the interview setting, modern subjects are those who are willing to engage in conversation with strangers but only in a manner predetermined by the expectations of those who set the terms of proper discourse.

Sticky Conversations

In their initial assessment of the Middle East surveys, Lerner and Riesman elaborate on the ideal survey respondent by way of illustrating what the interview subjects are *not*. Citing a part of the interview with the Chief of Balgat, who answers a question about whether he gives advice to fellow villagers ("Yes, that is my main duty, to give advice . . . about all that I or you could imagine, even about their wives and how to handle them, and how to cure their sick cow"), Lerner and Riesman immediately comment that "it would seem from this exchange that the Chief could not project himself into the interviewer's place (conceivably, he aggressively did not care to), else he would quickly have realized that the latter *could* imagine advice on other matters than the cure and care of females." Lerner and Riesman insist that it is the task of the respondent to offer unconditional cooperation by putting himself in the place of the interviewer; in the process, they reveal a profound misreading of the Chief's willingness to anticipate, perhaps even empathize with, his interlocutor's expectations regarding the requirements of his job. In the authors' account, by contrast, the Chief's refusal to abide by the terms of the proper interview exchange arrests him in traditional time, a time encapsulated in hierarchies, obsolete conceit, and an inability to "compare, equate or differentiate" personal and public problems.[45]

The respondent's attitudinal shortcomings are also linked to his cognitive and linguistic abilities in this account. Following their depiction of the episode with the Chief, who ostensibly could not imagine anything but the "cure and care of females," Lerner and Riesman comment on the centrality of sufficient communication skills in a footnote that cites an assessment of interviews conducted in Arkansas in the aftermath of a tornado. In that example, they observe that the "lower-class hillbilly respondents," who, like their Turkish counterparts, proved incapable of putting themselves in the interviewer's place, "would plunge him *in medias res* without telling him so, shift place or pronoun without realizing that he could not follow, and so on."[46] Seemingly surprised to find parallels between the "hillbilly" respondents of Arkansas and the traditional Chief of Balgat in Ankara, the authors nevertheless make a gesture towards recognizing the potential subversion and tactical prevarication that the survey unwittingly produces:

> To be sure, we realize that one must be wary of comparisons between the lower class and the less enlightened in a modern "mass society" like our own and the tradition-oriented, the leaders and followers alike, in a pre-industrial culture. We realize, too, that the disaster-study material is susceptible to varying interpretations; for example, the possibility that the lower-class respondents were resentfully and at least semiconsciously making fools of the interviewers while pretending cooperation (or, possibly, that linguistic difficulties in the narrow sense, rather than broadly semantic issues, were involved). Nevertheless, there would appear to be some similarity in the lacunae of self-other awareness in these historically quite separate settings—a similarity reflected in analogous metaphoric patterns.

In this turn of events, it is no longer the Chief preoccupied with cows or the lower-class witnesses of the Arkansas tornado, barely capable of keeping their pronouns straight, who are prone to ridicule. In the absence of interlocutors who will abide by their discursive and imaginary dictates, it is the interviewers themselves who are thrown into unfamiliar terrain. Still, Lerner finds it easier to equate the reframing strategies of Ankarans and Arkansans than to assign the same sense of traditionalism to the French elite and Arab peasants.[47] In both cases, a more nuanced account of the different respondent populations is purposefully extracted from the textual account lest it undermine the certitude of the archetypes that are carefully crafted and staged through the interview process.

The questionnaires used in the Turkey surveys, some of which are catalogued along with Lerner's papers at the Institute Archives and Special Collections at MIT, reveal a variety of resilient responses that did not make it into his musings on modernization in published form. These refusals to engage with the survey questions automatically disqualified the respondents from being categorized as modern subjects, capable of empathy in general and of conversing with the interviewer in a proper manner in particular. Oftentimes, however, their refusals indicated less a lack of capacity for imagination than a realistic assessment of their standing or interests in life. Some said they lacked the education or credentials for running a newspaper, others that they were not interested in that line of work. Another replied that he would resign immediately from the post of president since he considered himself unqualified for the job.

One particularly unruly respondent objected to the wording of the survey questions and the limited categories imposed by the answer range. Asked to provide two defining characteristics on five different nations (the United States, England, France, Germany, and the Soviet Union), the respondent demanded, "If I am to respond that the Americans are industrious and the British intelligent, would I be saying that it is not possible for the British to be industrious and the Americans to be intelligent?" He added, "I do not think questions of such importance and complexities should be answered in a condensed manner, like vitamin pills."[48] In fact, a lack of imagination in numerical terms, guaranteed to result in low scores on the Lerner modernity index, was a commonplace occurrence among those interviewed. "I am against statistics in general," another respondent insisted, but his aversion was directed towards the survey in particular: "The questions aren't judicious enough. In life, all is not black and white than is grey. And grey is a 'nuance.'"[49] In addition to being restrictive, the questions seemed demeaning to some. Told that he could ask about anything he wanted to find out about America, one respondent, otherwise reluctant to adopt the quantitative terminology of the survey, inquired, "What is the height of the Empire State Building? How many cars the Ford [*sic*] produces a year?" The interviewer added in parentheses, "Sarcastically, resents the question."[50]

Such occurrences suggest that the interviews were far from having proceeded along the impersonal and cordial lines envisioned by the researcher. No matter how hard the survey tried to produce a particular kind of verbal exchange and social interaction based on civility, tolerance, and empathy alike, such regulations were bound to be broken by the interview setting. Meanwhile, the retorts, silences, and refusals to think in numbers and condense all answers into statistically communicable "vitamin pills" remained antithetical to the categories proclaimed by the survey. That is why they were rendered inferior to the coded categories, erased from the narrative, and expelled from what Lerner believed to be his rigorous means of highly probable, empirically determined generalizations. The sample survey's claim to representation was achieved precisely through such exclusions and attenuations. For all the emphasis on empathy in Lerner's communicative theory of modernization, those not voicing opinions in the interview setting were presumed to not have any opinions at all.

What Lerner neglects to include in his scientific report is what the social scientist resorts to, albeit in a selective manner, as "qualitative support" or, as Lerner does quite elegantly in his own work, as narrative device. These partial inclusions, however, which surface as plot devices and intermittent depictions of the protagonists involved, only underscore what was expunged from the condensed, mediated, and codified account. Why else, we wonder, are people unlikely to want to move to the United States, indeed, wishing they would die instead, aside from a putative lack of capacity for imagining themselves elsewhere? Responded one, "I am convinced that living a mechanized life is far from agreeable."[51] Inquired another, "Why is it that while acquiring wealth [Americans] didn't acquire the necessary culture to go with this wealth? Why do they still insist on segregation while claiming to be the best democratic country?"[52] What else did these survey researchers sacrifice in their endless cataloguing and (re)coding?

The Grocer, the Chief, and the Interviewer

It would be inaccurate to suggest that Lerner neglected all mention of the verbatim answers recorded by the interviewers. A student of literature before the war, Lerner was no stranger to the narrative category, and he masterfully employed characters, chronotopes, and literary devices, evident in particular in his arresting parable of the Grocer and the Chief, which serves as the introduction to his *Passing of Traditional Society.* This story intrigued Lerner more than any other while he was working through hundreds of interviews, and it led him to proclaim that the "personal meaning of modernization in underdeveloped lands can be traced, in miniature, through the lives of Balgati—The Grocer and The Chief."[53]

A "prophet" ahead of his time, the Grocer "lives in a different world, an expansive world, populated more actively with imaginings and fantasies"; he "'sees' things the others do not see, 'lives' in a world populated by imaginings alien to the constrictive world of the others." In contrast to the Chief, who held the only radio in Balgat in 1950 and tuned in only for news from Korea, Lerner cites the Grocer's aesthetic preferences approvingly:

> It was in a movie that he had first glimpsed what a *real* Grocery store could be like—'with walls made of iron sheets, top to floor and side to side, and on them standing myriads of round boxes, clean and all the same dressed, like soldiers in a great parade.' This fleeting glimpse of what sounds like the Campbell Soup section of an A & P supermarket had provided the Grocer with an abiding image of how his fantasy world might look.[54]

In addition to providing an elaborate description of the supermarket shelves the Grocer pined for, the passage captures and confirms, for Lerner, the crucial link between a distinctly modern(izing) capacity for empathy and the ability to imagine otherwise foreign places, lifestyles, and, indeed, arrays of soup cans—in other words, the ability for psychic mobility.

The Grocer thus surfaces as the paragon of the proper interview subject. His wide range of imagination is accompanied by a capacity for anticipating *and* providing the responses that are expected of him. His capacity for psychic mobility takes into account the physical mobility of his fellow Balgati, resulting in his position as a vanguard in the interview setting and the modernization process and in a plot device that Lerner uses to celebrate the Marshall Plan–funded highway program in the country. Asked how he would rule, the Grocer responds that "he would make roads for the villagers to come to towns to see the world and would not let them stay in their holes all their life." Unlike the Chief, who cannot image leaving the place where he was born, the Grocer can readily imagine himself living in America: "Indeed he seemed fully prepared, as a man does when he has already posed the question to himself many times."[55] These instances, cited profusely and admiringly by Lerner, are indications of the survey method succeeding at its task, which is not merely to procure data but also to occasion the performance of modernizing subjectivities.

Although the Grocer, a proxy for all transitional Turks in Lerner's scheme, comes closest to embodying the ideal respondent in the village of Balgat, "he is not yet capable of the Modern Turk's *introjective* technique"; although he is "learning to project imaginatively, [he is] not yet stretching his imagination too far."[56] It is for this reason that the modernized native interviewer, Tosun, is perplexed by the effective means of communication on the part of his interlocutor, who otherwise seems "a very unimpressive type" and "even wore some sort of a necktie."[57] This detectable tone of distaste is telling for Lerner: Tosun's contempt for the Grocer must have stemmed from the latter's ability to "see himself as the interviewer saw him."[58] Lerner interprets the tension between the two characters as an indication of the throes and pangs of modernization. The Grocer is threatening to the interviewer precisely because he is in the midst of passing on to modernity, thereby providing an image of Tosun's own transitional (and once, presumably, traditional) past in flesh.

It is noteworthy that Lerner includes a member of the survey team in his array of protagonists inhabiting the "modernizing landscape," which "involves many Tosuns and shepherds, many Grocers and Chiefs, many sons of Chiefs."[59] The interviewer emerges as a full-fledged character in this account of the otherwise anonymous landscape; the Grocer and the Chief were the only titles granted to the respondents, with the rest reduced to their number, location, and rural/city distinction on the front page of the questionnaires.[60] In fact, the members of the survey team were asked to attach lengthy descriptions of the respondents at the beginning of the questionnaire forms, and the team members did not hesitate to provide comments on their physical appearance, education, eating habits, and seeming level of intelligence. At times, such observations gave the interviewers license to skip certain questions, especially if they were acquainted with their subjects beforehand. (In one case an interviewee was a close friend, and in another case, a domestic employee.) Some interviewers were flattering—if curiously—in their aesthetic assessments of the respondents: "He reminds me of a dignified silkworm inside his cocoon." Others were even more ruthless than Tosun: "He always gave me the impression of a jellyfish, physically. . . . When he speaks his mouth is wet. When he pronounces his *th*'s, *sh*'s and *ch*'s he spits in the air."[61]

In addition to recording physical depictions of their respondents, the interviewers frequently noted what they perceived to be attitudes of fear and intimidation. Some believed that this initial state of trepidation gradually became more relaxed once they explained that the project had nothing to do with politics. Yet the survey's motives were rarely so clarified, and most rural respondents continued to believe that the interviewers came from newspapers, aid agencies, or the government and that their answers would facilitate the arrival of roads, radios, and movies not unlike the ones they were being interrogated about. Some suggested that the questionnaire was unlikely to help and that American experts should come and see the situation for themselves, although one thought this had been done before, "with no result."[62]

The interviewers were not the only ones who communicated judgments about the survey setting. Once the questionnaires had been filled out, each respondent was asked what he or she thought about the interview. Although these often-detailed answers did not make it to Lerner's reported opinion range or empathy index, they revealed yet another instance of the unexpected results of the survey setting. Many found the questionnaire "silly," "lengthy," or "superfluous yet lacking," and for one person, it seemed "funny, queer . . . a most American thing."[63] Such respondents attempted to reframe the survey in both its meanings and context: it no longer measured progress along an abstract, placeless continuum of modernization but was instead a practice tethered to its place of origin—the United States. Other respondents questioned the lack of transparency intrinsic to the survey setting, and one suggested that "if sincerity is the rule between interviewer and respondent . . . it would be very interesting for those interviewed to know the results."[64] Still others seemed, like the Grocer, highly receptive to and appreciative of the interview process, and they suggested that they would have "loved to be able to ask questions too."[65] The catalogue of reactions to the interview comprises the range of reflective activity unfolding in real-time attitudes towards the discursive interaction. In the case of survey research, both recipients and practitioners negotiated interpretive frames as they tried to make sense of their communicative encounters. That Lerner erased the instances of respondents' reframing from his narrative of modernization speaks to his awareness of the necessity to write the script, cast the interviewers, and direct the performance of modern, traditional, and transitional subjectivities in overtly theatrical and staged terms.

In the context of Lerner's seminal work on modernization in the Middle East, then, the task of the survey is manifold. In his writing, replete with a preoccupation with models, literary imagery, and narrative structures, the imperative to survey is as crucially linked to sight as it is to cataloguing and numerical reduction. In this account, plot twists, "passings," and crossroads provide the "landscape" that the modernization narrative requires. But although Lerner masterfully performs the task of narrative chronicler, his discerning eye is principally that of the forecaster:

> There are villages to which, willy-nilly, the city comes—either via a new concrete road as in Turkey, or via road as in Egypt, or via adventurous young villagers who shuttle to and fro as in Lebanon. By whatever method the city invades the village... the poignancy is heightened for the modern observer, who knows that in some sense the city will always "win," by the great human cost added to these dramas because the actors are unaware that a rough draft of the third act is already written.[66]

The surveyor remains the ultimate "modern observer," at once responsible for delineating the categories that will inform the coding process and for knowing beforehand how the next chapter of modernization will play out. In the conclusion of Lerner's parable, which is a scaled-down version of Cold War development, he informs his readers that "the Grocer was dead. The Chief—'the last *Muhtar* of Balgat'—had reincarnated the Grocer in the flesh of his sons. Tosun was in North Africa studying the Berbers," presumably as an agent of survey-led modernization.[67]

Lerner's account of development rests on predetermined stages that unfold in progressive, linear fashion: urbanization, literacy, mass-media extension, and economic and political participation occur in that order simply because, in some sense, "they had to go together." The end point for this cluster of positive changes is an identifiable destination, since as Lerner famously claimed, the West—and in particular, America—was precisely what the "Middle East [sought] to become." In that process, the survey itself takes on a facilitating task as a measure of modernization:

"The Bureau questionnaire can serve as a model for future efforts to apply modern American research procedures in the less developed areas of the world."[68] As we will see, large-scale sample surveys conducted in Turkey throughout the 1950s and 1960s employed qualified versions of Lerner's procedures and his categories of tradition, transition, and modernity.

Survey Research in Turkey

The two surveys that served as a preamble to this chapter share a lineage in terms of content and methodology. By occasioning the production of proper interviewers who were conceived as modernizing agents, these and subsequent studies converged in their efforts to set the stage for the enactment of modernization. They also relied on earlier criteria laid out by works such as Lerner's, but their translation and adaptation of the original categories nonetheless contributed to the crystallization of modernization theory. As we will see, even growing skepticism towards the political implications of large-scale surveys did not impede the increasing prevalence and popularity of this method in Turkey's social scientific landscape over the following decades.

Frey's survey on high-school students, for instance, adopted the functionalist lexicon of modernization theory, comparing changes in value systems with the evolution of biological organisms.[69] He argued in the SSRC volume on Turkey and Japan that the high-school students retained "an immoderate amount of authoritarianism" but that their "growing ideological commitment to democratic forms" attested to the role that education played in modernization.[70] Although his questionnaire itself was of a reiterative nature, Frey manufactured a new coding system for personal-achievement categories, which were discerned through notions of future aspirations and assessments of the self and the material world, familiar themes in survey research.[71]

Nermin Abadan was more forthcoming in the disclosure of her intellectual predecessors, as her three-fold typology mapped not only onto the three universities whose students she investigated but also to the categories postulated by Lerner and Riesman: "The outer-oriented, materialist manager; the idealist, prospective administrative-leader; and the traditional, static implementer." Abadan, however, chastised the Middle East Technical University students, who fell under Riesman's outer-oriented and Lerner's modern categories, for being too steeped in the Anglo-American tradition; if these students could imagine themselves as the president of Turkey or citizens of another country, this was a testament to their "materialism," seeing as how the students remained "under the influence of the thought patterns of a society that has already tackled its trial of modernization."[72] She insisted that Turkey was, "as Daniel Lerner has correctly pointed out, 'not yet a modern society by our standards, but is no longer quite traditional either,'" and she did not hesitate to enroll Lerner's categories of attitude formation. While Abadan's interjections translated—that is, remade—the categories by rallying them for purposes beyond their initial intent; her work contributed to the "routinization" of these categories in survey research.[73]

Abadan's detailed explication of Lerner's findings was in keeping with her central role in the propagation in Turkey of recent trends in the American social sciences. In her memoirs, Abadan explains that she first learned about public opinion through an "assistant of Daniel Lerner's" who was conducting the Middle East surveys in 1950. She spent the 1953–1954 academic year as a Fulbright fellow at the University of Minnesota, where she "discovered political science" while studying with Herbert McClosky, whose work investigated political behavior through survey methodology.[74] It was through her dissertation on public opinion; her various articles on media research, public administration, and interest groups; and the elective courses she offered on American political parties that Abadan contributed to the new orientation of political science at Ankara University.[75] Although Abadan went on to conduct surveys on Turkish guest workers in West Germany, she remained critical of her earlier study on the spare-time activities of the university students; in particular, she was unhappy with her method of sampling, which, due to lack of funding and assistant personnel, did not entail a process of random selection and thus proceeded in an "incomplete and faulty" manner.[76]

Abadan assessed her sampling techniques on the basis of lecture notes from a course on social scientific methodology that was offered during the 1957–1958 academic year at the Faculty of Political Science at Ankara University, where Abadan taught at the time. That course, which Frederick Frey also attended during his time in Turkey as a Ford Foundation grant recipient, was co-taught by Arif Payaslıoğlu and Herbert Hyman within the purview of an exchange program between NYU and Ankara University that was under the auspices of the International Cooperation Administration (ICA).[77] In many respects, the trajectory of Hyman's career was intertwined with the proliferation of survey methodology in the social scientific circles of the United States. During World War II, Hyman participated in the US Department of Agriculture's Division of Program Surveys and the bombing surveys in Germany and Japan, and he later recalled that it was this experience that "led [him and his colleagues] to train survey researchers and help conduct the first postwar surveys in Japan, Turkey, Norway, and elsewhere against the frequent objections that the method would not work."[78] After the war, Hyman worked at the New York office of the National Opinion Research Center and was later recruited by Lazarsfeld to the BASR at Columbia.[79] Although Hyman made his research available to the SSRC's CCP and other venues, he cautioned against conducting surveys on subjects who may be "*unwilling* or *incompetent* to provide reliable answers."[80] Luckily for Hyman, the academic year he spent in Turkey presented two opportunities for conducting surveys on purportedly willing *and* competent subjects in the university setting. Abadan and Frey both cited these studies profusely.

The first of these works was a comparison between the values of the students of Robert College and the Faculty of Political Sciences at Ankara University; Hyman, along with Payaslıoğlu and Frey, presented the findings from this study in the special issue of *Public Opinion Quarterly,* which spoke to problems of attitude research in the developing world. The student of Robert College, not unlike the METU student in Abadan's study, was found to "resemble his American counterpart more than the Ankara student [did]." Hyman and his collaborators added that most of the university students could be considered modern given the behavioral indices of Lerner's study, but they did not refrain from introducing additional "historical and logical criteria" because of their assumption that Turkey was "presumably partaking both of traditional Middle Eastern culture and of modernized or Westernized culture." The "historical" criteria allowed the authors to compare the Turkish college youth with both the "traditional" youth Turkey's past and the "modern" youth in neighboring Europe. As the authors wrote, "At the level of symbols and practices of daily living, they are clear representatives of modern civilization. This is revealed, for example, in their dress, hygiene, health practices, possessions, and media behavior. Unlike an earlier educated generation, very few can use Arabic."[81] The signs of modernity were presumed to evade the pitfalls of what Hyman critically deemed "pseudo-crossnational research" elsewhere.[82]

This blend of modernity and tradition confirmed, for the authors, a reading of Turkey vis-à-vis Lerner's transitional framework. Reverberating through their account were categories of transition espoused in earlier work across the Middle East, the replication of questionnaires conducted on students of the West, and a confirmation of conjectures that guided the survey process in the first place. Hyman and his collaborators also emphasized the edifying character of their project, seeing as how it was conducted by "a group of Turkish students in the course of receiving training in social research."[83]

Hyman's course on methodology also produced a panel study that relied on two previous surveys targeting the graduates of Ankara University.[84] Since this method was ostensibly "new" to Turkey, the academic setting was necessarily its first venue of practice; the students of political science—indeed, the future administrators of Turkey—were designated as simultaneously the subjects and employers of this survey, thereby suggesting its benefits for both content and training. Because the students learned of the sample survey method not only by carrying it out but also by being interviewed, the metamethodological concerns of this study would familiarize them with the "realities of survey research," such as the scarcity of available sources, the necessity of accomplishing certain tasks at a designated time period, and the imperative to cooperate with others in a rational manner.[85]

In fact, mail-in questionnaires and self-administered surveys were employed by magazines and newspapers as early as the 1920s, acquainting interview subjects with the question-and-answer format prior to its use by American and Turkish researchers in the postwar period.[86] Throughout the 1940s, a group of faculty, including Niyazi Berkes, Behice Boran, and Muzaffer Şerif, that was working on rural sociology and social psychology at Ankara University also employed small-scale surveys that targeted villages and towns in the vicinity of Ankara.[87] Most of these scholars were trained in the United States in the early 1930s and were forced to resign from their posts following the "Red Scare" that culminated in the academic purge of 1948. The sacked authors' monographs and questionnaires, some of which were meant to capture attitudes towards time, measurement, and work, would selectively inform the categories of "tradition" used in the large-scale surveys carried out by American social scientists in Turkey in the following decades.[88] Hyman and Lerner relied especially on the writings of Şerif and Berkes; Berkes had in fact been one of the original interviewers for the VOA study.[89]

Payaslıoğlu and Frey not only erased the legacy of these earlier studies but also condensed, combined, and recategorized the answers offered by the Ankara students, thereby providing another instance of the erasure of local voices and the shrinking of particularities in survey research. The remaking of recorded categories ostensibly bolstered an analysis of change by discarding instances of incommensurability. As the substantive categories from the earlier surveys were tampered with—indeed, flattened out—their modification would abet the survey researchers-in-training in their quest for cycles and regularities. The task of the survey novice included not just procuring and presenting raw data but also tweaking information, redefining occupational categories, and disposing of irregularities and outliers.[90]

As social scientific surveys obtained greater visibility in Turkey, Hyman, Abadan, Frey, Payaslıoğlu, and others enlisted in their work the categories proclaimed by Lerner's seminal study while also introducing caveats and modifications to some of its formulations. Although the concepts were "transformed in translation," they nonetheless aided the popularization of survey methodology.[91] Throughout the 1950s and 1960s, the survey methodology was further spread by a series of novel academic and governmental institutions such as the Institute of Public Administration for Turkey and the Middle East (1952), the Test and Research Bureau of the Board of Education and Discipline (1953), the State Planning Organization (SPO, 1960), the Scientific and Technological Research Council of Turkey (1963), and the Institute of Population Studies at Hacettepe University (1967). The popularization of social scientific surveys came to fruition during the 1969 elections when the daily newspaper *Milliyet* commissioned a group of professors from Istanbul University to prepare a survey of workers' voting behaviors. Surveys were so prevalent by 1970 that at a conference about the development of the social sciences in Turkey, psychologist Şefik Uysal explained, "When one thinks of social research in our country, the method of data-gathering that comes to mind is the survey."[92]

During this period, American agencies also continued their investment in survey research. The United States Information Agency (USIA) was especially interested in "media habits" and entered a multiyear contract with Nezih Neyzi's Piyasa Etüd ve Araştırma Bürosu (PEVA, Institute of Market Studies and Research) for the measurement of radio, cinema, and press usage in major Turkish cities.[93] Researchers like Abadan, Hyman, and Payaslıoğlu followed Lerner's lead by not only adapting his categories of modernization but also volunteering their findings for governmental opinion research. Each scholar sold his or her university-student surveys to the Office of Research and Analysis at the USIA. Although these transactions could also be deployed for strategic purposes, as in the case of Abadan, who used her 1960 visit to USIA-Washington to chastise the agency for its lack of immediate support for the coup (which she described as a "revolution"), suspicions of the survey method grew alongside its popularity over the years.[94]

It Is Printed and It Circulates

In 1962, in the midst of the social scientific proliferation of surveys, came a study targeting a sample of eight thousand rural residents. Christened as the Rural Development Research Project, the survey, mostly funded by USAID, listed a familiar roster of consultants: Daniel Lerner, Herbert Hyman, Ithiel de Sola Pool, and Sloan Wayland, with Frederick Frey acting as the main rapporteur.[95] Frey's various accounts of this project reveal the ways in which survey methodology continued to be fraught with suspicions, alliances, and frailties when undertaken in foreign settings. Given the "sensitive and possibly volatile character of the investigation," Frey disclosed, the SPO was enlisted as an "official liaison" in order to assist in "dealing with delicate political situations," thus "leaving our nascent survey organization generally free to concentrate on the demanding technical tasks of the research."[96]

Frey's differentiation between the political and technical aspects of survey research appears hollow on closer inspection of the various institutions that were embedded in the complex economy of this study. The travels of the questionnaires between different agencies began with their dispatch from USAID to the Research and Measurement Bureau of the Turkish Ministry of Education, which conducted most of the data collection. After the questionnaires were filled out and collected from randomly selected households, they were sent for coding and card punching to MIT, where they were closely monitored for residual errors. It was at CENIS that Frey completed the reports, which were then submitted to USAID. The survey was shot through with obligations to sponsors and administrators, seemingly confirming Frey's contention that "an extensive multicultural survey demands the skills of a diplomat, financier and administrator, as well as technical and theoretical expertise."[97] The fact that Frey unreservedly used the terms *westernization* and *modernization* in the reports despite having denounced them in his own dissertation as concepts that were "vague, cosmic, unclear in their referents, and difficult to measure" is telling.[98]

The "technical" and ostensibly apolitical aspects of the survey pertained to the training of native interviewers. They were carefully chosen from among those with rural backgrounds—literate and "reasonably sophisticated" ones—and took a course that included "familiarization with the instruments and sampling plan, lectures and discussions on interviewing techniques, model interviews, role playing, coding practice, and pretest fieldwork."[99] Given the strenuous conditions for conducting research in mostly remote villages across Anatolia, supervisors paid regular visits to research sites to further ensure that team leaders abided by norms of randomness in selecting respondents.[100] At the end of this extensive training process, Frey could self-assuredly declare, "One of the oft-cited side benefits of the project was that we would bequeath to Turkey a sizable group of well-trained and experienced village interviewers who would be of great use to the government in future work with the peasantry."[101] There were unforeseen complications, though, such as the persistence of an unwritten language (Kurdish) that necessitated the employment of bilingual interviewers, "inevitably sacrificing, thereby, some control over interviewer performance."[102]

Once the results were tallied, the reports entailed an aesthetic reconfiguration: the verbal format of the questionnaire would now be translated into numerical and graphic form (see figure 2.1). Tables were crafted in accordance with the indices that were carefully conjured up by the coders. The distribution graphs propelled yet another shift in stylistic presentation: the categorization and ranking of coded preferences now mapped onto lines and curves representing the "rural mindset." The rapporteur's task was to furnish his policy recommendations with as much visual corroboration as possible, wherein the policy makers would have "insight" into the Turkish peasant's psyche through its display in mobile, stable, and combinable form.[103]

The USAID reports addressed issues as diverse as land ownership, national identification, regional variation, and mass media.[104] Although they found it "difficult to eliminate any item as being generally irrelevant" to the "villager's propensity to innovate," they concluded that the literate, male, young adults with higher degrees of exposure to mass me-

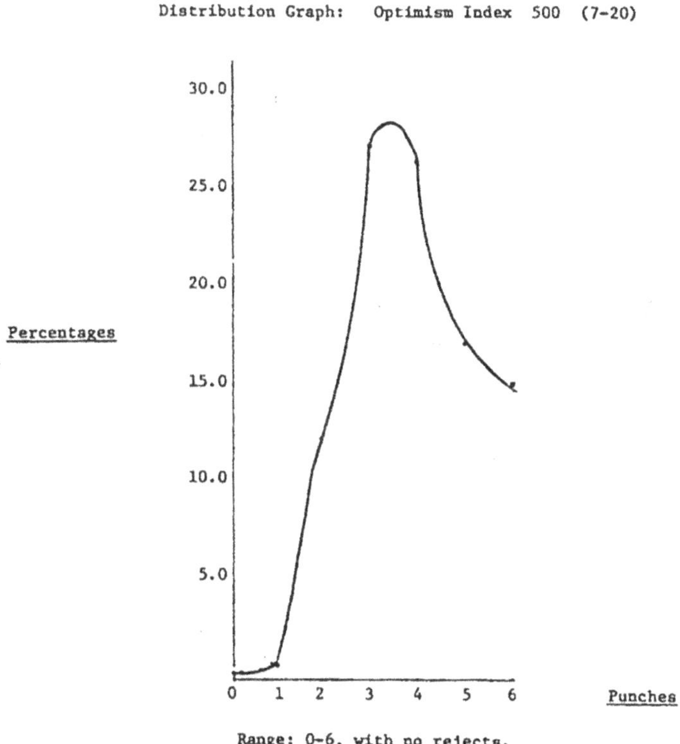

FIGURE 2.1. Measuring optimism. Reprinted with the permission of the MIT Center for International Studies, from *Rural Development Research Project No. 2: Index Construction and Validation* (Cambridge, MA: CENIS, 1967).

dia seemed more likely to be innovative, thus suggesting that those already considered "modern" by the standards of the survey were most likely to modernize.[105] The capacity for having an "open, imaginative mind" as well as degrees of "external mistrust" (discerned through interviewer evaluations that catalogued respondents' suspicion, sincerity, and cooperativeness) also figured into indices of modernization, further evoking Lerner's tautological standards for psychic mobility and interpersonal trust. High scores on the innovation index thus indicated a "relatively flexible cognitive structure"; the report concluded that "innovators appear to be people who are generally knowledgeable about their community, who can project their thoughts and stretch their imaginations, who are not distrustful of strangers coming into the village environment, and who are not restricted by parochial loyalties."[106] Once again, then, behavior in the interview setting came to connote exposure to and proclivity for modernization. Openness to a new cultural form (the survey situation), readiness to talk to a stranger (regardless of suspicions that might be validated by disclosure of the agencies involved), and willingness to identify with hypothetical situations were treated as both evidence and raw data. They at once confirmed and factored into the crafting of the categories of modern and traditional.

Conclusion

In the midst of the proliferation of social scientific surveys in 1968, a group of Turkish agencies collaborated on a study that measured the propensity for modernization among 5,244 villagers. USAID's Rural Development Research Project provided not only the guidelines for sampling methods but also a basis for comparison, since half of its questionnaire was replicated. Some of the original questions were omitted because they seemed too laden with connotations of prestige. Others remained, inquiring into the peasants' spare-time activities, levels of education, literacy, and attitudes about the future. Although the answers were evaluated through tropes of open society, mastery over nature, and technological change, concepts such as peasant innovation were coded differently.[107]

The replication of the Rural Development Research Project, however partial, may suggest a level of success in the conduct of its manifold safeguards. By 1968, though, Frey had published only two articles divulging the findings of the research, and the reasons for this scarcity remained a point of contention. The publication of the Turkish replication of the study presumably helped dispel some of this aggravation, but one scholar went so far as to censure the unavailability of the original research as a hindrance against the "development of social sciences in our country. Unless this is done, I have to express with sadness, this study can be deemed a form of 'intellectual neo-colonialism.'"[108] Edwin Cohn, who acted as economic adviser to Turkey under both the MSA and USAID missions, repeated the sentiment that the project, originally deemed attractive during the time of its conduct, gave "the impression that they regard the Turks as guinea pigs to be studied and analyzed for the benefit of the external scholarly community." This fostered the view that "Turkey is being exploited by foreign scholars for their own exclusive advantage—and, by implication, to Turkey's detriment—[which] is somewhat analogous to the attitude widely held by Turkish intellectuals . . . towards foreign enterprises in general and mining companies in particular."[109] Cohn's contextualization of the reception of the project within a broader atmosphere of suspicion is apt, given a growing anti-Americanism in universities during this period, including the "violent disruption" of a lecture Daniel Lerner was to give at Istanbul University in 1969 by a group of students led by Deniz Gezmiş, a founding member of the People's Liberation Army.[110] As for the interviewer Tosun, whom Lerner expected to engage in the manifest destiny of survey research in North Africa, he eventually left his diplomatic post in Morocco for New York City, where he staged "happenings" criticizing the Vietnam War.[111] He converted to Sufism in the 1980s and today lives as a proselytizing sheikh in Chestnut Ridge.[112]

The preceding account is not meant to detract from the import of Lerner's work in the propagation of survey methodology and modernization theory, wherein the coding of speech and regulation of attitudes suggested a tailored fit between survey research and that school of thought. The partial disclosure of research aims, through interviewer negligence, the concealment of VOA interests, or the enlistment of local agencies such as the SPO, was in fact central to the efforts to conceive of the survey setting as part of a modernizing edifice. Its practitioners viewed the technique as capable of producing modern interviewers and respondents alike. Sample surveys, growing out of collaborative enterprises between government agencies, research centers, and universities, were deployed as technologies through which American developmental schemes and attendant social scientific practices would be promulgated across the world. Yet there was not a wholesale acceptance of the premises and dictates of those practices, and they were not imbued with the ability to cultivate new subjectivities for their recipients. The simultaneous success and frailty of modernization theory can be discerned in its reliance on survey research for the crafting and dissemination of its categories. This knowledge practice crystallized despite and through the substitutions and translations that were endemic to practitioners' efforts to fix its categories' framings.

In the work of Lerner and later practitioners, we find a perseverance of hostile receptions of initially welcome projects, questionnaires overflowing their original intent, and disorderly interviewer behavior. The interviewees' responses entailed strategies of resistance and subversion through refusals to respond in the designated way, prevarication of opinions, and skepticism about the premises and categories proclaimed by the survey. Although those responses were misread or omitted in final accounts, the reported form of the surveys also remade questionnaires and coding procedures, denoting mutability in processes of translation, reiteration, and circulation. Still, Lerner explicitly linked the notion that surveys could enact empathy with other signifiers of modernity. In his parable, the Grocer was an exemplary subject who not only demonstrated the capacity for psychic and physical mobility but also extended hospitality to his interviewer. These additional traits of modern subjectivity were encouraged through the construction of highways and hotels across the country, the subject of the next chapters.

3

Material Encounters

Experts, Reports, and Machines

What the American Engineer does in the Middle East during the years 1948, '49 and '50 will be an important factor in determining the fate of the world for many years to come.

—Max Thornburg, "The Middle East and the American Engineer"

Mr. Hilts, desirous of buying a small carpet, was guided to a rug store in the old covered bazaar. The price tag indicated 800 Turkish liras. Mr. Hilts hesitated; it was rather expensive for him. The shopkeeper stared at him for a moment and seemed to recognize his face. "Aren't you the American who is here to help us with our highway problems?" he asked. Mr. Hilts replied "Yes," whereupon the shopkeeper said "You can have it for 700 liras. I'll cut my profit for you."

—*Turkish Roads and Highways*

IN A PROGRESS REPORT delivered to the Engineer's Joint Council in 1949, Max Thornburg laid out his vision for American engineers' contribution to the economic development of the Middle East, whose people were choosing between "our way and the Russian way." Speaking two months after President Truman's inaugural speech announcing the Point Four Program in technical cooperation, Thornburg argued that the transfer of technical knowledge, which could be "passed on freely without diminishing the supply," was a "public duty on a world scale." Even though obstacles, such as the lack of private capital and the prevalence of German techniques, stood in the way of what he called "racial and economic progress" in the region, he called on engineering societies and "our great national business associations" to act as an "important part of the 'brain' which must be grafted onto the Middle East body."[1]

Thornburg worked as a Standard Oil Company of California executive in Bahrain in the 1930s, as petroleum adviser to the State Department during World War II, and as a "self-styled 'foreign industrial consultant'" for private companies and local governments in Iran and Turkey in the postwar years.[2] A steadfast proponent of "private sector developmentalism," he eventually lost favor in Iran and was blamed for contributing to the process that led to the nationalization of oil in 1951. Thornburg had better luck in Turkey, where he was first commissioned by the Twentieth Century Fund to write a report assessing the country's economic climate. His report, which served as an important primary source for modernization theorists such as Daniel Lerner, chastised the policies of the Kemalist Republican People's Party (CHP), which was "under the spell of the Soviet passion for magnificent planning and construction of heavy industries."[3] Thornburg instead recommended encouraging foreign capital, privatization, and agricultural production by investing in infrastructure and especially a highway network, which he deemed necessary for "every possible advance in Turkey, whether for the development of agriculture and industry or for improvement of health, education and other social and political goods."[4] In order to secure American aid, the CHP gradually abandoned its railway-led, state-owned industrialization policies in favor of agricultural growth, privatization, and highways—an economic program that the Democrat Party (DP) fully implemented when it came to power in 1950.

Adnan Menderes, the new DP prime minister, appreciated Thornburg's vision of modernization and invited him back as his economic adviser in 1955, even as Menderes abolished other foreign consultants who criticized his policies. By the time of the 1960 coup that deposed Menderes, the oilman had reinvented himself as an academic and found a home at the Center for Middle Eastern Studies at Harvard University. In scholarly publications, he called on American policy makers who wanted to "understand or produce" change in the region to "at least possess what Edward Shils has said is the essence of sociology—an 'imaginative feeling for the patterns of life and conduct of people whose ways are different from one's own.'" As for the social scientists whose empathy should set a model for others, Thornburg counseled that they should unify their terminology and theories so as to be intelligible to policy makers who sought to comprehend and influence behavioral problems.[5]

Thornburg's 1949 speech summoning engineers to share their technical know-how and his encouragement for a "modern motor highway" in Turkey can be situated in a longer history of American interventionism, starting with the occupation of the Philippines, which Michael Adas has described as a "vast engineering project."[6] During the Cold War, the United States and the Soviet Union both invested in technology transfer and infrastructural projects across the global periphery.[7] Against the Soviet-funded Aswan Dam in Egypt and Bhilai Steel plant in India, the United States implemented aviation programs and replicas of the Tennessee Valley Authority (TVA), which became, as David Ekbladh put it, a "grand synecdoche, standing for a wider liberal approach to economic and social development both domestically and internationally."[8] Public works construction had been a central tool for reducing employment and shifting towards a Keynesian management of the economy during the New Deal.[9] In the postwar period, "mature federal resource agencies, born of Depression constituencies and war production schedules," were equipped with specific ideas about "what had caused the Great Depression, and what had fixed it," such as appropriate technologies and bureaucratic organization.[10] For its champions like David Lilienthal, TVA signified "democracy on the march," resonating across "the crossroad towns in the Ozarks, the trailer camps in Detroit, [the] oil fields across the Rio Grande, the collieries in Wales; [even] the villages on the Ganges and the caves beneath Chunking."[11] Despite its popularity in foreign policy circles, this symbol of liberal developmentalism was criticized as a symbol of "creeping socialism" to the detriment of "private enterprise" at home.[12] Cold War developmental technologies were ambivalent indexes, wavering between visions of planning and laissez faire, democracy and interventionism, public and private interests. But rather than growing out of insular American debates, such technologies also interacted with and were informed by local conversations about modernization.

In Turkey, the highway initiative commended by Thornburg and modernization theorists was an early example of technical cooperation with the United States, predating the Point Four Program by two years. The arrival of American aid, experts, and machinery through Truman Doctrine and Marshall Plan funds was expected to instigate modernization in administrative and mechanical terms by acquainting the new highway organization and its civil engineers with rational methods of record keeping, roadbuilding, and machine maintenance. Yet the interactions between the governmental agencies, such as the US Bureau of Public Roads (BPR), the Turkish General Directorate of Highways (KGM), and the Economic Cooperation Administration (ECA), were marked by tensions and conflicts. Experts disagreed about the pace and methods of modernization, whether private contractors should be employed, the amount of machinery to be circulated, and where and to whom roads should be delivered.

The extension of technical know-how in the field of highway building was an important component of Turkey's laboratization. The Marshall Plan required not a wholesale abandonment of etatism but an arrangement whereby the state would provide the infrastructure needed for capital accumulation by the private sector—in other words, a "deepening of capitalist relations."[13] This was consistent not only with the vision of development laid out in the pages of *Forum* and the "push" that modernization theorists like W. W. Rostow envisioned in the transition to the "take-off" stage but also the active state involvement encouraged in international development circles, such as Council on Foreign Relations planners.[14] Engineers' offices were microcosms in which debates about economic development, expertise, and bureaucracy were staged and worked upon.

The circulation of budgets, progress reports, and completion maps were instrumental to measuring and displaying the postwar economy. As Matthew Hull has argued, "Documents are not simply instruments of bureaucratic organizations" but are constitutive of bureaucratic "ideologies, knowledge, practices, subjectivities."[15] American engineers understood their Turkish counterparts to be in need of reorientation (in attitudinal, physical, and epistemic terms) before they could become the purveyors of modernization to the rest of the country. They were especially concerned with upgrading the Turkish engineers' temporal outlook and encouraging them to invest in realistic, short-term plans that could be carried out with patience in the immediate future. Through their relationship with material objects, such as reports, maps, highway equipment, and roads, experts were to cultivate mastery of concepts like foresight, expenditure, saving, and management.

The negotiations between the different agencies also pivoted around questions of teamwork, recognition, and intimacy. The literature on development has depicted experts as presenting their work as technical solutions and, in doing so, concealing the political implications of their interventions.[16] But in the highway initiative in Turkey, seemingly personal and corporeal interactions were equally central to the fashioning of expert knowledge and practices. Like the social scientists who grappled with the imperative to simplify the world in which they sought to intervene, engineers were enmeshed in social and material relationships that rendered their solutions provisional at best. As Harvey and Knox also find in their ethnography of highway construction between Brazil and Peru, documents of engineering are "themselves social forms, relational devices that are produced to serve a particular purpose."[17] Debates over paperwork and machinery not only addressed the imperatives to calculate and predict material realities but also pertained to the generation of interpersonal encounters.

Road construction brought together questions of modernization on multiple scales, including the direction of Turkey's postwar economy, the creation of a relationship between Turkey and the United States based on technical assistance, and the production of the civil engineer as a certain kind of social and temporal subject. In order to trace this example of laboratization in practice, this chapter foregrounds the individual and institutional recipients of ostensibly abstract and transcendent visions of development. Following an overview of the founding of the new Turkish highway organization after the image of the American BPR, I examine the tension-filled relationship between the latter institution's engineers and the Marshall Plan administrators. The location of highways, the circulation of reports, and the labeling of roadbuilding equipment were material sites where the agencies competed over the management of the Turkish economy and staked out their claims to authority and visibility. I then outline the American engineers' demands for record keeping, time management, teamwork, and manual labor from their Turkish counterparts, whose modernization was deemed to be contingent on their mastery over material devices, such as documents and machinery. The expertise and modernity of both sets of engineers were called into question over the course of their developmental negotiations, which are catalogued in the political, material, and personal encounters between them.

Mirrors for Engineers

Political economists of postwar Turkey generally cast three documents as the protagonists of its liberalization narrative: Thornburg's 1949 report for the Twentieth Century Fund, the 1951 "Barker" report for the International Bank for Reconstruction and Development (IBRD, the precursor to the World Bank), and *Turkey's Highway Situation*, penned in 1948 by Harold E. Hilts, deputy commissioner of the BPR in Washington.[18] As with Lerner's questionnaires, these reports were to occasion the enactment of modernization, in this case by restructuring Turkey's economy and altering its material and bureaucratic landscape. The Thornburg and Barker documents were more comprehensive in their recommendations, urging privatization and agricultural mechanization. Hilts's report paved the infrastructure for this new political economic order: a new administrative unit to oversee the extension of a highway network that would enable farm-to-market transportation, door-to-door delivery, and faster haulage relative to railroads.

The visibility of Hilts's recommendations obscures another document that preceded it by three years. The author of this earlier report was Vecdi Diker, an engineer at the Department of Roads and Bridges of the Turkish Ministry of Public Works. In 1945, Diker and another engineer, Vehbi Ekesan, spent two months in Washington, DC, where they inspected the federal BPR, and another two months traveling through a range of states, including New Jersey, North Carolina, Alabama, California, Texas, and Colorado, some of whose terrains were deemed similar to Turkey.[19] Over the course of their investigative trip, they also visited factories, universities, and research institutes across the country, having traveled 25,000 kilometers by car by the time of their departure.

Upon his return to Ankara, Diker presented a report on the American highway system to the Ministry of Public Works, depicting in detail the service stations, rest stops, restaurants, tourist camps, and repair shops he observed alongside highways. He also described various regulations regarding road taxes, the use of contractors, and laboratory research that ensured highway construction.[20] The BPR, Diker noted, was the prototype of the "modern highway organization" of which the Turkish "highway cause" was in dire need. Although he conceded that some adjustments would have to be made in modeling a new administrative unit after the American one, Diker raised the possibility of having American engineers brought to Turkey for personnel education.

It was Diker's follow-up visit to Washington in August 1947 that occasioned Hilts's report, which stands as a mirror image of his own. During this new trip, Diker successfully negotiated with the US State and War Departments for the purchase of highway equipment in the amount of $5 million from the recently announced Truman Doctrine funds.[21] A treaty was signed between the Turkish Ministry of Public Works and the

US Aid Commission on April 26, 1948, allowing for the arrival of American funding and machinery for road construction.[22] The initial equipment was immediately put to use in highway construction between the strategically important Erzurum and the commercial and military ports of Iskenderun, the first exercise in mechanized roadbuilding in Turkey.[23] On August 8, 1948, the cabinet approved the plan to build roads in the amount of 23,000 kilometers through a nine-year plan that would unfold over the course of 3 three-year stages.[24] (See figure 3.1.) After a series of negotiations and standstills in Parliament, a new, autonomous highway organization was founded, consciously modeled after the American one.

Diker, who was appointed the first director of the new organization, was an active participant in the making of postwar modernization, given his role as a translator between local and American engineers and policy makers. He was born in Istanbul in 1908 and attended Columbia University and the University of Missouri before he took a position with the Department of Roads and Bridges in Turkey in 1937. Diker explained that it was his initial stay in the United States as a student of engineering during the 1930s that "opened his eyes" and made him appreciate the American highway system that connected the country like a human body.[25] He was in the United States for its most sustained period of highway investment prior to the Federal Aid Highway Act of 1956, a time when the New Deal provided $4 billion dollars in federal funds for roadbuilding, making the daily commute increasingly synonymous with the American way of living.[26]

Soon after his return from his studies, Diker delivered speeches that depicted the American highway system as a replicable model at home: "A student or a teacher can go to a school that is 50–60 kilometers away each day. A businessman, an engineer, a doctor can work in cities where they do not reside. Provinces and villages about 150–200 kilometers away from the city can benefit from the goods of urban life. For instance, people can travel between cities as far away from each other as Ankara and Konya in order to attend a conference or play. These things are done [in the United States] all the time."[27] This speech from 1938 was an early valorization of highways and their facilitation of voluntary and leisurely movement at a time when travel was associated with trains, a much less individualistic method of transport in Turkey. Diker appreciated highways as an archetype of American modernization and "automobility," which historian

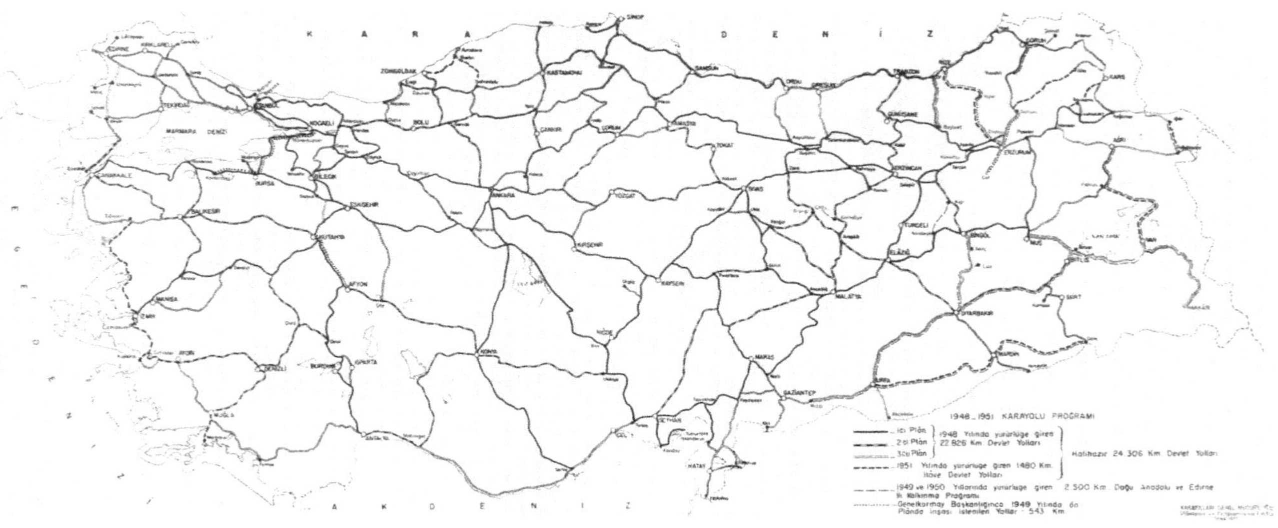

FIGURE 3.1. The nine-year highway plan. Courtesy of the Archives of the General Directorate of Highways, Ankara, Turkey.

Cotten Seiler defines as "the combined import of the motor vehicle, the automobile industry and the highway, plus the emotional connotations of this import for Americans."[28]

In administrative terms, Diker praised the American system as a model of expertise that was rational, applied, and experiential.[29] In line with his proposal in the 1945 report, the aid agreement secured funds for the formation of the American Public Roads Group (PRG), which stayed in Turkey between 1948 and 1959, with a personnel of more than one hundred, including engineers, mechanics, foremen, and stenographers.[30] The PRG provided guidance in the administration, planning, programming, and financing phases of highway construction in Ankara, with the federal BPR administering an engineer training program in Washington.[31] The sixteen-week-long curriculum included lectures on the role of highway transport in the American economy and technical subjects such as highway drainage, bridging, soil stabilization, and compaction.[32] Following the first phase, delegates were sent in groups of three or four on ten week-long field trips to states whose terrain was deemed similar to their country of origin. During these trips, they could observe construction and maintenance techniques, inspect testing labs, and study the administration of state and local highway departments. Urgent tasks awaited the engineers on their return home.

Engineering the Economy

In May 1950, F. G. Draper of the ECA delivered a speech to Turkish highway engineers on their way to the training center in Washington. Draper's speech linked Cold War exigencies with the promotion of development; he explained that the objective of the Marshall Plan was "to raise the standard of living of all peace loving democratic countries [so] as to preserve the basic elements of individual freedom and develop international and joint resistance against the disease of communism." One way of "fortifying [the free nations of the world] against those who would destroy freedom" was the establishment of the ECA, which regulated the "investment of money towards lasting results in the form of economic development" through technical assistance programs. Draper admonished the Turkish engineers: "Your studies in the United States . . . are an investment both in dollars and in lira. It is your responsibility to bring back information to Turkey and apply it to your work so as to increase the economic value of what you produce, whether it be designing, or blueprinting, or engineering or constructing or something else."[33]

Draper's depiction of the training program in terms of investment and economic value exemplified the administration's approach towards technical cooperation. Assistance for highways started under the auspices of the Joint American Mission for Military Aid to Turkey [JAMMAT], which founded its own engineering branch in 1949, and continued under the Marshall Plan. Russell Dorr, the chief of the ECA mission to Turkey, was initially conflicted about which agency the PRG would report to since it continued work on "strategic military roads" even as the program was being financed by ECA funds, with the organizational arrangement appearing "rather anomalous."[34] Although the changes that ECA representatives suggested to the initial program were implemented, highway building was never completely civilianized, as can be evinced from maps and progress reports chronicling the differences and overlaps between roads with military and economic "values" over the years.[35] As the Army Corps of Engineers and the US Engineer Group continued their operations in the country, the list of strategic roads planned and built by American engineers grew, even long after the Marshall Plan was discontinued.[36]

The ECA's understanding of the roads program reflected Turkey's place in the postwar world economy. The new highway network connected the hinterland to port cities and linked cities that were important for military and agricultural reasons to Ankara and Istanbul, with subsequent revisions in road construction emphasizing international road agreements with Europe and Iran. An early aid agreement with the United States underscored the necessity for moving agricultural and other products to "domestic markets and to Turkish ports for export to countries in urgent need of such Turkish surpluses as food and coal."[37] In communications with engineers, such as Jesse Williams, who was put in charge of the PRG in Ankara after Hilts's departure, Dorr insisted that his priority was the "European recovery point of view."[38] His organization took a special interest in roads built around a variety of industrial projects, such as the Zonguldak coal basin, the Ağaçlı lignite works, the Ereğli steel works, and the salt works at Tuz Gölü.[39] The PRG, by contrast, interpreted their mission as the extension of technical know-how. In a series of speeches delivered to engineers across the United States, Hilts described their program as a precocious case in technical cooperation—a "'Point Four' project initiated in late 1947."[40] These conflicting interpretations would lead to disagreements over the allocation, transfer, and dissemination of material things, such as machinery, meticulously kept records, and maps designating areas of economic interest.

An important point of contention between the two agencies was Dorr's suggestion that American private contractors be brought in to accelerate highway building. A clause allowing their arrival had indeed been included in the original agreement at the insistence of ECA representatives who believed that the PRG was not qualified to train Turkish engineers, administrators and laborers, given their tendency to teach the Turks too much "theory" and not enough "down-to-earth training."[41] The PRG opposed not only the import of contractors but also the sale of American road machinery to private Turkish contractors, maintaining that the Department of Highways' hold on equipment would ensure faster construction on roads.[42] The American engineers' approach was a compromised product of the New Deal, whose agencies bickered over whether to use the force account method of construction, which targeted unemployment, or to let private contractors bid for actual construction while the federal government remained in charge of purchasing materials.[43] The PRG thus viewed the Turkish program through the lens of New Deal debates about public versus private enrichment. But their experience in Turkey allowed them to adapt to the language of national security and economic development in their battle for a federal highway program at home, as the conversation about public works no longer addressed job creation or social welfare in the postwar period.[44]

The ECA mission's insistence on contractors, in turn, was consistent with their efforts to encourage foreign-capital investment and "[foster] private enterprise" in Turkey.[45] American contractors were ubiquitous in different sectors, with firms such as Parsons, Brinckerhoff, Thompson-Starrett, Skidmore, Owings, Merrill, Morrison-Knudsen, and Metcalfe involved in planning and building ports, dams, hotels, oil refineries, resort towns, and US Army Corps of Engineers bases over the years.[46] As İlhan Tekeli has pointed out, the PRG's insistence on public oversight presented the interesting situation in which "while Turkey was distancing itself from etatism in broad political strokes, it was shifting from private sector to state involvement in highway building."[47]

American engineers were resolute that their task was to help build an administrative organization and provide technical assistance up to

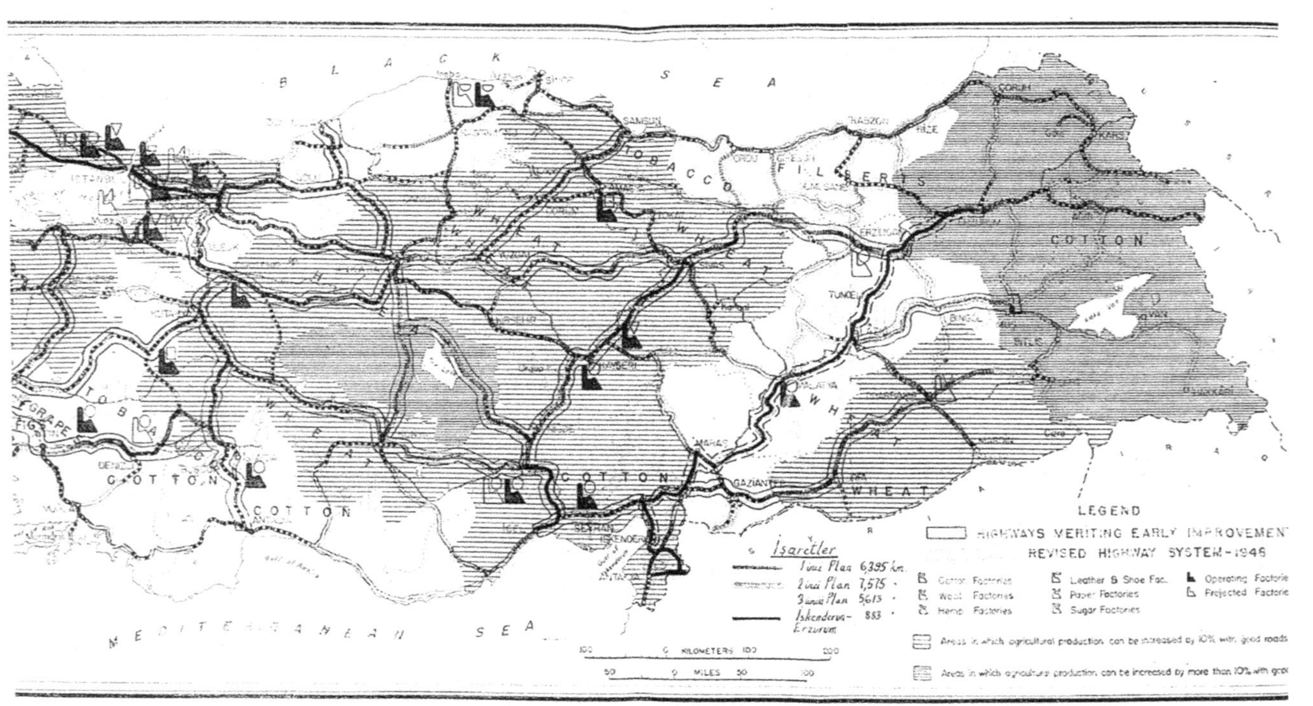

FIGURE 3.2. Highways to assist agricultural production. Courtesy of the Archives of the General Directorate of Highways, Ankara, Turkey.

the point at which Turkish experts and contractors would be able to take over. Hilts believed that Dorr lacked experience in "cooperative intergovernmental construction" and was "approaching the entire road problem in Turkey from the point of view of a contractor who wants to build a lot of high-priced roads."[48] Hilts went so far as to persuade Commissioner MacDonald that the PRG could not stay in Turkey should American contractors become involved, while Dorr complained of the "childish" and "far-from-conciliatory attitude" displayed by Hilts and the PRG, saying, "The word 'gradual' (which Hiltz [*sic*] kept using all the time) is no part of our ECA vocabulary."[49] Hilts was indeed invested in gradual learning and frequently counseled "patience and then more patience" to the Turkish engineers in their efforts in roadbuilding and cost accounting.[50]

Disagreements over the pace of roadbuilding also unfolded in the realm of paperwork and highway equipment. While Hilts insisted that the PRG in Turkey would report to the "Commissioner of the Bureau of Public Roads and no one else," Paul Hoffman, the head of the administration, informed Commissioner Macdonald that the recent isolation of the ECA from the details of the Turkish Roads Group had been "ill-advised."[51] Comprehensive knowledge of highway activity required the submission of monthly progress reports, inventories, lists of equipment, and project completion dates. These documents were then compiled in quarterly reports and juxtaposed with progress on other ECA-funded projects, such as the Istanbul Hilton Hotel. These publications and the internal memoranda regarding their timely submission and circulation amounted to what Mary Morgan has called "measuring instruments," tools of data collection that also work as analytical devices by arraying economic phenomena.[52] The aggregated figures and tables framed and envisioned the economy in a particular way, linking roadbuilding with projections about agricultural yield and industrial productivity. Maps prepared at the Department of Highways for the ECA catalogued import and export goods, such as wheat, cotton, timber, and tobacco by their respective regions. (See figure 3.2.) The spatial composites of the country and indices of production became interchangeable, condensed units of development. Such documents shed light on Dorr's insistence that Hilts and the Roads Groups "must be made to realize that the Turkish economy is our business and that when it comes down to questions of priorities, ours must be the last word."[53]

An additional way for the ECA to display ownership of the Turkish economy was its request that all equipment procured by the PRG be "conspicuously marked with the ECA emblem" so that "people of countries participating in the Marshall Plan [are] informed of the activities carried out under the plan." Dorr asked Robert Huse, the director of the Overseas Information Division of the ECA, to inform the BPR of "the requirement of adequately labeling ECA financed purchases. You might also point out the importance of the Road Program to the Turkish economy as a whole and the blunt fact that this Road Program is now underwritten by ECA, which fact ought also to be acknowledged *publicly*."[54] In other contexts, ECA representatives conceded to having been "irritated here at home by the *publicity* which BPR is giving to the Turkish project [without mentioning] the fact that ECA plays any part in making it possible."[55] The circulation of carefully marked machinery was to ensure exposure and gratitude in this particular microcosm where the Cold War was fought over alternative models of technical knowledge and economic development. A wide range of material objects, such as machines, paperwork, and maps were concrete channels through which ideas about modernization and expertise traversed and crystallized.

As we will see in the remainder of this chapter, ECA demands from the American PRG were projected onto expectations from Turkish engineers in an act of refraction. While the engineers were able to ward off American contractors, they were responsive to ECA requests for documentation of expenses and progress on projects; every time the ECA suggested that the engineers were not up to the task, they became stricter in their comportment towards their Turkish counterparts, who responded with their own set of demands.

Engineering Time

The press and public relations unit at the Turkish General Directorate of Highways (KGM) retains a plethora of reports, maps, and correspondences that catalogue the highway-assistance program. The records of the weekly meetings that took place between Turkish and American engineers, spanning the period between 1948 and 1950, are incomplete and intermittent. The gaps between various communications and the missing weekly summaries, which can be discerned through references to previous meetings that were either not recorded or could not be salvaged for archival purposes, are telling. Dispatches to regional directorates, it seems, did not make it to Ankara at all—a failure in centralized record keeping that would deeply trouble the American experts. The sporadic nature of the archival record is a testament to the frailty of demands for scrupulous documentation.

The standstills and disputes between the BPR and the ECA swiftly mapped onto the relations between the American PRG and the Department of Highways in Ankara. Once the PRG embarked on their work in Turkey, they enumerated their own expectations and demands from local engineers, which ranged from practices of bookkeeping and cost consciousness to the cultivation of cooperative skills. The civil engineer who was to carry out the material reconfiguration of the Turkish landscape by delivering highways to the countryside was to reorient himself physically, temporally, and attitudinally. He was to acquire a flair for cost analysis and be prepared to "get his hands dirty" if necessary, since the handling of spare parts and the maintenance of newly arrived machinery—and a concurrent grasp of waste, delay, and expenditure—were crucial components of American understandings of highway expertise. Related conceptions of rational organization, future-orientation, and linear thinking were questions that preoccupied the American experts, who argued among themselves, and the Turkish engineers, who were cast in their image.

While the temporal reorientation required of the highway engineer entailed acclimation to gradual and linear thinking, the Americans complained that the prevailing mindset was inflected with impatience and an excessive preoccupation with the future to the detriment of the expediencies of the present. The American group committed to the vision of a nine-year plan as laid out in the Turkish division's report, but they questioned the feasibility of such long-term and open-ended planning.[56] The prospect of a decade-long plan seemed bold and impetuous, particularly given uncertainties about the availability of funds, equipment, and classified personnel.

The cultivation of organized methods of roadbuilding proceeded along protracted lines, as one American engineer explained to a Turkish counterpart:

> For many months back emphasis has been made on the importance of the preparation of individual Province maps showing location and physical data of all Provincial roads. Before leaving for the States Mr. Burdick advised of the need for the early

> completion of the maps because of their value in the orderly planning and programming of highway activities and future construction and he instructed that this phase of the work be actively carried on during his absence. . . . On a recent check of the status of the progress of the mapping project I find that the work is now at a complete standstill.[57]

The requests for maps, which were meant to chronicle and ensure the timely completion of projects based on ECA expectations, were commonplace items on the agenda at the weekly meetings of the planning unit. In one instance, division engineer Chester Burdick, a vocal presence at these meetings, insisted that more work be done on a particular road between Aydın and Denizli along the Aegean coast, insisting that promises had been made to "the Marshall" and that these roads had to be completed in order for aid "not to be revoked." Burdick's requests for a specific timeline were met with dithering responses ("We need to think about it") and evasion at best ("That's quite difficult"). In response to the threat that it would be "disastrous" if the map displayed plans that "cannot be completed," Seyfi Tunga of KGM politely reassured Burdick that promises had also been made to an unnamed minister and that they would "work in a more rational manner from now on."[58] During another meeting also attended by Hilts, Diker reassured his American colleagues that "when Mr. Hilts returns next year, he will notice the progress."[59]

In fact, Harold Hilts periodically returned to Turkey during the early phases of the program, and his months-long visits were fervently chronicled in newspapers across the country. (See figure 3.3.) He took time to talk to reporters during these trips, providing updates on recent developments, such as the creation of a scientific commission at the Department of Roads and Bridges. This commission would be charged with identifying and examining industrial resources.[60] Hilts also attended weekly meetings at the Department of Highways, recounting his observations from various field trips across the country. During these meetings, he advised caution and patience to the Turkish engineers, but at the same time, he warned them of potential problems that awaited them in ten years, such as increasing volumes of traffic.[61] With design engineer Eric Erhart complaining of the weakness of the "organization on the planning side," Hilts insisted on the necessity of bookkeeping and contracts. The activities of the regional divisions should also be monitored closely by the center, he suggested, with stricter regulations regarding accounting

FIGURE 3.3. Harold Hilts (left) and Vecdi Diker. Courtesy of the Archives of the General Directorate of Highways, Ankara, Turkey.

and the collection of reports at the center in Ankara. As Hilts observed the waste of equipment, he often offered examples of standard procedures from the Bureau in Washington, not neglecting to turn to Turkish engineers who had just returned from training in the United States for confirmation. With the help of recently American-trained Turkish engineers, such as Cahit Őzgen, who had spent time in Kansas, Hilts could swiftly revert to the "hands-off" and gradual attitude that so frustrated ECA representatives. As he put it, "The only way for success is that you do your own job. You will find your own mistakes, which will help you succeed. God helps those who do their own job."[62]

Oftentimes, the Turkish engineers committed to the vision of an administrative unit incorporating meticulous organization and rationality. They responded to the PRG's requests for traffic surveys and field inventories and adopted their standards for operating speeds and the minimum width of road surfacing. KGM implemented stage construction development whereby each road was built and improved to meet present and future traffic needs, and bituminous surfaces were paved only if the volume of traffic required it. In correspondence with Williams, Hilts praised trainees such as Zafer Pamir, who seemed "thoroughly sold" on cost-accounting principles and will "take back with him some ideas that can be used."[63] Hilts's priorities were consistent with his initial report that launched the highway project, in which he likened the management of the personnel system to "the management of an industrial enterprise."[64] The preparation of budgets and the careful monitoring of expenses would ensure that good management and a grasp of financial matters proceeded in complementary fashion, combining scientific expertise with corporatism and bureaucratic planning, the hallmarks of the Marshall Plan.[65]

Hilts was also vocal about his dedication to gradual methods of highway building in private communications with engineers of higher ranking. He warned Diker, for instance, about roads being built around the Salt Lake in central Anatolia, which might be endangered by "your old slipshod methods of handling excavation and embankment."

> You will remember that we both commented on the excellent work that had been done by your maintenance division on one section of the route north of Konya where I told you this looked like a good American highway with 4 to 1 slopes, with ditches well removed from the roadbed, and with a good workmanlike appearance to the whole highway right-of-way. Unless you begin to instill pride into your men

for the appearance of the road you will be losing a golden opportunity to achieve results for which the traveling public would commend you highly.[66]

In addition to familiarizing both the Turkish engineers and the "traveling public" with methodically crafted American highways, commitment to realistic plans remained a priority. As Hilts put it, "We must continue to oppose schemes that from our experience we know cannot be carried out efficiently. We must do our best to stabilize their thoughts, and we must adhere strictly to the insistence that programmed items must be finished in workmanlike fashion before attempting to carry out other large schemes. You will never do any harm in opposing schemes which are paper schemes only."[67] The Turkish engineers' penchant for "paper schemes" was indicative at best of hasty methods and dreamscapes, which prevailed at the expense of punctual, assiduous, and precise workmanship. The distinction between the proper modernity of a gradual future orientation and an overly optimistic and impatient temporal outlook also had implications for the possibility of cooperation between the two engineering teams.

Teamwork in Question

Despite incompatible work habits that ostensibly warranted the disciplinary demands imposed on the Turkish engineers, Thomas MacDonald, the commissioner of the BPR, praised the harmonious atmosphere and "emotional proximity" that prevailed between the two countries: "My first impression of Turkey is the similarity in thinking and effort on the part of Turkish and American people. . . . Before coming to Turkey, I was in Ethiopia, Egypt and Iraq. But it is only in Turkey that I feel as though I am among my fellow compatriots in any city of the United States."[68] In speeches across the United States, Hilts praised the "characteristic cordiality of the Turkish technicians," adding that the Turks reacted to the highway program no different than "the average American" would.[69] Turkish engineers who participated in the training center also returned with accolades for the cordial reception they received in Washington.[70]

Conceived in concrete terms, the road network was expected to be an approximation of American standards. Yet the commitment to follow the highway template in administrative and technical terms was by no means uniform, given instances of mistranslation and frustrations about bureaucratic roadblocks. While MacDonald publicly reiterated the view of the technical exchange program as a success story in collaboration, there were disagreements among political figures as well as other engineers about the applicability of the American model and the nature of the Road Group's task. According to one member of Parliament, the unreflexive replication of the American template through such means as the replacement of "Makadam" (Macadam) roads with stabilized ones merely "resulted in errors and waste."[71] A similar point of contention pertained to techniques in bridge construction. Changes proposed by PRG engineer Fred Hartford to replace the durable yet costly stone- or steel-and-concrete structures with "a steel-pile bridge with timber deck and asphalt surfacing (or with reinforced-concrete deck)" were met with resistance.[72] One returnee from the training program, Mithat Bölgen, objected to American bridge construction methods on aesthetic grounds: "The lattice girders used at the top of bridges in some cities ruins the view. Cities like Pittsburgh have been divided in two by such bridges and have lost their original beauty."[73] The durability of these bridges was also of a dubious nature, the engineer noted, with the linings of bridges, "which are done according to the advice Mr. Hartford gives us," failing to retain water in rainy weather: "Whether or not this is a problem is a separate issue. But to let the beams get dirty and the hinges wet and soiled is not right." It was not just the material used in road construction that was under scrutiny but also the extent of American financial assistance: one issue of the *Highway Bulletin* was devoted to debunking rumors about the existence of "Marshall Boulevards, London Asphalt, and NATO Roads" across the country.[74]

During parliamentary debates, some members objected to extensive American involvement in the highway initiative. Emin Sazak bemoaned that "these days, our engineers have let themselves go. When a foreigner shows up, they lose themselves. . . . I cannot deny the benefits of American aid; I am grateful and obliged. But I would take their machinery, their advice, and tell them I will do the rest." Ahmet Ali Çınar also expressed appreciation for Americans' delivery of "a new thinking, a new understanding to our nation" but insisted that "this understanding and thought can arrive with one or two engineers, not through masses of engineers." Çınar suggested that the foreign experts should offer suggestions instead of dictates, since they only fully understood "the history, geography and economic conditions of their own nation." In the aftermath of the uproar, Şevket Adalan, the minister of public works, was put to the task of defending the entire aid program, and he explained that the Americans were present as "merely consultants." Turkish engineers benefited from their "knowledge and experience" without ceding authority to them.[75]

As for the Turkish engineers who were subject to this official rebuke, the first conversation regarding technical cooperation took place a year and a half into American presence at the Department of Roads and Bridges. Vecdi Diker breached the topic at a meeting of the planning unit and asked if there was truth to the complaints about Americans being "willful, stubborn, uninformed."[76] Mithat Özarar pointed out that "they think things are the same here as they are in America, and then they are furious with us." Confirming the concerns raised in Parliament, Cihat Başak added, "They are supposed to be cooperating with us but we treat their written requests as commands." Other engineers complained of problems with language and the Americans' lack of familiarity with Turkish conditions and their organization. Although Diker was sympathetic to these grievances, he added, "We are not behind them in terms of ideas, but the problem is that we do not know how to work in systematic fashion. . . . They have worked in American states for many years, they have much to teach us. As you know, there is specialization in America, a man doesn't know everything. You cannot call a man ignorant just because he doesn't know outside his field." (See figure 3.4.)

The American-trained Diker, who singlehandedly spearheaded the collaborative project, tried to appease the anxieties of the engineers in his division, who in turn questioned their American colleagues' insistence on standardized and abstract knowledge. Such assessments can be read against the American engineers' professionalization in a historical context. Michael Adas describes that professionalization as "command of esoteric knowledge, a specialized jargon by which to communicate that knowledge, and the technical skills to turn that knowledge to practical advantage."[77] The translation of esoteric knowledge into "technological universalism" was precisely what secured the engineers' self-presentation as the harbingers of progress and civilization across disparate sites of technical assistance and intervention, such as the Philippines, Turkey, or India.[78] At the same time, these "authoritative generalizations" cannot be

FIGURE 3.4. Vecdi Diker (second from left, seated) and the American Public Roads Group. Courtesy of the Archives of the General Directorate of Highways, Ankara, Turkey.

unmoored from the "specific relations" in which they are articulated—a testament to the perpetually provisional nature of expert practices in highway construction.[79]

The American PRG had its own set of grievances about tensions between universal and particular knowledge. If Turkish engineers provided bewilderingly vague answers to requests about progress reports and completion dates for projects, they did not necessarily remain quiet during the weekly meetings. Williams found the meetings "exceedingly long and cumbersome"; another division engineer who was responsible for taking notes in the meetings labeled them "confused," given "considerable cross talk in Turkish and English." He explained, "In these meetings the three deputies and other Turks present participate freely and at length in the discussions, all in Turkish, whether the subject is within their jurisdiction or not or whether they are informed or not." The American chairman was hesitant to interrupt the flow of conversation during the meetings, but he complained that "the issues are unnecessarily confused. Should not the deputy whose function is under consideration take the lead, talk briefly and to the point, with the other two deputies 'sitting on the sidelines' and participating only when the question affects their sections?"[80]

The contradiction between specific and general knowledge was found to characterize the bulk of administrative processes as well. Burdick wrote a memorandum outlining the various obstacles that the law for reorganizing the Department of Roads and Bridges met in Parliament, and he insisted that there was an "intentional and planned sabotage of the Turkish highway improvement program" being carried out by a "top-bracket group of Turkish persons."[81] He thought that their plans were "immediately reviewed by a group of unknown persons, and rewritten into largely unrecognizable and changed form," whereby "inadequate opinion has been substituted for factual reasoning and experience." Burdick formulated a conception of expertise that contrasted bookkeeping, rationality, and particularized experience with ignorance and slipshod methods. If promises made to the "Marshall" could not be kept on account of unreliable planning, gaps in record keeping were equally culpable. The most important way in which those gaps were manifest was the treatment and maintenance of machinery, which also figured into complaints about the competence, knowledge, and cooperative skills of the Turkish engineers.

Getting Hands Dirty

In his memoirs reflecting on Cold War–era Turkish-American relations, George McGhee, US ambassador and coordinator of aid to Turkey, recounted with pride that "soon there appeared all over Turkey highway equipment compounds with strong iron fences and locked gates painted the same distinctive orange colour as the equipment, just as the depots are built in the United States."[82] McGhee's recollections underscore the centrality of equipment to the highway initiative. As with the tensions between the ECA and the Roads Group, American and Turkish engineers also clashed over the use of roadbuilding machinery. The Turkish Department of Highway's requests for an increase in the amount of machinery resulted in maintenance units, portative buildings, and portable repair shops rapidly becoming visible across the country. The competitive bidding process for rollers, motor graders, and bulldozers benefited American equipment manufacturers, such as Huber and Caterpillar, as well as smaller companies from obscure Midwestern towns.[83] When American road-machine companies and their engineers returned from their global operations in Iran and Libya, they used their experience to undertake the ambitious interstate highway program at home.[84] But the onset of mechanized highway building also produced the problem of a shortage of available and qualified personnel who were familiar with the imperatives of machine maintenance in places such as Turkey. (See figures 3.5 and 3.6.)

Documents that were penned to assess the viability of American aid to Turkey frequently addressed the treatment of machines and vehicles. According to IBRD's Barker report, "Foreign visitors to Turkey, for example, are forcibly struck by the improvidence and recklessness with which trucks, tractors and automobiles are driven, used and maintained." Thornburg chimed in, "In 4,000 miles of travel over roads in nearly every region of Turkey, the author counted eleven power-driven road roll-

FIGURE 3.5. Road roller operated by hand, prior to the mechanization of roadbuilding. Courtesy of the Archives of the General Directorate of Highways, Ankara, Turkey.

FIGURE 3.6. An excavator. Courtesy of the Archives of the General Directorate of Highways, Ankara, Turkey.

ers. Four of these were abandoned by the roadside, and apparently were stripped of accessories. Of the remainder, only one was working on an important highway job." The problem, Thornburg cautioned, was the lack of operators who would maintain the machinery. He believed that "no further substantial dollar requirement is likely in the near future" until the highway personnel received proper training.[85]

Editorials in mainstream Turkish newspapers also noted the shortage of personnel and the need for specialized occupational schools, given the arrival of a "tremendous army of machinery."[86] The machinery called for not only a new mentality in roadbuilding methods but also an attunement to their biological life. As one editorial put it, "If we want to deter the machinery from turning into scrap before they complete their natural life cycle, we need to breed experienced personnel who know not only how they are used, but also appreciate how each one of them needs to be cared for."[87] In the lack of such personnel, the machinery would lead "abused, roughed up, miserable" lives, unable to endure until their "natural death."[88] In this anthropomorphized landscape, the worth of mechanical life was calculated in terms of monetary value, costing up to eighty thousand Turkish lira by one account, and twenty thousand to thirty thousand dollars a piece by another.[89]

Given the frequent depiction of machinery as living creatures whose worth was computed in dollars and liras in the public imagination, training mechanically attuned personnel became an increasingly pressing issue. The temporal reorientation expected of the civil engineer was thus equally about encounters with machinery. Insofar as linear thinking was a necessity in the prevention of waste and unnecessary expenditures, material objects proved central, once again, to the making of modern experts. The Turkish engineers' future-oriented temporal outlook, otherwise rash, brazen, and impatient, was apparently belied by their treatment of machinery. The maintenance of equipment, so intrinsically linked to questions of saving and rationally cautious behavior, was perceived to be alien to the Turkish mentality. According to Robert Kerwin, an Office of Strategic Services veteran who was working on his dissertation at Istanbul University as a Middle East Institute fellow, spare parts were requested at whim, regardless of gaps in written records and related repercussions:

> The idea of waste in terms of not properly using equipment for the work for which it is designed is not as easily apparent to the Turk as the concept of waste of labor or materials. Thus, for example, a large truck is often sent to do a small truck's job with no thought of the ton-mileage costs involved. Lack of standardized practices in use of equipment hampers the keeping of records and accounts on use and depreciation. When a tire blows on a truck, a replacement is frequently "cannibalized"—taken from another vehicle rather than ordered from the equipment depot.[90]

The interchangeability of equipment indicated a disregard for its proper function and life cycle as well as a lack of comprehension when it came to questions of cost consciousness and accountability.

For all their zest and impulsiveness in planning and building roads, the Turkish engineers, Kerwin wrote, did not wish to "get their hands dirty." Once again, it was the "engineer's inexperience" that interfered with the cultivation of knowledge about proper means of maintenance.[91] During the training program in Washington, at least one Turkish trainee wished to remain in the office at the BPR and refused to go out in the field.[92] Such occurrences fueled the perception among the Americans that the Turks refused to get "dirt under their nails," given their "executive attitude" and "caste attitudes rooted in a premechanical community." The breach between engineer and laborer was found to be persistent, particularly considering the former's perception of manual labor as "degrading." As Robert Lehman wrote, "The men [Turkish engineers attached to road-survey crews] seem to think that because they are graduates of engineering schools they do not have to do the minor jobs. . . . They think the work is beneath their dignity."[93] An article in the *New York Times*, which was full of praise for the program, was equally critical of the "deadweight of engineers with good theoretical training but whose white-collar pride keeps them from getting their hands dirty and mastering the new machines."[94] By most accounts, the culprit for "managerial" attitudes was the prior training of Turkish engineers by European, especially German, standards, which viewed "mechanical work" as degrading or vulgar.[95] The engineers developed a reputation as "desk executives," but it was hoped that mechanization would gradually diminish such attitudes by interposing "between the mass of unskilled laborers and the small elite a sizeable class of trained and skilled workers."[96]

At the "Spring Garden Project" for an automotive-repair school founded in 1955 in Izmir by the International Cooperation Administration (ICA), investigators found that the mechanics initially preferred "the classroom to the shop." Gradually, however, their suspicion of applied knowledge disappeared. As two researchers wrote, "Cooperation replaced hierarchical subservience in student-teacher relations. . . . Spring Garden instructors did not merely point to the engine. They crawled under the chassis and forced their students to do the same. Clean hands, the unsoiled white coat, reliance on the *Meister*, were things of the past."[97] This was consistent with the "spirit of teamwork" prescribed by Hilts and was seemingly internalized by local engineers such as Diker's successor, Orhan Mersinli, who wrote that "we need to conceive of ourselves as a member of the group, regardless of our task, be it a driver, a worker, or an administrator. . . . We should not weaken our team by dividing it into classes of chiefs and officers [civil servants]."[98] The American vision of expertise ostensibly challenged a division of labor that kept asunder the engineer and the worker, as mechanization alleviated the manifestations of uneven, classed habitus.

Whereas the efforts to foster a cooperative spirit were derailed by seeming presumptions about dignity, degradation, and refusal to associate with machinery and manual labor, the economist Kerwin related the "caste system on construction projects" to "the behavior patterns characteristic of Turkey, and [the] elementary stage of its economic development."[99] Such evaluations were commonplace in debates about military, technical, and educational assistance projects as well as in the prospects for development across the country at this time. At a CFR meeting on the "human factors of economic development," Edwin Cohn, who in the late 1960s criticized the imperialist implications of survey research, attributed the lack of preventative measures to the Turkish disinclination for collaboration. He believed that such attitudes were rooted in a "short time horizon" that suggested an "inability to visualize the consequences of non-maintenance, a tendency to live only in the present and ignore the future," which in turn interfered with capital formation in the country.[100] Elsewhere, Cohn wrote that "the distaste on the part of the educated for manual work, for getting one's hands dirty" had "unfavorable implications for bringing education, health, and other services to rural areas, for field work and experiment, and for establishing industries outside of metropolitan areas."[101] In these accounts, personal and physical involvement with the maintenance of machinery were requisites in laboratories of economic development.

Extending his analysis to the army, Kerwin wrote that Turkish officers who initially "objected violently to assignment to the task of greasing and cleaning equipment" were transformed by the unprecedented effects of mechanization.[102] Journalist Robert Hartmann, who reported on military cooperation during the Korean War for the *Los Angeles Times*, argued that the mission served as a "school-teaching operation" and helped "break down the traditional reluctance of Turkish officers to getting their hands dirty" that was rooted in the "old 'Pasha complex' which the American mission [was] trying subtly to eliminate." The officers' haughty attitude towards manual labor was exceeded only by the ignorance of "Turkey's peasant soldiers," as an American trainer explained: "Willing as the Turks are to learn, this is not something that can be corrected overnight. It's one thing to make a tank mechanic out of an American boy who has grown up with a tractor and a combine, and another thing to make one of a Turkish boy who has grown up with a donkey and a scythe."[103]

The image of "young Turkish farm lads" who returned to their villages to disseminate methods of mechanization captured the imagination of social scientists such as Daniel Lerner, who hailed the benefits of military modernization on the brink of the 1960 coup:

They acquired new habits of dress, of cleanliness, of teamwork. In the most profound sense, they acquired a new personality. Along with the physical and social mobility

> opened to them through the military training program, they acquired also the habits of *psychic mobility*. The military corps became, in this decade, a major agency of social change precisely because it spread among this key sector of the population a new sense of identity—and new skills and concepts as well as new machines.[104]

Thus, as the tractor replaced the wooden stick plough as "the most complicated piece of machinery" the peasant-soldier ever encountered, his participation in a "modern military formation" meant that he, too, could become, "upon his return to civilian life, a qualified modern man."[105] Along with survey questionnaires, the American military mission and centers for engineer training were to equip their recipients with psychic mobility. According to Turkish scholars, too, teaching the peasantry "how to operate a tractor" entailed the acquisition not just of new skills but of "a new system of habits, standards, and values peculiar to the thinking and behavior of a modern farmer."[106] It would then be incumbent upon him to share his modernized way of thinking and comportment with others on his return to the village.

The temporal dimensions of mechanization are manifold in these accounts. Surmounting technical glitches entails an outlook that is simultaneously future-oriented and rooted in the present, since it incorporates a grasp of waste, efficiency, and expenditure. The ever-feared breakdown of machines, given their status as always *too few* and prone to unnatural decay, can indicate only a lack of comprehension of severe repercussions down the line. As machinery surface as a "powerful supplement to the time-keeper," expert power demands an understanding of linear, cumulative time that is predicated on mastery over the equipment.[107] Preventive measures are ways of predicting the future as well as protections against the predicaments of technological change. The taming of machines amounts to their being rendered intelligible; they are no longer strange portents of a future inconceivable, a future simultaneously yearned for and yet relentlessly unpredictable. Machines shift from signifying the future to enacting it, but the imagery of debris continues to ail even provisional attempts at modernity.

Apprehension about risk, danger, and malfunctioning, coupled with the comprehension of probability and vigilance, indicate an acquaintance with machinery within the contours of a regime of calculation. As Patrick Carroll-Burke puts it, the machines themselves surface as "epistemic engines, . . . generative of knowledge production" within that regime.[108] In the parameters of expertise being exported to Turkey in this period, engineers are to achieve detached mastery over this knowledge and equipment. At the same time, the necessity for intimate familiarity—indeed, a personal engagement—with the equipment shows that there was simultaneously a corporeal component to these mechanized conceptions of expertise. The imperative to "get your hands dirty" is simultaneously a call for "going out on the field." Dirt is imagined here as a leveling force that will break down barriers of class, as against the suspect and hierarchical (European) vision of expertise that otherwise prevailed.

The new vision of engineering, with its requirement for mechanical erudition, required new educational institutions. Not unlike the army that was presumed to function as a school of mechanized modernization, KGM launched a program in Iskenderun to train machine operators. Zafer Pamir, who was director of the program, noted that the initiative produced "masses conscious of the import of mechanization. Other participants started having these training programs as well."[109] Such programs were hailed as creating mechanized mindsets, accommodating both conceptual familiarity and corporeal intimacy with machinery. If a machine was to break down and ECA headquarters were to deliver a spare part for its repair, the engineer ought to kneel down and show its delicacies to a group of technicians in the making. The dissolution of prevalent attitudes of arrogance, "managerial executives," and the "Pasha complex" was thus predicated on acquiring a working knowledge of tractors, excavators, and spare parts.

An additional site that showcased the status of highway engineers as applied educators was the Middle East Technical University (METU), which was founded in 1956 on the recommendation of UN consultant Charles Abrams with an advisory committee from the University of Pennsylvania and funding from the US Agency for International Development.[110] Among the enthusiastic benefactors of this project was Vecdi Diker, who helped secure a physical site for the university and served on its advisory board along with other central figures from KGM.[111] Over the years, METU would be hailed for its role in breeding generations of "socially engaged" engineers, architects, and urban planners, who got their hands dirty in local development projects but were also fluent in sociology and economics.[112]

Physical and personal familiarity with machinery, as measures of those who operated them, paved the way for designations of the engineer as a tutor of modernization for others. In the case of the highway organization in Turkey, which increasingly prevailed as a mirror image of the American one, observers spoke of an "experiment in grassroots technical assistance" that was to become a "model in the rapidly expanding sphere of technical cooperation."[113] Even the "variety and depth of the difficulties" encountered in this experiment would illuminate "the problems likely to arise if American assistance in the economic development of Middle Eastern countries [was] undertaken."[114] Commissioner Macdonald of the BPR expressed his desire "to do everything possible for the success of the Highway program of Turkey so that it may become an example for the neighboring countries and the whole Middle East."[115]

The foremost expression of such desires was the United Nations Highway Training Center, which convened annually in Ankara between 1954 and 1958. The program, overseen by KGM and initially attended by engineers from Middle Eastern countries, consisted of joint sessions, field trips, and specialized courses.[116] The center in Ankara was a reflection of the program in DC to such an extent that the *Highway Bulletin* proudly reported the words of an Iranian participant who had previously inspected the American roads administration and marveled at the similarities he found between the two organizations. During an inaugural ceremony, Charles Weitz, resident representative of the UN Technical Assistance Board, gave a speech that confirmed the positive assessments of the aid program and the possibilities for its extension across the Middle East:

> Turkey nominally is a country which receives technical assistance, and yet in many fields Turkey is also uniquely able to provide assistance for others. In the field of Highway development Turkey has made vast strides within the past ten years, and while she still continues to work shoulder to the wheel to expand and improve her highway system in every respect, she can at the same time offer a helping hand to other countries.[117]

Despite and through the various trials, miscommunications, and frailties characterizing the highway initiative, the two organizations mirrored each other in administrative terms and in their instructional capacity as centers of expertise. A final expression of similarity was found in accounts of the reception of the Turkish and American highway engineers across the country.

Intimacy in Expertise

The 1948 report that delineated the nine-year plan for roadbuilding also detailed the onerous nature of the work that awaited the highway engineer: a monotonous life working for meager wages on construction sites and in mountainous areas deprived of "civilized living standards." By 1961, a promotional pamphlet titled "Wouldn't you like to work at the Highways?" boasted of high salaries, social security provisions, and possibilities for rapid advancement and occupational development for potential recruits. The promise of "comfort" and a "western mentality" culminated in the description of a particular item: the country's first IBM 650 electronic data processing machine (acquired by KGM), also dubbed the "Electronic Brain." The IBM section's employment of experts from a wide range of disciplines, such as economics, mathematics, and engineering, was cast in terms of "civilizational" expediency. Having completed its own mechanical revolution at a level "comparable with the United States and many nations in Europe," KGM could now situate itself as the vanguard of modernization across the country and inquire of aspiring highway workers, "Wouldn't you also like to be an outstanding commander in this outstanding army?"[118] (See figure 3.7.)

Not unlike the peasant-soldier returning from duty to his village, the highway engineer was fully equipped to impart the boons of mechanization to the rest of the nation. This newfound responsibility for edification was a result of administrative arrangements that delegated rural roadbuilding to their primary beneficiaries on the condition that KGM would provide technical and material resources. Recruiting high-school graduates from particular provinces for the mechanical course in Iskenderun was one way of addressing the pressing dearth of technical personnel in villages.[119] The Turkish engineers' attitude towards the rural roads program was one of detached paternalism, echoing Hilts's dictums about "gradual learning" and the provision of technical knowledge. As an engineer put it in the Department's official publication, "There is no doubt that our rural citizens who have suffered from the lack of roads will work with body and soul on their own roads and succeed in this great cause as long as the government provides technical and material aid. Our task is to become their guide."[120] The Department of Highways, just like the American aid agencies, was content with the extension of technical know-how in lieu of concrete measures to address inequality in rural areas.

If the highway engineer could be viewed as akin to the military modernizer, previously unaccustomed to the intricacies of mechanization but familiar enough with its urgency, the engineer's task was now to spearhead its dissemination to otherwise remote and even less mechani-

FIGURE 3.7. "The Highway Directorate is the first institution to use an Electronic Brain in Turkey." From *Karayollarında Çalışmak İstemez Misiniz?* [Wouldn't you like to work at the highways?], 1961. Courtesy of the Archives of the General Directorate of Highways, Ankara, Turkey.

cally amenable rural populations. The disputes between the experts stationed at the three agencies did not unfold in a social vacuum or in the absence of recipients whose lives their projects transformed. It was the villagers as well as the engineers whose experience of space, time, and movement would be significantly altered through the highway project. According to official accounts, that transformation was already underway, since, as Orhan Mersinli proudly proclaimed:

The grasp for the need for roads is now rooted in the character of the people. . . . As Commissioner Mr. MacDonald has suggested, road work in a nation is a question of public philosophy. That is, if a people do not feel the need for roads and do not express that need, no matter what the administrators do, the roads in that nation will not develop. . . . As long as the love of roads prevails as it does in our nation, road administration becomes more than a service to the people; it becomes something more, something like a national treasure. Those who work on highways become the guardians of this treasure.[121]

Mersinli's statement found resonance in mainstream publications, which depicted rural populations as the joyful recipients of road projects. Newspapers assiduously reported road-opening ceremonies, which were greeted by "deeply grateful" local people who shed "tears of joy," as though they were celebrating a *bayram*, or Eid.[122]

The *Highway Bulletin* saw the enthusiastic reception on the part of "citizens asking for roads" as a distinct measure of success.[123] It was not "long examinations, analyses, [and] interpretations" that would help explicate the "positive character of our road cause on our economic and social system" but the mood of celebration that followed the delivery of roads across the countryside. As the publication put it, "The completion of roads in villages and towns result[s] in a true atmosphere of *bayram*. Citizens gather in squares, playing games and slaughtering hundreds of sheep, and celebrate this happy day. In the verse of local poets, one can find open expressions of the deep gratification of the people."[124] In the official imaginary, celebrations unfolded in a semireligious atmosphere, complete with the slaughter of sheep and shedding of tears. The festive occasion was one of enraptured communal experience, carefully chronicled in local games and poetry, and further established the engineer as the provider of goods to those in need.

The highway engineer's status as the purveyor of benefits, furthermore, did not relegate him to the ranks of anonymous civil service. The immediate and intimate recognition of both the Turkish and American experts across the country was a further indicator of the success of the highway initiative. Burdick, who was otherwise frustrated with bureaucratic roadblocks, boasted, "I know that the people of Turkey, the peasants of Rize, of Gaziantep, of Diyarbakir, of Afyonkarahisar, in fact of every city and village that I have visited, want an improved highway system. We have seen whole villages lay down their work to talk to American and Turkish road engineers and beg for quick highway improvements."[125] In the words of Herbert Cummings, the director of the Near Eastern and African Division of the US Department of Commerce, the delivery of roads was not among the "numerous changes which peasants resist or accept reluctantly." The wholehearted embrace of the roads program, in turn, was contingent on an appreciation for the hardships encountered by the highway engineer:

> Some [American engineers] would live in such unfamiliar places as [Elazığ], Iskenderun, and Konya. The bridge engineers and their families would for months at a time live in trailers and associate with Turkey's real hewers of wood and drawers of water—the Turkish peasants. Few, indeed, of the Bureau of Public Roads engineers and their families were to be exposed to the rigors of Ankara's nightly cocktail-party grind and the gossip of the capital city's smug foreign colony. . . . In many of the remote villages where it is doubtful whether a single inhabitant could name any of the numerous foreign Ambassadors accredited to his government in Ankara, dozens will be able to tell you when Marsh or Burdick or Hartford or Erhart of the United States Roads Group last visited them, and, furthermore, will tell you in specific terms what the new or greatly improved road through their villages meant to them.[126]

In one respect, Cummings's account seems to corroborate the image of the hubristic developmental expert who misrepresents his work in technical, apolitical terms. At the same time, though, he seems to conceive of engineering as a superior supplement to diplomacy, imbuing the engineers with a level of familiarity that the secluded circles of Foreign Service officers in Ankara could not fathom. It seems that Dorr's worries were confirmed in the end, with the experts' physical presence rivaling ECA-labeled machinery in the contest for public recognition.

Amid the sweeping declarations regarding the benefits of transportation to a modernizing nation's socioeconomic well-being, interpersonal encounters were central to designations of expertise. Alternately designated by others and identifying themselves as informal diplomats, civil servants, mechanics, military officers, and household names, the highway engineers were foremost agents of development. They conceived of themselves as extratechnical experts, spreading mechanized methods of modernity across the nation. Their delivery of roads to remote corners of the country was to put them on a first-name basis with their recipients, indicating an often neglected component of formulations of expertise: claims to intimacy. Engineers were to abandon their "managerial desk executive attitudes" and engage in face-to-face encounters with machinery and people alike.

The highway program thus served as a developmental laboratory where debates about public works and private enterprise were scaled down to the level of roadbuilding machinery, paperwork, and time management. The negotiations between the Marshall Plan administration, the American BPR, and the Turkish Department of Highways pivoted around components of proper expertise, which included not only cost consciousness and savings but also teamwork and intimacy. The conversations about bureaucratic organization and the management of the economy carried over from experiences of the New Deal and plans for postwar European reconstruction. But they were also informed by American engineers' previous involvement with colonial administration and by the efforts of the Ottoman and Turkish governments to manage their populations' mobility, which are discussed in the next chapter.

4

"It's Not Yours If You Can't Get There"
Modern Roads, Mobile Subjects

Your roads are changing the face of your own country, not because you are cutting down mountains and filling in valleys but because you are opening paths of communications between your own peoples. Health, education, economic activity—progress—are theoretical concepts so long as people are landlocked and unable to come together and move freely.

—Charles Weitz, Speech at the Second Annual UN Highway Training Center, Ankara, 1955

From the rich Mediterranean coastal plain the route crosses the Amanus range and heads northeast to Marash, Malatya and Elazig. It then cuts straight north through the highlands where the last serious Kurdish uprising was ruthlessly liquidated in 1937, and reaches the upper valley of the Euphrates at a point twenty-five miles east of Erzincan. . . . There is no mistaking the meaning of year-round roads to the villages along the way. Relief from isolation, a chance to move their produce to better markets, access to doctors and hospitals, conditions that would make more competent teachers and officials put up with the disadvantages of country life—all these come with the new roads.

—Farnsworth Fowle, "New Turkish Road Points Up US Aid"

IN 1952, Russell Dorr delivered a triumphant speech marking his departure from Turkey. Dorr's panoramic account entreated his audience to visualize "Turkish wheat being loaded abroad foreign ships" in Istanbul and Iskenderun, "ships passing through the Bosphorus carrying coal from Zonguldak and to France and copper from Hopa to many countries," and the large-scale assistance projects he had overseen during his term.[1] For Dorr, the transformation of the country was first to be envisioned at a general, bird's-eye-view level: "It works something like the dropping of a stone in a pool. Wave after wave spreads out from the point of impact, getting even larger and moving even further." Dorr's narrative then zoomed in through a microscopic lens and summed up the effects of the "expanding economy" in the "hypothetical case of a peasant in Central Anatolia":

> For the first time a year-round highway has penetrated his region. Three years ago it would have taken him days of difficult travel to reach a city. That made the idea of selling food to the city a little remote, if not possible, for him. Therefore there was no incentive for him to raise more than his own needs and those of his immediate community. Now he can get to the city or he can send his crops there more easily. He can get money in exchange for his crops. With the money he can buy household utensils, tools, furniture—any of the things that put together add up to a higher standard of living for himself and his family. Therefore he has the incentive to grow more, to open up new fields if necessary or to try to raise the yield of his present land. Along with the incentive, he now has the means to grow more—the agricultural tools provided through the agricultural banks at low interest rates . . . raise [his] standard of living.

In Dorr's account, the nameless Central Anatolian peasant is at once a testament to the palpable success of the American aid program and an indispensable contributor to postwar European recovery. The narrative is predicated on the assumption that the peasant owns the land he tills, but more vital for the purposes of the story is his newfound capacity for incentive, investment, and mobility. All-weather roads enlarge the scope of movement not only for his crop but also for the goods he has acquired, goods that will spell a higher standard of living on his return to the village. Although the acquisition of agricultural tools and furniture is primarily intended for his family, the peasant's face is also turned outward, whereby the barriers between him and the rest of the nation are seemingly surmounted. The unprecedented sense of mobility is not only posed as a corrective to previous problems of isolation and self-interest but also occasions the emergence of a new type of farmer. Now deemed a force of democracy and no longer sequestered in the outposts of the country, the new peasant is marked by the changes in the tools he acquires and uses.

Dorr's foregrounding of the new peasant at the heart of the Marshall Plan's achievements in Turkey was consistent with the program's rural orientation, such as its delivery of agricultural machinery and collaboration with the Turkish government's agricultural extension services.

Although modernization theorists tended to valorize urbanization, with the caveat that cities should not radicalize their new inhabitants, between the 1940s and 1960s, as Nicole Sackley has shown, "the 'village' and its presumed inhabitant, the 'peasant,' became both subjects and objects of expert and state campaigns to develop and secure the 'Third World.'"[2] In addition to categories like calories, birth rates, and the willingness to adopt new agricultural techniques, which were crucial indices in assembling the notion of rural underdevelopment, infrastructural projects, such as highways, were also important sites in the construction of developmental thought.[3]

The negotiations between engineers, Economic Cooperation Association (ECA) representatives, and Turkish and American officials—the subject of the previous chapter—did not unfold within the exclusive purview of expert knowledge and practice. The highway program was intended to remake not only the minds and habits of the engineers who were trained in novel and mechanized methods but also the recipients of roads across the countryside. Highways were crucial sites in the construction and enactment of modernization theory because it was through them that the habitual comportment of experts and peasants would be transformed and national space reshaped. Roads facilitated the spatial organization and circulation of bodies, goods, and ideas and, in doing so, occasioned the production of knowledge. Because of their interest in documenting the stagnant aspects of traditional societies and the transitions between different stages of development, social scientists factored indices and images of movement into their theories of modernization.[4] It was the bus service to Balgat that transformed the lives of the Grocer and the Chief; it was via roads that social scientific questionnaires were circulated across the country. Studies like Frederick Frey's Rural Development Research Project explicitly inquired after the capacity for geographic mobility. (See figure 4.1.) Yet such visions persistently neglected how "the ease of travel [that roads] facilitate is also a structure of confinement."[5] Highways connect and bring people together, but they also keep certain segments of the population asunder, making the mobility of some conditional on the immobility of others.

Scholars, engineers, and policy makers believed that roads would grant access to otherwise remote corners of the nation and shrink the distances between its members, thereby allowing them to participate in a shared national space and economy. Highways were capable of remak-

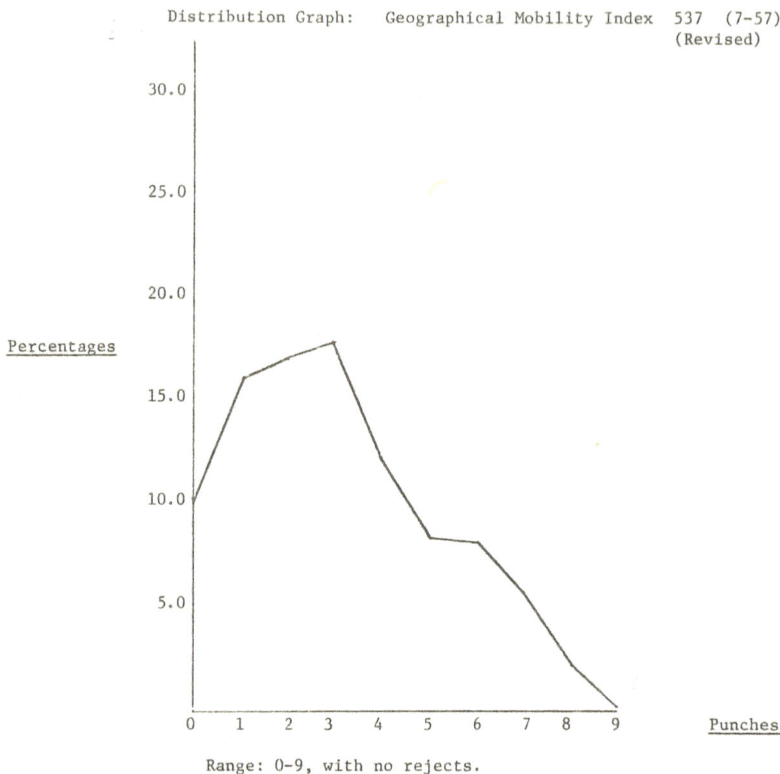

FIGURE 4.1. Geographical Mobility Index. Reprinted with the permission of the MIT Center for International Studies, from *Rural Development Research Project No. 2: Index Construction and Validation* (Cambridge, MA: CENIS, 1967).

ing the territory, demarcating *and* merging its discrete regions at the same time that they induced attitudinal changes in their beneficiaries, imbuing them with new spatial experiences and dispositions. The ability of highways to craft commercial and political ties between the people is a testament to what Brian Larkin calls the double function of technology—a technical one of "moving people faster from one place to another, and its ideological mode of address, hailing people as new sorts of subjects."[6]

Highways took on significance during the postwar liberalization of Turkey's political economy, which was initiated by the republican elite and further implemented by the Democrat Party (DP). As technologies of liberalism, roads enabled "society to come to know itself and govern itself on the basis of its own knowledge," seemingly minimizing intervention by the state.[7] They forced otherwise disparate units of governance into a single sphere of circulation, making it easier to manage the territory of the nation as well as to arrange the circulation and disposal of populations and things therein. The political economic and representational role of roads included facilitating *and* intervening in the movement of people and goods. Along with all its connotations of autonomy and freedom, mobility also produced differentiated categories of subjectivity and citizenship and highlighted the unevenness of the geography.[8]

Roads occasioned encounters between engineers and peasants, interviewers and respondents, politicians and voters, consumers and producers. But the "common language of the public road" could easily dissolve into practices of control.[9] The political and symbolic functions of roadbuilding have also included colonial projects of possession.[10] Roads have been mobilized in the exercise of classification and policing on account of their presumed civilizing utility in places like Indonesia, Ireland, and India.[11] In the Philippines, American rule meant that those in charge deployed roads as part of their military campaign against Filipino resistance and as an edifying force against "savagery" and "retarded progress" at the turn of the century.[12] Roads were the material backbone of "campaigns to eradicate epidemic diseases and improve health and hygiene, to 'modernize' Filipino agriculture, and to establish elementary schools with American-style sports programs throughout the islands."[13] William Cameron Forbes, the Boston businessman who served as governor-general of the islands from 1909 to 1913, implemented a policy of "material development," which "prioritized the construction of roads, bridges, harbors, and other infrastructure essential to opening the Philippine economy to export-oriented exploitation."[14] During the Cold War, developmental actors like David Lilienthal insisted that TVA replicas in India, Vietnam, and Iran would function as "an effective response to a world in the throes of decolonization," and yet their projects readily recycled these earlier colonial forms.[15]

Depictions of the highway initiative in Turkey were also propelled by attendant discourses about regional backwardness and modernity. The delivery of civilization was deemed to be particularly urgent for remaining outposts of the country, particularly Kurdish villages in eastern provinces that denied access and defied homogenization in physical, political, and linguistic terms. The highway project was to pick up where Kemalist nation building had left off with its railway-led offense into the dark corners of the country. Discourses of enlightenment designated the least accessible members of the nation as the primary beneficiaries of roads, and the task of folding the nation into one proceeded along both conceptual and concrete registers. Postwar developmental language and practice built on earlier discourses of civilizational deficiency and ethnic hierarchies, even as they ostensibly flattened out and homogenized the national space.

Highways were also to occasion the possibility of the emergence of new subjects who were amenable not just to regulation and measurement but also to individual mobility and leisure, which were promoted as correlates to the liberal restructuring of postwar economies.[16] Rural populations were expected to produce for an increasingly unified market at the same time that they became the consumers of commodities previously unavailable in villages and smaller towns. Unlike railroads, which privileged timetables for centralized production and regimented subjectivities, highways were believed to accommodate flexible schedules for volitional travel through a national space increasingly organized around the figure of the individual consumer. The role that roads played in the political imaginary was grafted onto a set of desires, hopes, and anxieties about the populace. In addition to enacting power relations, roads were to reshape social and sensory worlds, cultivating habits of mobile modernity for practitioners and recipients alike.

This chapter details the role that roads were assigned in the construction of a modern, civilized, democratic citizenry in postwar Turkey. At the same time, the text does not lose sight of the exclusionary, hierarchical, and disciplinary functions of roads or of their unexpected consequences. The planners aimed to produce the conditions and subjects of individual economic and political rights. In fact, their universalizing projects ended up enabling new critiques of inequality. As a laboratory for the enactment of modernization theory, the highway network was also a palimpsest on which practitioners encountered existing visions of development, nation, and statecraft. These different understandings were interweaved with a series of modernizing imaginaries—colonial, liberal, and civilizational missions marbled into one. The preexisting visions, each with its own set of temporalities and political constituencies, were shaped by histories and notions of tradition and progress, which were then worked out and repackaged into modernization theory.

Managing Mobility

The postwar highway program can be situated in a longer history in the regulation of movement by Ottoman and republican elites. During the early decades of the Ottoman Empire, mobility was alternately encouraged and restricted, depending on the need for labor, settlement, and control over newly acquired territories. By the end of the nineteenth century, demographic engineering projects involved policies such as deportation, involuntary displacement, and forced migration. Meanwhile, population exchanges following the loss of territory across the Balkans and the Caucuses and the persistence of recalcitrant nomadic groups led to sedentarization through land grants and tax exemptions.[17] As Muslim and Turkish *muhajirs* (immigrants) and nomadic Kurdish tribes were resettled across Anatolia, they were granted the expropriated possessions and agricultural lands of Armenian and Greek subjects who had been deposed or exterminated.[18] The spatial redistribution of populations coincided with the construction of railroads, for which labor was provided by the remaining immigrants who had not been settled on fertile land by the state.[19] The railway network was built both to ensure security and administration and to integrate the empire into the world economy.

During the Kemalist years of state building, railroads, which were nationalized in 1924, became symbols of the republican landscape, exemplified in the popular phrase, "Demir ağlarla ördük bu vatanı" ("We wove this country with webs of iron").[20] The 1930s were distinct for the Republican People's Party's (CHP) single-party rule and five-year developmental plans, which were often drawn up by Soviet experts, and that decade saw state-led attempts at industrialization, premised on the "extraction of agricultural surplus."[21] Railroads connected cereal-growing areas of central Anatolia to the ports of Istanbul and Izmir, but the agricultural sector was not favored in terms of government investment. During this period, planners saw roads as a "supplement" to railways, in a division of labor that accorded the latter the task of long-distance haulage.[22] The portrayal of roads as appendages to the main mode of transportation in the country was a recurrent formulation in bills that depicted them as "arteries" or "tributaries nourishing the railways."[23]

World War II saw a stagnation in agricultural prices, conscripts from the agricultural labor force, and ensuing disillusionment with the government on the part of the peasantry. After the war ended, CHP proposed the Law for Providing Land to Farmers in order to reestablish a rural electoral base. Although moderate in scope, the law contained the infamous Article 17, which sought to eliminate landlessness among the peasantry by redistributing the land of absentee landlords to the tenants and sharecroppers who worked it. The land-reform proposal was approved in June 1945 but never fully implemented; its gradual reversal would mark the beginning of a series of concessions to landowners on the part of an apprehensive CHP on the eve of the 1950 elections, which ultimately removed them from office.[24]

The law was consistent with earlier attempts at land redistribution in 1927 and 1929 (both in response to Kurdish uprisings) and initiatives such as the Village Institutes, which were founded in 1940 with the aim of modernizing the peasantry and propagating Turkish identity and Kemalist ideology across rural areas.[25] Particularly controversial in the 1945 bill was the farmer homestead (*çiftçi ocakları*) clause, which was excised shortly before it was voted on in Parliament. This particular clause aimed to create independent farmer families who would be required to cultivate the land they received for twenty-five years without being allowed to sell it or hire sharecroppers.[26] The clause on farmer homesteads is emblematic of CHP's desire to limit, or at least manage, mobility in rural areas and perhaps to create a "conservative peasant social fabric in the Turkish countryside," as Karaömerlioğlu has argued.[27] It was also the type of clause that opponents of the law, in particular, large landowners like Cavit Oral, Emin Sazak, and Adnan Menderes, would seize on during parliamentary debates.

Menderes was the most vocal and significant member of the opposition, and it was while debating land reform that a permanent rift within the CHP opened up, with Menderes, alongside Celal Bayar, Refik Koraltan, and Fuad Köprülü, splitting and founding the DP with "permission" from Ataturk's successor, President Inonu.[28] As Yahya Tezel has pointed out, Menderes's speeches during the land reform debates were the harbingers of the agricultural policies he would adopt during his term as prime minister between 1950 and 1960.[29] Menderes notoriously compared the homestead clause with Nazi Germany's Erbhof Law, which was a settlement-and-land law that restricted the mobility of farmers. Menderes argued that such laws were intended to sever the connections between urban residents and rural areas, that they were a plan to "erect insurmountable barriers between the village and the city" that would only "perpetuate the backwardness of our nation."[30] Removing the walls between urban and rural settings, as we will see, would become a central component of Menderes's liberalization policies and the subject of academic accolades for the highway network on both sides of the Atlantic. During this period, the transition to political and economic liberalism was on full display in the construction of roads, which were among the spaces that the state created "for the symbolic and spectacular performance in individual will and choice—such as voting, consumption, and mobility," with assistance from European Recovery Program funds.[31]

The allocation of Marshall Plan monies for road construction was anomalous compared with other recipients, such as Austria, France, Germany, and Italy, where counterpart funds were primarily spent on railway construction.[32] In order to secure these funds, in 1947, CHP drew up an economic development plan, which emphasized agricultural growth and foreign aid to the detriment of its previous policies of state-led industrialization.[33] When DP came to power with a similar policy agenda in 1950, the party would take the rural development plan to its logical conclusion. A basic agreement existed between the DP, the party of landowners, and the American experts who argued that highways would encourage agricultural productivity and "the marketization of agricultural products: the government [would invest] in infrastructure, and the motor car was to integrate the national market."[34]

During his decade in power, Menderes courted the rural vote through agricultural credits and price-support policies as well as programs that prioritized improvements in infrastructure and transportation for rural areas.[35] Proudly attuned to the "ideological and economic aspirations in the countryside" and, in particular, in the rich and middle strata of the peasantry, the DP often faulted its predecessor for having failed to fulfill the promise of the Kemalist maxim, "the peasant is the master of the country."[36] Since Marshall Plan tractors were sold on credit, the middle peasantry continued to be integrated into the market and to grow, along with DP's popularity.[37] Unlike the CHP, which "never allowed the nascent bourgeoisie a free hand," Menderes's party "promised to aid the birth of a similar class of capitalists in agriculture."[38] Although the Democrats adopted the rhetoric of physical and social mobility over the years, they resisted "even the most elementary laws and regulations concerning minimum wage, child labor, workers' safety and right to strike, . . . [and] larger issues such as land reform and directive economic planning."[39] Still, highway expansion was believed to facilitate participation in the market economy and the cultivation of democratic sensibilities throughout the 1950s.

The Path to Democracy

In the reports, accounts, and publications of Turkish and American experts and officials, the provision of roads, in particular to the countryside, was construed as a civilizational necessity, one that would deliver an increase in education and access to "open society."[40] Highways were framed as the "blood vessels" of the nation and the "coil spring" of economic movement, facilitating the creation of national markets and the uplift of culture.[41] Roads were the conduits for national unity and would bring commercial and agricultural development, an overall increase in life standards, and tourism flows.[42] Highway engineers themselves postulated a conception of roads as the solution to all problems ailing developing countries. As they put it, "Every nation wants to attain prosperity. It is now understood everywhere and by everyone that the fastest and surest way of delivering prosperity and accomplishment to nations is via roads."[43] Although conjured as indices of progress and modernity, roads were also framed as extending and providing passage into the past; dating from "the first caravan routes [that] linked the great population masses in Europe with those in Asia," they "broke down barriers of time and distance" and "hastened man's progress by promoting the exchange of ideas and making the movement of goods easier and cheaper."[44]

Given the simultaneity of the dissemination of the highway network and the transition to a multiparty regime, roads were easily invoked as a step in forging a democratic people, one in which the nation's "democratic will" would become the foremost "guarantee that the road cause [would] be completed." Thus, an engineer explained, it made sense for the highway project to come at the expense of railroads, which had failed to complete the task of democratization.[45] According to an editorial in a popular daily, roads ensured the spread of "civilization," which was suffused with "ideas of democracy." The editorial went on to say that "countries without roads, where cities, towns, villages are not connected, and where the people do not engage in close relations with one another, can never become forward nations, and democracy will not develop in such places either."[46] Roads were to enable the crystallization of new forms of political consciousness, dissolving obsolete allegiances and static hierarchies. The individual choice of political party would correspond to the individual choice for alternative modes of transportation.

At first sight, the alleged relationship between roads and the march of democracy mapped onto the seeming contrast between the DP populism that relied (and thrived) on rural votes and the CHP legacy of paternalistic nation building. *Forum* editor Aydın Yalçın faulted DP's populism for a tendency to "exploit village romanticism," and yet he also said at a CFR meeting that the extension of an all-weather road network was imperative for not only eliminating inequality but also "[shortening] the distance between the townsman and the villager." The process was intimately linked to democratization, he argued, and would ensure that the villager was "respected, [was] taken into account, and [had] his ideas inquired after."[47] As the two parties converged in their commitment to the highway program, the claim, popularized by the reports of the American experts, that railways lacked the "flexibility and extensiveness of highway transportation" found expression in parliamentary debates. If highways had been prioritized during the early days of the republic, many argued, the nation's "economic visage" would have been much more developed by the 1950s.[48]

One area in which the association between democracy and highways was called into question was a clause in the Law for the Department of Highways and Bridges that delegated the building and maintenance of rural roads to their recipients. The clause came under attack for leaving the great masses "to their own devices." This abandonment, according to one member of Parliament, did not go unnoticed by villagers who refrained from expressing gratitude to DP for the delivery of roads: "We all know how CHP used to build village schools. They had them built through force, pressure, and collective labor. This new method that is being used today is the same one that was responsible for the dissolution of the CHP."[49]

Despite occasional objections to the use of forced local labor, CHP and DP officials, along with American experts, recycled and agreed on a paternalistic attitude towards rural settings, whose dearth of "civilization" could be repaired with the extension of roads. Highways would transmit "culture, democracy, and technology" to villages; ignorance would leave the countryside traversing the same paths that carried teachers, medicine, and books.[50] Sociologists concurred that the extension of the "road network" was inseparable from "social and economic development" but also had to be "coupled with efforts for national education."[51] Otherwise, villagers were doomed to remain "outside of time": "Thanks to the development of transportation means, all nations benefit from new discoveries immediately, but in our villages, the years go by without a trace."[52] Since problems of backwardness, ignorance, and disease were linked in the minds of policy makers and experts, the civilizing thrust of roads was summed up in their capacity to purvey immediate benefits, such as "modern instruments and machines, which are the boons of the civilized world."[53]

This language of uplift was also adopted by the likes of Herbert Cummings, the director of the Near Eastern and African Division of the US Department of Commerce and an enthusiast of the highway program. Cummings explained that access to "better schools, better medical and hospital care, . . . better seeds and improved farm implements" via roads was bound to render the villagers grateful. He said that "to [the villager,] good roads constitute a new horizon; and his hopes for a better future, at least for his children, have been aroused."[54] Generational overturn would ensure the reproduction of an obliged, hardworking peasantry, who, in the words of a CHP minister of public works, "tell me that the province offices are late in delivering technical and material aid and . . . entreat me to mediate on their behalf so that assistance can be delivered. The truth of the matter is that we are unable to provide the necessary personnel, equipment and machinery to meet our villagers' desire to build the village roads."[55] Zeytinoğlu's praise for technical assistance was consistent with Point Four conceptions of development, which deemed rural populations unlikely to request health care, free education, or jobs instead of highway equipment or technical advice. In any case, the "village roads program" that both parties seemingly committed to during their terms in power remained incomplete; by 1960, only 11,000 kilometers out of the goal of 150,000 kilometers of rural roads had been built.[56]

Social scientists argued that the modernizing thrust of roads was crucial for providing outreach to rural populations, particularly those secluded in less developed outposts of the country. In addition to breaching the gap between urban and rural settings, highways were to "bring the isolated rural villages and provincial towns into direct contact with the national or 'great' society."[57] This entailed attunement to and an identification of the parts of the country that otherwise appeared to be "social oases," waiting to be integrated with the rest of the nation.[58] It was the "breakthrough" in transportation that would generate the "final change from one thousand Turkeys to one," Frey argued in a CCP publication.[59] Sociologist Cavit Orhan Tütengil concurred that roads would liberate these "severed cells" from the remote lives they were otherwise doomed to lead.[60] Providing access to territories that had previously been isolated, roads would now facilitate their possession, categorization, and regulation.

Measures of Colonization

A publication commemorating the twenty-fifth anniversary of the founding of the General Directorate of Highways (KGM) includes an anecdote by Tahsin Önalp, a mechanical engineer who accompanied Ralph Agnew of the Bureau of Public Roads on a trip across Van and Hakkari in eastern Turkey during the early phases of the highway initiative. During a stop at a coffeehouse, Önalp recounts, Agnew overheard a conversation and inquired as to its contents.

> I did not know how to respond, and blushing, I said: "Mr. Agnew, I could only understand what you understood." Our citizens in that neighborhood spoke every language but Turkish (Arabic, Farsi, Kurdish) and yet they did not understand Turkish. This truth made me realize what Halil Rifat Pasha, the Governor of Sivas, meant when he said "It's not yours if you can't get there," and why it was that we of the Highway Administration have chosen this meaningful maxim as our motto. Years later, when I visited Hakkari again, I saw that our highway district facilities were the most valuable work of art in that magical and beautiful corner of the nation, and hearing that Turkish was also being spoken in the streets, I was delivered from a great embarrassment.[61]

The colonial effects of the roads project are palpable in Önalp's account and are further encapsulated in the KGM motto, "It's not yours if you can't get there," which often decorated the header of *Highway Bulletin* issues. The statement is predicated on an assumption of possession: the ease of travel to otherwise inaccessible regions of the country will ensure their ownership. Yet, curiously, the negation entailed in the statement suggests a degree of recognition, perhaps resignation, of an originary state of lack that interferes with access and ownership. Önalp's concession to his personal embarrassment is also telling in this regard: his own modernity, premised on the possession of unified state territory, is revealed to be hollow. Given the prevalence of incomprehensible languages, the motto opens with a concession to that which refuses to be folded into the nation. The present tense of the formulation is a testament to the expediency of that refusal but also an indication of the engineer's certitude in the success of his task. Highways can be seen as part of the Turkish state's longstanding spatial approach to the "Kurdish issue," which has included policies of forced migration, resettlement, and territorial colonization.[62] Transportation and communication infrastructures were not merely metaphors of subjugation but had long been central components of a militarized Turkification project.[63]

The irreconcilable differences that characterized "eastern Turkey," with its foreign populations, customs, and languages, loomed large in the minds of social scientists who equipped highways with the power of social transformation. The persistence of difference was particularly urgent in contexts in which, according to a *Forum* writer, "Turkish culture, even Turkish language have not penetrated."[64] Roads were thus conceived as an investment in the creation of a new Turkey. As Tütengil put it, "The road has a remarkable role in eliminating the spirit of resignation, scant living, separatist differences, backwardness, and sectionalism."[65] It was for this reason that KGM should set an example to other "government agencies" in the country: "From the laborers to the high ranking engineers, all the members of this organization share an enthusiasm that comes from the knowledge of working with modern techniques, and they have a work ethic that conquers Anatolia again."[66]

As the engineers, too, reconciled themselves with the task of assimilating wayward portions of the country, the kinship between their task and military conquest came to characterize depictions of new projects, such as a road along the northeastern coast. As Lütfi Yeleşen wrote, "In our national struggle, we were saved from enemy servitude. In this new struggle, the great men of the highways have introduced the automobile from Rize to İspir and have gained a new victory. In this great war with mountains, we move closer to our target each day, thanks to our compressors which sound like rifles."[67] A publication of the Turkish Information Office in New York depicted the engineers "working tirelessly over their drafting tables or in the field, in high spirits despite the hardships of the rugged terrain or adverse climactic conditions," not unlike the "diligence of bulldozer operators, graders, etc., ploughing [*sic*] their way through the trails and paths which were to become the lifeline of a nation's prosperity."[68] Highway building, especially in the eastern provinces of the nation, was explicitly framed in terms of forays into foreign territory; this imagery was confirmed by American observers who readily offered up points of comparison, noting that "a road linking the eastern border provinces with the open Mediterranean ports of Mersin and Iskenderun would, for example, be of great value by either yardstick. East Turkey is, like the old American West, a pioneer region less developed than the rest of the country."[69] The analogy of the frontier, where "peopled space met empty space," was predicated on the possibility of movement, making order out of chaos and modernity out of wilderness.[70]

Although eastern Turkey was described as open territory waiting to be acquired, it still had to be rendered knowable and controllable. The planning unit at KGM carefully studied the population density and economic values of each region of the country; these studies were then dispatched to the eleven regional divisions within the Directorate.[71] The ordering of the material landscape was occasioned through a series of representational practices, such as maps that identified areas of economic interest in the country. As with Ottoman elites' efforts to survey and map Kurdish subjects at the brink of World War I, the demarcation of the country into regions entailed their classification and comparison in terms of progress.[72] The maps did not merely display the authority of the governing apparatus; they were classificatory exercises that secured that authority in the first place.[73] Conjured as efforts to conceptualize space as "abstract, homogeneous, and universal in its qualities," as David Harvey puts it, the effects of these maps amounted to a spatial and social ordering with material and palpable consequences.[74]

One such map that amounted to an exercise in cartographic ranking was a byproduct of the Rural Development Research Project of USAID and the Turkish State Planning Organization. One of Frey's reports for the Rural Development Research Project aimed to gauge the existence of "attitudinal regions" within "several Turkeys." Frey's study of the geographic regions imposed a developmental scale between them, with the Aegean and Marmara regions labeled the most modern, and Eastern regions labeled the most traditional. "Region," explained Frey, is a "concept

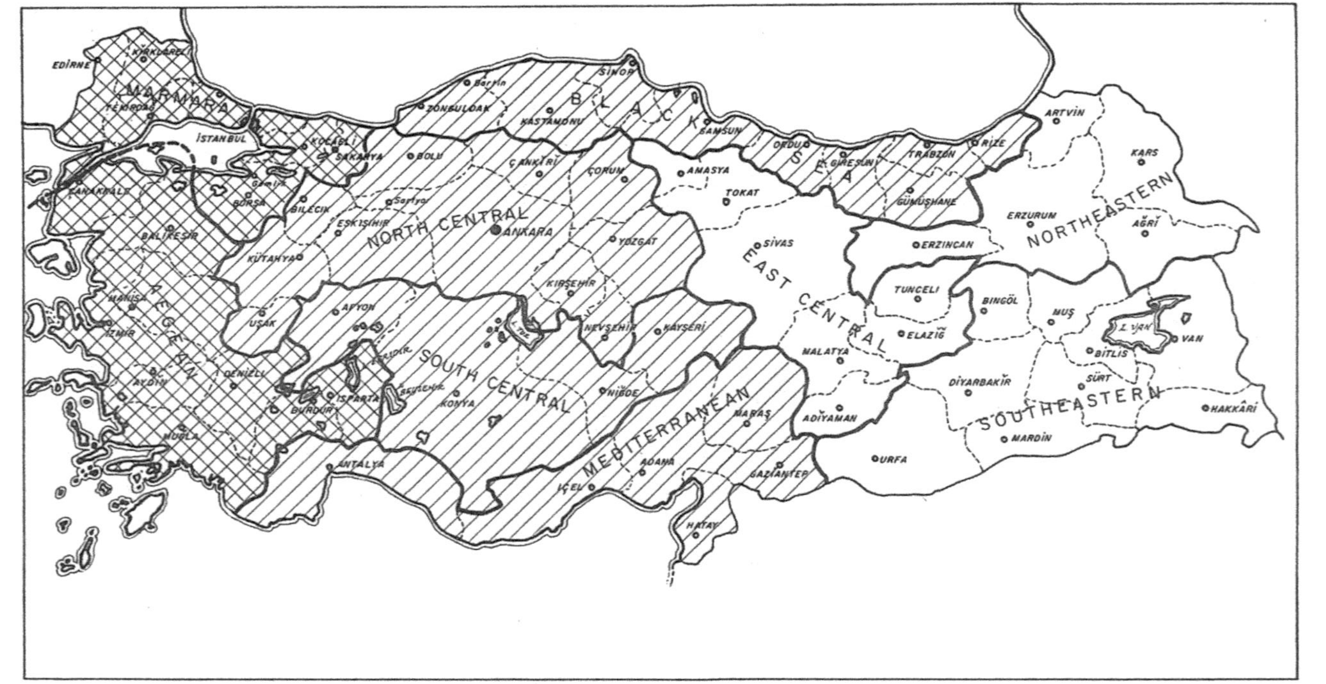

FIGURE 4.2. Mapping development by regions. Reprinted with the permission of the MIT Center for International Studies, from *Rural Development Research Project No. 2: Index Construction and Validation* (Cambridge, MA: CENIS, 1967).

that in some ways has more interest for the policy-maker than it does for the social scientist." It was for this reason that an account of regional variations, pertaining not merely to a different topography, climate, and level of economic development but also to "a different psychological atmosphere," would prove "critical for the policy maker." Of particular concern to those invested in the developmental progress of rural populations should be "the village's remoteness from the nearest regularly travelled road, the nearest kaza (prefectorial) center, [and] the nearest railway station."[75] The persistent underperformance of eastern regions by these criteria was troubling for those surveying regional development in conceptual and concrete terms. For such figures, maps and surveys served as distinct measures of modernization. (See figure 4.2.)

In another example, the General Directorate of Statistics provided data for Barbara and George Helling's Ford Foundation–funded "socio-statistical appraisal" of rural Turkey and translated their report into Turkish. The text's twenty-seven maps compared the country's regions in terms of population density, urbanness, hygiene, and agricultural factors. It was the three-fold cultural division that kept "recurring in our statistics," the Ford research scholars argued, separating the "Levant"—which included the littoral of the Aegean, the Mediterranean, and the Sea of Marmara—and where "Asia most frequently faced Europe in history" from the "Anatolian heartland" on the one hand and the "Southeast" on the other hand. The authors noted republican policy makers' efforts to overcome the first division: "The moving of the capital city from Istanbul in the Levant to Ankara on the plateau is symbolic of the forced flow of teachers, technicians, and managers into the Anatolian heartland, a flow that has been compensated by a continuing natural drift of Anatolians in the other direction." As for the more persistent "line cutting the eastern corner of the country off from the rest," it undermined the "solid linguistic uniformity of the rest of the country," given the presence of "Kurds, a Moslem people who retain an ancient tribal organization and speak a language of their own."[76] (See figure 4.3.)

Mastery over space was thus predicated on identifying and measuring the developmental gap between different parts of the country, given engineers' diagnosis of "centuries of difference" between eastern provinces and their western counterparts.[77] "The dreariest scenes" one encountered in eastern villages came at the "expense of making Ankara beautiful," an editor lamented, a favoritism that spelled not merely regional differences

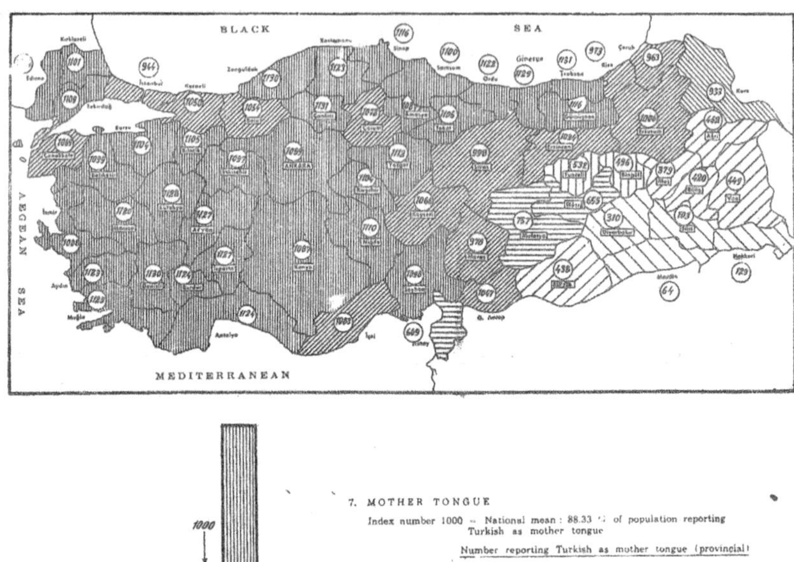

FIGURE 4.3. Mapping "mother tongue" by regions. From Barbara Helling and George Helling, *Rural Turkey: A New Socio-Statistical Approach* (Istanbul: Istanbul Üniversitesi İktisat Fakültesi, 1958).

but also the persistent segregation between rural and urban settings.[78] One way to ensure and accelerate the region's "progress" was CHP's short-lived "Eastern development project," which was approved by the cabinet on May 10, 1949, with a budget of 10 million Turkish liras allocated to the Ministries of Public Works, Education, and Health.[79] Although the three ministries prepared separate reports on the region in the period leading up to the project's implementation, priority was accorded to all-weather road networks, which received more than half of the allocated funds.[80] Tahsin Banguoğlu, the minister of education declared, "As you know, our eastern provinces are backwards in terms of civilization and economic development. A primary cause is the scarcity of means of transportation. The first condition for assessing land productivity and for establishing civilized institutions and facilities in these regions is building roads."[81]

Once again, the provision of roads would precede the delivery of hospitals and schools, which were apparently waiting in the wings to be transported off to faraway lands but simply lacked the means to get there.[82]

Although a commitment was made towards allocating 13 million liras for a second year of the eastern development project, it was abruptly terminated when DP came to power in 1950. The Democrats argued that the project perpetuated assumptions of difference between western and eastern parts of the country and had in fact been CHP's ruse to console the people of that region, "whose lives of neglect, injustice, and cruelty, [are] reminiscent of the Middle Ages."[83] CHP partisan Aydın Yalçın protested that such indictments only aided the separatism, specifically the "Kurdism" that ultimately benefited the Soviets: "There have always been uprisings in that region. Dersim is fresh in our memory. But it was CHP that took railways and the sleeping car," along with social development, peace, and order to the rest of the East.[84] Yalçın's objections are a reminder of how highways were expected to take on tasks that were once assigned to railways, among them national integration and "congruity of the national economy."[85] Throughout the 1930s, bill proposals for the extension of railways into eastern territories emphasized that it was through this mode of transportation that "the difference between eastern and western provinces [would] disappear."[86]

Yalçın argued in 1953 that the DP's suspension of regionally specific policies would exacerbate rather than erase the differences between urban and rural parts and western and eastern sections of the country:

> Naturally, sheikhs who perform miracles by handing out amulets to women and feudal lords who collect money by forcing people to drink horse urine will not be pleased with the awakening of the innocent people in their clutch; they will provoke and try to preserve the mentality and life of the Middle Ages. . . . This behavior will only increase as long as the Democrat Party people continue their blind and narrow-minded propaganda.[87]

When confronted with such criticism, Menderes demurred, saying that "as long as roads are extended, electricity and water are delivered to villages, as long as tractors and other machines enter the villager's life, these people will no longer get carried away with superstition."[88] Leaving the realm of superstition, in turn, amounted to entering the space of the nation: the DP's 1951–1954 cabinet program identified rural roads and schools, especially in eastern Turkey, as the government's "locus of action"

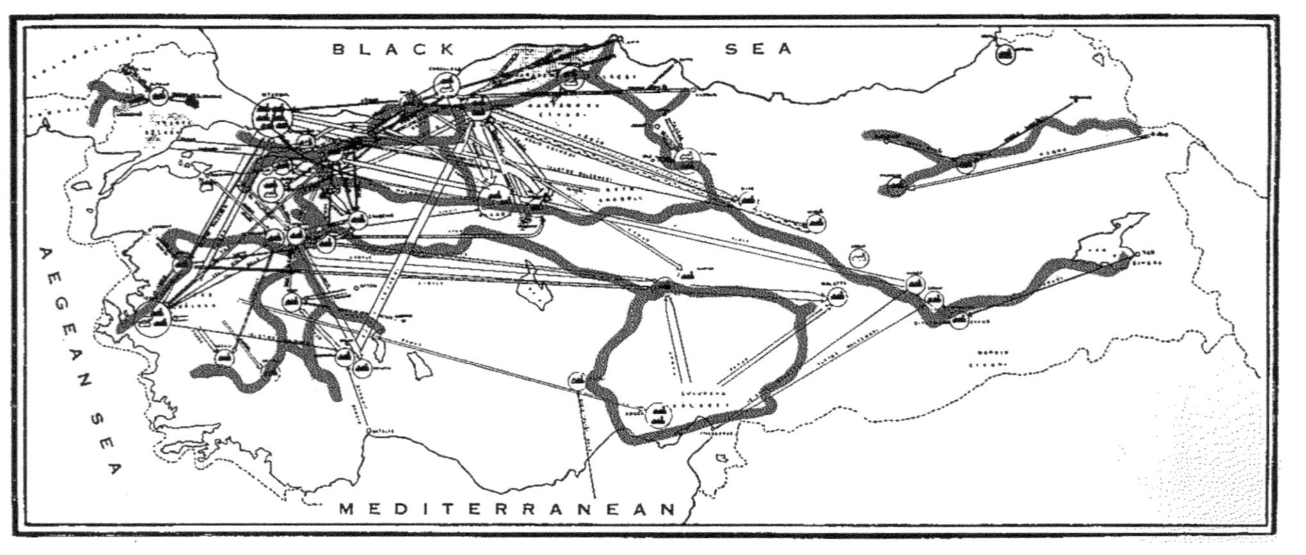

FIGURE 4.4. Uneven circulation. From *Turkish Roads and Highways* (New York: Turkish Information Office, 1950).

in order to "[mobilize] our youth around the ideal of 'Nation.'"[89] Between 1950 and 1953, the government committed to spending more than 55 million liras in three highway administrative units and in 2,451 kilometers of roads in the region.[90] In the words of one engineer, such investment was "a numerical harbinger of the social and economic development of the East. . . . The East, in a nearby future, will stop being the subject of gloom and grief, and will become a new source of respite in our hearts."[91]

Still, the extension of roads remained circumscribed in regionally differentiated terms, since priority was in fact accorded to areas of economic activity in western and central Anatolia.[92] (See figure 4.4.) Most state investments in eastern Turkey during this period were in the agriculture and energy sectors: "The role of the East in the regional division of labor in Turkey was to provide energy and agricultural products while being a market to the industry intensified in the West of Turkey."[93] As for agricultural credits and machinery, their main beneficiaries were feudal landowners who moved to Western cities, became absentee landlords, and began to engage in commercial activities that brought them closer to urban capitalists, as Ismail Beşikçi has shown.[94] Although some members of the Kurdish elite did join the DP during the 1950s, the coalition began to break towards the end of the decade, culminating in the arrest in 1959 of fifty-two Kurds, among them university students and members of Parliament.[95] The military government that came to power in the 1960 coup arrested an additional 485 prominent Kurds and detained them without trial for nine months in a concentration camp in central Turkey. A forced-settlement law came into force the next year, deporting the most influential of the detainees to western Turkey and stipulating that its mission was to "demolish the order of the Middle Ages that exist[s] in Turkey and eliminate bodies such as aghas and sheikdoms."[96] Populist democrats, republican elites, and the military all intervened, at one point or another, in the movement of what they perceived to be unruly populations.

Experts and policy makers envisioned a type of national unification that required not only the elimination but also the discursive delineation of particular "problems" or "issues"—hence the widespread circulation of phrases such as the "eastern issue" or the "rural problem," themselves acting as counterparts to and rendering necessary "causes" to rally behind, such as transportation or tourism. Allusions to the eastern issue remained markedly elliptical in nature, with occasional acknowledgment of linguistic difference substituting for the otherwise unspoken (and unspeakable) "problem" of Kurdish populations. The ineffability of the "Kurdish question" necessitated that it be cast in terms of "regional backwardness" instead of in terms of ethnic and political difference—a gesture of erasure that would characterize intellectual and public discourse throughout the following decades.[97] The seeming abstraction that characterized the delineation of such problems was leveled with the particularity and materiality of the solutions proposed to counteract them. If the problem could be framed as ignorance and superstition, experts could draw up technical solutions, such as highways and agricultural machinery, which ultimately benefited regional elites and central administrators. "It's not yours if you can't get there," the highway motto read. The "there" was a region marked by inscrutability but one that could nonetheless be folded back into the nation, given greater ease of travel and access.

It was expected, then, that villagers, especially those residing in the East, would greet their saviors with open arms and tears of joy, given the promise of modernity, democracy, and prosperity associated with roads. That promise, in turn, was contingent on the assumption of a profound lack characterizing those regions—a lack so patent and pressing that parliamentary records, newspaper editorials, and academic publications were devoted to its articulation, even in circuitous terms if necessary. Villages were accordingly depicted as the dark corners of civilization, desperately in need of reform and progress by way of their inclusion in the nation. Especially of concern were those regions in which different identities and languages persevered and were deemed to be in need of erasure. The efforts to tame, civilize, and enlighten particular segments of the population thus required a project of unification that was increasingly conceived in terms of spatial and colonial conquest. The foremost expression of that unification, as we have seen, was in the realm of the market.

A New Type of Farmer

In a 1948 report requesting American assistance, the Turkish Ministry of Public Works argued that improvement in the highway system was "a basic step in the economic development of agriculture, of productive enterprise, and of world trade."[98] Engineers celebrated highways' contribution to intraregional circulation, emphasizing their ability to transport perishable goods, minimize distribution costs, and offer wider geographical coverage over the years than trains could.[99] Securing passage in both summer and winter months guaranteed the development of an internal market, enabling farmers to move their produce at lower costs. The heightened degree of connectivity facilitated price uniformity and an unprecedented speed in the circulation of staples and commodities. The seemingly incessant circulation of trucks was the foremost expression of the new division of labor between the country's regions. Highway construction was the new "organizational form of capitalist accumulation," as Faruk Birtek has argued. It was "what railways had been to the Etatist expansion."[100]

Problems of integration in physical and linguistic terms could also be addressed by increasing networks of commercial connectivity. Given the incentive to grow crops for the rest of the country, the villager would be invested in other parts of Turkey: the crafting of a national imaginary, discussed in this chapter's previous section in terms of regional unification, also entailed investment in one's neighbors through the terms of production. The idea of villagers producing cash crops for distant markets amid this sweeping economic integration captured the imagination of social scientists and policy makers alike. Daniel Lerner wrote approvingly that "along the main highways trucks are moving fruits, vegetables, wine, and fish from producing areas, especially the Çukurova and Aegean, to Istanbul, Ankara, Izmir, and secondary cities and transporting a reverse flow of manufactured goods from Istanbul and other industrial centers for use on farms, in construction activities, in other industries, and for personal consumption."[101] The most arresting depictions detailing the emergence of the national market concerned the new farmer. In these narratives, the historically "bashful peasant" was "awakening" and "demanding service in return for his vote"; his entry into the "money economy for the first time" prompted accounts of the emergence of a "new type of farmer."[102] As Helling and Helling put it, the peasant who "has a much more direct relationship to the land" was increasingly replaced with the farmer, a "businessman whose business happens to be agriculture."[103] The new farmer's mobility marked him as not only the subject of a new political economy that could be described as agrarian capitalism but also an object of expert scrutiny and American propaganda.

In a series of articles published in the *Los Angeles Times*, Robert Hartmann, the reporter of Turkish-American military cooperation, told of an encounter with a peasant whose life was seemingly transformed by roads: "One such beneficiary is Gazi Esen, a 32-year-old farmer who works 100 acres of wheatland along the highway. Gazi owns his land and hires a couple of hands for the harvest, now in full swing all over Turkey. His house of mud-plastered adobe brick stands at the edge of the new road. . . . With the new road, he can easily transport his surplus melons to market not only in the nearest village, Ahiboz, but also to Ankara."[104] Another promotional pamphlet, published by the Turkish Information Office in New York, described the plight of Huseyin, an Anatolian schoolteacher who struggled to convey American farming techniques to his village. Before the villagers built the rural road connecting to the Marshall Plan–funded main artery, Huseyin lamented, "I raised a wonderful crop of water-melons such as nobody's ever seen in Surek before. But could I sell them, as I'd hoped? No! There was no way of getting them to the nearest market. . . . If only there was a road."[105] The pamphlet concludes with Huseyin getting his road and teaching his father, the initially "conservative and suspicious" Muhtar (presumably a kindred spirit to Lerner's Chief), how to spell: "P.R.O.G.R.E.S.S. . . . The word is 'Progress,' father, and it spells a better future for Turkey."

A decade later, modernization theorists built on these embellished accounts, arguing that the sale of surplus produce was now easier through relatively swift access to wholesale markets in nearby cities and through wholesalers' increased ability to drive their citrus fruit–loaded trucks to distant villages in spite of previously debilitating weather conditions.[106] According to such narratives, the space of production and circulation was increasingly homogenized. One measure of the country's material reconfiguration was its expression in terms of speed, savings, and efficiency, mediated through new means of transportation such as the truck and the bus.

Trains, Trucks, and Buses

In 1945, Ibrahim Yasa of Ankara University penned a monograph examining the effects of railroads on the temporal and spatial perceptions of the inhabitants of Hasanoğlan village. Before the extension of the railway system, explained Yasa, it took villagers eight to twelve hours to commute to Ankara by donkey and up to fourteen hours by oxcart in wintertime: "Today he can reach Ankara by horse-cart in three to four hours, and by train in one hour. Trucks and cars cover the same distance in three-quarters of an hour." The railway, accompanied by the proliferation of other means of communication, such as "letters, the telephone, the telegraph, the radio, newspapers and magazines," facilitated immediate contact with the outside world and led the villagers to "reevaluate their idea of time and space."[107] Fifteen years later, Cavit Orhan Tütengil conducted a similar study, identifying changing perceptions of time, measurement, and space among the population of the town of Adapazarı in western Turkey, which, in his view, was transitioning from a "closed society" to an open one. In Tütengil's text, the impetus for change was highways, which brought about a "new conception of time and space. In villages and towns which are close to highways, and in places where means of transportation are punctual, 'alaturka' time is being forgotten. The speed with which papers spread the news is an accessory to the way in which the radio is making Turkey and the world smaller. The convergence that we see in terms of 'time' between the cities and towns of Turkey within the past century is captivating."[108]

The fifteen-year period between the two studies was marked, as we have seen, by a sweeping reconfiguration of the country, which can also be expressed in quantitative terms. In 1950, highways were responsible for 32.5 percent of the haulage of goods across the country, with 63 percent of that task performed by railways. By 1970, the percentage that roads transported increased to 73.9, as opposed to the 25.8 delivered by trains.[109] The truck became a symbol in the rhetoric of modernization: as the purveyor of "material and moral values alike," it indexed the renewal of the country.[110] If the truck stood for economic unification, enabling the likes of Gazi to bring his surplus melon to the nearest city, the task of transporting people in an equally orderly manner fell to the bus. Like the truck, which displaced the train and the obsolete oxcart that preceded it, the bus became the unmistakable means for a reduction of intracity travel time and costs.[111] The relatively frequent departure time for buses as well as the more convenient routes for pickup and drop-off increasingly made them the preferred mode of transportation. At the same time, they contributed to shrinking distances across the country.[112] As trucks and buses became more visible, travel time between Ankara and Istanbul was reduced from fifteen to six hours between 1948 and 1959, that between Ankara and Iskenderun from twenty-one to nine hours.[113] (See figure 4.5.)

For the modernizers, peasants producing cash crops for distant markets signified national unity, whereas sovereignty was predicated on mastery over nature and the prospect of territorial control; remote corners

FIGURE 4.5. Intercity bus. Courtesy of the Archives of the General Directorate of Highways, Ankara, Turkey.

of the nation, otherwise impenetrable over lengthy stretches of wintry months, were now permeated with the imperative for openness and swift exposure. The contraction of the landscape was enabled by the mounting circulation of goods, people, and capital insofar as proximity itself was measured in terms of efficiency. The people of Balgat finally attained the bus service to Ankara they had been coveting. Coal uncovered in Ereğli reached its destination in Zonguldak. Newspapers of Istanbul were delivered to the denizens of Edirne.[114] Each novelty was a step towards condensing and commanding the space of the nation. Measures of space were formulated not merely in terms of travel time but also in terms of the tonnage of material atop trucks, the cost of intercity bus transportation, and the profit-generating capacities of door-to-door delivery, presumed, in turn, to exceed the abilities of railway haulage. At the level of individual perception, the compression of space was presumed to have the effect of telescoping the layout of the nation. Once unable to identify the neighboring cities within their province, residents would now be able to accommodate far-flung regions within their dreamscape. That dreamscape, in turn, was rendered amenable to leisure, travel, and amusement as well as greater familiarity with other members of the nation.

Leisurely Times

The discourse about the efficiency of the new buses soon morphed into discussions about their comfort. The *Highway Bulletin* acclaimed the comfort of newly launched bus services between Izmit and Istanbul.[115] Members of Parliament marveled at the smoothness of the ride: "There was a time when I considered myself fortunate when it took me eight hours to commute between Antalya and Burdur. There were times when the driver would curse the day he was born and sob. The last time I traveled, it took me 50 minutes, not a single jolt." Even eastern provinces benefited from the transformation, according to Feridun Fikri Düşünsel's account of his trip between Bingöl and Elazığ: "I did not feel a single jolt; if it were possible I would have been able to drink tea on the bus."[116]

The smoothness of the bus ride was no doubt permeated with connotations of access and uplift in the minds of policy makers. The convenience of travel indicated that provinces previously deemed to be frozen in the Middle Ages could now be targeted for moral and temporal reform. Consider Rudolph Mrázek's depiction of colonial roadbuilding in Indonesia: "The newness, the hardness and cleanness—it was the roads' modernity. Cleanness of the roads, in this logic, was purity of times, democracy even, we might say. . . . New roads through Java and in the whole colony, to Kartini, were to be fully made of progress, and, as long as they were made of that hard and clean stuff, nothing could stop the wheels."[117] The jolt-free ride and the attendant promise of cleanliness would deliver the peasants from filth, backwardness, and slavish deference to the authority of tradition. The lack of bumps on the trip, the reduction of agony for the driver, and the desire to consume tea on the ride were also indicative of a novel sense of pleasure associated with travel. Signs of comfort accompanied this new conception of leisure, crucial in the context of the initiative to develop a tourism industry, which is the subject of the next chapter. (See figure 4.6.)

The awakened peasantry was to cultivate a penchant for spare-time activities rather than passively await the delivery of doctors, medicine, books, or manufactured goods to their village. Throughout the 1950s and 1960s, modernization theorists produced romanticized depictions of the

FIGURE 4.6. The road between Izmit and Istanbul, 1957. Courtesy of the Archives of the General Directorate of Highways, Ankara, Turkey.

peasant traveling in his free time in order "simply to pass the time of day, . . . go to a motion picture," or "see wrestling matches," thanks to the dissemination of highways.[118] The desire to travel and "investigate new avenues for pleasure and enjoyment," they argued, would eventually lead to the building of "bars, restaurants, and tea gardens," especially in prosperous rural regions.[119] For those with "extra time and income," amusement would no longer be at the exclusive disposal of the city dweller. Mobile subjects were expected to participate in the exercise of this novel and self-chosen leisure. It was for this reason that inquiries after spare-time activities began to populate surveys targeting not only students and administrators but also rural populations, as we have seen in the work of Abadan and others. These new inquiries borne out of the postwar social scientific imaginary can also be considered in light of the perceived effects of the

Marshall Plan in Europe, where an emergent class of managers and executives came to redefine "values of efficiency, relaxation, and democratic manners," popularizing "the habit of the 'week-end,' the 'barbecue,' or Saturday supermarket shopping."[120] As Tütengil, the sociologist of highways, argued, it was the middle classes that benefited the most from their construction, thanks not only to new opportunities in construction, imports, and repair but also to the heightened possibility for horizontal and vertical mobility.[121]

In scholarly accounts of rural Turkey, leisurely conduct was equated with practices of conspicuous consumption. Social scientists carefully chronicled the items decorating the shelves of the new grocery stores in villages and small towns. Peasants, now equipped with the means to transport their excess produce, also had access to commodities previously deemed unimaginable in rural settings. A geographer studying Boğaçay recorded the array of items that arrived from the neighboring city of Antalya by way of peddlers and artisans. The list included "cotton seed, fertilizers, silkworms, bread, fuel, tools, clay, hardware, tiles, window glass, candy, dry goods, cotton cloth and so forth."[122] In Şile, outside of Istanbul, Tütengil observed new brands of cigarettes, margarine, soda, canned food, baby food, bar soaps, and toothpaste.[123] When Lerner returned to Balgat four years after the initial set of VOA interviews, he found not only the original grocery store but also a clothing shop in the "newer part of the village, just across the new road from the 'bus station.'" It displayed "dungarees, levis, coveralls" and "ready-made suits, shirts, even a rack of neckties."[124] As the tangible benefits associated with roads broadened to include luxury items, depictions of the peasantry, too, came to address their covetous and curious conduct.

The villager, otherwise deemed to be distrustful of strangers, appeared to acquire a "yearning for communication," Karpat noted, surely "a symptom, too, of a nascent confidence in life and people."[125] Even Rustow set aside his skepticism of nonpolitical measures of development and marveled at the frequency and regularity with which the peasant could visit town, bringing him into "weekly contact with the Westernized ways of the urban population." He reported that "the terminal of the overland bus lines at the cobble-stone corner has joined the bazaar, and in part replaced it, as a center for urban-rural communication."[126] Frey went further and argued that the transformative effect of highways exceeded other means of communication:

Railways, airplanes, the telegraph and telephone, the press, and even radio seem to have been trivial in their force compared to the real revolution created by the motor vehicle. The peasant appears to need tangible evidence of previously unexperienced and strange phenomena introduced to him from outside his environment—to need to see and touch—before he believes. Moreover, the ideas emanating from the newspaper that is read to him or from the radio on the coffee house wall are always very strongly filtered through a cognitive screen manufactured from his own limited experience. . . . Such selective interpretation is much less able to mitigate the impression that visiting the town or city and seeing [something] with his own eyes, feeling it with his own hands, and stumbling over it with his own feet make on him. The development of road transportation in the past decade or so has made this experience possible for untold villagers who formerly remained immured behind mud-brick walls even though only five miles from town.[127]

For behavioralists interested in the "communications revolution," roads broadened the peasant's vision by enabling the sensory experience of novelty items. Familiarization with foreign phenomena, lifestyles, and consumption habits removed the barrier of otherwise insurmountable mud-brick walls. Visual and physical interaction with neighboring towns was the true measure of mobility, which could be exercised in cognitive and affective terms as well. Unlike the train, which remained sluggish and inconvenient by comparison, or the radio, which merely served as a "one-way street," highways facilitated intimate and immediate encounters, making it possible for "villagers to get to the cities and at the same time bring city people, especially politicians and civil servants, to the villages."[128]

Familiar Places

Social scientists such as Kemal Karpat viewed the farmers' desire to visit neighboring towns and cities "whenever they have time or pretext to do so" as a further testament to the modernizing thrust of highways.[129] Roads were capable of introducing urban ways to rural populations by rendering such trips easier and more alluring than before. Given increasing familiarity with novel means of transportation, peasants could display and act on their curiosity about foreign places. The punctuality of the bus rendered it a recognizable item that could then be employed to discover other novelties. In Lerner's account,

Tosun's words of 1950 returned to us: "It could have been half an hour to Ankara if it had a road." Now it did have a road. What was more, a bus was coming down the road. As it passed, jammed full, none of the passengers waved or even so much as stuck out a tongue at us. Without these unfailing signs of villagers out on a rare chartered bus, to celebrate a great occasion of some sort, we could only make the wild guess that Balgat had acquired a regular bus service.[130]

No longer an occasion for playful or festive behavior, the sighting of the bus was depicted as an unmistakably pedestrian incident in such passages. The prevalence of travel—its frequent and punctual nature—was not limited to the circulation of agricultural produce or consumer goods. Itinerant demeanor would become another feature of the landscape, eliminating "problems" such as inertia, "a lethargic state of mind, and a stagnant life."[131] Bodies moved regularly in space, lacking even the punctuation of a hand wave or stuck-out tongue. As the bus and the tractor became familiar sights, the physical mobility they facilitated would be inscribed on rural mindsets, imbuing them with a cognitive capacity ineluctably linked to psychic movement and empathy, seeing as how "*mobility tends to be systemic*, i.e., physical, social and psychic mobility 'go together' in every village."[132]

The "mobile person" would be capable of "identification with new aspects of his environment" and of putting himself in the place of the other. Empathy itself, as the foremost signifier of modernity, entailed not only a flair for answering survey questions or displaying hospitable behavior to guests but also a desire to travel to otherwise alien settings. Anticipating the other's needs and wishes was akin to an ability to imagine the nation as compact and easy to traverse. Given the ease and speed of travel, the shrinking of physical space was subsumed within the psychic imaginary. Spatial (and interpersonal) proximity in turn was a question of scale, prevailing at the local, national, and global levels alike. In Tüengil's Adapazarı, increased opportunities for travel generated attitudinal change in domestic interactions: children learned to speak directly to their fathers without fear and husbands and wives referred to each other on a first-name basis. The removal of psychic barriers at home was inevitable in "the age of Sputnik," when the "world itself [was] shrinking" and "the stereotyped notion of the peasant as a man unaware of the world beyond his horizon" was beginning to erode.[133] Once again, the leveling of domestic hierarchies and new possibilities for travel went hand in hand, merging economic and political freedom for individuals.

Modernization theorists were invested in chronicling how the condensed landscape led to changes in the "sense of space, distance, time—

the geotemporal universal." According to Daniel Lerner, "Only in the measure that they come into contact with urban society do villagers acquire the concepts, indeed the language, of precise and standard units."[134] Accuracy in measurement would bring the peasants not just into the space but also into the time of the nation, time that encapsulated both regularity and leisure within its dimensions. Orderly bus schedules and punctual delivery times for trucks were ways of ensuring this precision. But such passages distilled earlier studies, such as Yasa's account of railway-induced transformation in Hasanoğlan or Şerif's and Berkes's surveys of rural Ankara. When Cohn and Lerner wrote of the disappearance of seasonal and cyclical conceptions of time or the replacement of the farming routine and the call to prayer with synchronized and linear understandings, they reworked existing accounts of modernization.[135] The earlier narratives had recounted the day's division into standardized units and depicted trains instigating changes in perceptions of space and measurement. In Yasa's account, "The 'step' as a measure for length, the 'height of a man or a minaret' as a measure for depth . . . [were] things of the past."[136] Distances were no longer formulated as "within a bullet's reach, 'as far as my voice can go,' 'as far as (it takes) to smoke a cigarette.'" Şerif, the psychologist, wrote that the dissemination of these new standards was also a measure of "what is familiar and what is 'strange.'"[137] Tütengil added seventeen years later that the "new vehicles do not only 'change the conception of time and space' and lead to the forgetting of the old clock, but also increase the field of movement for people. . . . Contact between people increases in intensity, public opinion is born, etiquette and experience spread in a larger field."[138] As with their shared colonial functions, railroads and highways took on similar roles in social scientific imaginaries of modernization.

According to the reports of social scientists and policy makers, the peasants' demand for roads did not merely derive from an urge to leave their villages:

> As related by Niyazi Aki, the governor of Antalya, villagers themselves come to the district seat and propose road-building projects in their respective areas, offering to pay whatever is necessary. In one village visited during the trip, peasants demanded that a small hill obstructing the view from the highway be removed, so that everyone could "see that we also live in this world."[139]

At first sight, the governor's proclamation amounts to official propaganda, echoing the public works minister's insistence on the peasant's insatiable desire for roads. Yet the account culminates in the suggestion that the longing of the villagers to see other places and to be closer to their neighbors was also motivated by a drive to be seen. The demand for visibility unhinges the certitude of the roads project that was to render eastern regions more western, rural populations more urban, and the peasantry eager participants in market practices. The request for the delivery of roads, at the expense of conquering and drastically remaking the physical landscape, was also a means to overcome the obscurity associated with mud-brick walls and hills along the highway. Roads could convey a plea for recognition, providing visual and concrete proof that "we also live in this world."

Wayward Subjects

Between 1948 and 1957, Richard Robinson, working as an area specialist for the American Universities Field Staff, dispatched a series of letters detailing rural transformation in Turkey.[140] The content of his missives ranged from the physical features of Turkish people ("all physical types from out and out Oriental complete with slanting eyes to what is generally called Nordic or North European, blonde and blue-eyed") to detailed descriptions of village houses, dietary habits, and clothing. On the subject of the rapid onset of agricultural mechanization, Robinson adopted a wary tone, writing that "I have always raised a skeptical eyebrow at the manner in which some would bring 'help' to primitive and semi-primitive peoples. It seems to me that bringing only an isolated feature of 20th century civilization—such as farm machinery—into a primitive society is lifting something from context and turning it into a dangerous weapon for destruction."[141] Robinson's hesitant stance would be repeated in increasingly skeptical accounts of the pace of modernization in Turkey throughout the following decades. American experts involved in building highways or the Hilton hotel viewed the speed with which such projects were embarked on as indicative of an impatient mindset in their Turkish counterparts. Edwin Cohn believed that the incessant demands for agricultural or roadbuilding machinery or "the desire to move directly from ox-cart to jet airplane, ignoring the intervening steps or, at best, compressing them into too short a period, exemplifies this inability to grasp the nature of growth."[142] The expansion of the road network, Robinson argued elsewhere, joined forces with the perilous tractor, resulting in uninhibited levels of urbanization.[143] If the truck and the tractor were potential weapons of destruction, rural displacement, and urban overpopulation, they could also be put to use for purposes that exceeded the original intent of their creators.

While social scientists and policy makers celebrated leisurely visits into town or the city, it was the means by which such trips were undertaken that continued to be a matter of debate. By one account, transportation between "country seats and the capital" was pregnant with ingenuity, evident in the implementation of a daily truck service: "This latter service is a matter of local entrepreneurship and usually consists of a large flat-bed truck into which all the travelers crowd for their trip to town. Trucks leave the villages early in the morning, and return from the town by four or five o'clock in the afternoon. Fares depend roughly upon the distance traveled, but no schedule of rates is enforced by the local government."[144] Freed from official regulation, villagers devised their own times and costs for travel at the same time that they reappropriated the truck (and the tractor) as vehicles for passenger transportation—a misuse that could spell more than mere mischief if engaged in excessive terms. According to Frey,

> The tremendously increased number of inter-city buses are still packed to the luggage racks, and the number of extra passengers hitching rides on trucks mounts daily. Even remote villages are within striking distance of roads along which come two or three trucks per day which will let them clamber aboard. Moreover, most of the 40,000 tractors which have been wisely or unwisely injected into the Turkish economy by American aid are used for regular excursions from villages to towns and cities—though most peasants still refrain from taking their relatives to Germany on the family tractor as one atavistically bold Turk did not long ago.[145]

No longer confined to its designated terms of use within the village boundaries, the tractor readily became a mark of unmanageable behavior. Innocuous curiosity about foreign places was undercut by innovative excess, reverting the villager back to obsolete audacity rather than advancing him into the future. The use of tractors to commute to "weddings or even movies" was also suggestive of a sinister materialism, according to sociologist Sabri Űlgener: "The satisfaction derived from the tractor is not an indirect one related to the increase in production, but a direct satisfaction connected with the form and size of the machine."[146]

Familiarity with the material dimensions of travel, furthermore, resulted in corporeal playfulness rather than in the properly measured units of movement and gesture it was expected to inculcate. As Ülgener wrote, "Instead of pulling a bell, conductors shout at the top of their voices when somebody wants to get off the bus. Drivers use their hands and arms; taxi drivers keep their left arms outside the car to be able to make any signs required by the traffic rules or not."[147] It was not just traffic rules that physical demeanor defied. Despite his accolades for the peasant deemed to be eagerly anticipating the delivery of roads, Howard Reed related that there were those who feigned ignorance about the Village Law, which required that each village "construct its own feeder road to connect it to the nearest highway or to the next village": "Many peasants questioned on this point grinned and replied that they 'hadn't read' the law, although failure to know its provisions is an offence."[148] The peasants' refusal to abide by the law and their proclivity to replace it with their own set of rules led to further ambivalence in assessments of the "far-reaching effects the highways are having." As Helling and Helling commented, "The old Turkish custom of free hospitality to the stranger cannot survive beside a busy highway, and with the developing commercialisms this and other virtues of the old way of life are passing."[149] Mobility could undercut rather than induce empathy, it seems, thus frustrating the expectations of its adherents.

By the 1960s, highways initiated a sweeping reconfiguration of Turkey, facilitating a vast urban migration that resulted in a 75 percent increase in the population of the four largest cities of Turkey, "battering the imaginary city walls that had been jealously guarded by the bureaucratic elite in previous decades and centuries."[150] Still, the anxieties of modernization theorists seemed to be confirmed by the continuing rift between the urban and the rural, which was identified as the culprit for the country's persistent underdevelopment. Kemal Karpat had cautioned in *Forum* in 1957 that "the dual social structure of the village-city will continue for a long time despite the pace and influence of industrialization."[151] In a 1970 book, Edwin Cohn lamented that "the educated Turk from the city tends to look down on the villager, whom he considers to be ignorant, lazy, and dirty, while villagers, in turn, do not concede the city man the superior status to which he thinks his education, clothing, and style of life entitle him." The urban Turks, in this narrative, did not desire to learn about their rural counterparts, "perhaps because these aspects remind them painfully of how backward much of Turkey remains."[152]

One study that was optimistic about the bundled effects of modernization was Mübeccel Kıray's survey of Ereğli, a coastal town on the Black Sea that was about to become the site of a steel and iron factory. Kıray held a PhD in anthropology from Northwestern University and had briefly worked at Voice of America upon her return to Turkey in 1950.[153] The Ereğli study was commissioned in 1962 by Cohn in his role as economic advisor to the State Planning Organization; the study inquired about the effects that changing means of communication and transportation had on the worldviews and perceptions of the town's inhabitants. The participants were asked to identify the farthest place from Ereğli in the country, and those who were able to name regions other than their own were hailed as the fortunate beneficiaries of the expanding steel industry in the adjacent city of Zonguldak, which was the destination of a recently launched bus service.[154] Evaluating the respondents' knowledge of Hakkari's location in southeastern Turkey and that of Berlin, London, Tokyo, and New York as signs of Ereğli's "openness to the outside world," the functionalist Kıray approvingly noted that the inhabitants appeared to be cognizant of their place in an exceedingly mobile and connected world.

Kıray was also hopeful about the prospects for a longitudinal survey that she planned to conduct in Ereğli after twenty years. This study was never completed, but according to one of her research assistants who recounted their preliminary trip for this follow-up study, "as the bus entered Ereğli, Kıray pointed at the villas on the hills and told us: 'Look! When you have proper industrialization, you get villas, not slums.' A few days later, a group of research assistants discovered that these villas belonged to guest workers in Germany who were from Ereğli, and that they were built on treasury land, and were legally in slum status."[155] The attempts by social scientists to capture, measure, and predict processes of industrialization and urbanization persisted along with the frailty of their efforts to label what they observed as modernization.

In perhaps the most telling example of the unexpected consequences of mobility, Kurdish migration to western cities presented an opportunity for "interaction with fellow Kurds and different social groups in an urban context, sharing and reproducing common memories about state practices in the Kurdish regions."[156] As Azat Zana Gündoğan has argued, these encounters paved the way for the eastern meetings of 1967, in which Kurdish contenders clamored for roads and factories rather than police stations and gendarmerie in rallies across major eastern cities.[157] When the participants demanded infrastructural development, they did so on their own terms and held the state accountable for regional underdevelopment, which they associated not with primordial "backwardness" but with the unequal distribution of resources and services.[158]

For the policy makers, experts, and social scientists, the modernizing function of roads ranged from raising "the level of citizens' prosperity" to the delivery of "doctors, medicine, modern tools and machinery; the various boons of the civilized world."[159] The roads that engineers built were to bring villages back into the nation, folding it into one along political, economic, and social registers. But the forward march of roads in enabling circulation and demarcation, in designating some sections of the population as filthy or backward, could be hindered by an unforeseen turn of events. The very democratic process that was seen as the hallmark of the roads project was curtailed by Menderes's increasingly authoritarian measures and a military coup in 1960. Still, resilient subjects refused the directives of a state that attempted to dictate which of its subjects could move, and when and where. Mountains, relentlessly inaccessible by highways, became the venue for the flourishing instead of the eradication of prohibited languages and identities. Cities, now flooded by rural inhabitants, would turn into sites of leftist mobilization and fascist backlash in the following decades. Such detours accompanied the delivery of highways, further rendering them seminal exercises in representation and governance alike. Modernizers' interest in enabling international mobility in turn continued in the realm of the tourism industry.

5

The Innkeepers of Peace
Hospitality and the Istanbul Hilton

A Hotel is much more than a collection of materials of steel, bricks, and furniture.

—*Welcome to the Istanbul Hilton* (employee handbook, 1955)

We hope that the opposition to Jewish subjects in Germany becomes a lesson for us. Turks are hospitable today because we have been masters in the past. But shouldn't guests either mix with the hosts or keep their visits short? Our minorities have never mixed with the hosts, they have never bothered to learn how to do this.

—Burhan Belge, "Our Minorities"

THE PROMOTIONAL CAMPAIGN for the Istanbul Hilton presented the hotel as a showcase of westernization and a challenge to Communism. An architectural magazine reported in 1953 that "modern buildings" were becoming so prevalent in Turkey's landscape that "mosques and minarets, earlier native architecture of Istanbul, will one day soon be scenic contrast" to the hotel.[1] Another publication situated the building at the clichéd crossroads of the East and the West: "To many Turks, who long discarded the fez and the veil in favor of Western ways, the new Istanbul Hilton symbolizes something else: the hope that Turkey, once called the 'sick man of Europe,' will become a healthy, wealthy and much-visited member of the international family."[2] Conrad Hilton's inaugural speech, a discussion of which opens this book, described each hotel in his international enterprise as a "little America" and a sentinel against the malicious spread of Communism: "We mean these hotels too as a challenge—not to the peoples who have so cordially welcomed us into their midst—but to the way of life preached by the Communist world. Each hotel spells out friendship between nations which is an alien word in the vocabulary of the Iron Curtain."[3] Erected as a showcase for amity and freedom, the hotels were to embody the proverbial motto of Hilton Hotels International

FIGURE 5.1. Advertisement for the Istanbul Hilton. Courtesy of the Hospitality Industry Archives, Massad Family Library Research Center, University of Houston, Conrad N. Hilton College of Hotel and Restaurant Management, Houston, Texas.

Corporation: "World Peace through International Trade and Travel."[4] (See figure 5.1.)

The Hilton enterprise can be situated at the cultural front of the Cold War, during which the American "arsenal of weapons" included art exhibitions, news services, and high-profile international conferences with musicians and artists. The CIA-funded Congress for Cultural Freedom, USIA publications, Fulbright educational exchange programs, VOA broadcasts, and Goodwill Ambassador tours with jazz artists such as Louis Armstrong and Dizzy Gillespie were all components of American cultural diplomacy and propaganda infrastructure. In addition to these government initiatives, private sector actors, such as Hilton International and

Pan American Airways (Pan Am), also participated in the commercial and cultural outreach of what Victoria de Grazia has called "market empire." As Hilton franchises multiplied across Athens, Cairo, Tel Aviv, and other cities, the hotel mogul seems to have internalized the vernacular of that empire ("efficiency, progress, service"), all the while claiming government funds and public spaces for his enterprise.[5]

The Istanbul Hilton was financed by Emekli Sandığı (Turkish Pension Fund) and the Economic Cooperation Administration (ECA) of the US government. Securing funding from the latter required outmaneuvering other suitors, such as the Park Hotel of Istanbul and the Intercontinental Hotels Corporation, then a subsidiary of Pan Am. The design of the Hilton building grew out of a fraught collaboration between Turkish architect Sedad Hakkı Eldem and Gordon Bunshaft of the American firm Skidmore, Owings and Merrill (SOM). Although its reinforced concrete and white cubic forms would be imitated across the country, the domineering iconic status of the building, inscribed with traces of the local and the global alike, was challenged at each turn. Rather than surfacing as a medium for the top-down imposition of an Americanized modernity or as the material expression of the ideological concerns of its builders, the Hilton was marked by contention from the outset.

The hotel fueled debates about foreign expertise, private enterprise, and the parameters of the people, which were carved with the ongoing history of expropriation from the country's non-Muslim minorities. For the Turkish government, the Hilton was a turning point in its efforts to establish and expand the tourism industry amid postwar disputes about public spaces and urban development. For ECA representatives, it helped deflect criticism over its neglect of tourism promotion and presented an opportunity for cultural diplomacy. It was the simultaneous expression of and blueprint for Turkish hospitality, which was seen as existing prior to the ventures of American investment and yet in need of being modified and perfected by the standards of the tourism industry from across the Atlantic. The hotel was thus an object that occasioned the possibility for the emergence of complex networks of commercial competition, complicity between the private sector and government agencies, and the entanglements of imperialism and xenophobia. Not unlike survey research and roadbuilding, it also rendered concrete the protean visions of modernization conjured by transnational and local actors.

Sociologists of science Susan Leigh Star and James Griesemer have written about boundary objects that "inhabit several intersecting social worlds . . . *and* satisfy the informal requirements of each of them." In the world of science, such objects may include publications, specimens, field notes, repositories, maps, and ideal types. They are elastic enough to accommodate local needs and thus serve to bridge the particular and the abstract and the multiple constituencies they bring to bear. International icons such as the Istanbul Hilton participate in a similar work of translation, rendering projects of development recognizable across different settings, given their dual status as "concrete and abstract, specific and general, conventionalized and customized" artifacts.[6] The Istanbul Hilton Hotel ostensibly incorporated local and global elements in its design, at once recuperating "authentic" motifs such as tiles and opulent architectural effects and signifying the aspiration to the International Style and consumerism in their American iterations. The hotel was a boundary object between visions of development, power, and hospitality, existing in multiple worlds and retaining different yet common enough identities in each.

The Istanbul Hilton was self-consciously manufactured to be hybrid in its financing, cultural elements, and design. The hotel's status as a hybrid space of travel and flows can be glimpsed through the movement of its modernist aesthetic between Turkey and the United States as well as through the commodities used in its construction and running. It was conceived as a temporary haven for tourists, but it also served as a conduit for mobility, with people, capital, and competing visions of modernity flowing through it. Although the Hilton was merely an addition to an existing landscape of hotels, which included imperial grand hotels and early Republican-era facilities like the Ankara Palas and the Istanbul Pera Palas, its architectural style and American amenities, such as soda fountains, tennis courts, and spacious lobby, were novelties that produced new ideals of leisure and consumption.[7] Overlooking the Bosphorus and highly visible (and transparent, given its crafting out of reinforced concrete and glass), the Hilton became a template for the urban landscape, disseminating an aesthetic of modernism in the International Style. Yet its hybrid forms resulted in undermining, if not altogether subverting, the very modernism it was expected to prescribe and proliferate. Although boundary objects foster translation across multiple sites, they can "also allow others to resist translation and to construct other facts."[8] The hotel's construction, too, was marked by instances of mistranslation between funders and experts, calling into question the very coherence and stability of the meanings it was expected to convey.

This chapter traces the attempts to cultivate a hospitable mindset in the context of the Hilton's implementation in Istanbul. Hospitality required openness to foreign capital and expertise. Modernizing subjects, whose capacity for empathy in business dealings and propensity to travel made them welcoming hosts, were to showcase local artifacts that were simultaneously available for global consumption. Claims to hospitality, however, were offset by disruptions in the flows and allocation of capital, the hesitations of traveling experts, and misunderstandings between the various actors involved in the hotel initiative. They were also belied by the ferocious dispossession of those deemed to be the country's internal "foreigners." An account of the tensions and failures encapsulating the biography of the Istanbul Hilton helps dislodge the seeming success and certitude of that project, also revealing the fragility of the competing visions of development and diplomacy that it was presumed to communicate.

I begin with an overview of the purported alignment of interests between the Hilton Corporation, the ECA, and the Turkish government in the context of tourism promotion in the aftermath of World War II. Thereafter, I examine episodes in the life of the building that unsettle the veracity of the claims regarding its status as a showcase of American modernism and the uncontested reception of foreign capital and expertise. These latter interludes, such as Turkish architects' protests, parliamentary debates about the desirability of American conceptions of hospitality, and rival projects in the tourism industry, are a testament to the circuitous trajectory of the Istanbul Hilton.

Dollar-Earning Tourism

The broader milieu for the Istanbul Hilton project was the breakthrough of mass international tourism throughout the 1950s and 1960s. During the early phases of this process, the Marshall Plan, launched in 1947 and put into effect the following year with the establishment of the European Recovery Program (ERP), played a crucial role in the configuration of its recipient countries as tourism destinations for American travelers. As a Travel Development Section (TDS) was created within the ECA, the Department of Commerce opened a Travel Branch, and the two organizations often collaborated in their efforts to promote tourism across Europe.[9] The endeavors of these organizations included the encouragement of transatlantic transportation through tourist-class airfares, the near-elimination of visa requirements, and the "modernization" of accommodation facilities in recipient countries through ECA-funded trips to the United States for delegations of European hotel and restaurant owners.[10] These measures were in line with Section 117(b) of the Foreign Assistance Act of 1948, which instructed the ECA to "facilitate and encourage, through private and public travel, transport, and other agencies, the promotion and development of travel by citizens of the United States to and within participating countries."[11] Accordingly, ECA grants, loans, and counterpart funds were rendered available for the restoration of transportation systems; the survey, rehabilitation, and construction of hotels and tourism facilities; and the adoption of travel promotion techniques across Europe.

The tourism promotion program also found support from Congress, with allies such as Senator William Fulbright, who reiterated the view of tourism as an asset in the reduction of the "dollar gap" and a stable "dollar earner" that would contribute to the economic reconstruction of ERP countries long after the Marshall Plan was terminated.[12] For war-stricken Europe, tourism not only guaranteed the arrival of much-needed hard currency but also proved an "easier political sell than foreign aid" in the policy circles of the United States.[13] As tourism continued to function as a crucial component of foreign policy under the Truman and Eisenhower administrations, it both helped dispel the skepticism of "fiscal conservatives fearful of conventional foreign aid" and consolidated the linkage between "tourism and US global expansion."[14] This linkage was particularly salient in light of the postwar status of the United States as a world power, wherein the promulgation of the standards and methods of American tourism were likely to conjure up images of colonial dependency across European and other tourist destinations.[15] This did not deter the proponents of tourism from underscoring its importance as a measure for "breaking down the barriers of ignorant prejudice between ourselves and our allies" and as a means of fostering international understanding and harmony.[16] In the end, American conservatives accepted it as a privatized panacea for economic problems, whereas liberals embraced it as a benevolent form of developmental assistance.[17]

The tourism question was becoming increasingly visible in the circles of Turkish policy makers and the popular press against this backdrop of ECA representatives' bid to sponsor travel to Marshall Plan beneficiary countries. Unlike in Turkey's European counterparts, in which the industry had entered stagnation following the war, tourism in Turkey was in dire need of wholesale construction.[18] The sole step taken in this direction during the early Republican era was the founding of the Türkiye Seyahhin Cemiyeti (later, Turing [*sic*] Club) in 1923 under the auspices of Mustafa Kemal. Süreyya Ergün, the chief of the Tourism Branch of the Directorate of the Press and Broadcasting, called attention to this state of neglect in the immediate aftermath of the war, articulating a vision of tourism as a *dava* (cause) of civilization and national honor. Recommending, among other things, measures of stimulus and protection and of credit provision for the creation of a national hotel industry, Ergün contended that tourism was more than a commercial enterprise and would help foster the capacity for national mobility, political and cultural unity, and the spiritual and physical well-being of the nation. Ergün's avowal of the need to cultivate a sense of "leisure time" among the "hardworking new generations" of Turkey and his insistence on the need to promote "cultural capital, tourism etiquette, and a climate of hospitality" prefigured the debates pertaining to the tourism industry throughout the following decades.[19]

In August 1949, the ECA commissioned Charles White, a tourism expert, to survey the prospects for tourism development in Turkey.[20] In his report, White proposed a series of legislative measures, such as visa exemptions, improvements to transportation, and the construction of accommodation facilities, that would help ameliorate the shortage of tourism facilities in Turkey. In particular, these measures would be enacted through the implementation of laws to encourage local private and foreign capital investment. White suggested that the ECA mission to Turkey actively set up a tourism program for the year 1950–1951, making available "5 million dollars to be used for loans in the erection of first-class hotels . . . on the basis that private capital invests a minimum of 50 percent and the loans be made on a 20 year basis with very attractive interest rates."[21]

A series of institutional arrangements followed on the heels of White's report and the proclaimed interest in extending ECA funds to Turkey's tourism initiative.[22] A Tourism Advisory Board was formed and held its first annual meeting in December 1949. Among its tasks would be to review the draft of the law for encouraging tourism development and to determine qualifications for touristic hotels.[23] In March 1951, the

Travel Association of Turkey was founded with Vedat Nedim Tör appointed as its general secretary. During the 1930s, Tör had been a prolific contributor to the Kemalist-socialist journal *Kadro* and a proponent of land reform and state-led industrialization. His organization was now in frequent contact with Russell Dorr, informing him of their efforts, such as assisting pilgrimages to Ephesus, collaborating with the interparliamentary tourist union, and opening a school for hotel management.[24] The recently established Aegean Tourism Association was another organization that requested more active involvement from "American enterprise and know-how."[25] Also in accordance with the dictates of White's report, the Directorate of the Press and Broadcasting was expanded to include tourism under its title, with Ahmet Şükrü Esmer, its director, joining representatives from other Marshall Plan recipients on a trip to New York and Washington, DC in order to discuss the possibilities for the takeoff of the tourism initiative.[26] Among the activities of the newly expanded Directorate of Press, Broadcasting and Tourism was the creation of a Commission for Tourism Education and Etiquette in 1951.

Selahattin Çoruh, a participant of that commission and the author of several textbooks on tourism education, prepared a series of reports that were published by the Turing Club in Ankara. Drawing on the earlier report by White, Çoruh framed the "tourism cause" in terms of attracting foreign capital to the country, since Americans' lack of knowledge about the country (for example, their beliefs that Turks are "dark-skinned" and that "they still have harems") led to low levels of investment.[27] He also offered examples from the American tourism industry as the standards by which the Turkish initiative was to be evaluated. He described, in detail, for instance, the interior structure of American hotels, complete with a "lobby that is as spacious as possible," a cloakroom, an easily accessible reception area, phone cabins, shops selling postcards and cigarettes, as well as barbers, florists, and dry-cleaning facilities.[28] Çoruh compared the ideal lobby of the American hotel with that of existing Turkish facilities:

> Squeaky stairs lead to the lobby of the hotel. At the corner is a tin faucet, painted an ugly green or red, erected on a darkened, filthy base made of zinc, irritating the eye. On the walls are worn-out mirrors that distort the human face. Next to the mirror are twisted, humpy little tables. When one enters the rooms, it is as though one is entering third class hospital wards. . . . The clothes of the employees are miserable. Most are round bearded baldheads, with clogs on their feet, and gawking glares in their eyes. . . . It is impossible not to be revolted, disgusted.[29]

He finds that the appearance, hygiene, and conduct of the Turkish personnel all fail by the standards of the American hospitality industry. Failure to abide by the American norms, he believed, had repercussions for both the role of tourism within the development of the national economy and the reputation of the nation. In another report, Çoruh emphasized the need to cultivate a mentality and understanding of hospitality for primary, middle, and high school students. The integration of tourism into school curricula would ensure that foreigners would no longer be met with nonchalance, diffidence, or internalized feelings of animosity. The delegation of tourism expertise to the students fit into a larger project of the cultivation of hospitality and empathy. Among the after-school activities Çoruh recommended were trips to touristic centers in the students' towns, which would ensure the provision of accurate directions to such places as well as the cultivation of principles of courtesy for strangers and the practice of commercial integrity and honesty in business interactions with them.[30]

Çoruh's emphasis on hospitable mindsets was consistent with the editorials of leading newspapers in Turkey throughout the 1950s. The foremost concern shared by these figures was the shortage of adequate accommodation facilities, despite the "good fortune" of the landscape's natural attractions.[31] The editors of these newspapers, which otherwise reflected a broad political spectrum, concurred that it was the task of the Turkish state to encourage potential investors by means as varied as tax exemptions, provision of land to hotel builders, stimulus policies, and the founding of a tourism bank.[32] Other questions of concern were the treatment of tourists, particularly of Americans who were believed to fear being deceived as a result of haggling practices or losing money due to the gap between the official and black-market dollar-exchange rates. Indeed, the idea that the tourist was often viewed as "a wretch bound to be robbed and duped" tied into the notion that the necessities of tourism were factors that would elevate the level of civil manners, professional ethics, national order, conduct, and hygiene, further positing tourism as a "public question of etiquette and civilization."[33]

Highway engineers made up an additional set of interlocutors in the tourism debate. Vecdi Diker's early reports and speeches praised "the service stations, rest stops, restaurants, tourist camps with hot water and garages, and above all, the clean and cheap hotels one can find even in the smallest town" as "indispensable facilities that complete the road network" in the United States.[34] Soon after the passing of the Law for the Encouragement of Tourism, the Directorate of Highways published a bulletin called the *Touristic Roads Program*, which promoted the extension of all-weather roads as a precondition for hotels, restaurants, and service stations.[35] Subsequent highway plans frequently cited the encouragement of domestic and transcontinental tourism as a rationale, ranked third after the goals of economic development and national security. As vacations became more popular among the middle classes in the 1950s and 1960s, KGM repaired and asphalted roads to summer resorts, beaches, vacation camps, and summerhouse complexes.[36]

The highway group also considered the diplomatic implications of travel. For instance, a pamphlet entitled *Etiquette and Counsel for Travelers to America* instructed Turkish engineers headed to the training center in Washington on issues as diverse as table manners, gender relations, small talk, and dress code. According to this document, etiquette involved avoiding mockery of Americans' ignorance and respecting their personal liberties. Seeing as how each engineer was traveling to the United States as an unofficial ambassador of his country, every mistake on his part would reflect on and denigrate not just himself but Turkishness as a whole.[37] The group's anxieties were mirrored in Washington in the age of mass travel. As Jenifer Van Vleck relates, "Beginning in the late 1940s, the State Department inserted a booklet into U.S. passports that warned, 'Tourists who assume an air of arrogance or who transcend the bounds of decency in human conduct can do more in the course of an hour to break down the elements of friendly approach between peoples than the Government can do in the course of a year in trying to stimulate friendly relations.'"[38] In the midst of these mutual apprehensions, the attempts to initiate a hitherto underdeveloped tourism industry, and ECA avowal to aid such causes came a venture that seemingly answered the prayers of all the parties involved. A brief foray into the motivating vision behind the various projects undertaken by Conrad Hilton casts light on how the Istanbul Hilton emerged as a seemingly serendipitous and auspicious endeavor in this context.

The Innkeepers of Peace

Born in San Antonio in 1887, Conrad Hilton purchased the Mobley Hotel in Cisco, Texas, in 1919. That marked his initial foray into the hotel industry. The Hilton Hotels Corporation was founded in 1946 and quickly expanded with the purchase of the Waldorf-Astoria of New York in 1949. That same year, Hilton also won the contract to operate the Caribe Hotel in San Juan, Puerto Rico.[39] The Caribe would present the formula for further ventures abroad, wherein local investors were expected to build and equip the hotel. Hilton International provided technical assistance and consultants in the planning, design, and building phases, and it also operated the hotel under a long-term agreement, keeping one third of the profits for itself while giving the rest to local owners.

In his autobiography, *Be My Guest,* and in various speeches he delivered throughout the 1950s, Conrad Hilton elucidated the manifold meanings he attributed to the expansion of the hotel industry. In one respect, the hotel business abroad was part and parcel of the romance of profit making that exemplified his endeavors at home, which commenced by "developing a real crush on each perspective hotel. . . . Romance blossomed the minute I could see through a frowsy façade to potential glamour—the inherent ability to make money. I had no interest in hitching onto any hotel without a dowry."[40] In the case of the international hotels, the quest for financial gain was coupled with the desire to display "the fruits of the free world" to the "countries most exposed to Communism."[41] Otherwise, Hilton argued, Western civilization might be at risk of extinction: "I am convinced that it is to be our business in the next half of the twentieth century to see to it that our civilization continues, that our revolution spreads over the world, that our western spark ignites and lights the world of the orient, Africa and northern Europe." [42]

Hilton's use of imperial imagery took on a particular meaning in the context of decolonization and the battle over the hearts and minds of the newly independent countries. Given his lifelong insistence on "the necessity of prayer and work" as well as on the annual prayer breakfasts he hosted, which were attended by the likes of Dwight Eisenhower and Richard Nixon, Hilton could devoutly proclaim that the battle was characterized not by "the Suez Canal, oil, trade, atomic bomb tests, even the great markets of Africa and Asia" but rather by the conflict between "spiritual movements [extending] into eternity."[43] In a speech delivered soon after the Asian-African Conference in Bandung, Hilton described a rapidly changing world order in which a "billion faceless men are standing up and demanding to be counted—[their faces] black and yellow and brown." This demand, he believed, was reminiscent of 1776.

Hilton assigned a specific role to the hotel industry in his gesture to appreciate the petition of Third World populations. The buildings were marked as "edifices of peace," bringing about the circulation of "trade and ideas and men around the world."[44] Among the ideas they disseminated was a specific conception of hospitality:

> We are all innkeepers, you and I—innkeepers of the most sturdy and hospitable inn ever erected for a human guest, the United States of America. A world-famous hostess stands at the door, her torch held high to light the way for seekers of freedom and opportunity. Our inn has sheltered the hungry and homeless, princes and potentates, and the victims of religious purges and persecutions. Each guest on arrival is given a complimentary gift—the gift of individual freedom. And the price? Guests pay as they stay—they work for their keep and are expected to become self-sustaining. They keep the inn clean. They defend it and above all, they learn to love it.[45]

The vision of geopolitics-as-hospitality is exacting in its demarcation of appropriate guest behavior, which is characterized by self-sufficiency, diligence, and gratitude. As Hilton's inns proliferated across the world, preaching the dictates of the proper relationship between guest and host, he also adopted the vernacular of Point Four developmentalism in his speeches.

Hilton called for the dispatch not only of "bulldozers instead of tanks" but also of a "stream of good men around the world, scientists, technicians, doctors, crop experts, yes even hotelmen and Rotarians."[46] Having started "its own little spearhead of the economic offensive across the world," the company could thus "assist Mr. Dulles [secretary of state] in his foreign policy. . . . President Eisenhower concisely summarized the economic and political policy of Hilton International when he said 'aid, which we wish to curtail; investment, which we wish to encourage; convertibility, which we wish to facilitate; and trade, which we wish to expand.'" [47] Indeed, the mogul took great pride in having been approached by "both the State Department and the Department of Commerce" in order to build hotels that would "stimulate trade and travel, bringing American dollars into the economies of the countries needing help" and would "create international good will."[48] Given Hilton representatives' pledge to the Travel Development Section of the ECA of their commitment to "the importance of creating dollar earners in Western European countries" and "helping bridge the dollar gap," it seemed that there was, indeed, a tailored fit between the interests of the two institutions.[49]

Conrad Hilton presented himself and his company as "inn-keepers" and "peace-makers" at the service of American foreign policy. In addition to showcasing American modernity against the dangers of Communism, the Hilton hotels were uniquely equipped to disseminate the dictates of the tourism industry. One place Hilton claimed to have uncovered the "authentic" display of hospitality was Istanbul, where local traditions had to be worked upon in order to meet the demands of modern tourism.

Milkshakes at the Old Seraglio

The agreement for the construction and leasing of the Istanbul Hilton was signed on December 15, 1950, between Hilton and the General Directorate of the Pension Fund of the Turkish Republic for a period of twenty years.[50] Subsequently, an agreement for architectural services was signed between the republic and the firm Skidmore, Owings and Merrill (SOM) and Turkish architect, Sedad Eldem.[51] The services of SOM were covered by ECA counterpart funds in the amount of $210,000.[52] The Istanbul Hilton project was announced at the Waldorf-Astoria on October 29, 1951. Standing before the model of the building, Hilton labeled it a "monument to the foresight, courage, and international cooperation of the new Turkey."[53] (See figures 5.2 and 5.3.)

Hilton, now granted the key to the city of Istanbul, an honor "never before [bestowed on] an innkeeper," found the Turkish landscape already prepared to receive the hotel enterprise.[54] The hotel had been a "sound business investment" and became the "social and diplomatic focal point for local residents and distinguished visitors" hailing from the United States and Europe as well as China, Pakistan, Thailand, Trinidad, and India. Hilton wrote in his memoirs,

> I found myself hoping that they had found time at least to drink a cup of coffee together. Drinking a cup of coffee in Turkey has a very special significance. It was explained to me the first time I was offered a demitasse of the strong local brew. 'After you drink a cup of coffee with me,' said my host, 'that commits you to friendship for thirty years.' Imagine what would happen if everyone in that hotel (from thirty-eight different countries) were to drink coffee together in the Turkish tradition![55]

Hilton's romanticized account, with a horizon that exceeds the fleeting nature of the guest-host relationship and gestures towards a commitment to long-term friendship, was likely informed by the various reports sent

FIGURE 5.2. Conrad Hilton with the model of the Istanbul Hilton. Courtesy of the Hospitality Industry Archives, Massad Family Library Research Center, University of Houston, Conrad N. Hilton College of Hotel and Restaurant Management, Houston, Texas.

FIGURE 5.3. The building under construction. Courtesy of the Hospitality Industry Archives, Massad Family Library Research Center, University of Houston, Conrad N. Hilton College of Hotel and Restaurant Management, Houston, Texas.

by John Houser following his negotiations with the ECA and the Turkish government. In these letters, Houser, the vice president and general manager of Hilton Hotels International, praised not only the assistance of the ambassador and the "ECA people" but also the enthusiasm of Turkish officials, who "like the idea since it appeals to their pride. . . . They will agree to American architects and I believe contractors as well, if we feel they are needed. This is the real crossroads of the East and West and if there isn't a war, we will be in for a great advance and development." Two years after his initial encounters in Turkey, Houser insisted that "the top people are really enthusiastic about the hotel. . . . It is one of the most popular efforts of Americans in that vital country." Houser was particularly pleased with his conversation with Fahrettin Kerim Gökay, the eugenicist mayor-governor of Istanbul, who explained to him that the Hilton was perceived not "as just a hotel" but also as an expression of Turkey's commitment to its participation in the United Nations and the Atlantic Pact to "nations from other free countries."[56] As Houser wrote to Hilton, "It's a big and serious thing to them and a responsibility. The new ambassador, [George] McGhee, is equally laudatory, [and] said to the head of press etc. that we were establishing a pattern for private enterprise he hoped would be followed by others."[57]

Turkish officials reiterated visions of the hotel as a landmark in the recently burgeoning tourism industry and a signifier of Turkey's status as a staunch ally. Prime Minister Menderes described it as a cornerstone in overturning the neglect that the tourism industry had endured through the years, while Halim Alyot, the director of Press, Broadcasting and Tourism, hailed the contract as "the first triumph of the Turkish tourism cause."[58] The hotel can also be seen as an early step in Menderes's ambitious plan for Istanbul's redevelopment, which he personally oversaw between 1956 and 1960, and which became one of his most contested legacies. During this period, an estimated five to seven thousand buildings were demolished in the city in order to make way for grand boulevards and major arteries and to clear the areas around mosques and other Ottoman era monuments so they would be visible for tourists and Istanbulites.[59] Architectural journals depicted the hotel as a catalyst for the burgeoning tourism industry in this context and a remedy for the previous lack of hosting space for diplomatic functions and international conferences. Professional events could themselves contribute to the tourism cause, as in the case of the Tenth International Road Congress, which took place in Istanbul in 1955 and was followed by "new and modern" bus convoys taking the delegates to tourist sites across the city.[60]

Other accounts of the Hilton were embellished with paeans to the building's modernity, which was reportedly "Corbusian" in character—"raised on concrete *pilotis*, faced with box-like balconies, and capped with shaped equipment housing and a domed nightclub."[61] Built of reinforced concrete (given the shortage of steel in the country), the hotel housed three hundred guest rooms, which sprawled across eight floors extending over the "lower floor which contains shops, offices, and lounges around an enclosed patio."[62] Tennis courts, a swimming pool, a roof terrace bar, a cocktail lounge, and a spacious lobby, not unlike the one Çoruh yearningly described in his reports during the initial phase of the tourism cause, were among the luxurious surroundings that would make the American tourist feel at home, as Annabel Wharton has put it, importing the "suburban United States" to "the core of urban Istanbul."[63] Other amenities that would ensure a sense of familiarity included specialty items on the menu, such as milkshakes, cheeseburgers, and soda fountains. Steam-heated and automated coffee-making machines, "revolving hors d'oeuvres trolleys, [and] mobile service tables with electric food warmers [permitted] a personalized service at all guest tables."[64] Like abstract art exhibitions, jazz concerts, and Hollywood movies, the hotel exposed its visitors to "the way of life of a nation in which . . . liberty was shown not as some abstract right but as exposure to the concrete freedom of making choices by selecting among a myriad of spectacles and artifacts."[65]

Depictions of the hotel also praised its technological convenience, such as "high velocity Hobart mixers, dishwashing machines and bake ovens."[66] Turkish architectural magazines provided detailed accounts of plumbing, climatization, and the private bathrooms in guest rooms: "Each bathroom contains a shiny, enamel built-in bathtub, a counter around the washbasin, a modern 'a la franca' toilet with a flush, and a bidet. The plumbing contains a safe mixing system that prevents getting scalded. The showers have mechanisms that help adjust the flow and pressure of the water. A third faucet added to the sink will provide ice cold drinking water."[67] In stark contrast to Çoruh's "tin faucet, painted an ugly green or red . . . irritating the eye," the Hilton bathroom's utilities were put on display precisely on account of the hotel's embodiment of hygiene and efficiency.

The Hilton experience also incorporated an international outlook: from Holland came the linen, from France the glass, and from Switzerland the silver, china, and elevators. Hailing from England were bathtubs, furniture, and kitchen equipment, with Sweden providing draperies and laundry machines.[68] But hotel publications insisted that the simultaneously global and American modernity of the hotel was mingled with local elements, "adapting many Turkish features of styling and design."[69] The foremost expression of this blend was the *Lalezar* (Tulip Room), in which Turkish coffee was served by local women wearing "traditional clothes."[70] Highly publicized were the pavilions bracketing the cocktail terrace, "cupolas with golden pinnacles," and the infamous canopy at the gate, which was dubbed the "Flying Carpet" and believed to be "inspired by the gate of the Old Seraglio."[71] (See figure 5.4.) Even the Marmara Roof Bar, which boasted a dance floor and an American-designed garden, came with a dome believed to convey distinctly Turkish characteristics. As one description put it, "Hundreds of small lights concealed from behind shimmer through the perforations, creating a fairy tale effect."[72]

FIGURE 5.4. "The Flying Carpet" and the lobby. From "Hilton's Newest Hotel," *Architectural Forum*, December 1955.

The Orientalist depictions were leveled with official accounts of the hotel's contribution to otherwise forgotten local industries, such as carpet weaving and tile making, which Conrad Hilton insisted had "largely died out" until his company sought artists out.[73]

The hotel surfaces, in these depictions, as an object of consumption that also enables the consumption of authentic and modern artifacts. In the process, it rehabilitates local or regional form, as can be evinced by the canopy at the entrance and the details of the roof garden, which are offered as markers of authenticity. By these accounts, while the Hilton exudes American modernity, its authenticity is spontaneously fabricated, or "staged," on the spot.[74] Dichotomies like the global and the local unravel in the body of the building as times are hybridized in this space of mobility: people in the hotel move in time to a supposedly authentic past that has been recovered and folded into the present, to a technological present marked by the flow of steam-heated coffee and frosted milkshakes, and to an aesthetic future populated by replicas of Corbusian modernism across the urban fabric, as we will see. The duration of the present in such a place can only be brief, momentary, fleeting, not unlike the transience circumscribing the stay of its guests. Folded into that brief instantiation are green and blue tiles decorating the building and coffee girls in "traditional" attire, alongside novelty items such as the fountain soda, burgers, and ice cubes.

The accounts of the hotel belie a tone of certitude with regard to its function and symbolism. It is the already hospitable gesture of coffee sharing that enables commitment to a friendship that is to endure for thirty years; it is local politicians and experts who have been clamoring for the International Style; and it is the desperate lack of adequate facilities that makes the Hilton investment a much-awaited grant finally bestowed on Istanbul. Unsettling the veracity of such claims is the way that each proclamation invokes its opposite, suggesting that the seemingly concentric circuits of amity and hospitality were in fact undercut by conscious efforts to cultivate each.

The remaining sections of this chapter detract from the seemingly coherent narrative arc of the Hilton enterprise. The collaboration behind the building and its reception did not signal the top-down imposition of the International Style onto the Turkish architectural scene. The tourism industry did not encounter a readily hospitable environment in Turkey from its inception, as parliamentary debates for its encouragement were undercut by conversations about foreign capital and expertise as well as by previous and contemporaneous acts of expropriation. An earlier venture to build a hotel in Istanbul, undertaken by the Intercontinental Corporation, further reveals a series of standstills and diplomatic roadblocks behind the portrait of the country as a willing ally and pliable receptacle for private investment. The following interludes and the series of events they spun thus weave a net of entanglements around the Hilton enterprise, at once disrupting the otherwise linear biography of the hotel and revealing the forebodings attendant to the travels of foreign ventures into unknown lands. Each claim about the hospitable landscape (the Turkish government's enthusiasm for foreignness, the relentless demand for American modernism, the tailored fit with ECA interest in tourism promotion) is overturned by these intermissions.

Hilton's Reception

In his memoir, Nathaniel Owings, partner at the architectural firm Skidmore, Owings and Merrill (SOM), repeated an account of the Istanbul Hilton that was consistent with depictions that romanticized the hotel's "fairy tale effects." He wrote, "Again, entirely conceived by Louis Skidmore, through his imaginative use of Marshall Plan funds for foreign building designs, like a meteor in the sky came an Arabian Nights' job. . . . Sedad Eldem is famous for having defeated Bunshaft on his own ground, maintaining the supremacy of rich, lush, romantic Turkish architecture over Bun's more classic international predilections."[75] Carol Krinsky, the author of a monograph on Gordon Bunshaft, contradicts this account and points out that it was Eldem, the Turkish architect, who "insisted on teakwood for balcony grilles, reflecting his interest in regional wooden houses," while Skidmore suggested "the domed rooms, which he considered similar to those of the madrasahs, schools adjacent to mosques."[76] According to Krinsky, the collaboration between the two architects was amicable, with them concurring about the use of characteristic features of American modernism, such as reinforced concrete, and the "Ottoman-inspired" opulent effects. A closer look at the professional trajectories of the two architects suggests overlaps between their careers and stylistic proclivities.

Sedad Eldem was trained at the Academy of Fine Arts at Istanbul University between 1924 and 1928, and then he studied in Paris and Berlin between 1929 and 1930, where he discovered the work of Frank Lloyd Wright and Le Corbusier, whom he visited occasionally. Upon his return to Turkey, he designed the iconic Taşlık Coffee House in 1947, which was meant as a "showpiece of all the essentially modern qualities of the traditional Turkish House; a demonstration of the contemporary potential of history." Eldem also collaborated throughout the 1940s with foreign professors, such as Paul Bonatz and Clemens Holzmeister, an alignment that consolidated his status within the profession.[77] Under the influence of Bonatz, Eldem began to design public edifices and government buildings, culminating in his collaboration with Emin Onat on the Istanbul Palace of Justice (1949), which signaled the turn towards the International Style in the Turkish architectural scene.

Given this change in the trajectory of Eldem's career during the 1940s and 1950s, his match with Gordon Bunshaft could be deemed a customized fit. Bunshaft traveled across Europe on a Rotch Traveling Fellowship between 1935 and 1937, where he met Walter Gropius, and returned to Paris as part of the Army Corps of Engineers between 1942 and 1945, where, like Eldem, he made the acquaintance of Le Corbusier, the vanguard of International Style.[78] His long-standing tenure with the architectural firm SOM, which was renowned for postwar office buildings, and with various American embassies and diplomatic posts across Europe also resulted in landmarks such as the Lever House in New York, the Chase Manhattan Bank headquarters, and the Lyndon B. Johnson Library and Museum in Austin, Texas.

The end product of Eldem and Bunshaft's work has been singled out as the "precursor of high-rise hotels in Turkey" and for having contributed to the belief that the International Style could be applied in Turkey.[79] That style incorporated prismatic forms, geometric elements, and extensive use of the grid system—trends for which the Istanbul Hilton was deemed the "forerunner." Hilton's reinforced concrete and white cubic forms would indeed be replicated in buildings such as the Istanbul City Hall (1953) and the Anadolu Club (1959) as well as in housing blocks in Ataköy and Levent, which were built with the extension of low-interest credit by the Emlak Kredi Bank as a means to alleviate the housing shortage in Turkey throughout the 1950s.[80] Still, Eldem's "involvement with modernism 'proper,' while designing as a regionalist, must not be interpreted as diversion or compromise."[81] Although it has been suggested that the hotel could be construed as "a training ground in Modernity for both Turkish architects," the dissemination of that style was not imposed from without.[82] As Sibel Bozdoğan has cogently demonstrated, the propagation of the International Style did not have the Turkish architects as the "passive recipients of an imported aesthetic," and there was not a singular Americanization to speak of. Instead, "mediterraneanized" forms with perforated bricks, precast concrete grills, and geometric grids were combined, as in the Hilton, with shells and curves, which were not "oriental" in outlook but rather international, further destabilizing binarized accounts of the building's visage.[83]

Furthermore, neither the commission of a foreign expert nor the proliferation of the International Style took place in the absence of resistance. The import of German and Austrian architects to design state buildings had begun as early as 1927, along with criticisms by their Turkish counterparts in the professional journal *Mimar* in 1931. Throughout the 1930s and up to the end of World War II, fascist architecture remained influential in Turkey, with local experts comparing the "commissioning of German-speaking architects in republican Ankara to the employment of Armenian and Greek minority architects by the Ottoman Court in the nineteenth century." In this context, the opposition between the local and the global, seen through the prism of hospitality, took on a xenophobic tone as the fabricated category of the "native" was described to be in need of rescue from internal and external "foreigners" alike. Even Eldem participated in this double expulsion: his student diary from a tour across Europe contained the (later crossed-out) observation that Turkish art had been "colonized" and destroyed by European products. When he returned and started working on the modern "Turkish house" style, he became invested in his own project of erasure, a project that was marked with "as much amnesia as memory," given its "absorption of all the ethnic and religious groups including Armenians, Greeks, Kurds, Jews and Alevis under one overarching nationality of 'Turkish.'"[84]

The year 1949 saw a series of further protests organized by Turkish architects and engineers across Istanbul, Izmir, and Ankara in response to the hiring of American architects for the construction of the Faculty of Medicine at Istanbul University. As Ela Kaçel relates, these public outbursts resurfaced in 1953, while the Hilton was still being built, when the Ministry of Public Works decided to import experts from Germany for construction work.[85] This was an era when the profession was becoming autonomous from the state for the first time. In the latter half of the decade, the Chamber of Architects criticized the Menderes government for working with the KGM rather than with the "appropriate expertise"—that is, architects—on Istanbul's redevelopment program.[86] An early and vocal opponent during this time was renowned architect Şevki Vanlı, who was also concerned about the delegation of Hilton's operation to an American firm prior to its building. "To hand over the management of a hotel that does not yet exist expresses an American mentality," Vanlı noted, and he inquired, "What is this rush?"[87]

Vanlı was especially critical of the style that the building spurred in Turkey's architectural scene, dubbing that trend "Hiltonculuk."[88] He argued that it was easy to identify the "legitimate children" of the Hilton, given their façades decorated with rectangular balconies and the addition of "eccentric, flamboyant touches" to the protruded corners of the entrances and terraces of various buildings. Such addenda were expected to instill the new modernist buildings with "personality," as could be discerned in the imposition of pavilions, canopies, cupolas, and domes onto the otherwise "easy façade." These "children," however, failed to see that SOM employees were "merchant-architects" at best. Vanlı understood the "local" flourishes of the hotel to be embellishments "staged" as afterthoughts to the increasingly popular International Style. The discomfort of him and other architects with the project was also mirrored in the apprehensions of the American actors who were responsible for building the hotel.

Mistranslations

At the behest of the Turkish Republic and in connection with the technical assistance program of the ECA, Gordon Bunshaft spent two months in 1951 in Turkey with Bill Brown, the housing expert and partner at SOM, soon after SOM's assignment to the design of the Istanbul Hilton.[89] Their task was to offer an overview of the housing, public building construction, and town planning problems in Turkey, with their main recommendation being the creation of a national planning agency charged with the responsibility of "coordinating all programs for the creation of physical facilities required in carrying out the national policies for economic and social development." The rapporteurs noted the "wide gap between the technical proficiency of architects and engineers and their ability to use that proficiency for the improvement of building construction." They also reported on problems within the labor force, given "social attitudes centuries old, political moves and the industrial revolution [which] have had an unfortunate effect on the development of craftsmanship in Turkey."[90]

Bunshaft's diagnoses of the shortcomings of the Turkish building industry are illuminating in light of his account of his collaboration with Eldem:

> During the design stage, [Eldem] came here for six months. We had our problems. I remember we would do designs and stick them up on the wall for us to discuss with him. I would walk around and point out things and he kept saying, "Yes, yes, yes"; I thought he was approving it. After about three months he came up to me and said, "You know, we go around looking at these things, and I make some comments and you pay no attention to me. You just proceed the way you want to go." I said to him,

"But you keep saying 'yes.'" He said, "No, in Turkey, or in that part of the world, when we say 'yes, yes,' that means, 'yes, yes, I understand what you are saying,' not that I agree." That was unfortunate for him, but I'm glad it ended up that way, or we would still be designing the building.[91]

Contrary to Owings's triumphant proclamation of a "satisfactory compromise" between the two distinct styles of the architects, Eldem's unwitting consent seems to have resulted from a foreign mode of communication that eluded him.

Bunshaft immediately follows his depiction of this muddle with his own trip to Turkey:

I went with him, when the building was designed, with a huge model to present to the Turkish people of the Pension Fund. . . . This meeting of three days drove me up a wall, because Sedad was doing all the talking in Turkish, naturally—none of them spoke English—and every once in a while I would whisper to him and say, "What's going on?" He would say [that] "it's not important that you know; it's important that they understand."[92]

The tables are turned in this mirror image of Eldem's term as an interloper at SOM, in New York. In Turkey, it is Bunshaft who surfaces as the unwanted guest, literally lost in translation and frustrated by the silence imposed on him. Stripped even of the capacity for saying yes to the project that is now being pitched to Turkish officials, the corporate architect loses his authority, which requires familiarity with local norms.

The uncomplicated narrative of the collaboration begins to disintegrate in this version that pays heed to silences, outsiders, and misunderstandings. In his memoir, Conrad Hilton praised the local work ethic and insisted on the presence of a "common interpretation of words," despite the absence of a shared language: "For instance when a Turk used the Turkish word for 'immediate' he meant, as we do, 'right now.' When their government offered us 'full cooperation' they gave us exactly that."[93] Yet this was a skillful misrepresentation of the experiences of the personnel responsible for overseeing the hotel's construction in Istanbul. The crew included his brother, Carl Hilton, who wrote Conrad of the "headaches Americans used to American ideas have in dealing in a business way with these people. Appointment hours mean nothing; agreement with you and yessing you mean nothing; there is a great gap between promise and achievement." In another letter, he described the "strange attitude" he encountered in Turkey, where people "won't advertise; the theory being that if you advertise your product is of dubious quality. You find out about them by the grapevine or various and devious means. This characteristic also marks most business transactions."[94]

In another example, Dean Carpenter, who was Hilton's brother-in-law and replaced John Houser as vice president of Hilton Hotels International, seems to have become increasingly skeptical of their endeavors abroad, particularly across the Middle East:

> I have read two 600 page books, plus much else on the Arabs, the ancient Saracanic influences and the Middle East. How little we of the west, particularly in the US, understand Islam! . . . After two years of experience and association in this area of the world, I wonder if a second look of appraisal of our own position, and [of that] in Europe, may not be in order? In many ways I am disenchanted by the frustrations I have had, and also by those had by other large companies, even those with much money of their own to invest or spend. When we first came, there was trust. Now there isn't. Then, these countries had all to gain and nothing to lose. Now I think they take a dimmer view, when it is a matter of investing their own. . . . Many times have I been asked why, if we think prospects are so good, and our know-how so productive, don't we back them up with cash? . . . I think many of these people are quite content and happy with their own know-how and in some ways, of service for instance, they can teach us a little. They like some of their standards better than they do ours, and are happy to do without some of our ideas of luxury in other things. Maybe I am in danger of becoming disillusioned—maybe the disillusionment unconsciously concerns our own personal future.[95]

The otherwise smooth hotel initiative is under scrutiny in these correspondences, which are reminiscent of highways engineers' frustrations over machine maintenance and of CFR presentations that identified "human factors," particularly conceptions of "time," as hindrances to economic development. Expectations of eager receptivity are once again derailed by the shortcomings of the host, whose understanding of time is vague and for whom, as Edwin Cohn put it, "tomorrow" means "some other time" or simply "not now."[96] No matter how much official statements and publicity efforts insisted on receptivity, differences in business conduct, conceptions of time, and language were indications of the contentious responses to the Hilton project, which also surfaced during parliamentary debates.

The Hotel's Expropriations

At the time of the hotel's opening, Ahmet Emin Yalman, the Columbia University–trained editor of the daily *Vatan*, penned an article in defense of Conrad Hilton, whose honorary citizenship in Istanbul had become a contentious matter. Yalman argued that Hilton added "ideals, art, taste, knowledge and experience" to the hotel business, yet he was insufficiently appreciated. "Our context in particular presents a difficult frontier of resistance," Yalman lamented, "given its stationary methods, static viewpoints, and habits that pay no heed to time. In order to enter the age of modern tourism, we need a foothold and vaccine like the Hilton. Of course the troubles are not over: the Hilton initiative will meet obstacles, such as backwards mentality, demagogy, stagnant thinking, and jealousy."[97]

Yalman's reference to "stationary methods" and "static viewpoints" echoes his writings in the context of debates over the foreign investment law (1951), the law for the encouragement of foreign capital (1954), and the petroleum law (1954), which implemented a fifty-fifty split of oil profits following the Aramco arrangement in Saudi Arabia. As Max Thornburg returned to the country to encourage the adoption of such legislation, Yalman, who made an appearance in Lerner's *Passing of Traditional Society* as a source and a "demokrat man," used his editorial post to endorse these laws and to gripe that the critics were "buttering Moscow's bread."[98] The Pension Fund's acquisition of the Bellevue site overlooking the Bosphorus from the Istanbul Metropolitan Municipality, its previous owner, required a law for which consideration was also rife with dispute.

Hikmet Fırat, a Republican member of Parliament from Malatya, protested that the "Bellevue location" had been "promised to the people" for the purpose of building a public park.[99] Fırat believed that although building hotels was a "lofty cause," it need not entail an assault on citizens' rights: "Have you ever slaughtered a rooster? I have. Perhaps you have as well. We trample its feet and wings when we do. . . . We do this, and it cannot flutter. But we don't hold down its throat, it screams. Nobody can interfere with its scream. But this law bans the citizen's yelling." Fırat's analogy reflected a broader concern about the transfer of public property into the hands of a private American firm. Although the speech is laudable in its defense of public space, however, said space stood next to the Taksim Promenade, which today also abuts the Gezi Park of the 2013 protests. The park was the creation of a major urban renewal project led by the French architect Henri Prost in the 1930s and was in fact built on the ruins of an Armenian cemetery that was confiscated by the state.[100] In that sense, Fırat's anti-imperial outcry obscured prior dispossessionary violence wrought by the state on its minority communities. Once again, the rejection of the "Western foreigner" in defense of the public was predicated on the previous erasure of "foreign" elements not deemed proper to the nation project.

The next year saw the Turkish Parliament discussing the Tourism Encouragement Law, which contained a special clause pertaining to the Hilton Hotel.[101] The debates over this law addressed concerns about the arrival of foreign tourism experts and the very meaning of notions of hospitality and the tourist. Hikmet Fırat was once again the prominent critical voice and pointed out that the new law would follow the precedent set by the previous one, allowing foreigners to purchase public land for the purpose of building hotels with a payment option over the course of twenty years. Feridun Fikri Düşünsel joined Fırat in labeling the law thoroughly "anti-democratic," despite proponents referring to the Hilton as an example of a venue that would provide as many as five hundred Turkish workers with new opportunities.[102]

The question of hotel personnel took on a particularly contentious nature since the law also included a clause that would allow foreigners to work at tourism facilities for three years, provided they remained under 15 percent of the entire workforce at those facilities. This particular clause occasioned discussions about the very definition of experts, given concerns raised by some that the law would pave the way for hospitals and other public institutions to employ them. But lengthy debates limited the definition of "expertise" to waiters, maîtres d'hôtel, bartenders, porters, cooks, and jazz musicians.[103] Hidayet Aydıner objected that the law was increasingly reminiscent of capitulations, but others retorted that this would not be the first time that foreign experts were summoned during the Republican era. They cited Ataturk's invitation of German architects, engineers, and professors, such as Alexander Rüstow, during the reconstruction of Istanbul University.

The much-celebrated invitation of German and Austrian experts, some of whom were Jewish, conceals the darker history of the war years, which saw the establishment of Varlik Vergisi, a capital tax targeting non-Muslims between November 1942 and March 1944, and the dismissal of

Jewish workers from the hospitality industry and railway construction.[104] Furthermore, just three months after the opening of the Hilton hotel, the ruthless campaign against non-Muslim minorities entered yet another phase with the anti-Greek pogroms of 1955. On September 6, the state radio and various newspapers reported that Greek nationalists had bombed Ataturk's house in Thessaloniki. Over the next two days, thousands of properties, homes, shops, and schools belonging to Greek and other non-Muslim inhabitants in Istanbul and Izmir were looted and burned down, while churches and graveyards were desecrated and many injured. Members of the "Cyprus Is Turkish Association (CTA)," whose local branches included DP members, were arrested, along with "Red provocateurs," who were singled out by the government as the real culprits. It was "hostile elements" within who were to blame, but certain foreigners, those who seemingly did not overstay their status as temporary guests, were immune to the violence. The American consulate was untouched, and while the police reportedly stood by during the major phase of the destruction, a troop of cavalry was posted on the Hilton lawn the next day. Yalman, the defendant of foreign investment and the "tourism cause," had been a prominent member of the CTA and acted as an instigator with his patriotic editorials about the "Cyprus cause" in the months leading up to the events. His foremost concern about the pogrom was that it would put US-Turkish relations at an impasse and turn the "Free World against us." Luckily for him, American authorities publicly praised the reparation attempts (which remained minimal) and, in private, questioned the Menderes government's efforts to pin the atrocities on Communists (since they were not believed to have a significant presence in the country at that time). American diplomats quickly reverted to the language of security and worried thereafter about prospects for the Balkan Pact and NATO, of which Turkey and Greece were both members.[105]

In the buildup to the violent destruction of Greek and other minorities' properties and right to exist in public spaces, leading intellectuals and politicians were looking for ways to entice foreign capital and tourists to the country. While some members of Parliament, such as Senihi Yürüten, objected to the importation of jazz-musician experts ("Let those foreigners come and see our customs . . . why this need to Europeanize our mentality?"), Burhanettin Onat defended the "refined" preferences of the tourist by saying that "a tourist is a person who indulges his own tastes, his own needs. We are obliged to bring musicians who can play music that he is accustomed to, just as we are obliged to bring in cooks who can cook the food he is accustomed to. The Christian tourist who goes to Ephesus to see Mary's tomb does not read the Bible all day long; he completes his pilgrimage during the day, and goes to a bar to dance at night."[106] Namık Gedik concurred that although the tourist's day might be taken up by visits to historical sites, he preferred going back to establishments like the Hilton at the end of a demanding day of sightseeing, establishments that would provide the comfort and ease he was accustomed to. The staged meeting of the local and the global resurfaced in this official imagining of the daily schedule and movement of the tourist. The conversations once again evoked the principles of empathy and mobility as the hallmarks of a modernized hospitality industry; at the same time, the extension of those principles remained circumscribed to Muslim, "Turkish" elements of the country and their transient guests.

Cemal Kıpçak's attempt to relate the debate to broader understandings of hospitality dovetailed with the prioritization of the tourist's preferences over the interests of workers and non-Muslim communities:

> Are we going to entice tourists? First we need to adapt our mentality to the formula required by tourism. . . . What if the law pertained not to the building of hotels but to the incitement of our hospitality? For instance, if a tourist was coming to visit us at home, we would first ask someone who knows what kind of food he wants, what time he goes to bed and wakes up. We would sacrifice our customs to prove our hospitality to this man and create the system he is accustomed to. When we go to the countryside, the villager brings us forks, knives, plates as a treat since he knows that is our need. We have to do the same. Otherwise, this law would not be the tourism law but the law of protecting the Turkish worker. The thesis we are defending here is the encouragement of the tourism industry.[107]

Kıpçak's intervention is reminiscent of the earlier studies prepared by the likes of Çoruh and Ergün. The cultivation of a hospitable mindset is an arduous task that requires insight into the tourist's standards of living and comfort as well as into his artistic and culinary predilections. Those norms, furthermore, are as foreign to the Parliament members in Ankara as the customs of the Anatolian villager, who will apparently resort to cutlery only in the presence of esteemed guests from the capital. Concerns about public space and labor rights are to be jettisoned in this formulation of tourism as an enterprise that is first and foremost about empathy for the needs of specific others.

In another example, from 1964, the State Planning Organization commissioned Mübeccel Kıray, the surveyor of industrializing Ereğli, to study the feasibility of a tourism industry in seven towns on the Aegean coast. The survey measured levels of outer-orientation and tolerance as well as breakfast and personal hygiene habits. Kıray found low levels of xenophobia among the inhabitants, who were recently settled from the Balkans and the Caucuses, but she was displeased with their habit of eating olives for breakfast and the frequency with which they bathed their children and did their laundry.[108] In this assessment, the efforts to cultivate hospitality pivoted around questions of hygiene and civilization, which have also been defining features of colonial encounters.[109]

It was accommodation facilities such as the Hilton that would take on the task of familiarizing the nation with the tastes and needs of the tourist in postwar developmental efforts. As members of Parliament grappled with the meaning and desirability of foreigners, expertise, and the quotidian pastimes of tourists, their debates revolved around the shortcomings of waiters who remained uncertain of the etiquette for serving wine or villagers who lacked proper table manners and hygiene habits. These debates in fact concealed the darker underside of the republic's history of intolerance for lifestyles it deemed to be foreign. Such erasures of national history were also mirrored on the American side.

The Spearpoint of Imperialism

On June 22, 1950, Henry Mitchell relayed a letter to Russell Dorr suggesting that he catalogue the enclosed memorandum in the mission's "Moore file." The author of the original memorandum, entitled "Obtaining Private Investment Capital from the United States for Turkey for Hotel Building and Tourism" and addressed "apparently" to a "Minister of the Turkish government," was Dan Tyler Moore Jr., representative of the Intercontinental Hotels Corporation.[110] In his letter, Moore inquired about whether "investment of American capital in Turkey [would] be a good thing for Turkey," only to arrive at an answer in the affirmative. A disjointed account of the purported affinity between Turkey and the United States, Moore's missive included lessons from the history of both countries, citing the former's negative experiences with England, France, and Germany in the era of capitulations and the latter's long-standing and "violently anti-imperialistic" proclivities, traced through encounters in Cuba, Canada, Mexico, and the Philippines. In this revisionist history of empire, Moore insisted that "the U.S. business man has never been the spearpoint of imperialism nor will he ever be," but he "must be assured that a fundamental change has occurred in the attitude of the Turkish people, and their newly elected government, to foreign capital, and that it is now realized that foreign contractors can be enormously helpful to Turkey in her task of converting her economy into a modern capitalist one based somewhat on the U.S. model."

Moore had expressed his concern for the prospects of American business interests abroad in an earlier letter dispatched to George Wadsworth, the American ambassador to Turkey. In that letter, he cited the misfortunes of other companies, such as the J. G. White Corporation, the Socony Vacuum Corporation, the Coca-Cola Corporation, and the Middle East Company. Moore picked up the theme of Turkish temporal deficiency and chidingly inquired, "What is the reason for this almost complete failure of the American capitalist system to achieve anything in Turkey? One American businessman oversimplified the problem the other day by saying that American business in Turkey is dying from 'yarinitus' ('yarin' means tomorrow)."[111] According to him, the State Department and the ECA had been "lamentably negligent" to the extent of "seriously [injuring] the oil companies and the Pan American Airways System [which] certainly represent two of the most significant American capitalist developments abroad."[112] The piecemeal awkwardness of Moore's missives and the failure of the Intercontinental initiative in Istanbul between 1948 and 1950 serve as a coda to Hilton's seeming success story during the same period.

Dan Tyler Moore Jr. arrived in Istanbul as a representative of the Intercontinental Hotel Corporation in 1948, but that was not his first time in the Middle East.[113] During World War II, he served in the Office of Strategic Services and as deputy to James Landis, head of the American Economic Mission to the Middle East in Cairo. It was after his term as a stockholder in the Middle East Company of Cleveland, Ohio, which he cofounded with Landis, that Moore's tenure as a representative for the Intercontinental Hotels Corporation started. Although initial contacts with Republican Prime Minister Nihat Erim seemed in favor of a hotel project in Istanbul, Moore believed that his efforts were sidelined by the arrival of Charles White, the ECA tourism expert whose 1949 report was crucial for jump-starting the industry. When irate correspondence with Dorr and Wadsworth, the ambassador, proved futile, Moore turned to various US Congressmen to alert them to the fact that "Marshall Plan money, although designed for emergency use only, is being used to stifle the normal flow of American private and Export-Import Bank capital to nations abroad."[114]

Even if it was Moore's personal connections that secured these critical outbursts, his reprobation of the ECA resonated in certain circles of the American government and press, bringing the organization under public scrutiny.[115] Congressmen Claude Pepper and Mike Mansfield wrote ECA officials, such as Director Paul Hoffman, and inquired about the use of counterpart funds for tourism promotion, taking a special interest in Turkey. Dorr defended ECA-recommended legislation in the country, such as simplified visa and passport restrictions. "I should like to point out," he added, "that the adoption of this legislation is a rather revolutionary step in Turkey since up to now, the general philosophy has been one of state capitalism."[116] As Moore's various missives succeeded in catapulting the discussion to an investigation of Turkish capitalism, the Democrat Party came to power in Turkey, avowing its support for the expansion of private enterprise and the encouragement of foreign investment.

It was soon after Moore's demand that the prevailing mindset towards American business be overhauled that negotiations between the newly elected Turkish government and the Hilton Hotels International Corporation commenced in August 1950. Congressman Mansfield, a family friend of Moore's, found the timing of the Hilton negotiations suspicious, in fact, an "*unbelievable coincidence*" that attested to the Marshall Plan personnel's desire to "get in on the act," and he believed the deal warranted an investigation into the agency.[117] Although Dorr insisted that the mission did not interfere "with a legitimate American business interest," there were suspicions of the possibility of "shut[ting] out competitive bidding" and of the mission "knowingly [competing] with legitimate reasonable private capital."[118] During a meeting with a Turkish minister of State, Dorr conceded that the mission was in a "ticklish situation" because of the uncertainties in the hotel situation, given two "very influential American firms contending over the project in Istanbul. The firm which would not win the issue would, very likely, create great furor in the States. . . . Being very influential, they would press some Congressmen to take a belligerent attitude against the ECA."[119] Dorr was careful to explain that any assault on the ECA would have repercussions for Turkey's allocations, and he demanded that a decision be made between the two firms as soon as possible. Soon after Dorr's ultimatum to the Turkish government, the Intercontinental Hotel Corporation also indicated that it was growing weary of the repeated failures and "long tirades" of Moore, who soon became a "former employee."[120] Two months later, the lease between the Hilton and the Turkish government was signed, and the ECA began to reject any proposals by other tourism facilities, such as the Istanbul Park Hotel, with the "Korean situation" providing the convenient excuse that "counterpart funds are to be utilized for projects directly in support of a defense economy" and no longer for tourism.[121]

The interludes of the Intercontinental episode and Moore's misfortunes are fruitfully compared with the seeming certitude and orderliness of Conrad Hilton's speeches. Not unlike Hilton, who insisted that his hotels would help cultivate proper hospitality, Moore, too, believed that the incursion of traveling figures—whether American capital, businessmen, or hoteliers—would help discipline the Turkish government into receptivity to American business ventures. Their preoccupation with fostering openness to foreign experts and capital recalls not only the survey researchers' concerns about respondents' willingness to speak to interviewers but also the engineers' insistence that rural populations awaited roads with open arms.

As a boundary object, the Istanbul Hilton took on multiple meanings. For Conrad Hilton, the hotel was a safeguard against the perilous march of Communism and an opportunity to participate in the market empire. For Bunshaft and Eldem, it was the venue for stylistic contestation and reconciliation, occasioning the fabrication of global and local forms alike. For ECA representatives, the Hilton indexed the success of foreign aid while imbuing its allocation with partisanship. For the Turkish government, it signaled a turning point in the tourism industry. At the same time, however, the hotel remained enmeshed in the country's long history of dispossession in urban development schemes. The functions of the Istanbul Hilton were manifold, ably negotiating visions of diplomacy, modernity, and hospitality, all under the shadow of empire and xenophobia.

Conclusion

> It is to the credit of American empathy and generosity, as well as to our naiveté, that we have been willing to promote that theory, and to stand throughout the world as apostles of modernity.
>
> —David Riesman, *Passing of Traditional Society*

> Tourists are criticized for having a superficial view of the things that interest them—and so are social scientists. Tourists are purveyors of modern values the world over—and so are social scientists. And modern tourists share with social scientists their curiosity about primitive peoples, poor peoples and ethnic and other minorities.
>
> —Dean MacCannell, *The Tourist*

IN 1959, survey researcher Frederick Frey published a two-part article in *Forum*, the Ankara political science venue. In it, he chronicled his experiences during the two years he spent in Turkey as a Ford Foundation grant recipient. Frey explained that the title of his article, "Why Turkey?," came from a query he frequently encountered from Turkish and American interlocutors alike: "Why did he choose Turkey for investigation when, as a social researcher, he had the whole world at his disposal to use as a laboratory?"[1] Frey's answer was consistent with the social scientific and political treatment of Turkey as an exception and model of modernization during this period: "Turkey is singular in today's world—singular in a way that helps illuminate all our future."

In the second installment of his article, Frey elaborated on the country's "exceptional" transition to multiparty politics and affirmed his status as a "modern" expert by relaying anecdotes that demonstrated his intimate familiarity with the social and material features of his field of examination:

> We have traveled more than 20,000 miles in two years. Though we were subject to improper treatment in the back streets of Istanbul and our car parts were stolen in Kayseri, the memory I recall most vividly is the image of polite and smiling children

who saluted us on the side of the road, who tipped their hats at us in the Black Sea Region, who helped us locate the sites we wanted to see near Mersin, who ran hundreds of meters to inform us when we took a wrong turn.[2]

Still, Frey noted that Turkish hospitality was partial at best, given the wretched state in which he found Anatolian hotels and the personal interactions he observed in urban settings. Frey admonished an overall "failure to apply the rules of common courtesy to strangers," which he found manifest in people cutting lines, trucks not giving priority to buses in traffic, and women being mistreated in public transportation. He acknowledged preexisting notions of empathy and hospitality among obliging children but found that these traits needed to be updated by the standards of American modernization. Doing so required building new infrastructures, such as "better decorated and advertised hotels," and disseminating new knowledge practices that would encourage rational thinking and "auto-criticism."

As I have argued in this book, Frey's account resonated with the other developmental theorists and practitioners who were involved with the laboratization of Turkey during the Cold War. These included communications and propaganda scholar Daniel Lerner, who did not appreciate the Balgat Chief's ability to imagine the wants and needs of others and erased or recoded as "traditional" the answers that did not confirm his definition of "modernization." Although hotel mogul Conrad Hilton publicly celebrated the "authentic" notions of hospitality he discovered, his building's suburban American features and amenities were intended to upgrade the domestic tourism industry. Although the engineers who paved the roads were told that they ought to cultivate a future-oriented temporal outlook, they were chastised for their impatience and the long time frame of their plans. The engineers were also advised that "getting their hands dirty" was essential to modern practices of roadbuilding and that the embrace of American—rather than European or "traditional"—models would carry with it the reward of being cast as a regional model, with the prestige and money that this entailed. The short-lived implementation of a United Nations highway training center in Ankara for the purpose of assisting neighbors across the Middle East was an exemplary developmental measure.

The urgency of the modernization project made the tension between the accumulation of knowledge and its implementation particularly acute in Turkey. The laboratories of development varied in size and purpose, but each provided a crucial site in which the Cold War could be reduced in scale, effectively managed, and, through manipulation, won. Survey research tested attitudes towards Voice of America broadcasts and, by extension, American modernity. Hotel lobbies showcased the fruits of free-market-oriented empire and undermined the appeals of the command economy. Highways promised territorial and commercial integration. Engineers' offices assembled the economy and rationalized expertise. Punctual buses, hygienic hotels, orderly questionnaires, and properly maintained machinery were all means to produce model subjects of modernization, capable of conceiving of time in linear, noncyclical terms. As the theories and methods of the social scientists traveled, their loci of application, whether masses of peasants residing in rural Turkey, the engineers of Ankara, or the students of Istanbul, were expected to envision themselves as subjects of empathy, mobility, and hospitality.

In their production of a particular version of modernization as truth, these laboratories also crisscrossed with local ideas and political projects. They became testing sites for debates about public versus private sector developmentalism, internal colonialism, and foreign investment, among other topics. Local politicians' and architects' complicated reception of the Istanbul Hilton intersected with policies of urban redevelopment, dispossession, and enticement of foreign capital and expertise, highlighting the distinctions between transient guests (Western experts) and permanent outsiders (non-Muslim minorities) in the country. Experts and policy makers agreed that highways would cultivate the individual capacity for physical and psychic mobility. And yet, pockets of difference persisted for Kurdish populations whose movement continued to be closely managed through policies of forced migration and settlement. The implementation of these projects was further offset not only by the negotiations and disagreements between Turkish and American social scientists, government practitioners, and private sector capitalists but also by their hesitations and anxieties.

The modernizers did not simply conduct surveys to tally responses, and they did not simply draw regional maps for evaluative purposes. Each computational exercise was an effort to occasion the performance of modern subjectivities. Each experiment was also a test of modernity for those who ran them. But the frailty of expert practices could well result in the untethering of modern selves. The shortcomings of explanatory models and the inapplicability of their methods were manifest to the experts, rendering them wary about the reception of their various projects.

The fragility of theories like modernization and their attendant models is not irreconcilable with their tenacity, seeing as how they work by building sturdy material spaces they can traverse. To take into account the precarious status of the experts' thinking and work is not to absolve their entanglements with Cold War politics but rather to highlight instances of doubt that were not merely conducive to, but in fact central to, the production of social scientific knowledge and identities. As models, methods, and theories travel, they are refracted and shot through with instances of reflection: scholarly and technical certitude is undercut by the anxieties of the experts, the coterminous success and failure of their projects, and their subversion on execution. If travelers craft knowledge about themselves as well as about their objects of study, encounters within "contact zones" can turn out to be "heterogeneous," "unequal," and "awkward."[3] Participation in such exchanges is a risky business, fraught with uncertainty, mistranslation, and anxiety, at best. Selves, theories, and plans are made, unraveled, and remade over the course of their travels rather than being safely lodged in a singular location from which they can be wrested and taken elsewhere.

It was not the case, as some global histories of development have suggested, that theories and projects were securely crafted during New Deal debates and taken abroad intact; the practitioners were not confident Cold Warriors who had to ward off alternative plans that periodically emerged from the intellectual margins. Modernization was not imposed in a uniform or unidirectional fashion; rather, it was characterized by contentions and internal dissent.

Still, in their retrospective assessments of their work, practitioners like Gabriel Almond continued to disavow both their privately disclosed uncertainties and their political agendas. Almond found particular affront in the charges that Social Science Research Council's Committee on Comparative Politics volumes had legitimized the existing order, projecting "Anglo-American and capitalist values on the outside world."[4] The political scientist's prevarication about the interventionist nature of his and his collaborators' research seems whimsical in light of their positions as consultants in psychological warfare, propaganda, and intelligence institutions, such as the Psychological Strategy Board.[5] Far from producing objective scholarship, unified theories of modernization often undermined possibilities for democratic and equitable ways of living, as they valorized elite-led development and authoritarian reform in their policy recommendations. Their models were seen as windows into the mindsets and attitudes of potentially subversive subjects, as Joy Rohde has shown, "whether the behavior in question took place at a polling station in New York City or in a guerrilla conflict in rural Indonesia."[6] Throughout the 1960s, developmental and counterinsurgency methods were also transplanted to the United States, as urban problems and social welfare came to be framed in military terms.[7] Domestic deprivation and overseas underdevelopment were explicitly linked, as community development projects were recycled in the War on Poverty, whose architects, such as Daniel Patrick Moynihan, cited the Point Four Program as an inspiration.[8] Claims to objectivity justified interventions at home and abroad, casting a dark shadow over celebratory tributes to disciplinary progress.

Recent cohorts of political scientists have generally refrained from invoking the language of modernization and have presented its theorists as a mortifying, historical episode in field seminars. But many of its core tenets were invoked to describe and legitimize the reconstruction projects of post-invasion Iraq and Afghanistan, bolstering the association between development and security and also between nation building and democracy promotion. The battles of counterinsurgency experts once again proved to be both ideological and political, as their efforts in institution building were entwined with projects geared to shape the attitudes and beliefs of local populations, whether through "money as a weapons system" or other means.[9]

An example of this approach was the Caravan Hotel at the Baghdad International Airport (BIAP); the US Army financed the hotel through seized Iraqi assets and American funds in 2007. The army envisioned the hotel as a central part of the new Baghdad International Airport Economic Zone, which would be spotlighted as the gateway to Iraq and the Middle East. The area would also host a modern business and convention center that would attract international investment. As occupied Iraq became a playground for contractors, reconstruction firms, and private army and security corporations, optimistic actors cited tourism as a major growth sector and an investment opportunity.[10] Still, the Caravan Hotel, which cost $4.2 million, soon became the object of scrutiny in a series of reports issued by the Special Inspector General for Iraq Reconstruction, exemplifying not the new Iraq its planners had imagined but the mismanagement and wasted funds that characterized the war and its aftermath.[11]

The lamentations in the inspector general's reports echoed other accounts by participants in the War on Terror, such as army officials, State Department employees, and social scientists. Observers identified incompetence, lack of personnel, or the infighting between the Defense and State Departments as the culprits for failure. Others were adamant that the outcome of the occupation would have been favorable if only the Pentagon had listened to Middle East experts and their plans.[12] Political scientist Larry Diamond of Stanford University, for instance, had gone to Iraq as a senior advisor to the Coalition Provisional Authority (CPA) in 2004 only to return a few months later, disillusioned and disenchanted. Diamond denounced the endeavor as a "pipe dream," full of "miscalculations" and "blunders."[13] In a pointedly titled book, *Squandered Victory,* he blamed the senior Pentagon leadership and Paul Bremer, who was in charge of the CPA, and questioned the decisions that Bremer implemented with "a high degree of confidence but little knowledge of the country."[14] In order to remedy the problematic lack of familiarity with local conditions, a group of civilian social scientists was brought in and embedded in military brigades in 2007.[15] Although official and academic participants expounded on the "hard lessons" learned in Iraq, their belief in the responsibility to intervene and invest in political and economic reconstruction remained intact. As Larry Diamond put it, "Although the American people will have little appetite, in the coming years, for another nation-building venture of this scale, humanitarian and geopolitical circumstances are bound to compel us to become involved again somewhere, sometime, in post-conflict reconstruction."[16] As we have seen throughout the book, Diamond was not the first political scientist to report on local conditions for foreign-policy initiatives and emerge from the experience with reservations and anxieties, however limited, about the links between empire, capital, and knowledge.

The 2010s saw the return of yet another trope of modernization theory, namely the "Turkish model," which resurfaced following a half century of dormancy. After the 1960 coup, Turkey was still cited as a "successful" example of military modernization, but the possibility of a "Turco-centric" regional strategy was increasingly called into question by policy makers who sought to accommodate the rising tide of Arab nationalism.[17] The military regime in Turkey—although in power for only a year and a half—held a referendum on a more liberal constitution, which was drafted in part by *Forum* authors and included rights for unionization and collective bargaining. The 1960s also saw the establishment of the State Planning Organization, which adopted import-substitution industrialization as official government policy and instituted a series of five-year economic plans that stayed in effect until as late as 1980.

Throughout the 1960s, strains on the once exemplary Turkish-American alliance also grew more severe. Problems ranged from the Cuban Missile Crisis (1962) and Lyndon Johnson's censure of Ismet Inonu regarding Cyprus (1964) to growing anti-American sentiment among Turkey's youth. Faculty and students at the Middle East Technical University (METU), which had been conceived as an institution that would make Turkey a regional center, increasingly turned to public solutions for the housing shortage instigated by the highway network. By the 1970s, the Chamber of Turkish Architects and the Turkish Union of the Chambers of Engineers also began to debate the merits of collective housing settlements, equal rights to minimal housing, and the "right to the city" and public services for the growing migrant workforce. Engineers, especially, adopted an anti-imperialist, revolutionary discourse, one that nonetheless relied on the formation of a "technical intelligentsia."[18] METU itself became the site of anti-American protests, which culminated when Robert Komer's car was set on fire during his visit to the campus at the time of his brief yet highly contested post as US ambassador to Turkey. This post came right after he had served as the head of the Civil Operations and Revolutionary Development Support program in South Vietnam. In 1965, which marked the year of the eastern meetings and the onset of Kurdish separatist mobilization, the Turkish Workers' Party took fifteen seats in Parliament, even as the Justice Party that came to power in 1967 reproduced the more conservative elements of the Democrat Party's (DP) politics. The crises and class struggles of the following decades were violently cut short with yet another coup in 1980, which severely curtailed trade unions, stepped up the militarization of Kurdish areas, and expanded the privatization of public institutions. When the Justice and Development Party (AKP) came to power in 2002, it continued the neoliberal policies of the 1980s and 1990s while also promising a process of civilianization.

The forgotten trope of Turkey as a model of democracy and modernity in the Middle East resurfaced in the aftermath of the Arab uprisings in 2011.[19] If all goes well, we were told, the revolts would turn Egypt, Tunisia, and the others into states like Turkey: prosperous, economically liberal, and capable of "integrating Islamists into democratic institutions."[20] The Turkish model was hailed as the "great multicultural hope for mankind, an Islamic modern democracy . . . the new world of Islamic modernity."[21] Still, there were ambiguities about the contents of the Turkish template. Those who cited Turkey's 1982 constitution—drafted after its bloodiest coup—as worthy of emulation envisioned an active role for the Egyptian military in the post-Mubarak landscape. For them, the Turkish military had been the active guardian of secularism, carving a space of "moderation" for Islamic parties in that country. For others, such as the Muslim Brotherhood, Egypt's trajectory could be modeled after the reign of the AKP, with its steadfast program of neoliberalism and success in luring foreign capital and increasing growth rates.

In 2013, however, the governing AKP faced its own set of crises, as the proposal for an urban development plan in Istanbul's Taksim Gezi Park resulted in months-long protests. The Gezi renewal plan was emblematic of AKP's construction-based preoccupation with economic growth, which has provoked comparisons with the DP's Menderes—a comparison Erdoğan has welcomed in his perennial struggle with the military. Of particular note is the Public Mass Housing Administration (TOKI), which has in fact partnered with private contractors to rise to the top of the real-estate market, dispossessing the most vulnerable populations (often in predominantly working-class, Kurdish, Alevi, and LGBT neighborhoods) and turning potentially valuable areas into lucrative sites for speculation and rent extraction. The Gezi protests quickly metastasized into a far-reaching critique not simply of the Taksim development scheme but also of the AKP's governing vision and its domestic and foreign policies. Prime Minister Erdoğan's less-than-tolerant response to the protests apparently came as a surprise to "experts" who had so recently been extolling his model of neoliberal democracy. The persistent incarceration of leftist, primarily Kurdish, activists, journalists, and students, which started as early as 2008 and intensified after the elections of 2011, had somehow not found its way into policy-oriented scholarly analyses on the other side of the Atlantic. Commentators have also been silent about the replacement of the military tutelage with a massive police state and the ongoing urban warfare in Kurdish areas, which have been subject to, but have been resisting, prolonged curfews, infrastructure destruction, and urban renewal programs since 2015.[22]

This should come as no surprise. During the Cold War, upholding the replicability of the Turkish model required the erasure of its authoritarian, hierarchical elements. Experts and policy makers relied on this model to promote the developmental and capitalistic vision of American foreign policy and its core ideological offering, modernization theory. The crafting of this theory and its Turkish model worked in tandem through the implementation of concrete yet tentative measures of modernization.

Frailties of theory construction are not obstructions to be surmounted on the path to all-explanatory theories and models; rather, they are endemic features of knowledge production, whose tensions can be navigated but never surpassed. In their disregard for the histories and political effects of their theories and research agendas, political scientists have, for the most part, abandoned inquiry of a crucial domain of political practice: the work of uncertain experts such as themselves. Modernization theory, whose premises continue to guide international development, democracy promotion, and reconstruction projects, was an important product of that work, one whose study should not be delegated to historians but should be embraced by political scientists themselves. Taking up its study might provide a focal point for a query into the politics of knowledge production and our role in it.

Notes

Introduction

1. Conrad Hilton, "The City of the Golden Horn," June 1955, box 16, folder: Turkey-Istanbul, Records of the Hilton Hotels International, Hospitality Industry Archives, Massad Family Library Research Center, University of Houston, Conrad N. Hilton College of Hotel and Restaurant Management (hereafter cited as HHI); "Expansion in Turkey," *Hilton Items* 15, no. 8 (January 1952): 5. See also Annabel Wharton, *Building the Cold War: Hilton International Hotels and Modern Architecture* (Chicago: University of Chicago Press, 2001).

2. Conrad Hilton, "Towards a Foreign Policy for Hotels" (speech, Los Angeles Rotary Club, July 27, 1956), box 6, HHI.

3. Hilton, "City of the Golden Horn," June 1955, box 16, folder: Turkey-Istanbul, HHI.

4. Odd Arne Westad, *The Global Cold War: Third World Interventions and the Making of Our Times* (Cambridge, UK: Cambridge University Press, 2009).

5. On the making of the Third World, see Vijay Prashad, *The Darker Nations: A People's History of the Third World* (New York: New Press, 2007). For an earlier periodization, see L. S. Stravrianos, *Global Rift: The Third World Comes of Age* (New York: William Morrow, 1981).

6. Between 1948 and 1952, Turkey received $100 million from Truman Doctrine funds, $349 million from Marshall Plan funds, and an estimated $587 million in military aid (some of which was used for highway construction).

7. Daniel Lerner, *The Passing of Traditional Society: Modernizing the Middle East* (Glencoe, IL: Free Press, 1958); Robert Ward and Dankwart Rustow, eds., *Political Modernization in Japan and Turkey* (Princeton, NJ: Princeton University Press, 1964).

8. Nils Gilman, *Mandarins of the Future: Modernization Theory in Cold War America* (Baltimore: Johns Hopkins University Press, 2003); Michael Latham, *Modernization as Ideology: American Social Science and "Nation Building" in the Kennedy Era* (Chapel Hill: The University of North Carolina Press, 2000); S. M. Amadae, *Rationalizing Capitalist*

Democracy: The Cold War Origins of Rational Choice Liberalism (Chicago: University of Chicago Press, 2003); David Milne, *America's Rasputin: Walt Rostow and the Vietnam War* (New York: Hill and Wang, 2008); David Ekbladh, *The Great American Mission: Modernization and the Construction of an American World Order* (Princeton, NJ: Princeton University Press, 2010); Hemant Shah, *The Production of Modernization: Daniel Lerner, Mass Media, and the Passing of Traditional Society* (Philadelphia: Temple University Press, 2011).

9. Nick Cullather, *The Hungry World: America's Cold War Battle Against Poverty in Asia* (Cambridge, MA: Harvard University Press, 2010), p. 183.

10. Michel Callon, Pierre Lascoumes, and Yannick Barthe, *Acting in an Uncertain World: An Essay on Technical Democracy*, trans. Graham Burchell (Cambridge, MA: MIT Press, 2009), pp. 58–59. For this account, I also draw on Bruno Latour, *The Pasteurization of France* (Cambridge, MA: Harvard University Press, 1988); and Timothy Mitchell, *Carbon Democracy: Political Power in the Age of Oil* (New York: Verso, 2013).

11. "Expansion in Turkey," *Hilton Items* 15, no. 8 (January 1952): 5.

12. Turkey joined the International Monetary Fund and the International Bank for Reconstruction and Development in 1947, and signed the Baghdad Pact with Iraq in 1955. Following the coup in 1958, Iraq left the Pact, which became the Central Treaty Organization (CENTO) with the inclusion of Pakistan, Iran, and Britain. The United States was not an official member but encouraged the organization's role in protecting the "Northern Tier."

13. William Hitchcock, "The Marshall Plan and the Creation of the West," in *Cambridge History of the Cold War*, eds. Melvyn Leffler and Odd Arne Westad (Cambridge, UK: Cambridge University Press, 2012).

14. Bradford De Long and Barry Eichengreen argue that Marshall Plan "conditionality" pushed European political economy "in a direction that left its post–World War II 'mixed economies' with more 'market' and less 'controls' in the mix" and can thus be seen as a successful structural adjustment program. "The Marshall Plan: History's Most Successful Structural Adjustment Program" (working paper no. 3899, National Bureau of Economic Research, 1991).

15. Victoria de Grazia, *Irresistible Empire: America's Advance Through Twentieth-Century Europe* (Cambridge, MA: Harvard University Press, 2005), p. 349.

16. Keyder and Pamuk have pointed out that between 1947 and 1972, about 8 percent of cultivated land was redistributed, with only two-thousandths of this having been private land. Çağlar Keyder and Şevket Pamuk, "1945 Çiftçiyi Topraklandırma Kanunu Üzerine Tezler" [Theses on the 1945 law for providing land to farmers], *Yapıt* (Ocak 1984): 52–64. All translations from Turkish are mine, unless otherwise noted.

17. Harry S. Truman, "Inaugural Speech," January 20, 1949, https://www.trumanlibrary.org/whistlestop/50yr_archive/inagural20jan1949.htm.

18. Mitchell, *Carbon Democracy*, p. 121.

19. Cited in Westad, *Global Cold War*, p. 25. On Hoffman's role as president of the Ford Foundation in the 1950s and his approach to philanthropy as an "imaginative weapon in the Cold War," see Zachary Lockman, *Field Notes: The Making of Middle East Studies in the United States* (Stanford, CA: Stanford University Press, 2016), p. 114.

20. Baskın Oran, ed., *Türk Dış Politikası: Kurtuluş Savaşından Bugüne Olgular, Belgeler, Yorumlar, Cilt 1: 1919–1980* [Turkish foreign policy: Events, documents, interpretations from the War of Independence to today] (Istanbul: İletişim Yayınları, 2001), pp. 495–96.

21. Robert Vitalis, "The Midnight Ride of Kwame Nkrumah and Other Fables of Bandung (Ban-doong)," *Humanity* 4, no. 2 (2013).

22. Reşat Kasaba, "Populism and Democracy in Turkey, 1946–1961," in *Rules and Rights in the Middle East: Democracy, Law, and Society*, eds. Ellis Goldberg, Reşat Kasaba, and Joel Migdal (Seattle: University of Washington Press, 1993).

23. Max Thornburg, *Turkey: An Economic Appraisal* (New York: The Twentieth Century Fund, 1949).

24. See Ilham Khuri-Makdisi, *The Eastern Mediterranean and the Making of Global Radicalism, 1860–1914* (Oakland: University of California Press, 2010); Keith David Watenpaugh, *Being Modern in the Middle East: Revolution, Nationalism, Colonialism, and the Arab Middle Class* (Princeton, NJ: Princeton University Press, 2012); Marwa Elshakry, *Reading Darwin in Arabic, 1860–1950* (Chicago: University of Chicago Press, 2013); Nathan Citino, "The 'Crush' of Ideologies: The United States, the Arab World, and Cold War Modernization," *Cold War History* 12, no. 1 (2012); and Jeffrey James Byrne, "Our Own Special Brand of Socialism: Algeria and the Contest of Modernities in the 1960s," *Diplomatic History* 33, no. 3 (2009), among others.

25. Cihan Tuğal discusses the shortcomings of the model but treats it only as a phenomenon of the 2000s. See *The Fall of the Turkish Model: How the Arab Uprisings Brought Down Islamic Liberalism* (New York: Verso, 2016).

26. For recent critics, see Ismet Akça, Ahmet Bekmen, and Barış Ozden, eds., *Turkey Reframed: Constituting Neoliberal Hegemony* (London: Pluto Press, 2014); Erdem Yörük, "Welfare Provision as Political Containment: The Politics of Social Assistance and the Kurdish Conflict in Turkey," *Politics & Society* 40, no. 517 (2012): 517–47.

27. Kadir Yıldırım and Marc Lynch, "Is There Still Hope for Turkish Democracy?," *POMEPS Studies 22: Contemporary Turkish Politics* (December 7, 2016); Jason Brownlee, "Why Turkey's Authoritarian Descent Shakes Up Democratic Theory," *Washington Post*, March 23, 2016, https://www.washingtonpost.com/news/monkey-cage/wp/2016/03/23/why-turkeys-authoritarian-descent-shakes-up-democratic-theory/?utm_term=.8a57a13c390d; Berk Esen and Sebnem Gümüsçü, "Rising Competitive Authoritarianism in Turkey," *Third World Quarterly* 37, no. 9 (2016): 1581–606.

28. Richard Robinson, "The Lessons of Turkey," *Middle East Journal* 5, no. 4 (1951); George McGhee, "Turkey Joins the West," *Foreign Affairs* 32, no. 4 (July 1954): 617–30.

29. On Turkey's continuing diplomatic, cultural, and commercial relations with Germany—for instance, in the form of chrome shipments well into 1944—see John Vanderlippe, *The Politics of Turkish Democracy: Ismet Inönü and the Formation of the Multi-Party System, 1938–1950* (Albany: State University of New York Press, 2005).

30. Those who could not pay the capital tax were sent to labor camps in eastern Turkey. Asım Karaömerlioğlu, "Turkey's 'Return' to Multi-Party Politics: A Social Interpretation," *East European Quarterly* 40, no. 1 (2006): 97. Between 1912 and 1927, the

Christian population of Anatolia decreased from 20 to 3 percent. Soner Çağaptay, "Reconfiguring the Turkish Nation in the 1930s," *Nationalism and Ethnic Politics* 8, no. 2 (2002): 68.

31. Daniel Lerner and Richard Robinson, "Swords and Ploughshares: The Turkish Army as a Modernizing Force," *World Politics* 13, no. 1 (October 1960): 19–44; Dankwart Rustow, "Ataturk as Founder of a State," *Daedalus* 97, no. 3 (Summer 1968); Walter Weiker, *The Turkish Revolution, 1960–1961: Aspects of Military Politics* (Washington, DC: Brookings Institution, 1963).

32. Nadia Abu El-Haj, *Facts on the Ground: Archaeological Practice and Territorial Self-Fashioning in Israeli Society* (Chicago: University of Chicago Press, 2001); Timothy Mitchell, *Rule of Experts: Egypt, Technopolitics, Modernity* (Berkeley: University of California Press, 2002); Bruno Latour, *Reassembling the Social: An Introduction to Actor-Network-Theory* (Oxford, UK: Oxford University Press, 2005); Michel Callon, "What Does It Mean to Say That Economics Is Performative?" (working papers series 5, Centre de Sociologie de l'Innovation, 2006); Donald Mackenzie, Fabian Muniesa, and Lucia Siu, eds., *Do Economists Make Markets? On the Performativity of Economics* (Princeton, NJ: Princeton University Press, 2007).

33. Michel Foucault, *Madness and Civilization: A History of Insanity in the Age of Reason* (New York: Vintage, 1988); Ian Hacking, *The Taming of Chance* (Cambridge, UK: Cambridge University Press, 1990); Lorraine Daston and Peter Galison, "The Image of Objectivity," *Representations* 40 (Autumn 1992); Mary Poovey, *A History of the Modern Fact: Problems of Knowledge in the Sciences of Wealth and Society* (Chicago: University of Chicago Press, 1998).

34. Lisa Wedeen, "Scientific Knowledge, Liberalism, and Empire: American Political Science in the Modern Middle East," in *Middle East Studies for the New Millennium: Infrastructures of Knowledge*, eds. Shami Seteney and Cynthia Miller-Idris (New York: Social Science Research Council, 2016).

35. Richard Rottenburg, *Far-Fetched Facts: A Parable of Development Aid*, trans. Allison Brown and Tom Lampert (Cambridge, MA: MIT Press, 2009), p. 74.

36. Theodore Porter, *Trust in Numbers: The Pursuit of Objectivity in Science and Public Life* (Princeton, NJ: Princeton University Press, 1996). There is a growing literature on the relationship between such technologies and their deployment in governance. On maps, see James Scott, *Seeing like a State: How Certain Schemes to Improve the Human Condition Have Failed* (New Haven, CT: Yale University Press, 1998); Manu Goswami, *Producing India: From Colonial Economy to National Space*, Chicago Studies in Practices of Meaning (Chicago: University of Chicago Press, 2004); and Patrick Joyce, *The Rule of Freedom: Liberalism and the Modern City* (London: Verso, 2003). On surveys, see Sarah Igo, *The Averaged American: Surveys, Citizens, and the Making of a Mass Public* (Cambridge, MA: Harvard University Press, 2007); Matthew Hull, "Democratic Technologies of Speech: From World War II America to Postcolonial Delhi," *Journal of Linguistic Anthropology* 20, no. 2 (2010): 257–82; John Law, "Seeing like a Survey," *Cultural Sociology* 3, no. 2 (2009): 239–56; and Michael Savage, *Identities and Social Change in Britain*

since 1940: The Politics of Method (Oxford, UK: Oxford University Press, 2010). On bureaucratic documents, see Miles Ogborn, *Indian Ink: Script and Print in the Making of the English East India Company* (Chicago: The University of Chicago Press, 2007); Ilana Feldman, *Governing Gaza: Bureaucracy, Authority, and the Work of Rule, 1917–1967* (Durham, NC: Duke University Press, 2008); and Matthew Hull, *Government of Paper: The Materiality of Bureaucracy in Urban Pakistan* (Berkeley: University of California Press, 2012).

37. Bruno Latour, *Science in Action: How to Follow Scientists and Engineers through Society* (Cambridge, MA: Harvard University Press, 1987), p. 223.

38. John Law, *After Method: Mess in Social Science Research* (New York: Routledge, 2004), pp. 20–21.

39. Latour, *Science in Action*, p. 216.

40. See Melani McAlister, *Epic Encounters: Culture, Media, and US Interests in the Middle East since 1945* (Berkeley: University of California Press, 2005); Robert Vitalis, *America's Kingdom: Mythmaking on the Saudi Oil Frontier* (Stanford, CA: Stanford University Press, 2006); Ussama Makdisi, *Artillery of Heaven: American Missionaries and the Failed Conversion of the Middle East* (Ithaca, NY: Cornell University Press, 2009); Keith Feldman, *A Shadow Over Palestine: The Imperial Life of Race in America* (Minneapolis: University of Minnesota Press, 2015); Alex Lubin, *Geographies of Liberation: The Making of an Afro-Arab Imaginary* (Chapel Hill: University of North Carolina Press, 2014); Anne McClintock, "Paranoid Empire: Specters from Guantánamo and Abu Ghraib," *Small Axe* 13, no. 1 (2009): 50–74; Toby Jones, *Desert Kingdom: How Oil and Water Forged Modern Saudi Arabia* (Cambridge, MA: Harvard University Press, 2011); Cyrus Schayegh, "Iran's Karaj Dam Affair: Emerging Mass Consumerism, the Politics of Promise, and the Cold War in the Third World," *Comparative Studies in Society and History* 54, no. 3 (2012): 612–43; and others.

41. Joseph Morgan Hodge, "Writing the History of Development (Part 2: Longer, Deeper, Wider)," *Humanity* 7, no. 1 (2016): 125; David Engerman and Corinna Unger, "Introduction: Towards a Global History of Modernization," *Diplomatic History* 33, no. 3 (June 2009): 380.

42. David Engerman, *Modernization from the Other Shore: American Intellectuals and the Romance of Russian Development* (Cambridge, MA: Harvard University Press, 2003); Nicole Sackley, "Village Models: Etawah, India, and the Making and Remaking of Development in the Early Cold War," *Diplomatic History* 37, no. 4 (2013); Nathan Citino, *Envisioning the Arab Future: Modernization in US-Arab Relations, 1945–1967* (Cambridge, UK: Cambridge University Press, 2017).

43. Michel Callon, "Some Elements of a Sociology of Translation: Domestication of the Scallops and the Fishermen of St. Brieuc Bay," in *Power, Action, Belief: A New Sociology of Knowledge?*, ed. John Law (New York: Routledge, 1986).

44. Latour, *Science in Action*.

45. See Asım Karaömerlioğlu, "The Village Institutes Experience in Turkey," *British Journal of Middle Eastern Studies* 25, no. 1 (1998) for an excellent account.

46. Lewis Thomas, foreword to *A Village in Anatolia*, by Mahmut Makal, ed. Paul Stirling, trans. Wyndham Deedes (London: Vallentine, Mitchell, 1954), p. xiv.

47. Mahmut Makal, *A Village in Anatolia*, ed. Paul Stirling, trans. Wyndham Deedes (London: Vallentine, Mitchell, 1954), pp. 69, 121.

48. Richard Robinson to Walter S. Rogers, March 20, 1954, in Robinson, *Letters from Turkey*, reprinted for the Peace Corps by permission of the Institute for Current World Affairs (Istanbul: Robert College, 1965).

49. Metin And, "Toplumbilimci Makal" [Makal the social scientist], *Forum* 3, no. 28 (1955).

50. Lerner, *Passing*, p. 122. For a comparison of the two authors' depictions of certain aspects of "traditional" life, such as the use of clocks as mere "decorative" devices, see Makal, *A Village in Anatolia*, p. 58; and Lerner, p. 39.

51. Mahmut Makal, *Kalkınma Masalı* (Istanbul: Varlık, 1960). On the erasure of passage points, see Johanna Bockman and Gil Eyal, "Eastern Europe as a Laboratory for Economic Knowledge: The Transnational Roots of Neoliberalism," *American Journal of Sociology* 108, no. 2 (September 2002).

52. Anna Tsing, *Friction: An Ethnography of Global Connection* (Princeton, NJ: Princeton University Press, 2005).

53. For the growing literature on colonial developmentalism that dates the notion to the 1930s and 1940s, see Frederick Cooper and Randall Packard, eds., *International Development and the Social Sciences: Essays on the History and Politics of Knowledge* (Berkeley: University of California Press, 1997); Frederick Cooper, "Writing the History of Development," *Journal of Modern European History* 8 (2010); Joseph Morgan Hodge, *Triumph of the Expert: Agrarian Doctrines of Development and the Legacies of British Colonialism* (Athens: Ohio University Press, 2007); Jacob Norris, *Land of Progress: Palestine in the Age of Colonial Development, 1905–1948* (Oxford, UK: Oxford University Press, 2013); and Sherene Seikaly, *Men of Capital: Scarcity and Economy in Mandate Palestine* (Stanford, CA: Stanford University Press, 2015). For earlier periodizations, see Helen Tilley, *Africa as a Living Laboratory: Empire, Development, and the Problem of Scientific Knowledge, 1870–1950* (Chicago: University of Chicago Press, 2011); Andrew Zimmerman, *Alabama in Africa: Booker T. Washington, the German Empire, and the Globalization of the New South* (Princeton, NJ: Princeton University Press, 2012); and Paul Kramer, *The Blood of Government: Race, Empire, the United States, and the Philippines* (Chapel Hill: The University of North Carolina Press, 2006).

54. On the role of German engineers in building Ottoman and early Republican infrastructure, see Mustafa Gencer, *Jön Türk Modernizmi ve "Alman Ruhu"* [Young Turk modernism and the German spirit] (Istanbul: Iletisim, 2003).

55. The decade of the 1950s saw a 75 percent increase in the population of the four largest cities of Turkey.

56. Joyce, *The Rule of Freedom*, p. 72. For other insightful accounts of infrastructural breakdown, see also Brian Larkin, *Signal and Noise: Media, Infrastructure, and Urban Culture in Nigeria* (Durham, NC: Duke University Press, 2008); Julia Elyachar, "Upend-

ing Infrastructure: *Tamarod*, Resistance, and Agency after the January 25th Revolution in Egypt," *History and Anthropology* 25, no. 4 (2014): 452–71; and Joanne Nucho, *Everyday Sectarianism in Urban Lebanon: Infrastructures, Public Services, and Power* (Princeton, NJ: Princeton University Press, 2016).

57. Arturo Escobar, *Encountering Development: The Making and Unmaking of the Third World* (Princeton, NJ: Princeton University Press, 1995), pp. 40–41, 44.

58. James Ferguson, *The Anti-Politics Machine: "Development," Depoliticization and Bureaucratic Power in Lesotho* (Cambridge, UK: Cambridge University Press, 1990), pp. 20–21.

59. Scott, *Seeing like a State*, p. 4.

60. Mitchell, *Rule of Experts*, p. 43.

61. Ibid., p. 233.

62. Tania Li, *The Will to Improve: Governmentality, Development, and the Practice of Politics* (Durham, NC: Duke University Press, 2007), p. 10.

63. Anne Norton, "Political Science as a Vocation," in *Problems and Methods in the Study of Politics*, eds. Ian Shapiro, Rogers Smith, and Tarek Masoud (Cambridge, UK: Cambridge University Press, 2004), p. 71.

64. Ann Stoler, *Along the Archival Grain: Epistemic Anxieties and Colonial Common Sense* (Princeton, NJ: Princeton University Press, 2009), p. 43.

65. On the relationship between writing and authority, see Jacques Derrida, *Dissemination*, trans. Barbara Johnson (Chicago: University of Chicago Press, 1981); and Michel Foucault, *The Archaeology of Knowledge and the Discourse on Language*, trans. A. M. Sheridan Smith (New York: Pantheon, 1982).

66. Jacques Derrida, "Archive Fever: A Freudian Impression," *Diacritics* 25, no. 2 (1995).

67. Talal Asad, *Anthropology and the Colonial Encounter* (London: Ithaca Press, 1973); Paul Rabinow, *Reflections on Fieldwork in Morocco* (Berkeley: University of California Press, 1977); Johannes Fabian, *Time and the Other: How Anthropology Makes Its Object* (New York: Columbia University Press, 1983); James Clifford, *Writing Culture: The Poetics and Politics of Ethnography* (Berkeley: University of California Press, 1986); Peter Novick, *That Noble Dream: The "Objectivity Question" and the American Historical Profession* (Cambridge, UK: Cambridge University Press, 1988); Cooper and Packard, *International Development and the Social Sciences*; George Steinmetz, ed., *Sociology and Empire: The Imperial Entanglements of a Discipline* (Durham, NC: Duke University Press, 2013).

68. For exceptions, see Irene Gendzier, *Managing Political Change: Social Scientists and the Third World* (Boulder, CO: Westview Press, 1985); David Ricci, *The Tragedy of Political Science: Politics, Scholarship, and Democracy* (New Haven, CT: Yale University Press, 1984); John Gunnell, *The Descent of Political Theory: The Genealogy of an American Vocation* (Chicago: Chicago University Press, 1993); Ido Oren, *Our Enemies and US: America's Rivalries and the Making of Political Science* (Ithaca, NY: Cornell University Press, 2003); David Long and Brian Schmidt, eds., *Imperialism and Internationalism*

in the Discipline of International Relations (Albany: State University of New York Press, 2005); Robert Vitalis, *White World Order, Black Power Politics* (Ithaca, NY: Cornell University Press, 2015); and others.

69. Steven Shapin and Simon Schaffer, *Leviathan and the Air-Pump: Hobbes, Boyle, and the Experimental Life* (Princeton, NJ: Princeton University Press, 1985).

Chapter 1

1. Dankwart A. Rustow, "Mukayeseli Devlet İdaresi ve Türkiye Üzerine Bir Seminer" [A seminar on comparative government and Turkey], *Ankara Üniversitesi SBF Dergisi* 16, no. 4 (1961): 197.

2. Ibid., pp. 193, 199.

3. Duncan Bell, "Writing the World: Disciplinary History and Beyond," *International Affairs* 85, no. 10 (2009): 5.

4. For insightful critiques of this process, see Masao Miyoshi and Harry Harootunian, eds., *Learning Places: The Afterlives of Area Studies* (Durham, NC: Duke University Press, 2002); Timothy Mitchell, "The Middle East in the Past and Future of Social Science," in *The Politics of Knowledge: Area Studies and the Disciplines*, ed., David Szanton (Berkeley: University of California Press, 2004); and Wedeen, "Scientific Knowledge, Liberalism, and Empire."

5. Lucian Pye, "The Non-Western Political Process," *The Journal of Politics* 20, no. 3 (August 1958): 468. For similar accounts, see Roy Macridis and Richard Cox, "Seminar Report," *The American Political Science Review* 47, no. 3 (September 1953); Gabriel Almond, Cole Taylor, and Roy Macridis, "A Suggested Research Strategy in Western European Government and Politics," *The American Political Science Review* 49, no. 4 (December 1955); Gabriel Almond, "Comparative Political Systems," *The Journal of Politics* 18, no. 3 (August 1956); George McT. Kahin, Guy Pauker, and Lucian Pye, "Comparative Politics of Non-Western Countries," *The American Political Science Review* 49, no. 4 (December 1955).

6. On traveling theories, see Edward Said, *The World, the Text, and the Critic* (Cambridge, MA: Harvard University Press, 1983); Mary Louise Pratt, *Imperial Eyes: Travel Writing and Transculturation* (London: Routledge, 1992); and James Secord, "Knowledge in Transit," *Isis* 95, no. 4 (December 2004).

7. Nils Gilman, "Modernization Theory, the Highest Stage of American Intellectual History" in *Staging Growth: Modernization, Development and the Global Cold War*, ed. David Engerman, Nils Gilman, Mark Haefele, and Michael Latham (Amherst: University of Massachusetts Press, 2003).

8. Callon, "Some Elements of a Sociology of Translation"; Latour, *Science in Action*.

9. See, for instance, Gilman's account of Roy Macridis, Popp's discussion of Manfred Halpern, and Immerwahr's take on proponents of community development. Gilman, *Mandarins of the Future*; Roland Popp, "An Application of Modernization Theory during the Cold War? The Case of Pahlavi Iran," *The International History Review* 30, no. 1 (2008): 76–98; Daniel Immerwahr, *Thinking Small: The United States and the Lure of Community Development* (Cambridge, MA: Harvard University Press, 2015).

10. Pendleton Herring, "The Social Sciences in Modern Society," *Items* 1, no. 1 (March 1947): 2, 4, 5.

11. Joy Rohde, "Social Science and Foreign Affairs," in *The Oxford Research Encyclopedia of American History*, ed. Jon Butler (New York: Oxford University Press, 2015).

12. David Engerman, "Bernath Lecture: American Knowledge and Global Power," *Diplomatic History* 31, no. 4 (2007): 605.

13. Oren, *Our Enemies and US*, p. 13.

14. Mitchell, "The Middle East," p. 86.

15. Karl Loewenstein, "Report on the Research Panel on Comparative Government," *The American Political Science Review* 38, no. 3 (June 1944): 540–41.

16. Udi Greenberg, *The Weimar Century: German Emigres and the Ideological Foundations of the Cold War* (Princeton, NJ: Princeton University Press, 2014).

17. Dankwart Rustow, "New Horizons for Comparative Politics," *World Politics* 9, no. 4 (July 1957). Neumann wrote in 1959: "Comparative Government—only yesterday to many a remote discipline of curiosity collectors—receives a new impetus and becomes for the mature citizen an imperative interest." Sigmund Neumann, "The Comparative Study of Politics," *Comparative Studies in Society and History* 1, no. 2 (January 1959): 105.

18. On the SSRC's own Committee on International Relations, which was founded in 1926 and encouraged overseas research, for instance, see Vitalis, *White World Order, Black Power Politics*.

19. For a comprehensive account of the contributions of Parsons, Shils, and their colleagues at the Harvard Department of Social Relations to the making of modernization theory, see Gilman, *Mandarins of the Future*, chap. 3.

20. Jessica Blatt, "'To Bring Out the Best That Is in Their Blood': Race, Reform, and Civilization in the *Journal of Race Development* (1910–1919)," *Ethnic and Racial Studies* 27, no. 5 (2004): 691–709; Vitalis, *White World Order, Black Power Politics*.

21. Rohde, "Social Science and Foreign Affairs."

22. W. W. Rostow, *The Stages of Economic Growth: A Non-Communist Manifesto* (Cambridge, UK: Cambridge University Press, 1960); Karl Deutsch, "Social Mobilization and Political Development," *The American Political Science Review* 55, no. 3 (1961).

23. Gabriel Almond, "Political Theory and Political Science," *American Political Science Review* 60, no. 4 (December 1966): 877–78.

24. The CIA used the Ford Foundation to "covertly channel funds to anti-communist organizations and periodicals and to support research of interest to US intelligence," and thus it made a crucial difference for the trajectories of area studies in general and Middle East studies in particular. Lockman, *Field Notes*, p. 114.

25. See Latham, *Modernization as Ideology;* and Milne, *America's Rasputin* for detailed accounts of Rostow's policy tenure.

26. Latham, "Modernization," in *The Cambridge History of Social Science Vol. 7: The Modern Social Sciences*, eds. Theodore Porter and Dorothy Ross (Cambridge, UK: Cambridge University Press, 2008), p. 727.

27. Gabriel Almond, "Research in Comparative Politics: Plans of a New Council Committee," *Items* 8, no. 1 (March 1954): 2.

28. On the interest in the shortcomings of Ottoman land reform, see Nathan Citino, "The Ottoman Legacy in Cold War Modernization," *International Journal of Middle East Studies* 40, no. 4 (2008): 579–97.

29. Dankwart Rustow, "Connections," in *Paths to the Middle East: Ten Scholars Look Back*, ed. Thomas Naff (Albany: State University of New York Press, 1993), p. 272.

30. Ibid., p. 270.

31. Alexander Rüstow returned to Heidelberg to head the Institute of Social and Political Science. Greenberg, *The Weimar Century*, p. 69.

32. Dankwart Rustow, "The Politics of the Near East: Southwest Asia and Northern Africa," in *The Politics of the Developing Areas*, eds. Gabriel Almond and James Coleman (Princeton, NJ: Princeton University Press, 1960); Ward and Rustow, *Political Modernization in Japan and Turkey*; Rustow, "Turkey: The Modernity of Tradition," in *Political Culture and Political Development*, eds. Lucian Pye and Sidney Verba (Princeton, NJ: Princeton University Press, 1965); Rustow, "The Development of Parties in Turkey," in *Political Parties and Political Development*, eds. Myron Weiner and Joseph LaPalombara (Princeton, NJ: Princeton University Press, 1966).

33. Irving Leonard Markovitz, "In Memoriam: Dankwart A. Rustow: Personal Remembrances," *Comparative Politics* 29, no. 3 (1996): 119.

34. Gilman, *Mandarins of the Future*; Latham, *Modernization as Ideology*; Citino, "The Ottoman Legacy." It is interesting that early critics of modernization theory enlisted Rustow as an ally in their accounts, categorizing his work as historical comparative analysis rather than as modernization theory. See Samuel Huntington, "Change to Change: Modernization, Development and Politics," *Comparative Politics* 3 (1971); Dean Tipps, "Modernization Theory and the Comparative Study of Societies: A Critical Perspective," *Comparative Studies in Society and History* 15, no. 2 (March 1973); Robert Packenham, *Liberal America and the Third World: Political Development Ideas in Foreign Aid and Social Science* (Princeton, NJ: Princeton University Press, 1973).

35. Rustow, "Turkey: The Modernity of Tradition"; Rustow, *A World of Nations: Problems of Political Modernization* (Washington, DC: The Brookings Institution, 1967).

36. Rustow, *Politics of Modernization and Westernization in the Near East* (Princeton, NJ: Center for International Studies, 1956), p. 5.

37. Lockman, *Field Notes*, p. 77.

38. Abstract of the paper presented at the Conference on Research in the Middle East, sponsored by the SSRC, Tehran, February–March 1959, Dankwart Rustow Private Papers, New York (hereafter cited as DRP).

39. The positing of continuity between Ottoman and Turkish processes of modernization became a fad in the next decades in the work of Bernard Lewis, *The Emergence of Modern Turkey* (Oxford, UK: Oxford University Press, 1961); Kemal Karpat, *Turkey's Politics: The Transition to a Multi-Party System* (Princeton, NJ: Princeton University Press, 1959); Niyazi Berkes, *The Development of Secularism in Turkey* (Montreal: McGill University Press, 1964); Berkes, *Türkiye'de Çağdaşlaşma* [Modernization in Turkey] (Ankara: Bilgi Yayınevi, 1973); Kemal Karpat, ed., *Social Change and Politics in Turkey: A*

Structural-Historical Analysis (Leiden: E. J. Brill, 1973); Şerif Mardin, *Türk Modernleşmesi* [Turkish modernization] (Istanbul: İletişim Yayınları, 1991).

40. The initial committee consisted of Gabriel Almond, Cole Taylor, George McT. Kahin, Roy Macridis, Guy Pauker, and Lucian Pye. The CCP stayed active between 1954 and 1972.

41. Gabriel Almond to Dankwart Rustow, November 6, 1953, DRP.

42. Robert Ward, ed., *Studying Politics Abroad: Field Research in the Developing Areas* (Boston: Little, Brown, 1964), p. 4.

43. Almond to Rustow, May 27, 1954, DRP.

44. In an edited volume that offered counsel to the political scientist abroad, it was noted: "He is apt to find also, however, that this factor of novelty—and the distrust instinctively aroused thereby—may to some extent be offset by the fact that he is a foreigner. Foreigners, especially Americans, are popularly expected to deport themselves in strange, i.e. foreign ways." Ward, *Studying Politics Abroad*, p. 47.

45. Gabriel Almond, "Memorandum: Suggested Terms of Reference for Your Conference on Research Strategy for the non-Western Areas," enclosed in Almond to Rustow, June 10, 1954, DRP.

46. Rustow to Almond, June 13, 1954, DRP.

47. Rustow, "New Horizons for Comparative Politics," pp. 530–32.

48. Ibid., p. 530.

49. Gilman, *Mandarins of the Future*, p. 151.

50. Almond, introduction to Almond and Coleman, *Politics of the Developing Areas*, p. 4.

51. Almond, "Comparative Political Systems."

52. Almond, introduction to Almond and Coleman, *Politics of the Developing Areas*, pp. 10, 16, 64.

53. I borrow the phrase "epistemic anxieties" from Stoler, *Along the Archival Grain*.

54. Rustow to Coleman, December 24, 1958, DRP.

55. Coleman, memorandum, May 1, 1959, DRP.

56. Rustow to Coleman, December 24, 1958, DRP.

57. Rustow's severe anxiety about the reception of this work prompted him to suggest and succeed in procuring a title change dangerously close to the publication date of the book. He said, "I feel very strongly that the adjective 'underdeveloped' is both scientifically inaccurate (because it imports an unwarranted value judgment) and, what is more important, is extremely offensive in practice to the inhabitants of countries commonly so described." Rustow to Almond, Coleman, and Herbert Bailey, memorandum on title of book, November 18, 1959, DRP. Almond responded, "It occurred to me that the title 'Politics of Developing Areas' might solve all of our problems and get us away from the fuzziness and clichéd quality of 'Political Systems in Transition.' If you still have problems let us know." Almond to Rustow, December 7, 1959, DRP.

58. Coleman, memorandum, January 19, 1959, DRP.

59. Ibid.; Oren, *Our Enemies and US*, p. 147.

60. Coleman, conclusion to Almond and Coleman, *Politics of Developing Areas*, pp. 558, 561.

61. In characteristic fashion, and consistent with his poetic sensibilities, Rustow continued, saying, "Except that, after one long and intense summer that we spent at Stanford University, I could not resist venting my dissent at a 'fun and farewell party' with an adaptation of a song from *Porgy and Bess:* 'It ain't necessarily so / Structures and functions / Parsonian disjunctions / They ain't necessarily so. . . . Little matrix was small, but, oh my! / When it got debated / It got so inflated.'" Rustow, "Connections," p. 280.

62. Rustow, "The Politics of the Near East," p. 452.

63. "Turkey at Mid-Century," unpublished, n.d., DRP. The books under review included Thornburg, *Turkey: An Economic Appraisal*; Eleanor Bisbee, *The New Turks: Pioneers of the Republic, 1920–1950* (Philadelphia: University of Pennsylvania Press, 1951); Lewis Thomas and Richard Frye, *The United States and Turkey and Iran* (Cambridge, MA: Harvard University Press, 1951); and James S. Barker et al., *The Economy of Turkey: An Analysis and Recommendations for a Development Program* (Washington, DC: IBRD, 1951).

64. Titles of the SSRC CCP series in political development include Pye and Verba, *Political Culture and Political Development*; Weiner and LaPalombara, *Political Parties and Political Development*; Lucian Pye, ed., *Communications and Political Development* (Princeton, NJ: Princeton University Press, 1963); Joseph LaPalombara, ed., *Bureaucracy and Political Development* (Princeton, NJ: Princeton University Press, 1963); James Coleman, *Education and Political Development* (Princeton, NJ: Princeton University Press, 1965).

65. See Paul Cammack, *Capitalism and Democracy in the Third World: The Doctrine for Political Development* (London: Leicester University Press, 1997) for a detailed assessment of the series.

66. Almond, preface to Ward and Rustow, *Political Modernization in Japan and Turkey*, pp. v–vi.

67. Those who contributed to the volume with writings on Turkey were Halil Inalcık, Roderic Davison, Peter Sugar, Frederick Frey, Kemal Karpat, Richard Chambers, and Arif Payaslıoğlu. Other names initially considered to attend the conference were Bernard Lewis, Nermin Abadan, Şerif Mardin, and Aydın Yalçın.

68. Minutes of the Seminar on Political Development on Japan and Turkey, Dobbs Ferry, New York, September 10–14, 1962, DRP.

69. Ward and Rustow, introduction and conclusion to *Political Modernization in Japan and Turkey*, pp. 3–4, 464, 467.

70. Halil İnalcık, "Türkiye ve Japonya'nın Siyasi Modernleşmesi Üzerine Bir Konferans" [A conference on the political modernization of Turkey and Japan], *Türk Kültürü* 1 (November 1962): 50.

71. "Neden Iki Memleket?" [Why two nations?], *Milliyet*, January 29, 1963; "Önderlik Ordudaydı" [The leadership was with the army], *Milliyet*, February 5, 1963.

72. Berkes ended up teaching at McGill University. Niyazi Berkes, *Unutulan Yıllar* [The forgotten years] (Istanbul: Iletişim, 1997).

73. Niyazi Berkes, "Review Essay: Political Modernization in Japan and Turkey," *International Journal* 20, no. 2 (1965): 271.

74. Nermin Abadan, "Siyasal İlimlerde Gelişim Eğilimleri: Birleşik Amerika, İngiltere, Batı Almanya ve Fransa'daki Çalışmaların Mukayeseli İncelenmesi" [Developments in the social sciences: A comparative analysis of research in the United States, England, West Germany and France], *Ankara Üniversitesi SBF Dergisi* 17, no. 3 (1962): 188.

75. Yavuz Abadan, "Mukayeseli Devlet İdaresinin Ana Konuları ve Ortadoğu" [Issues in comparative government and the Middle East), *Ankara Üniversitesi SBF Dergisi* 17, no. 3 (1962): 114, 122.

76. Şerif Mardin, "Türkiye'de Muhalefet ve Kontrol," in *Türk Modernleşmesi* (Istanbul: İletişim Yayinlari, 1991), p. 177. For his assessment of behavioralism, see Mardin, *Din ve Ideoloji* [Religion and ideology] (Istanbul: Iletişim, 1983).

77. Özer Ozankaya, "Japonya'nın Modernleşme Denemesi" [Japan's attempt at modernization], *Ankara Üniversitesi SBF Dergisi* 20, no. 1 (1965): 307; Ozankaya, "Toplumsal Değişme Olarak İktisadi Gelişme" [Economic development as social change], *Ankara Üniversitesi SBF Dergisi* 20, no. 1 (1965); Ozankaya, "The Stages of Economic Growth," *Ankara Üniversitesi SBF Dergisi* 20, no. 2 (1965).

78. Frey, "Niçin Türkiye?" [Why Turkey?], *Forum* 11, no. 128 (1959); Dankwart Rustow, "1954 Seçimleriyle ilgili Mutalaalar" [Some observations regarding the 1954 elections], *Forum* 4, no. 15 (1954). Essays by Howard Reed and Richard Robinson were also translated.

79. Mümtaz Soysal, "Eksik Kalmış Kitaplar" [The missing books], *Forum* 8, no. 59 (1958); Kemal Karpat, "Köy Kalkınmasının Esasları" [The principles of rural development], *Forum* 7, no. 82 (1957); Karpat, "Köy Kalkınmasında Bilim Metodu" [The scientific method in rural development], *Forum* 7, no. 78 (1957); Şerif Mardin, "Köprü Kurmak" [To build a bridge], *Forum* 13, no. 140 (1960); Aydın Yalçın, "Aydınların Sorumluluğu" [Intellectuals' responsibility], *Forum* 4, no. 37 (1955).

80. Rustow insisted that Kemal's political victims were far fewer than those of comparable regimes, numbering "several dozen, at most a few hundred (or, if we include the risings in Anatolia in 1920 and in Kurdistan in 1925, a few thousand)." Rustow, "Ataturk as Founder," p. 806.

81. Andrew Cordier to Rustow, February 5, 1965, DRP.

82. Their acquaintance dated to 1957 when Rustow reviewed Karpat's *Politics in Turkey* for Princeton University Press. Rustow went so far as to appease the worries of the Press regarding Karpat's visa problems in the late 1950s when he was teaching at Montana State University. Karpat to Rustow, September 8, 1958, DRP; Rustow to Karpat, November 29, 1958, DRP; Gordon Hubel to Rustow, November 17, 1958, DRP; Rustow to Hubel, December 3, 1958, DRP.

83. Emin Tanrıyar, *Dağı Delen Irmak: Kemal H. Karpat Söyleşi Kitabı* [The river that runs through the mountain: A conversation with Kemal Karpat] (Ankara: Imge, 2008), p. 273.

84. Proposal for a Program of Social-Science Research on Turkey at Columbia University, December 1964, DRP.

85. Proposal for a Center of Turkish Studies, n.d., DRP. The efforts of Karpat and Rustow to "stimulate new scholarly interest" in Turkey also gave rise to a conference sponsored by the SSRC and the Department of Politics at NYU. Proposal for a Conference on Democracy and Economic Development in Turkey, November 1964, DRP. The findings of this conference were published in Karpat, *Social Change and Politics in Turkey.*

86. In 1957, Celal Bayar, the president and founder of the Democrat Party in Turkey, said, "It is our hope that in thirty years with a population of fifty million, Turkey will become a small America." Nihat Erim, secretary general of the Kemalist Republican People's Party, had already proclaimed in 1949 that "barring some unforeseen catastrophe . . . in the near future Turkey will become a 'little America.'" Feroz Ahmad and Bedia Turgay Ahmad, *Türkiye'de Çok Partili Politikanın Açıklamalı Kronolojisi (1945–1971)* [A chronological account of multiparty politics in Turkey] (Ankara: Bilgi, 1976), pp. 50, 175.

87. Lerner, *Passing*, pp. viii, 79.

88. Fourth Meeting, Group on American Policy in the Middle East, 1951–1952, March 3, 1952, box 148, folder 4, Records of the Council on Foreign Relations, Series 3, Seely G. Mudd Library, Princeton University, Princeton (hereafter cited as CFR Records). Thomas gave the matter of Turkey's racial makeup considerable thought: "The Turks are definitely 'white,' although this has never seemed very important to them. . . . It is not very unusual to find light blonds as well as dark brunets, and even flaming redheads represented in a single family group, and eye color, too, has a comparable range" (Thomas and Frye, *The United States and Turkey and Iran*, p. 29).

89. First Meeting, Group on the Middle East and Modern Islam, 1958–1959, November 5, 1958, box 76, folder 1, CFR Records.

90. Aydın Yalçın, "Türkiye'de Demokrasi" [Democracy in Turkey], reprinted in *Forum* 10, no. 119 (1959).

91. McGhee to State, May 11, 1952, Record Group 59, 782.11/5-1952, General Records of the Department of State, National Archives.

92. McGhee, "Turkey Joins the West," pp. 617–30.

93. George McGhee, *On the Frontline in the Cold War: An Ambassador Reports* (Westport, CT: Praeger, 1997), pp. 12–13.

94. George C. McGhee, oral history interview by Richard McKinzie, June 11, 1975, Truman Library Online, Washington DC, https://www.trumanlibrary.org/oralhist/mcgheeg.htm.

95. Citino, *Envisioning the Arab Future*, pp. 83–89.

96. Edwin Cohn, "Some Propositions Concerning the Role of Human Factors in Economic Development," October 14, 1957, box 164, folder 4, CFR Records.

97. US policy makers also encouraged limited strategies in import substitution industrialization in places like the Philippines and Argentina in order to create favorable conditions for foreign direct investment. Sylvia Maxfield and James H. Nolt, "Protectionism and the Internationalization of Capital: US Sponsorship of Import Substitution Industrialization in the Philippines, Turkey and Argentina," *International Studies Quarterly* 34, no. 1 (March 1990): 49–81; Guy Laron, *Origins of the Suez Crisis: Postwar De-*

velopment Diplomacy and the Struggle over Third World Industrialization, 1945–56 (Baltimore: Johns Hopkins University Press, 2013).

98. According to Çağlar Keyder, "In one of the first instances when international organizations forced a developing country's government to adopt more planning, World Bank and OECD experts urged Menderes to form a planning board in order to impose some logic and control over public spending and the allocation of foreign exchange." *State and Class in Turkey: A Study in Capitalist Development* (London: Verso, 1987), p. 135.

99. Hurewitz, "Varying Military Styles in the Middle East," background paper, First Meeting, Group on the Military in the Middle East, 1963–1964, October 23, 1963, box 174, folder 3, CFR Records; Hurewitz, "Military Modernizers: Similarity and Difference in the Turkish and Egyptian Experiences," background paper, Second Meeting, Group on the Military in the Middle East, 1963–1964, November 26, 1963, folder 3, box 174, CFR Records.

100. First Meeting, Group on the Military in the Middle East, 1963–1964, October 23, 1963, box 174, folder 3, CFR Records.

101. Some Japan scholars, such as Inoki, suggested that the army had actually been a factor of nonmodernization in Japan. Peter Sugar argued that the army could retard modernization as well. Minutes of the Seminar on Political Development on Japan and Turkey, September 10–14, 1962, Dobbs Ferry, New York, DRP.

102. Rustow to editor, *New York Times*, May 5, 1960, DRP.

103. Second Meeting, Group on the Military in the Middle East, 1963–1964, November 26, 1963, folder 3, box 174, CFR Records; Lerner and Robinson, "Swords and Ploughshares"; Richard Robinson, *The First Turkish Republic: A Case Study in National Development* (Cambridge, MA: Harvard University Press, 1963); Haluk Ülman and Frank Tachau, "Turkish Politics: The Attempt to Reconcile Rapid Modernization with Democracy," *Middle East Journal* 19, no. 2 (Spring 1965).

104. Rustow, "Transitions to Democracy: Turkey's Experience in Historical and Comparative Perspective," in *State, Democracy, and the Military: Turkey in the 1980s*, eds. Metin Heper and Ahmet Evin (New York: Walter de Gruyter, 1988), pp. 242–43.

105. Citino, *Envisioning the Arab Future*, pp. 90–92; Osamah Khalil, *America's Dream Palace: Middle East Expertise and the Rise of the National Security State* (Cambridge, MA: Harvard University Press, 2016), pp. 196–99; Weldon Matthews, "The Kennedy Administration, Counterinsurgency, and Iraq's First Ba'thist Regime," *International Journal of Middle East Studies* 43 (2011): 635–53; Bradley Simpson, *Economists with Guns: Authoritarian Development and US-Indonesian Relations, 1960–1968* (Stanford, CA: Stanford University Press, 2008); Cammack, *Capitalism and Democracy*.

106. Oren, *Our Enemies and US*; Engerman, *Modernization from the Other Shore*.

107. Rustow, *A World of Nations*, pp. 3, 5, 8.

108. Ibid., p. 143.

109. Ibid., p. 141.

110. Ibid., pp. 131–32.

111. Rustow, "Modernization and Comparative Politics: Prospects in Research and Theory," *Comparative Politics* 1, no. 1 (October 1968): 43.

112. Ibid., pp. 42, 43, 45.

113. Joy Rohde, *Armed with Expertise: The Militarization of American Social Research during the Cold War* (Ithaca, NY: Cornell University Press, 2013), p. 112.

114. Rustow, "Days of Crisis," *The New Leader*, May 20, 1968.

115. Rustow, "Relevance in Social Science, or the Proper Study of Mankind," *American Scholar* 40, no. 3 (1971): 487, 496.

116. Ibid., pp. 489, 492–93.

117. Benjamin W. Smith to Dankwart Rustow, October 18, 1971, DRP.

118. Benjamin Smith, "Some Notes on the Social Science Research Council and the Governing Class Theory of American Politics," in *Political Science Enters the 1970s: Abstracts of Papers Presented at the 66th Annual Meeting of the American Political Science Association, September 8–12, 1970, Los Angeles, California*, ed. Richard L. Merritt (Washington, DC: American Political Science Association, 1971), p. 17.

119. Ibid., p. 208.

120. Rustow, "Transitions to Democracy: Towards a Dynamic Model," *Comparative Politics* 2, no. 3 (April 1970).

121. Rustow, *Turkey: America's Forgotten Ally* (New York: Council on Foreign Relations, 1987).

Chapter 2

Portions of this chapter are adapted from Begüm Adalet, "Questions of Modernization: Coding Speech, Regulating Attitude in Survey Research," *Comparative Studies in Society and History* 57, no. 4 (October 2015) and reprinted with permission from Cambridge University Press.

1. Frederick Frey, George Angell, and Abdurrahman Sanay, *Lise Seviyesindeki Öğrencilerin Değer Sistemleri: Öğrencilerin Meslek Gruplarına Bağladıkları Değerler* [The value systems of high-school students: The values students ascribe to occupational groups] (Ankara: MEB Talim ve Terbiye Dairesi Eğitim Araştırmaları ve Değerlendirme Merkezi, 1962).

2. Nermin Abadan, *Üniversite Öğrencilerinin Serbest Zaman Faaliyetleri: Ankara Yüksek Öğrenim Gençliği Üzerinde Bir Araştırma* [The spare-time activities of university students: A study of Ankara higher-education youth] (Ankara: Ankara Universitesi SBF Yayınları, 1962).

3. Arif Payaslıoğlu and Frederick Frey, "Babalarının Mensup Olduğu Meslekler Bakımından Siyasal Bilgiler Fakültesi Öğrencileri Üzerinde Bir İnceleme" [A study of political-science students in terms of their fathers' occupations], *Ankara Üniversitesi SBF Dergisi* 13, no. 3 (1958); A. T. J. Matthews, *Emergent Turkish Administrators: A Study of the Vocational and Social Attitudes of Junior and Potential Administrators* (Ankara: Turk Tarih Kurumu Basimevi, 1955); Fahir H. Armaoğlu and Guthrie G. Birkhead, *Siyasal Bilgiler Fakültesi 1946–55 Mezunları Hakkında Bir Araştırma* [A study of the 1946–55 graduates of the political-science faculty] (Ankara: TODAIE, 1956); A Committee of the Ankara University Faculty of Political Science, *Economic and Social Aspects of Farm Mechanization in Turkey* (Ankara: Ankara Üniversitesi SBF, 1953); Frey, "Survey-

ing Peasant Attitudes in Turkey," *The Public Opinion Quarterly* 27, no. 3 (1963); A Committee of the Ankara University Faculty of Political Science and New York University Graduate School of Public Administration and Social Service, *Kaza ve Vilayet İdaresi Üzerinde Bir Araştırma* [A study of the administration of provinces and districts] (Ankara: Ankara Üniversitesi SBF Yayınları, 1957); Nermin Abadan, *Batı Almanya'daki Türk İşçileri ve Sorunları* [Turkish workers and their problems in Western Germany] (Ankara: T. C. Başbakanlık Devlet Planlama Teşkilatı, 1964); Leslie Roos, "Development versus Distribution: An Attitudinal Study of Turkish Local Administration," *Economic Development and Cultural Change* 17, no. 4 (July 1969).

4. Latour, *Reassembling the Social*, p. 85. On documents as knowledge practices, see Annelise Riles, ed., *Documents: Artifacts of Modern Knowledge* (Ann Arbor: The University of Michigan Press, 2006); Foucault, *The Archaeology of Knowledge*.

5. Shah, *The Production of Modernization;* Khalil, *America's Dream Palace*, chap. 6.

6. Herbert Hyman, *Taking Society's Measure: A Personal History of Survey Research* (New York: Russell Sage Foundation, 1991), pp. 157–58.

7. Lucian Pye, "The Developing Areas: Field Research in the Developing Areas," in Ward, *Studying Politics Abroad*, pp. 5, 11.

8. Mitchell, "The Middle East," pp. 85–86.

9. The practice of survey methodology in political science was not a novelty in the aftermath of the war: "pioneering survey work" was already conducted in Charles Merriam's program at the University of Chicago in the 1920s. Jean Converse, *Survey Research in the United States: Roots and Emergence* (Berkeley: University of California Press, 1987).

10. Herbert Hyman, "Studying Expert Informants by Survey Methods: A Cross-National Inquiry," *The Public Opinion Quarterly* 31, no. 1 (Spring 1967): 9.

11. Converse, *Survey Research*.

12. Herbert Hyman, "The Sample Survey: Its Nature, History, Utilization and Effects" (a preliminary report to the National Science Board, February 1979), box 2, folder 5, Herbert Hyman Papers, Rare Book & Manuscript Library, Columbia University (hereafter cited as HHP).

13. Sidney Verba, "The Uses of Survey Research in the Study of Comparative Politics: Issues and Strategies," *Historical Social Research* 18, no. 2 (1993): 56–59; Frederick Frey, "Cross-Cultural Survey Research in Political Science," in *The Methodology of Comparative Research*, eds. Robert T. Holt and John E. Turner (New York: The Free Press, 1970).

14. Herbert Hyman, "Research Design," in Ward, *Studying Politics Abroad*, p. 182.

15. Frey, "Cross-Cultural Survey Research," p. 179 (emphasis in the original).

16. Payaslıoğlu and Frey, "Babalarının Mensup Olduğu Meslekler," p. 229; Herbert McClosky, *Political Inquiry: The Nature and Uses of Survey Research* (New York: MacMillan, 1969), p. 2.

17. Stein Rokkan, ed., "Comparative Survey Analysis: Trends, Issues, Strategies," in *Comparative Survey Analysis*, vol. 12, Confluence; Surveys of Research in the Social Sciences (The Hague: Mouton, 1969), p. 15.

18. Frey, "Surveying Peasant Attitudes," pp. 335–36.

19. Herbert Hyman, Arif Payaslıoğlu, and Frederick Frey, "The Values of Turkish College Youth," *The Public Opinion Quarterly* 22, no. 3 (Autumn 1958): 276.

20. Verba, "The Uses of Survey Research," p. 69; Myron Weiner, "Political Interviewing," in Ward, *Studying Politics Abroad*, pp. 127–28; Robert E. Mitchell, "Survey Materials Collected in the Developing Countries," in *Comparative Research Across Cultures and Nations*, ed. Stein Rokkan, Publications of the International Social Science Council, no. 8. (The Hague: Mouton, 1968), p. 224.

21. Daniel Lerner, introduction to "Attitude Research in Modernizing Areas," *Public Opinion Quarterly* 22, no. 3 (1958): 221.

22. Lloyd Rudolph and Susanne Rudolph, "Surveys in India: Field Experience in Madras State," *Public Opinion Quarterly* 22, no. 3 (Autumn 1958): 236.

23. Verba, "The Uses of Survey Research," pp. 67–68.

24. Frank Bonilla, "Survey Techniques," in Ward, *Studying Politics Abroad*, p. 140.

25. Tsing, *Friction*, p. 4.

26. Verba, "The Uses of Survey Research," p. 81.

27. Daniel Lerner, "Survey Research on Political Modernization," 1949–1976, box 13, folder 1, Daniel Lerner Papers, Manuscript Collection-MC 336, MIT Institute Archives and Special Collections (hereafter cited as DLP).

28. Popp, "An Application of Modernization Theory," p. 82; Oren, *Our Enemies and US*. Almond's major foray into cross-national survey research on political attitudes was coauthored by Sidney Verba. See Gabriel Almond and Sidney Verba, *The Civic Culture: Political Attitudes and Democracy in Five Nations* (Princeton, NJ: Princeton University Press, 1963).

29. Christopher Simpson, *Science of Coercion: Communication Research and Psychological Warfare, 1945–1960* (New York: Oxford University Press, 1994), p. 180. I would like to thank an anonymous CSSH reviewer for bringing this to my attention.

30. Daniel Lerner and David Riesman, "Self and Society: Reflections on Some Turks in Transition," *Explorations* 5 (June 1955): 68.

31. Shah, *The Production of Modernization*, p. 101.

32. Lerner, *Passing*, p. 45.

33. Lerner's dissertation, *Sykewar* (1948), chronicles his military research. Box 1, folders 3 and 5, DLP. It was Joseph Stycos, the chief of the BASR project, who described the rationale of the project as psychological warfare. See American Association for Public Opinion Research Conference Proceedings, "Contributions of Opinion Research to Psychological Warfare," in Simpson, *Science of Coercion*, p. 66.

34. The original contract between BASR and VOA, signed in 1949, stipulated the conduct of research in France, Italy, Germany, Austria, Sweden, Greece, Brazil, Spain, and Egypt. It was after a series of replacements that the Middle East survey was arrived at, and the content of the study was changed to inquire after the role of mass media in the orientation of respondents towards their own government and foreign countries engaging in propaganda activities. See Shah, *The Production of Modernization*, pp. 83–84.

35. Other rapporteurs included Elihu Katz, Siegfried Kracauer, and Mayone Stycos.

36. Shah, *The Production of Modernization*, chaps. 4 and 5.

37. Lerner and Riesman, "Self and Society," p. 74. On the link between CENIS and the CIA, see Bruce Cummings, "Boundary Displacement: Area Studies and International Studies During and After the Cold War," in *Universities and Empire: Money and Politics in the Social Sciences During the Cold War*, ed. Christopher Simpson (New York: New Press, 1998).

38. Daniel Lerner, "A Scale Pattern of Opinion Correlates: Communication Networks, Media Exposure, and Concomitant Response," *Sociometry* 16, no. 3 (August 1953): 269.

39. Lerner, *Passing*, pp. 54, 69–70, 144.

40. Ibid., p. 147.

41. Lerner and Riesman, "Self and Society," p. 78

42. Daniel Lerner and Suzanne Keller, "Empathy in Cross-National and Occupational Perspective," July 1957, box 11, folder 42, CENIS, MIT, DLP (my emphasis).

43. Lerner, "Interviewing Frenchmen," *American Journal of Sociology* 62, no. 2 (1956): 191–92.

44. Lerner, *Passing*, p. 148.

45. Lerner and Riesman, "Self and Society," pp. 70 and 77.

46. Ibid., p. 70.

47. I would like to thank one of the anonymous reviewers at *CSSH* for this turn of phrase.

48. Box 9, folder 7, Ist-35-City, "Middle East Surveys," ca. 1950, DLP. The same respondent refused to quantify and rank his newspaper reading experience, saying, "I am not accustomed to make reckonings by figures even in material matters. I leave it to you to derive the answers of these questions, from the [descriptive] answers I gave concerning movies, newspapers, and radios." Asked about his opinion of the interview as a whole, he deplored that "human nature is not to be treated, in my opinion, as a calculating machine which is the case with regards [*sic*] the majority of the questions involved in this questionnaire."

49. Box 9, folder 2, Ist-13-City, "Middle East Surveys," ca. 1950, DLP.

50. Box 12, folder 13, Ank-71-City, "Middle East Surveys," ca. 1950, DLP.

51. Box 9, folder 2, Ist-13-City, "Middle East Surveys," ca. 1950, DLP.

52. Box 9, folder 3, Izmir-47-City, "Middle East Surveys," ca. 1950, DLP.

53. Lerner, *Passing*, p. 19.

54. Ibid., pp. 23, 27–28, 41, 72.

55. Lerner, *Passing*, pp. 24–25.

56. Lerner, "A Scale Pattern of Opinion Correlates," pp. 269–70.

57. Lerner, *Passing*, p. 22.

58. Lerner and Riesman, "Self and Society," p. 72.

59. Lerner, *Passing*, pp. 43, 77.

60. In his account of his follow-up visit to Balgat, Lerner also provides descriptions of the two additional interviewers who accompanied him. One was Tahir S., who received an accolade from Lerner because of his composed deportment in the question-and-answer setting. Lerner said he was "always the American trained interviewer." The

other was Zilla K., who fits the profile of the female interviewer Lerner had "ordered 'by the numbers': thirtyish, semitrained, alert, compliant with instructions, not sexy enough to impede our relations with the men of Balgat but chic enough to provoke the women" (*Passing*, pp. 29, 34). Lerner's meticulous instructions suggest that the amount of work that went into obtaining the kind of interlocutor that would occasion the interview process was emblematic of survey research functioning as the stage for modernity itself.

61. Box 9, folder 8, Ist-40-city, "Middle East Surveys," ca. 1950, DLP; Box 9, folder 13, Ank-70-city, "Middle East Surveys," ca. 1950, DLP.

62. Box 9, folder 2, Ist-18-rural, "Middle East Surveys," ca. 1950, DLP.

63. Box 9, folder 5, Izmir-31-city, "Middle East Surveys," ca. 1950, DLP.

64. Box 8, folder 12, Ist-27-city, "Middle East Surveys," ca. 1950, DLP.

65. Box 9, folder 3, Ist-42-rural, "Middle East Surveys," ca. 1950, DLP; Box 9, folder 7, Ist-35-city, "Middle East Surveys," ca. 1950, DLP.

66. Lerner, *Passing*, p. 76.

67. Ibid., pp. 42, 76.

68. Ibid., pp. 47, 79, 105.

69. Frey, Angell, and Sanay, *Lise Seviyesi*, p. 3.

70. Frederick W. Frey, "Education," in Ward and Rustow, *Political Modernization in Japan and Turkey*, pp. 224, 225, 230.

71. On the commitment to democratic forms, Frey's questionnaire repeated verbatim the questions from a previous, cross-national survey. For example, one question read as follows: "Democracy is often defined in the words of Abraham Lincoln as 'government of the people, by the people, and for the people.' If you were forced to do so, would you personally give greater emphasis to the conception 'by the people' or 'for the people'?" James Gillespie and Gordon Allport, *Youth's Outlook on the Future* (Garden City, NY: Doubleday, 1955), p. 51. On Frey's recoding of the questionnaire, see "Democratic Potential/Values Study (Turkey)," enclosed in Frederick Frey to Herbert Hyman, June 27, 1959, box 2, folder 5, HHP.

72. Abadan, *Üniversite Öğrencileri*, pp. 6, 44, 87, 124. Abadan's hypothetical questions drew from Lerner's. One question was, for example, "What do you dream about becoming?" The options ranged from excelling at one's job to becoming a millionaire or a great artist to acting as the president or the prime minister to living as a citizen of another state (p. 147).

73. Ibid., p. 63; Latour, *Science in Action*, p. 43.

74. Nermin Abadan-Unat, *Kum Saatini İzlerken* [Watching the hourglass] (Istanbul: İletişim Yayınları, 1996), p. 174.

75. Nermin Abadan, *Halk Efkarı* [Public opinion] (Ankara: Ankara Üniversitesi SBF Yayınları, 1956); Abadan, "Devlet İdaresinde Menfaat Gruplarının Rolü" [The role of interest groups in government], *Ankara Üniversitesi SBF Dergisi* 14, no. 1 (1959); "Radyonun Görevi ve Tesir Alanı" [The function of the radio and its sphere of influence], *Forum* 4, no. 47 (1956).

76. Abadan, *Üniversite Öğrencileri*, pp. 8–10.

77. Herbert Hyman, "Sosyal Bilimler Metodolojisine Giriş Ders Notları" [Introduction to the methodology of the social sciences: 1957–1958], trans. Arif Payaslıoğlu, box 1, folder 2, HHP.

78. Hyman, *Taking Society's Measure*, pp. 128–29. Hyman returned to Japan in 1947 as a member of the expert mission on public opinion and sociological research, and he spent the 1950–1951 academic year in Oslo as a visiting professor in methodology. Box 7, folder 15, HHP.

79. Herbert Hyman, *Interviewing in Social Research* (Chicago: University of Chicago Press, 1954).

80. Hyman, "Sosyal Bilimler Metodolojisi," p. 85 (emphasis in original).

81. Hyman, Payaslıoğlu, and Frey, "The Values of Turkish College Youth," pp. 278–79, 280, 281.

82. "Strategies in Comparative Survey Research," presented at the Inter-University Consortium for Political Research, 1963, box 1, folder 11, HHP. Interestingly, Hyman found Lerner's empathy index to be an instance of such haphazard comparative work, which, despite the latter's "meticulous" method, led the reader to "somehow *contrast [the empathy index] mentally* [emphasis in original] with a Western, modern society, of which we have no empirical example." Hyman continued, "Wouldn't it be ironic if he subsequently found a lot of immobile personalities, nonparticipant types in the United States or Great Britain?" The irony seems to have eluded Hyman and his collaborators when they presumed Arabic-speaking youth to be imbued with a traditional mindset.

83. Hyman, Payaslıoğlu, and Frey, "The Values of Turkish College Youth," p. 275.

84. Matthews, *Emergent Turkish Administrators;* Armaoğlu and Birkhead, *Siyasal Bilgiler Fakültesi 1946–55 Mezunları.*

85. Payaslıoğlu and Frey, "Babalarının Mensup Olduğu Meslekler," p. 229.

86. Holly Shissler, "'If You Ask Me': Sabiha Sertel's Advice Column, Gender Equity, and Social Engineering in the Early Turkish Republic," *Journal of Middle East Women's Studies* 3, no. 2 (Spring 2007): 8. Sabiha Sertel, who published questions about particular topics and asked the readers to mail in their responses in *Resimli Ay* through the 1920s, had studied survey methodology with William Ogburn at the New York School of Social Work. Ogburn would later move to the University of Chicago, where he trained other survey methodologists, most notably, Samuel Stouffer.

87. Niyazi Berkes, *Bazı Ankara Köyleri Üzerinde Bir Araştırma* [A study of some Ankara villages] (Ankara: Uzluk Basımevi, 1942); Muzaffer Şerif, *An Outline of Social Psychology*, rev. ed. (New York: Harper, 1956); Behice Boran, *Toplumsal Yapı Araştırmaları: İki Köy Çeşidinin Mukayeseli Tetkiki* [Studies in social structure: A comparative analysis of two village types] (Ankara: Türk Tarih Kurumu Basımevi, 1945).

88. Şerif and Berkes continued teaching in the United States and Canada, respectively, whereas Boran stayed in Turkey and led the Workers' Party in the 1960s.

89. Lerner, *Passing*, pp. 122, 127, 131–33; Hyman, "Research Design," p. 176; Herbert Hyman, "Mass Media and Political Socialization: The Role of Patterns of Communication," in Pye, *Communications and Political Development*, p. 145. On Berkes' partic-

ipation, see Charles Glock to Emily Krueger, July 17, 1956, entry 1021, box 20, Country Project Correspondence, 1952–1963, Record Group 306, Records of the US Information Agency, National Archives (hereafter cited as RG 306).

90. Payaslıoğlu and Frey, "Babalarının Mensup Olduğu Meslekler," pp. 241–43.

91. Tsing, *Friction*, p. 3.

92. Şefik Uysal, "Türkiye'de Yapılan Sosyolojik Araştırmalar" [*Sociological research in Turkey*], in *Türkiye'de Sosyal Araştırmaların Gelişmesi: Hacettepe Nüfus Etütleri Enstitüsü ve Türk Sosyal Bilimler Derneği Seminerinde Sunulan Bildiriler* [The development of social research in Turkey: Proceedings of the seminar by the Turkish Social Sciences Association and the Institute of Population Studies at Hacettepe University] (Ankara: Hacettepe Üniversitesi Yayınları, 1971), p. 151.

93. The agreement with PEVA continued between 1965 and 1968. RG 306, entry 1021, box 17, Office of Research, Western Europe, 1964–1973.

94. Arif Payaslıoğlu to Leo Crespi, March 19, 1959; Leo Crespi to Herbert Hyman, June 23, 1958; George Schweller to Helen Crossley, August 22, 1960. All in RG 306, entry 1021, box 20, Country Project Correspondence, 1952–1963.

95. Frey was a frequent State Department consultant. Gail Matthews, "Modern-Day Role Explored: The Political Scientist and Society," *The Christian Science Monitor*, July 11, 1964.

96. Frey "Surveying Peasant Attitudes," pp. 338–39

97. Frey, "Cross-Cultural Survey Research," p. 202.

98. Frey, "Political Leadership in Turkey: The Social Backgrounds of Deputies to the Grand National Assembly, 1920–1957" (PhD diss., Princeton University, 1962), 13, 77.

99. Frey, "Surveying Peasant Attitudes," pp. 350–51.

100. Frederick Frey and Herbert Hyman, *Rural Development Research Project Report 1: General Description and Evaluation* (Cambridge, MA: MIT, 1967).

101. Frey, "Surveying Peasant Attitudes," p. 348.

102. Ibid., p. 353. This admission of employing Kurdish-speaking interviewers would have been controversial: Frey once complained to Hyman that Nermin Abadan was contacted by the Rockefeller Foundation to do a study on informal social communication on "some Kurds," and "she was incensed by the idea that there were Kurds in Turkey and that a 'foreign' agency (by innuendo probably a tool of the CIA) should want to investigate any such people" (Frey to Hyman, June 27, 1959, HHP, box 2, folder 5). I have not been able to locate this survey.

103. Latour, *Science in Action*, 223.

104. Frederick Frey and Ayşe Sertel, *Rural Development Research Project Report No. 6: Land Ownership and Peasant Orientations in Rural Turkey* (Cambridge, MA: CENIS, 1967); Frey, *Rural Development Research Project Report No. 3: The Mass Media and Rural Development in Turkey* (Cambridge, MA: CENIS, 1966); Frey, *Rural Development Research Project Report No. 4: Regional Variations in Rural Turkey* (Cambridge, MA: CENIS, 1966).

105. Frederick Frey and Noralou Roos, *Rural Development Research Project Report*

No. 7: The Propensity to Innovate among Turkish Peasants (Cambridge, MA: CENIS, 1967), pp. 8, 16.

106. Frederick Frey, Allan Kessler, and Joan Rothschild, *Rural Development Research Project Report No. 2: Index Construction and Validation* (Cambridge, MA: CENIS, 1967), p. 16.

107. The researchers refrained from inquiring directly about the ownership of land and radios, for instance. Araştırma Şubesi Toplum Yapısı Araştırma Grubu, *Türk Köyünde Modernleşme Eğilimleri Araştırması* [A study of tendencies of modernization in the Turkish village] (Ankara: Devlet Planlama Teşkilatı, 1970), pp. 8, 209–10, 253.

108. Çiğdem Kağıtçıbaşı, "Sosyal İlim Metodolojisi" [Social science methodology], in *Türkiye'de Sosyal Araştırmalar Gelişmesi: Hacettepe Nüfus Etütleri Enstitüsü ve Türk Sosyal Bilimler Derneği Seminerinde Sunulan Bildiriler* (Ankara: Hacettepe Üniversitesi Yayınları, 1971), p. 178.

109. Edwin Cohn, "The Climate for Research in the Social Sciences in Turkey," *Middle East Journal* 22, no. 2 (Spring 1968): 205.

110. Untitled, n.d., DLP, box 13, folder 27.

111. "Episode on Prince Street," *New York Times*, November 16, 1970.

112. Oğuz Erten, *Sıradışı Bir Hayattan Sıradışı Bir Sanata: Tosun Bayrak* [From an extraordinary life to an extraordinary art] (Istanbul: Galeri Baraz Yayınları, 2014). When I asked Bayrak about the questionnaires, he wrote that he remembered being paid to conduct the surveys as a USIS employee in Ankara, but he could not recall the questions he asked or the answers he collected (personal correspondence, April 29, 2017). I would like to thank Rüya Baraz for putting us in touch.

Chapter 3

1. Max Thornburg, "The Middle East and the American Engineer," *Journal of Engineering Education* 39 (March 1949): 333, 341, 343. Truman's speech, which inaugurated the Point Four Program, urged sharing Americans' inexhaustible, "imponderable resources in technical knowledge." Harry S. Truman, "Inaugural Address," January 20, 1949, https://www.trumanlibrary.org/whistlestop/50yr_archive/inagural20jan1949.htm.

2. Linda Williams Qaimmaqami, "The Catalyst of Nationalization: Max Thornburg and the Failure of Private Sector Developmentalism in Iran, 1947–1951," *Diplomatic History* 19, no. 1 (1995): 4.

3. Thornburg, *Turkey: An Economic Appraisal*, p. 109.

4. Ibid., p. 76.

5. Max Thornburg, *People and Policy in the Middle East: A Study of Political Change as a Basis for United States Policy* (New York: Norton, 1964).

6. Michael Adas, *Dominance by Design: Technological Imperatives and America's Civilizing Mission* (Cambridge, MA: The Belknap Press of Harvard University Press, 2006), p. 145.

7. Westad, *Global Cold War*. For a preliminary overview of Soviet projects, see David Engerman, "The Second World's Third World," *Kritika: Explorations in Russian and*

Eurasian History 12, no. 1 (2011): 183–211. As Engerman points out, the two superpowers were not alone in their bid for influence through technical-aid programs. For example, see Massimiliano Trentin, "Modernization as State-Building: The Two Germanies in Syria, 1962–1972," *Diplomatic History* 33, no. 3 (2009): 487–505; and Abou Bamba, "Triangulating a Modernization Experiment: The United States, France, and the Making of the Kossou Project in Central Ivory Coast," *Journal of Modern European History* 8, no. 1 (2010): 66–84.

8. Ekbladh, *The Great American Mission*, p. 8. On TVA replicas across Vietnam, Afghanistan, and India, among others, see Citino, *Envisioning the Arab Future*; Nick Cullather, "Damming Afghanistan: Modernization in a Buffer State," *The Journal of American History* 89, no. 9 (2002): 512–37; and Daniel Klingensmith, *"One Valley and a Thousand": Dams, Nationalism, and Development* (New Delhi: Oxford University Press, 2007). On aviation, see Jenifer Van Vleck, "An Airline at the Crossroads of the World: Ariana Afghan Airlines, Modernization, and the Global Cold War," *History and Technology* 25, no. 1 (2009): 3–24.

9. Jason Scott Smith, *Building New Deal Liberalism: The Political Economy of Public Works, 1933–1956* (Cambridge, UK: Cambridge University Press, 2006), p. 3.

10. Sarah Phillips, *This Land, This Nation: Conservation, Rural America and the New Deal* (Cambridge, UK: Cambridge University Press, 2007), pp. 244–45.

11. David Lilienthal, *TVA: Democracy on the March* (New York: Harper and Brothers, 1944), pp. 4–5.

12. See Gordon Clapp, *The TVA: An Approach to the Development of a Region* (Chicago: University of Chicago Press, 1955) for an overview of the critics and a defense.

13. Tolga Tőren, *Yeniden Yapılanan Dünya Ekonomisinde Marshall Planı ve Türkiye Uygulaması* [The Marshall Plan and its application in Turkey in the restructured world economy] (Istanbul: Sosyal Araştırmalar Vakfı, 2007), p. 174.

14. Laron, *Origins of the Suez Crisis*, p. 49.

15. Matthew Hull, "Documents and Bureaucracy," *Annual Review of Anthropology* 41 (2012): 253.

16. Ferguson, *The Anti-Politics Machine*; Escobar, *Encountering Development;* Scott, *Seeing Like a State*; Mitchell, *Rule of Experts*. See Li, *The Will to Improve* for an overview and a critique.

17. Penny Harvey and Hannah Knox, *Roads: An Anthropology of Infrastructure and Expertise* (Ithaca, NY: Cornell University Press, 2015), p. 198.

18. Thornburg, *Turkey: An Economic Appraisal*; Barker et al., *The Economy of Turkey*; Harold Hilts, *Türkiye'nin Yol Durumu* [Turkey's highway situation], p. 27, report delivered to the Ministry of Public Works, February 1948, Records of the General Directorate of Highways, Ankara (hereafter cited as KGM Records).

19. Diker was already in contact with the BPR prior to his trip, requesting monthly bulletins and publications pertaining to highway construction. See Vecdi Diker to Thomas MacDonald, November 1, 1944, box 510, record group 30, Bureau of Public Roads classified central files, 1912–1950, 015 Russia-Turkey—1942–1950, National Archives (hereafter cited as RG 30); MacDonald to Diker, April 28, 1945, RG 30.

20. Vecdi Diker, *Amerika Birleşik Devletleri Yol İşlerinde Yapılan Tetkikat Hakkında Rapor* [Report on the investigation at the US Bureau of Public Roads], Ankara, September 20, 1945, KGM Records.

21. Leyla Şen, *Türkiye'de Demiryolları ve Karayollarının Gelişim Süreci* [The development of railroads and highways in Turkey] (Ankara: Tesav Yayınları, 2003), p. 119.

22. *TC Bayındırlık Bakanlığı ile Amerikan Yardım Heyeti Arasında 26 Nisan 1948 Tarihinde Yapılan Antlaşmanın Kopyası* [Copy of the agreement signed between the Turkish Ministry of Public Works and the American Aid Group on April 26, 1948] (Ankara: TC Bayındırlık Bakanlığı Şose ve Köprüler Reisliği), KGM Records. The amount of American aid for highway construction totaled $43,101,226 between 1948 and 1959. Geoffrey Ireland, *Türkiye'de Karayolları Nakliyat İdaresi* [The administration of highway transportation in Turkey] (Ankara: Karayolları Genel Müdürlüğü, 1961), p. 257.

23. Yücel Mutlu, *Bayındırlık Bakanlığı Tarihi* [The history of the Ministry of Public Works] (Ankara: Bayındırlık ve İskan Bakanlığı, 2005), p. 337.

24. *1948–1960 KGM Çalışmaları Hakkında Rapor* [Report on the work of KGM between 1948 and 1960], KGM Records.

25. Interview with Vecdi Diker (1989) in Yollar Türk Milli Komitesi, *Karayolları Genel Müdürlüğü'nün Kurucusu Vecdi Diker'in Ardından* [After Vecdi Diker, the founder of the Directorate of Highways] (Ankara: YTKM, 1998), p. 67.

26. Matthew Huber, *Lifeblood: Oil, Freedom, and the Forces of Capital* (Minneapolis: University of Minnesota Press, 2013), p. 40.

27. Vecdi Diker, "Amerika'da Yol Sistemi ve Türkiye'de Tatbiki İktisadi Olabilecek Yol Tipleri" [The roads system in America and economically viable road types for Turkey (1938)], in Yollar Türk Milli Komitesi, *Vecdi Diker'in Ardından*, p. 16.

28. Cotten Seiler, *Republic of Drivers: A Cultural History of Automobility in America* (Chicago: University of Chicago Press, 2008), p. 5.

29. Diker, "Amerika'da Yol Sistemi," p. 29.

30. Robert Lehman, "Building Roads and a Highway Administration in Turkey," in *Hands Across Frontiers: Case Studies in Technical Cooperation*, eds. Howard M. Teaf and Peter G. Franck (Ithaca, NY: Publications of the Netherlands Universities Foundation for International Cooperation, 1955), p. 375.

31. Between 1949 and 1954, 509 engineers from thirty-five countries participated in the training programs. Bruce Seely, Donald Klinger, and Gary Klein, "'Push' and 'Pull' Factors in Technology Transfer: Moving American-Style Highway Engineering to Europe, 1945–1965," *Comparative Technology Transfer and Society* 2, no. 3 (December 2004): 236.

32. Jack Killalee, division engineer, to Aziz Torun, "Regarding Turkish Engineers Attending the Highway Course at DC Starting on May 16," March 4, 1949, KGM Records.

33. Talk presented to Turkish engineers at the General Directorate of Highways by F. G. Draper during their preparation for highway studies in the United States under the ECA Technical Assistance Program, May 2, 1950, Ankara, Turkey, KGM Records.

34. Russell Dorr to Ambassador George Wadsworth, August 27, 1949, entry 1399,

box 27, folder: Roads—1948–1949, Record Group 469, Records of US Foreign Assistance Agencies, 1948–1961, National Archives (hereafter cited as RG 469).

35. *Bakanlar Kurulunca Tasdik Edilen Devlet Yolları Ağı, Marshall Planı için Kabul Edilen Devlet Yolları, Bu Yolların Birbiriyle Mukayesesi* [The network of state roads approved by the cabinet, state roads approved for the Marshall Plan, a comparison of these roads], 1949, KGM Records; *Nafia İşlerinin Askeri Kıymetleri* [The military value of public works], 1952, KGM Records.

36. Robert P. Grathwol and Donita M. Moorhus, *Bricks, Sand, and Marble: US Army Corps of Engineers Construction in the Mediterranean and Middle East, 1947–1991* (Washington, DC: Center of Military History and Corps of Engineers, United States Army, 2009).

37. United States Department of State, *Aid to Turkey: Agreement between the United States of America and Turkey* (Washington, DC: Government Printing Office, 1947), p. 7.

38. Russell Dorr to Jesse Williams, November 15, 1949, entry 1399, box 27, folder: Roads—1948–1949, RG 469.

39. Orren McJunkins (deputy chief of ECA mission to Turkey) to Fevzi Lütfi Karaosmanoğlu (minister of state), November 22, 1950, entry 1399, box 26, folder: Roads—1952, RG 469; McJunkins to Vecdi Diker, September 9, 1950, entry 1399, box 26, folder: Roads—1952, RG 469.

40. Harold Hilts, "Highway Planning in Turkey" (speech, fall meeting of the American Society of Civil Engineers, November 3, 1949), box 4, Papers and Speeches of Harold Hilts, Office Files and Correspondence Concerning Particular Bureau Activities, RG 30. Hilts delivered different versions of the speech at engineering conferences in New Jersey; Harrisburg, Pennsylvania; and Utah.

41. Memorandum on Public Roads Program for Turkey, December 14, 1949, entry 1399, box 27, folder: Roads—1948–1949, RG 469.

42. Lehman, "Building Roads," p. 401. Private contractors had in fact been active in Turkey before the onset of the assistance program, with the Department of Roads and Bridges overseeing routine maintenance "on 'force account'—i.e., by the Department directly, hiring and supervising its own labor force" (p. 398). The new arrangement gave KGM the task of not only maintenance work but also engineering control and inspection rights over heavy construction, now undertaken by Turkish contractors, who were subject to stricter qualification tests. Robert Kerwin, "The Turkish Roads Program," *Middle East Journal* 4, no. 2 (April 1950): 203.

43. Smith, *Building New Deal Liberalism*, pp. 40–41.

44. Ibid., p. 232; see, for instance, Joint Committee on the Economic Report, *Highways and the Nation's Economy*, prepared with BPR representatives (Washington, DC: US Government Printing Office, 1950).

45. Russell Dorr to Edward Dickinson, November 28, 1949, entry 1399, box 25, folder: Roads—1950, RG 469.

46. Jeffrey Cody, *Exporting American Architecture, 1870–2000* (New York: Routledge, 2003), p. 139.

47. İlhan Tekeli and Selim Ilkin, *Cumhuriyetin Harcı: Modernin Altyapısı Oluşurken*

[The plaster of the republic: Forming the modern's infrastructure] (Istanbul: Bilgi Üniversitesi Yayınları, 2004), p. 413.

48. Harold Hilts to Jesse Williams, November 8, 1949, box 508, folder 2, RG 30. Hilts was confident in his organization's experience in the Pan-American Highway system (1930s) and postwar initiatives in the Philippines, Iran, Jordan, Yemen, Pakistan, and Europe. Seely, Klinger, and Klein, "'Push' and 'Pull' Factors."

49. Hilts to Williams, November 8, 1949, box 508, folder 2, RG 30; Dorr to Dickinson, December 8, 1949, entry 1399, box 25, folder: Roads—1950, RG 469.

50. Hilts to Diker, November 9, 1950, box 507, Turkey folders, RG 30.

51. Hilts to Williams, March 8, 1949, box 508, Turkey folders, RG 30; Paul Hoffmann to Thomas MacDonald, March 3, 1950, entry 1399, box 26, folder: Roads—1950, RG 469.

52. Mary Morgan, "Making Measuring Instruments," *History of Political Economy* 33 (2001): 235–251.

53. Dorr to Dickinson, December 8, 1949, entry 1399, box 25, folder: Roads—1950, RG 469.

54. Dorr to Huse, December 2, 1949, entry 1399, box 27, folder: Roads—1948–1949, RG 469 (emphasis in the original).

55. Memorandum on Public Roads Program for Turkey, December 14, 1949, entry 1399, box 27, folder: Roads—1948–1949, RG 469 (my emphasis).

56. Kerwin, "The Turkish Roads Program," pp. 206–7.

57. R. W. Gehring, highway engineer of the Bureau of Public Roads, to Lütfi Göze, chief of the planning and programming section, September 7, 1949, KGM Records.

58. Planlama Şube Müdürlüğü Toplantı Tutanağı, Minutes of the Planning Unit Meeting, June 6, 1949, KGM Records.

59. Planlama Şube Müdürlüğü Toplantı Tutanağı, Minutes of the Planning Unit Meeting, February 16, 1949, KGM Records.

60. "1948'de Yapılacak yol ve Limanlarımız" [The roads and ports to be built in 1948], *Ulus*, January 13, 1948. For reports on Hilts's various visits, see "Mr. Hilts'in Demeci" [Mr. Hilts's speech], *Ulus*, April 7, 1948; "Mr. Hilts Gidiyor" [Mr. Hilts is leaving], *Ulus*, December 21, 1949; "Türkiye'nin Yol Programı" [Turkey's road program], *Vatan*, February 13, 1948; "Türkiye Yolları" [Turkey's roads], *Ulus*, November 13, 1948 (in which Hilts was reported as calling Turkey his "home in the Middle East"); "Mr. Hilts İntibalarını Anlatıyor" [Mr. Hilts relates his impressions], *Ulus*, November 18, 1948; "Amerikan Yol Heyeti Başkanının Demeci" [The speech of the head of the American Roads Group], *Ulus*, December 27, 1947; and "Mr. Hilts Dün Ankara'dan Hareket Etti" [Mr. Hilts left Ankara yesterday], *Ulus*, April 27, 1948.

61. Planlama Şube Müdürlüğü Toplantı Tutanağı, Minutes of the Planning Unit Meeting, February 16, 1949, KGM Records.

62. Planlama Şube Müdürlüğü Toplantı Tutanağı, Minutes of the Planning Unit Meeting, December 14, 1949, KGM Records.

63. Pamir became a regional director upon his return to Turkey and was in charge of organizing the UN Highway Training Center in Ankara. Hilts to Williams, Septem-

ber 19, 1950, box 507, Turkey folders, RG 30. In 1962, the US Engineer Group, which supervised and administered contracts for military construction in Turkey, also developed an engineer student-apprenticeship program that continued for two years.

64. Hilts, *Türkiye'nin Yol Durumu*, pp. 41–42, KGM Records.

65. Michael Hogan, *The Marshall Plan: America, Britain, and the Construction of Western Europe, 1947–1952* (Cambridge, UK: Cambridge University Press, 1987).

66. Hilts to Diker, May 26, 1950, box 508, RG 30.

67. Hilts to Williams, August 29, 1950, box 507, RG 30.

68. "Thomas MacDonald Türkiye'de" [Thomas MacDonald in Turkey], *Karayolları Bülteni* [Highway Bulletin] 2, no. 20 (June 1952).

69. Hilts, "Highway Planning in Turkey" (speech, fall meeting of the American Society of Civil Engineers, November 3, 1949), box 4, Papers and Speeches of Harold Hilts, Office Files and Correspondence Concerning Particular Bureau Activities, RG 30.

70. Şükrü Kaya, "Amerika Dönüşü" [The return from America], *Karayolları Bülteni* 3, no. 28 (February 1953). See also entries in *Karayolları Bülteni* 3, no. 27 (January 1953).

71. *TBMM Meclis Tutanakları*, Dönem 9, Cilt 3, December 11, 1950, Parliamentary Records, Grand National Assembly Archives, Ankara, Turkey.

72. Lehman, "Building Roads," p. 395.

73. Bölgen, "The Reports of Those Who Went to America," 1949–1950, KGM Records. Bölgen also objected to copying American roads with no regard for differences in conditions, such as the number of pedestrians on Turkish roads, which far exceeded those on the Pennsylvania Turnpike, which had a weekly volume of traffic that could be observed only in a year on the busiest roads in Turkey.

74. "Yol Faaliyetleri ve Amerikan Yardımı" [Road activities and American aid], *Karayolları Bülteni* 5, no. 54 (April 1955). Perhaps the most telling example of scrutiny regarding excessive American visibility on Turkish roads was a highly publicized incident involving a Colonel Morrison, who killed one and injured eleven while driving under the influence outside of the Incirlik military base in 1959.

75. *TBMM Meclis Tutanakları*, Dönem 8, Cilt 24, February 1, 1950, Parliamentary Records, Grand National Assembly Archives, Ankara, Turkey.

76. Planlama Şube Müdürlüğü Toplantı Tutanağı, Minutes of the Planning Unit Meeting, August 31, 1949, KGM Records.

77. Adas, *Dominance by Design*, p. 142.

78. Klingensmith, *One Valley and a Thousand*, p. 75.

79. Harvey and Knox, *Roads*, p. 203.

80. Jesse Williams to all staff members, office memorandum, February 11, 1949, KGM Records; Jack Killalee, office memorandum, May 8, n.d., KGM Records.

81. Chester Burdick to Jesse Williams, Memorandum: Outline of the Provisions of Turkish Highway Finance Laws, March 3, 1949, KGM Records.

82. George McGhee, *The US-Turkish-NATO-Middle East Connection: How the Truman Doctrine Contained the Soviets in the Middle East* (New York: St. Martin's Press, 1990), pp. 48–49. The amount of highway machinery in Turkey increased from 1,127

in 1948 to 3,812 in 1951, with the aid program bringing a total of $23.5 million worth of machinery.

83. Keith Aksel, "The Engineering Generation: The Story of the Technicians Who Enabled American Cold War Foreign Policy, 1945–1961" (PhD diss., University of Colorado, 2016), pp. 214–18.

84. Ibid., p. 267.

85. Barker et al., *The Economy of Turkey*, p. 135; Thornburg, *Turkey: An Economic Appraisal*, pp. 82, 86.

86. Nazım Berksan, "Yollar Kanunu Görüşülürken" [As the highway law is being debated], *Ulus*, January 5, 1950.

87. "Yol İnşaatımızda Yeni Bir Zihniyet" [A new mentality in our roadbuilding], *Ulus*, July 26, 1948.

88. Ahmet Emin Yalman, "Türkiye'de Makine Devri" [Machinery age in Turkey], *Vatan*, March 5, 1948.

89. "Yol İnşaatımızda Yeni Bir Zihniyet," *Ulus*, July 26, 1948; "Iskenderun-Erzurum Yolunun İnşası" [The construction of the Iskenderun-Erzurum highway], *Vatan*, July 22, 1948.

90. Kerwin, "The Turkish Roads Program," p. 207. Kerwin's article incorporates anecdotes relayed to him by the American PRG.

91. Ibid., p. 205. The "dirty hands ethic" was also central to postwar agricultural development programs such as the Etawah pilot project in Uttar Pradesh, India. See Cullather, *The Hungry World*.

92. Zeyyat Inaloğlu was the subject of fervent communication between Daniş Koper and Arthur Williamson, who replaced Mersinli and Jesse Williams as directors of the KGM and the American PRG, respectively (1952 Communication Folders, KGM Records).

93. Lehman, "Building Roads," p. 390.

94. Farnsworth Fowle, "New Turkish Road Points Up US Aid," *The New York Times*, May 7, 1950.

95. Patrick Carroll-Burke, "Tools, Instruments and Engines: Getting a Handle on the Specificity of Engine Science," *Social Studies of Science* 31, no. 4 (August 2001), p. 600.

96. Public Roads Group and Ministry of Public Works representatives, Conference Minutes, February 7, 1948, cited in Lehman, "Building Roads," pp. 386–87.

97. Walter Adams and John Garraty, *Is the World Our Campus?* (Michigan: Michigan State University Press, 1960), p. 21.

98. Orhan Mersinli, "Karayolu Takımı" [The highway team], *Karayolları Bülteni* 1, no. 2 (December 1950). Hilts told Turkish engineers that "one of the most crucial aspects of efficiency is to work as a group. Nothing is more important than working as a team, be it in football, in industry or in the planning and building of a road network" ("Yol Yapım İşleri ile Yolların Kullanılışına Ait Bugünkü Görüşler" [Contemporary views on the building and use of highways], *Arkitekt* 193, no. 4 [1948]: 42).

99. Kerwin, "The Turkish Roads Program," p. 204.

100. Edwin Cohn, "Group Action and Economic Development" and "Time, the Future and Economic Development," November 12, 1957, box 164, folder 4, CFR Records.

101. Edwin Cohn, "Social and Cultural Factors Affecting the Emergence and Functioning of Innovators," in *Social Aspects of Economic Development: A Report of the International Conference on Social Aspects of Economic Development*, Istanbul, August 4–24, 1963, sponsored by the Economic and Social Studies Conference Board (Istanbul: Istanbul Matbaasi, 1964), p. 104.

102. Kerwin, "The Turkish Roads Program," p. 204.

103. Robert Hartmann, "Turks Pick Up U.S. Methods Speedily" and "Fight? Turks are Ready and Willing" in *Uncle Sam in Turkey*, (New York: Turkish Information Office, 1951), pp. 6 and 14. On Marshall Plan officials' frequent criticism of the "Pasha complex," see also Burçak Keskin Kozat, "Negotiating Modernization through US Foreign Assistance: Turkey's Marshall Plan (1948–1952) Reinterpreted" (PhD diss., University of Michigan, 2007).

104. Lerner and Robinson, "Swords and Ploughshares," p. 32.

105. Ibid., pp. 29, 30, 33, 35.

106. İlhan Özdil, "A Causative-Diagnostic Analysis of Turkey's Major Problems and a Communicative Approach to Their Solution" (PhD diss., Ohio State University, 1954), pp. 159–60.

107. E. P. Thompson, "Time, Work-Discipline, and Industrial Capitalism," *Past and Present* 38 (December 1967): 82.

108. Carroll-Burke, "Tools, Instruments and Engines," p. 594.

109. Interview with Zafer Pamir, *Anılarla Karayolları Tarihi* [History of highways in memoirs] (Ankara: Karayolları Genel Müdürlüğü, 2007), p. 31.

110. Charles Abrams, *The Need for Training and Education for Housing and Planning*, TAA 173/57/018, Report No: TAA/TUR/13 (New York: United Nations Technical Assistance Program, August 23, 1955).

111. The other names were Daniş Koper and Orhan Mersinli, both of whom succeeded Diker as the Director of Highways, and Zafer Pamir, who oversaw the UN Highway Training Center and virtually acted as the president of METU between 1957 and 1958. Komitesi, *Vecdi Diker'in Ardından*.

112. Sevgi Aktüre, Sevin Osmay, and Ayşen Savaş, *1956'dan 2006'ya ODTU Mimarlık Fakültesinin 50 Yılı* [Fifty years of METU Faculty of Architecture] (Ankara: ODTU Mimarlık Fakültesi, 2007).

113. Herbert Cummings, "Turkish Highway Program—An Interim Economic Appraisal," *Foreign Commerce Weekly* 45, no. 8 (November 19, 1951): 3.

114. Kerwin, "The Turkish Roads Program," p. 196.

115. Memorandum: A Summary of the Subjects Discussed with Various Officials and Statesmen during Commissioner MacDonald's Stay in Turkey from May 30 until June 20, 1952, KGM Records.

116. The first program only had five people attending (from Egypt, Iran, Jordan, Lebanon, and Syria). Subsequent programs added participants from China, Pakistan,

Iraq, Japan, Sudan, and Afghanistan, with the final program in 1957 hosting sixteen people. *Karayolları Bülteni* 5, no. 47 (September 1954); *Karayolları Bülteni* 5, no. 55 (May 1955); *Karayolları Bülteni* 6, no. 70 (August 1956); *Karayolları Bülteni* 7, no. 83 (September 1957).

117. *Karayolları Bülteni* 5, no. 47 (September 1954).

118. *Yol Davamız: 9 Yılda 23000 Kilometre* [Our road cause: 23,000 kilometers in 9 years] (Ankara: Bayındırlık Bakanlığı, 1948), p. 28; *Karayollarında Çalışmak İstemez Misiniz?* [Wouldn't you like to work at the highways?], 1961, KGM Records.

119. "Köy Yolları Çalışmaları" [Village roads program], *Karayolları Bülteni* 1, no. 1 (November 1950).

120. Niyazi Kiper, "Köy Yolları," *Karayolları Bülteni* 1, no. 5 (March 1951).

121. Orhan Mersinli, "Yol Mühendisliğinin Türkiye'de Son Otuz Sene Zarfındaki İnkişafları" [The development of highway engineering in the past thirty years in Turkey], *Karayollari Bülteni* 6, no. 72 (October 1956).

122. *Bayram* is a word that denotes Muslim holidays (eid) as well as secular and official ones ("the Republican *Bayram*," commemorating the proclamation of the republic). *Ulus*, November 18, 1949, and October 22, 1949.

123. Kemal Cündübeyoğlu, "Şark, Garp, Şimal, Cenup Hepsi Vatan" [East, west, north, south, all is our land], *Karayollari Bülteni* 3, no. 36 (October 1953).

124. "Yol Davasının Gerçek Manası" [The true meaning of the road cause], *Karayollari Bülteni* 3, no. 30 (April 1953).

125. Chester Burdick to Jesse Williams, Memorandum: Outline of the Provisions of Turkish Highway Finance Laws, March 3, 1949, KGM Records.

126. Cummings, "Turkish Highway Program," pp. 32, 33. The article was reprinted in the *Highway Bulletin* shortly thereafter as "Türkiye'nin Karayolları Programı ve Geçici bir İktisadi Tahlili," *Karayolları Bülteni* 2, no. 14 (December 1951).

Chapter 4

1. Russell Dorr (speech in the wake of his departure from Turkey, 1952), entry 1399, box 41, folder: Russell Dorr Speeches, RG 469.

2. Nicole Sackley, "The Village as Cold War Site: Experts, Development, and the History of Rural Reconstruction," *Journal of Global History* 6, no. 3 (2011): p. 481.

3. Ibid., p. 489; Mitchell, *Rule of Experts*; Cullather, *The Hungry World*; Immerwahr, *Thinking Small*. Although highway construction can also be studied in relation to questions of urbanization, Fordism, and oil dependency, this chapter addresses their utilization in modernizing the countryside.

4. Lerner, *Passing*; Almond and Coleman, eds. *The Politics of the Developing Areas;* Rostow, *The Stages of Economic Growth*; Karl Deutsch, "Social Mobilization and Political Development"; Rustow, "Transitions to Democracy."

5. Tsing, *Friction*, p. 6.

6. Larkin, *Signal and Noise*, p. 43.

7. Andrew Barry, "Lines of Communication and Spaces of Rule," in *Foucault and*

Political Reason: Liberalism, Neo-Liberalism and Rationalities of Government, eds. Andrew Barry, Thomas Osborne, and Nikolas Rose (Chicago: University of Chicago Press, 1996), p. 128.

8. Foucault, *Security, Territory, Population: Lectures at the College de France 1977–1978*, trans. Graham Burchell (New York: Palgrave, 2007); Joyce, *The Rule of Freedom*; Hagar Kotef, *Movement and the Ordering of Freedom: On Liberal Governances of Mobility* (Durham, NC: Duke University Press, 2015).

9. Rudolph Mrázek, *Engineers of Happy Land: Technology and Nationalism in a Colony* (Princeton, NJ: Princeton University Press, 2002), p. 28.

10. On the affinity between liberalism and imperialism, see Uday Mehta, *Liberalism and Empire: A Study in Nineteenth-Century British Liberal Thought.* (Chicago: University of Chicago Press, 1999); and Jennifer Pitts, A *Turn to Empire: The Rise of Imperial Liberalism in Britain and France* (Princeton: Princeton University Press, 2005).

11. Mrázek, *Engineers of Happyland*; Patrick Carroll-Burke, *Science, Culture, and Modern State Formation* (Berkeley: University of California Press, 2006); Jo Guldi, *Roads to Power: Britain Invents the Infrastructure State* (Cambridge: Harvard University Press, 2012).

12. Ekbladh, *The Great American Mission*, pp. 20–21.

13. Adas, *Dominance by Design*, pp. 169–70.

14. Kramer, *The Blood of Government*, p. 309.

15. For more on Lilienthal's international consultant group, *Development and Resources*, which was founded in 1955, see David Ekbladh, "Mr. TVA": Grass-Roots Development, David Lilienthal, and the Rise and Fall of the Tennessee Valley Authority as a Symbol for US Overseas Development, 1933–1973," *Diplomatic History*, 26, no. 3 (2002): 335–374.

16. On the relationship between driving and new patterns of leisure and recreation, see Kristin Ross, *Fast Cars, Clean Bodies: Decolonization and the Reordering of French Culture* (Cambridge, MA: MIT Press, 1995); Kristin Monroe, "Automobility and Citizenship in Interwar Lebanon," *Comparative Studies of South Asia, Africa, and the Middle East* 34 no. 3 (2014): 518–31.

17. Reşat Kasaba explains that the resettlement of Muslim and Turkish communities became a way of limiting the mobility of others: "Some of the new muhajir (immigrant) villages in central Anatolia were designed in a way that formed ribbon-like patterns around the lower reaches of the mountains, so that the migration routes of the local tribes would be blocked and the tribes would have to alter their nomadic lives." *A Moveable Empire: Ottoman Nomads, Migrants and Refugees* (Seattle: University of Washington Press, 2009), p. 110.

18. Uğur Űmit Űngőr, *The Making of Modern Turkey: Nation and State in Eastern Anatolia, 1913–1950* (Oxford, UK: Oxford University Press, 2011); Fuat Dündar, *Ittihat ve Terakki'nin Müslümanları Iskan Politikası 1913–1919* [The Committee of Union and Progress's policy of settling Muslims] (Istanbul: İletişim, 2001).

19. Ilhan Tekeli, "Involuntary Displacement and the Problem of Resettlement in

Turkey from the Ottoman Empire to the Present," *Center for Migration Studies* 11, no. 4 (2012): 202–26.

20. This line appeared in the "Tenth Year Anthem," which was composed to celebrate the achievements of the first decade of the Republic and can be heard to this day on loudspeakers on secular holidays and international soccer matches. I would like to thank Aslı Iğsız for reminding me to emphasize this point.

21. Faruk Birtek and Çağlar Keyder, "Agriculture and the State: An Inquiry into Agricultural Differentiation and Political Alliances: The Case of Turkey," *Journal of Peasant Studies* 2, no. 4 (July 1975): 446.

22. Tekeli and Ilkin, *Cumhuriyetin Harcı*, p. 381.

23. Law Proposal 1/431 Regarding Roads and Bridges, April 10, 1929, cited in Bilsay Kuruç, *Belgelerle Türkiye İktisat Politikası (1929–1932)* [Turkey's political economy with documents] (Ankara: Ankara Üniversitesi Siyasal Bilgiler Fakültesi, 1988); Law Proposal 1/979 Regarding the Administration of the Ministry of Public Works, May 9, 1934, cited in Bilsay Kuruç, *Belgelerle Türkiye İktisat Politikası (1933–1935)* [Turkey's political economy with documents] (Ankara: Ankara Üniversitesi SBF Yayınları, 1988), pp. 337, 531–32.

24. One such concession was President Inonu's approval of Cavit Oral as the minister of agriculture; Oral had previously condemned the bill as a dangerous "extremity." This appointment was in stark contrast to Inonu's initial enthusiasm for the bill, to the extent of denouncing those MPs who opposed it as "not his own." Yahya Tezel, *Cumhuriyet Döneminin İktisadi Tarihi (1923–1950)* [An economic history of the republican era] (Ankara: Yurt Yayıncılık, 1982), pp. 327–31.

25. Asım Karaömerlioğlu, "The Village Institutes Experience in Turkey," *British Journal of Middle East Studies* 25, no 1 (1998): 47–73.

26. In the event of noncultivation by the one designated member of the family who was allowed to inherit the land by law, the state would be able to reclaim it and transfer it to another family member.

27. Asım Karaömerlioğlu, "Elite Perceptions of Land Reform in Early Republican Turkey," *Journal of Peasant Studies* 27, no. 3 (2000): 130.

28. See Vanderlippe, *The Politics of Turkish Democracy* for a full account.

29. Tezel, *Cumhuriyet Döneminin İktisadi Tarihi*, pp. 328–29.

30. *TBMM Meclis Tutanakları*, Dönem 7, Cilt 17, May 16, 1945.

31. Seiler, *Republic of Drivers*, p. 131.

32. Frank Schipper, "Changing the Face of Europe: European Road Mobility during the Marshall Plan Years," *Journal of Transport History* 28, no. 2 (2007): 215.

33. İlhan Tekeli and Selim İlkin, *Savaş Sonrası Ortamında 1947 Türkiye İktisadi Kalkınma Planı* [Turkey's 1947 economic development plan in the postwar context] (Ankara: ODTÜ, 1974).

34. Keyder, *State and Class*, pp. 127–28. Both the Thornburg and Barker reports emphasize the link between highways and commercial agriculture (Thornburg, *Turkey: An Economic Appraisal*, pp. 76 and 86; Barker et al., *The Economy of Turkey*, p. 121).

35. See the cabinet programs announced for May 22, 1950, and March 8, 1951, cited

in Faik Kırbaşlı, *1920–1972 Döneminde Kalkınmada Öncelikli Yörelere İlişkin Hükümet Programları* [Government programs pertaining to regions of priority for development between 1920 and 1972] (Ankara: TC Başbakanlık Devlet Planlama Teşkilatı, 1973), p. 108.

36. Çağlar Keyder, "The Political Economy of Turkish Democracy," *New Left Review* 115 (1979): 16–17.

37. Between 1948 and 1958, the number of tractors in the country increased from 1,750 to 40,000. Ecehan Balta, "1945 Çiftçiyi Topraklandırma Kanunu: Reform Mu Karşı Reform Mu?" [The 1945 law for providing land to farmers: Reform or counter-reform?], *Praksis* 5 (2002): 277–98.

38. Keyder, "The Political Economy of Turkish Democracy," p. 19.

39. Kasaba, "Populism and Democracy in Turkey," p. 55.

40. "Karayolları Çalışmaları" [Work on highways], *Arkitekt* 253–54 (1954): 245.

41. *Yol Davamız*, p. 13.

42. Yavuz Abadan, "Yol Siyasetimiz" [Our road politics], *Ulus*, September 5, 1948; *1948–1960 KGM Çalışmaları Hakkında Rapor* [Report on the work of KGM between 1948 and 1960], KGM Records, pp. 8–9.

43. *Karayolları Bülteni* 6, no. 70 (August 1956).

44. *Highway Transportation in Turkey* (Ankara: Turkish General Directorate of Highways, 1957), p. 1.

45. Kemal Cündübeyoğlu, "Türkiye'nin Yol Davası" [The road cause of Turkey], *Karayollari Bülteni* 5, no. 50 (October 1955).

46. Şevket Rado, "Türkiye'nin Yol Davası Hal Yoluna Girmiştir" [Turkey's road cause is going to be solved], *Akşam*, October 12, 1950.

47. Aydın Yalçın, "Köyü Kalkındırma Muamması" [The conundrum of village development], *Forum* 4, no. 43 (January 1, 1956): 13–14; Aydın Yalçın, "Türkiye'de Demokrasi" [Democracy in Turkey], reprinted in *Forum* 10, no. 119 (1959): 7–8.

48. *TBMM Meclis Tutanakları*, Dönem 9, Cilt 5, February 25, 1951. Proponents of this view of belatedness were MPs Himmet Őlçmen and Ahmet Tokuş.

49. *TBMM Meclis Tutanakları*, Dönem 9, Cilt 3, December 11, 1950; *TBMM Meclis Tutanakları*, Dönem 8, Cilt 24, February 1, 1950; *TBMM Meclis Tutanakları*, Dönem 8, Cilt 24, February 3, 1950; *TBMM Meclis Tutanakları*, Dönem 9, Cilt 28, February 4, 1954. The reference is to the employment of local students in building the Village Institutes.

50. "Köye Gidecek Yol" [The road to the village], *Hürriyet*, September 2, 1950.

51. Cavit Orhan Tütengil, *İçtimai ve İktisadi Bakımdan Türkiye'nin Karayolları* [Turkey's highways from a sociological and economic perspective] (Istanbul: Elif Kitabevi, 1961), p. 161.

52. Süha Somer, "Ana Davalarımız" [Our primary causes], *Vatan*, March 6, 1948.

53. "Yol Davasının Gerçek Manası" [The true meaning of the road cause], *Karayolları Bülteni* 3, no. 30 (April 1953).

54. Cummings, "Turkish Highway Program," p. 32.

55. *TBMM Meclis Tutanakları*, Dönem 8, Cilt 24, February 1, 1950.

56. A new organization called The General Directorate of Road, Water, and Electricity took over the task of building and maintaining rural roads in 1965. Şen, *Türkiye'de Demiryolları ve Karayolları*, p. 169.

57. Ülman and Tachau, "Turkish Politics," p. 154.

58. Tütengil, *İçtimai ve İktisadi Bakımdan*, p. 131.

59. Frederick Frey, "Political Development, Power, and Communications in Turkey" in Pye, *Communications and Political Development*, p. 319.

60. Tütengil, *İçtimai ve İktisadi Bakımdan*, p. 9.

61. Mustafa Babur, İsmet İlter, and Nevzat Erdoğdu, eds., *Karayolları Genel Müdürlüğü 25 Yaşında* [The Highway Directorate is 25 years old] (Ankara: Karayolları Genel Müdürlüğü, 1975), p. 16.

62. Zeynep Gambetti and Joost Jongerden, eds., *The Kurdish Issue in Turkey: A Spatial Perspective* (New York: Routledge, 2015); Joost Jongerden, *The Settlement Issue in Turkey and the Kurds: An Analysis of Spatial Policies, Modernity and War* (Leiden: Brill, 2007).

63. Azat Zana Gündoğan, "Space, State-Making and Contentious Kurdish Politics in the East of Turkey: The Case of Eastern Meetings, 1967," *Journal of Balkan and Near Eastern Studies* 13, no. 4 (2011): 399.

64. Turhan Feyzioğlu, "Iki Türkiye" [Two Turkeys], *Forum* 1, no. 7 (July 1, 1954): 8. By one account, this was particularly true of regions to the east of the Euphrates, with Kurdish being spoken by 65 percent of the people, followed by Turkish at 27 percent and other languages at 8 percent. Tütengil, *İçtimai ve İktisadi Bakımdan*, p. 134.

65. Tütengil, *İçtimai ve İktisadi Bakımdan*, p. 163.

66. Ibid., p. 136.

67. Lütfi Yeleşen, *Karayolları Bülteni* 4, no. 38 (December 1953).

68. *Turkish Roads and Highways* (New York: Turkish Information Office, 1950), p. 4.

69. Hartmann, *Uncle Sam in Turkey*, p. 29.

70. Daniel Rodgers, "American Exceptionalism Revisited," *Raritan* 24, no. 2 (Fall 2004): 37.

71. *1948–1960 KGM Çalışmaları Hakkında Rapor* [Report on the work of KGM between 1948 and 1960], KGM Records, p. 26.

72. Fuat Dündar, *Modern Türkiye'nin Şifresi: Ittihat ve Terakki'nin Etnitiste Mühendisliği (1913–1918)* [The code of modern Turkey: Ethnicity engineering by the Committee of Union and Progress] (Istanbul: İletişim, 2008).

73. See Scott, *Seeing Like a State;* Joyce, *The Rule of Freedom;* and Mitchell, *Rule of Experts*, among others, for more on the classificatory and regulatory work that maps perform.

74. David Harvey, *The Condition of Postmodernity: An Enquiry into the Origins of Cultural Change* (Cambridge, MA: Blackwell, 1990).

75. Frey, *Regional Variations in Rural Turkey*, pp. 1, 3, 4, 9, 10, 11, 34.

76. When the Turkish translation went out of print in 1957, the Economic Institute at Istanbul University printed the original. Barbara Helling and George Helling, *Rural Turkey: A New Socio-Statistical Approach* (Istanbul: Istanbul Üniversitesi İktisat Fakültesi, 1958), pp. 8–9, 13.

77. Kemal Cündübeyoğlu, "Şark, Garp, Şimal, Cenup, Hepsi Vatan" [East, west, north, south, all is our homeland], *Karayolları Bülteni* 3, no. 36 (October 1953).

78. "Doğu Vilayetleri" [Eastern provinces], *Hürriyet*, November 14, 1948.

79. Şen, *Türkiye'de Demiryolları ve Karayolları*, p. 145.

80. Out of that ten million, the Ministry of Education was allocated 1,940,000 liras (for school buildings and teacher housing), the Ministry of Public Works was given 5,260,000 liras (for all-weather roads between Nizip and Silvan and between Rize and Erzurum, Bitlis, Hakkari, and Ağrı, among others), and the remaining 1,200,000 was allocated to the Ministry of Health (for local health centers and a traveling hospital). *TBMM Meclis Tutanakları*, Dönem 8, Cilt 19, May 9, 1949. Some of the money appears to have been spent on housing for civil servants in Diyarbakir, Mardin and Urfa. "Doğu Kalkınma Planı Gerçekleşiyor" [The eastern development plan is implemented], *Ulus*, January 1, 1950.

81. "Doğudaki İllerimizin Kalkındırılması İçin" [For our eastern provinces to develop], *Ulus*, September 3, 1948.

82. "Doğuda Yapılacak Yeni Yollar" [New roads to be built in the east], *Vatan*, October 21, 1948.

83. *TBMM Meclis Tutanakları*, Dönem 9, Cilt 14, June 28, 1950.

84. Aydın Yalçın, "İhmal Edilen Doğu İlleri" [The neglected eastern provinces], *Ulus*, September 24, 1953. The Dersim uprisings of 1937–1938 and ensuing atrocities on the part of the Turkish state, including the displacement and deaths of tens of thousands of Kurdish and Alevi subjects in the region, were erased from the official narrative in the following decades.

85. Mühendis Nazır, "Demiryollarımızda Nakil Ücretleri" [Transportation costs in our railroads], *Kadro* 18 (June 1933): 13.

86. Meeting on the Law Proposal for a Railway to Connect the Sivas-Erzurum Line with Malatya, parliamentary debate, May 20, 1933, cited in Kuruç, *Belgelerle Türkiye İktisat Politikası, 1933–1935*, p. 41.

87. Aydın Yalçın, "İhmal Edilen Doğu İlleri" [The neglected eastern provinces], *Ulus*, September 24, 1953.

88. Menderes's statement to the press, December 21, 1952, cited in Ahmad and Ahmad, *Türkiye'de Çok Partili Politika*, p. 105.

89. Kırbaşlı, *1920–1972 Döneminde Kalkınma*, p. 111.

90. "Doğudaki İllerimizin Kalkındırılması İçin" [For our eastern provinces to develop], *Ulus*, September 3, 1948.

91. Kemal Cündübeyoğlu, "Şark, Garp, Şimal, Cenup, Hepsi Vatan" [East, west, north, south, all is our homeland], *Karayolları Bülteni* 3, no. 36 (October 1953).

92. Reports on early project completion dates included the road between Pendik, Gebze, and Izmit, just outside of Istanbul, or the road between Akhisar and Gördes, which would deliver the industrial and agricultural goods of Izmir and the Aegean region to central Anatolia and back to the port of Izmir. *Karayolları Bülteni* [Highway Bulletin] 1, no. 3 (January 1951). Between 1948 and 1958, the length of all-weather roads across the country increased from 9,264 kilometers to 22,000 kilometers, but by 1967,

only 10 out of 253 villages had roads in the eastern city of Bitlis, and a total of only 39 kilometers had been paved across the city. In Mardin, 21 out of 708 villages received roads. İsmail Beşikçi, *Doğu Mitingleri'nin Analizi* [Analysis of the eastern meetings] (Istanbul: Yurt, 1967), p. 102

93. Gündoğan, "Space and State-Making," p. 403.

94. İsmail Beşikçi, *Doğuda Değişim ve Yapısal Sorunlar* [Change and structural problems in the east] (Ankara: Sevinç, 1969).

95. Kerem Yavaşça, "'Sark Meselesi'nden 'Doğu Sorunu'na: Ellili Yıllarda Kürt Sorunu" [From the eastern issue to the eastern problem: the Kurdish problem during the 1950s], in *Türkiye'nin 1950'li Yılları* [Turkey's 1950s decade], ed. Mete Kaan Kaynar (Istanbul: Iletişim, 2015), pp. 585–87.

96. Welat Zeydanlıoğlu, "The White Turkish Man's Burden: Orientalism, Kemalism and the Kurds in Turkey," in *Neo-Colonial Mentalities in Contemporary Europe? Language and Discourse in the Construction of Identities*, eds. Guido Rings and Anne Ife (Newcastle upon Tyne: Cambridge Scholars Publishing, 2008), pp. 155-174.

97. Mesut Yeğen, "Turkish Nationalism and the Kurdish Question," *Ethnic and Racial Studies* 30, no. 1 (2007): 599.

98. "Why Turkey Should Negotiate a Hard Currency Loan to Finance Modern Road-Building Equipment," prepared by the Turkish Ministry of Public Works, 1948, entry 1399, box 27, folder: Roads—1948–49, RG 469.

99. *1948-1960 KGM Çalışmaları Hakkında Rapor* [Report on the work of KGM between 1948 and 1960], KGM Records; *Yol Davamız* [Our road cause], prepared for the Izmir International Fair, 1949, KGM Records; "Functions of the Divisions and Offices of the General Directorate of Highways," March 1, 1950, KGM Records.

100. Faruk Birtek, "The Rise and Fall of Etatism in Turkey, 1932–1950: The Uncertain Road in the Restructuring of a Semiperipheral Economy," *Review (Fernand Braudel Center)* 8, no. 3 (1985): 412, 436.

101. Lerner, *Passing*, pp. 29, 56.

102. The trope would continue well into the 1960s, and the marketized peasant was almost always imagined as a man. Howard Reed, "A New Force at Work in Democratic Turkey," *Middle East Journal* 7, no. 1 (Winter 1953): 35; Tütengil, *İçtimai ve İktisadi Bakımdan*, p. 50; Edwin Cohn, "Turkish Development 1922–57," box 164, folder 4, CFR Records; Ülman and Tachau, "Turkish Politics," p. 154.

103. Helling and Helling, *Rural Turkey*, p. 20.

104. Hartmann, *Uncle Sam in Turkey*, pp. 25–26.

105. *Sketches from Turkish Life: The Road Comes to the Village* (New York: Turkish Information Office, 1950).

106. John Kolars, *Tradition, Season, and Change in a Turkish Village* (Chicago: University of Chicago Press, 1963), pp. 113–14, 187.

107. İbrahim Yasa, *Hasanoğlan: Socio-Economic Structure of a Turkish Village* (Ankara: TODAIE, 1957), pp. 30, 34.

108. Tütengil, *İçtimai ve İktisadi Bakımdan*, p. 97

109. Tekeli and Ilkin, *Cumhuriyetin Harcı*, p. 444. Between 1950 and 1956, the

amount of goods transported by highways increased from 957,059 tons per kilometer to 2,234,229. During the same period, the number of highway passengers increased from 2,597,311 to 12,910,634. See "Türkiye Karayolları İstatistik Bülteni," 1958, cited in Ireland, *Türkiye'de Karayolları.*

110. Tütengil, *İçtimai ve İktisadi Bakımdan*, p. 42.

111. Whereas the express train took twenty-three hours to travel between Ankara and Istanbul, the truck covered the same distance in ten hours. Haulage costs in turn were thirteen and eight kuruş for the train and the truck, respectively. As for passenger transportation, the bus cost twenty-five lira, as opposed to the first-class-train rate of eighty-five lira, with travel times of eight and fourteen hours respectively. Ireland, *Türkiye'de Karayolları*, pp. 254–55.

112. Tütengil, *İçtimai ve İktisadi Bakımdan*, p. 79.

113. Between 1948 and 1959, the number of buses increased from 2,198 to 8,291, and trucks from 10,596 to 36,919. Ireland, *Türkiye'de Karayolları*, pp. 258, 262.

114. The daily *Hürriyet* started the first distribution service in 1955—a truck would leave Istanbul at 3:00 a.m. and deliver copies of the newspaper to Edirne by 7:00 a.m. Tekeli and Ilkin, *Cumhuriyetin Harcı*, p. 423. For a discussion of the relationship between nation making and print capitalism, see Benedict Anderson, *Imagined Communities* (London: Verso, 1983).

115. *Karayollari Bülteni* 5, no. 52 (April 1954).

116. *TBMM Meclis Tutanakları*, Dönem 9, Cilt 5, February 25, 1951; *TBMM Meclis Tutanakları*, Dönem 9, Cilt 28, February 25, 1954. Tea is a customary treat on intracity buses today.

117. Mrázek, *Engineers of Happy Land*, p. 8.

118. Lerner and Robinson, "Swords and Ploughshares" p. 35; Richard Robinson, *The First Turkish Republic: A Case Study in National Development* (Cambridge, MA: Harvard University Press, 1963), p. 140; Kolars, *Tradition, Season, and Change*, p. 112.

119. Kemal Karpat, "Social Effects of Farm Mechanization in Turkish Villages," *Social Research* 27, no. 1 (1960): 95.

120. De Grazia, *Irresistible Empire*, p. 363.

121. Tütengil, *İçtimai ve İktisadi Bakımdan*, p. 67. Keyder also argues that roads created "a new concentration of small non-urban capital around the leading sector of automotive transport." "The Political Economy of Turkish Democracy," p. 22.

122. Kolars, *Tradition, Season, and Change*, p. 111

123. Tütengil, *İçtimai ve İktisadi Bakımdan*, pp. 125–26

124. Lerner, *Passing*, pp. 39–40

125. Karpat, "Social Effects," p. 87

126. Rustow, "The Politics of the Near East," p. 442

127. Frey, "Political Development, Power, and Communications in Turkey," pp. 321–22.

128. Edwin Cohn, *Turkish Economic, Social, and Political Change: The Development of a More Prosperous and Open Society* (New York: Praeger Publishers, 1970), p. 56.

129. Karpat, "Social Effects," p. 88.

130. Lerner, *Passing*, p. 29.

131. Karpat, "Social Effects," p. 103

132. Lerner, *Passing*, p. 132 (emphasis in the original).

133. Ibid., p. 49; Tütengil, *İçtimai ve İktisadi Bakımdan*, p. 143; Aydın Yalçın, "Türkiye'de Demokrasi," reprinted in *Forum* 10, no. 119 (1959): 8; Kolars, *Tradition, Season, and Change*, p. 110.

134. Lerner, *Passing*, p. 132.

135. Edwin Cohn, "Time, the Future and Economic Development," November 12, 1957, box 164, folder 4, CFR Records; Lerner, *Passing*, p. 133; Yasa, *Hasanoğlan*, p. 34; Berkes, *Bazı Ankara Köyleri*, pp. 58–59; Makal, *A Village in Anatolia*, p. 58.

136. Yasa, *Hasanoğlan*, p. 180.

137. Şerif, *An Outline of Social Psychology*, pp. 692–93.

138. Tütengil, *İçtimai ve İktisadi Bakımdan*, p. 100.

139. Karpat, "Social Effects," p. 88.

140. Robinson's initial assignment had been with the Institute of Current World Affairs. For an overview of his career, which culminated in a joint appointment at the Harvard Business School and the Middle East Center, see Richard Robinson, "A Personal Journey through Time and Space," *Journal of International Business Studies* 25, no. 3 (1994).

141. Richard Robinson to Walter S. Rogers, December 15, 1948; March 1, 1949; October 25, 1949; March 15, 1949; August 8, 1949, *Letters from Turkey*, reprinted for the Peace Corps by permission of the Institute for Current World Affairs (Istanbul: Robert College, 1965).

142. Edwin Cohn, "Some Propositions Concerning the Role of Human Factors in Economic Development," October 14, 1957, box 164, folder 4, CFR Records.

143. Robinson, "Turkey's Agrarian Revolution and the Problem of Urbanization," *The Public Opinion Quarterly* 22, no. 3 (Autumn 1958); Robinson, "Tractors in the Village: A Study in Turkey," *Journal of Farm Economics* 34, no. 4 (1952).

144. Kolars, *Tradition, Season, and Change*, pp. 16–17.

145. Frey, "Political Development, Power, and Communications in Turkey," p. 322. Frey seems to have been made aware of this particular peasant through Karpat's article: "Tractors are being extensively used for transportation between villages and towns; the extreme example concerns a peasant from Pamukova, a village in western Anatolia, who used his tractor for a family trip to Germany." Karpat, "Social Effects," p. 92.

146. Sabri Ülgener, "Value Patterns of Traditional Societies: Turkish Experience," in *Social Aspects of Economic Development*, p. 128.

147. Ibid., p. 129.

148. Reed, "A New Force at Work," p. 42.

149. Helling and Helling, *Rural Turkey*, p. 10.

150. Kasaba, "Populism and Democracy in Turkey," p. 58. The figure comes from Keyder, *State and Class*, p. 135.

151. Kemal Karpat, "Köy Kalkınmasının Esasları" [The principles of village development], *Forum* 7, no. 81 (August 1, 1957): 15.

152. Cohn, *Turkish Economic, Social, and Political Change*, p. 82.

153. Mübeccel Kıray, *Hayatımda Hiç Arkaya Bakmadım* [I never looked back in my life] (Istanbul: Bağlam, 2001).

154. Mübeccel Kıray, *Ereğli: Ağır Sanayiden Önce Bir Sahil Kasabası* [A coastal town prior to heavy industry] (Ankara: TC Başbakanlık Devlet Planlama Teşkilatı, 1964) pp. 165, 168.

155. "Demir Leblebi Gibi Kadin!" [A woman of steel], *Radikal*, November 17, 2007, cited in Lütfi Sunar, "Türkiye'de Sosyal Bilimlerde Toplumsal Değişim," *Sosyoloji Dergisi* 29, no. 3 (2014): 83–116.

156. Gündoğan, "Space and State-Making," p. 408.

157. Ibid., p. 411.

158. On modernization as a "claim-making concept," see Frederick Cooper, *Colonialism in Question: Theory, Knowledge, History* (Berkeley: University of California Press, 2005), p. 132; and James Ferguson, *Global Shadows: Africa in the Neoliberal World Order* (Durham, NC: Duke University Press, 2006).

159. "Yol Davasının Gerçek Manası" [The true meaning of the road cause], *Karayollari Bülteni* 3, no. 30 (April 1953).

Chapter 5

1. "Tourist Hotel for Istanbul, Turkey," *Architectural Record* 113 (1953).

2. "Hilton's Newest Hotel," *Architectural Forum* (December 1955): 122.

3. Conrad Hilton, "The City of the Golden Horn," HHI.

4. Conrad Hilton, *Be My Guest* (New York: Simon & Schuster, 1994), p. 234.

5. Frances Stonor Saunders, *The Cultural Cold War: The CIA and the World of Arts and Letters* (New York: New Press, 1999); Penny Von Eschen, *Satchmo Blows Up the World: Jazz Ambassadors Play the Cold War* (Cambridge, MA: Harvard University Press, 2006); Uta Poiger, *Jazz, Rock, and Rebels: Cold War Politics and American Culture in a Divided Germany* (Berkeley: University of California Press, 2000); De Grazia, *Irresistible Empire;* Jenifer Van Vleck, *Empire of the Air: Aviation and the American Ascendancy* (Cambridge, MA: Harvard University Press, 2013). On the other hotels, see Annabel Wharton's excellent *Building the Cold War: Hilton International Hotels and Modern Architecture* (Chicago: University of Chicago Press, 2001).

6. Susan Leigh Star and James Griesemer, "Institutional Ecology, 'Translations' and Boundary Objects: Amateurs and Professionals in Berkeley's Museum of Vertebrate Zoology, 1907–39," *Social Studies of Science* 19, no. 3 (August 1989): 393, 408.

7. For a preliminary background on the older hotels, see Zeynep Çelik, *The Remaking of Istanbul: Portrait of an Ottoman City in the Nineteenth Century* (Berkeley: University of California Press, 1986); and Sibel Bozdoğan, *Modernism and Nation Building: Turkish Architectural Culture in the Early Republic* (Seattle: University of Washington Press, 2001).

8. Joan Fujimura, "Crafting Science: Standardized Packages, Boundary Objects, and 'Translation,'" in *Science as Practice and Culture*, ed. Andrew Pickering (Chicago: University of Chicago Press, 1992), p. 175.

9. Christopher Endy, *Cold War Holidays: American Tourism in France* (Chapel Hill: University of North Carolina Press, 2004), p. 45.

10. Brian Angus McKenzie, *Remaking France: Americanization, Public Diplomacy, and the Marshall Plan* (New York: Berghahn Books, 2005); Gunter Binschof, "Conquering the Foreigner: The Marshall Plan and the Revival of Postwar Austrian Tourism," in *The Marshall Plan in Austria*, eds. Gunter Binschof, Anton Pelinka, and Dieter Stiefel (Livingston, NJ: Transaction Publishers, 2000).

11. "Tourism in the European Recovery Program," June 1950, the Statistics and Reports Division of the ECA, enclosed in Theodore Pozzy to Halim Tevfik Alyot, August 10, 1950, entry 1399, box 58, reports—T–Z, RG 469.

12. William Fulbright, "Promotion of Tourism Can Supply Europe," Wednesday, 26 April, legislative day of 29 March 1950, US Congressional Record. The "dollar gap" referred to the imbalance in trade between the United States and Europe. The Marshall Plan was supposed to alleviate the trade deficit on the part of Europe and the trade surplus on the part of the United States by enabling Europe to earn enough dollars so they could purchase American goods through a series of measures facilitating the influx of dollars into Europe as well as through the elimination of tariffs, import quotas, and bilateral trade agreements.

13. Christina Klein, *Cold War Orientalism: Asia in the Middlebrow Imagination, 1945–1961* (Berkeley: University of California Press, 2003), p. 108.

14. Endy, *Cold War Holidays*, p. 34.

15. For Europe's postwar participation in the spread of mass beach tourism across the Middle East, see Waleed Hazbun, *Beaches, Ruins, Resorts: The Politics of Tourism in the Arab World* (Minneapolis: University of Minnesota Press, 2008). For further reflections on tourism as a "neo-colonial political economy," perpetuating uneven relations between a traveling center and the "pleasure periphery," see Malcolm Crick, "Representations of International Tourism in the Social Sciences: Sun, Sex, Sights, Savings, and Servility," *Annual Review of Anthropology* 18 (1989); and Louis Turner and John Ash, *The Golden Hordes: International Tourism and the Pleasure Periphery* (New York: St. Martin's, 1975).

16. Fulbright, "Promotion of Tourism."

17. Van Vleck, *Empire of the Air*, p. 213.

18. "Memorandum on the Tourism Requirements of Turkey," undated, central files: 1948–56, entry 1399, box 58, reports—T–Z, RG 469.

19. Süreyya Ergün, *Milli Kalkınma Vasıtalarından Otelcilik ve Turizm Milli Kredisi* [The hotel business and the tourism national credit as a vehicle for national development] (Ankara: Başvekalet Basın Yayın ve Umum Müdürlüğü Turizm Dairesi Yayınları, 1944), pp. 149, 152, 158–59.

20. "Turizm Uzmanı Raporunu Verdi" [Tourism expert delivers report], *Ulus*, August 30, 1949.

21. Charles White, "Tourism Survey of Turkey," August 1, 1949, central files: 1948–56, entry 1399, box 58, reports—T–Z, RG 469.

22. Theodore Pozzy, the chief of the TDS of the ECA, based in Paris, also took an

interest in the development of tourism in Turkey, periodically requesting, among other things, information for hotel-equipment surveys and free dollar expenditures for tourism promotion in the United States. See Pozzy to Dorr, February 27, 1951, and March 15, 1951, central files: 1948–56, entry 1399, box 59, reports—Z-Trade, RG 469.

23. Out of sixty-one hotels that applied to the board to be qualified as a "touristic hotel," only ten were approved. "Turizm İnkişafı İçin Tedbirler" [Measures for the development of tourism], *Ulus*, September 28, 1953.

24. Süreyya Ergün to Russell Dorr, June 11, 1951, central files: 1948–56, entry 1399, box 59, reports—Z-Trade, RG 469.

25. Suad Yurdkoru to Dorr, June 25, 1951, central files: 1948–56, entry 1399, box 59, reports—Z-Trade, RG 469.

26. "Ahmet Şükrü Esmer New York'ta" [Ahmet Şükrü Esmer in New York], *Vatan*, January 18, 1950.

27. Selahattin Çoruh, *Turizm ve Propaganda* (Ankara: Turing Yayinlari, 1958), pp. 13, 34–35.

28. Selahattin Çoruh, *Herkes İçin Turizm Bilgisi* [Tourism knowledge for everyone] (Ankara: Turing Yayınları, 1954), pp. 57, 61–62.

29. Ibid., p. 95–96.

30. Selahattin Çoruh, *Turizm Bilgi ve Terbiyesi: Turizm Öğretimi* [The knowledge and etiquette of tourism: Tourism education] (Ankara: Turing Yayınları, 1958), pp. 3, 13–17.

31. Şevket Rado, "Oteller Nasıl Çoğalabilir?" [How to increase hotels?], *Akşam*, December 21, 1950; Hüseyin Cahit Yalçın, "Seyahat Mevsimi" [Travel season], *Ulus*, July 21, 1955; Enis Tahsin Til, "Turist Gelmesini Temin İçin Neler Yapılmalıdır?" [What should be done to ensure the arrival of tourists?], *Vatan*, January 20, 1951; "Turist Celbi Meselesi" [The tourist enticement question], *Vatan*, January 21, 1951; Sedat Simavi, "Turistlere Kolaylık" [Convenience for tourists], *Hürriyet*, October 11, 1949; "Yine Turizm" [Tourism again], *Hürriyet*, July 22, 1950; and "Otelcilik" [Hotel management], *Hürriyet*, November 20, 1950.

32. Hüseyin Cahit Yalçın, "Döviz Açığı ve Turizm" [The dollar gap and tourism], *Ulus*, September 20, 1953; Sedat Simavi, "Turist Otelleri" [Tourist hotels], *Hürriyet*, October 6, 1948; "Turizme Yeni Veçhe" [New direction for tourism], *Hürriyet*, December 12, 1948.

33. Sedat Simavi, "Turist Kafilesi" [The tourist convoy], *Hürriyet*, February 26, 1950; Yalçın, "Turizm Bahsinde Canlı Nokta" [Vital point in tourism talk], *Ulus*, May 15, 1953; Ahmet Emin Yalman, "Yeni Ufuklar" [New horizons], *Vatan*, January 13, 1952; "Turizme Ehemmiyet Verilmesi İstendi" [Request that tourism be emphasized], *Vatan*, March 14, 1952.

34. Diker, *Amerika Birleşik Devletleri Yol İşleri.*

35. *Turistik Yollar Programı* [Touristic roads program], KGM Records.

36. Meltem Ö. Gürel, "Seashore Readings: The Road from Sea Baths to Summerhouses in Mid-Twentieth Century Izmir," in *Mid-Century Modernism in Turkey: Archi-*

tecture Across Cultures in the 1950s and 1960s, ed. Meltem Ö. Gürel (New York: Routledge, 2016).

37. Orhan Bayçu, *Amerika'ya Gideceklere Etiket ve Tavsiyeler* [Etiquette and advice for those traveling to America], KGM Records.

38. Van Vleck, *Empire of the Air*, p. 225.

39. The Hilton Hotels International Corporation started as a subsidiary of Hilton Hotels Corporation, until 1964, when it became an independent, publicly owned company. By that date, the Hilton International enterprise had spread to major European cities as well as to Tehran, Cairo, Jamaica, Panama, Hawaii, Hong Kong, and Tokyo, among others.

40. Hilton, *Be My Guest*, p. 112.

41. Ibid., p. 236.

42. Conrad Hilton, "Towards a Foreign Policy for Hotels" (speech, Los Angeles Rotary Club, July 27, 1956), box 6, HHI.

43. Hilton, *Be My Guest*, p. 21; Hilton, "The Uncommitted Third" (speech, National Conference of Christians and Jews, El Paso, March 7, 1957), box 16, file 5, speeches—1957–1962, Conrad N. Hilton Papers, Hospitality Industry Archives, Massad Family Library Research Center, University of Houston, Conrad N. Hilton College of Hotel and Restaurant Management (hereafter cited as CNH).

44. Hilton, "The Battle for Peace," *Hilton Items* 5, no. 12 (May 1952).

45. Hilton, "We Are the Innkeepers" (speech, Junior Chamber of Commerce, Kansas City, January 11, 1962), box 16, file 3, speeches—1957–1962, CNH.

46. Hilton, "Towards a Foreign Policy for Hotels" (speech, Los Angeles Rotary Club, July 27, 1956), box 6, HHI.

47. Hilton (speech, Ezra Cornell Dinner, May 8, 1954), box 12, folder 5, CNH.

48. Hilton, *Be My Guest*, p. 233.

49. "Memorandum of Hilton Hotel Project for ERP Countries," enclosed in Theodore Pozzy to Russell Dorr, June 6, 1950, central files: 1948–56, entry 1399, box 35, folder: Hilton Hotel—Private Projects, RG 469.

50. The lease follows the formula developed at the Caribe. Box 137, file 6: Istanbul Hilton Hotel, CNH.

51. "Agreement for Architectural Services between the Republic of Turkey and Skidmore, Owings and Merrill and Sedad Eldem," central files: 1948–56, entry 1399, box 35, folder: Hilton Hotel—Private Projects, RG 469.

52. *Quarterly Report on the Marshall Plan in Turkey*, number 7 (4/1/1951–6/30/1951) and number 13 (10/1/1952–12/31/1952) (Ankara: Günes, 1964).

53. "Expansion in Turkey," *Hilton Items* 15, no. 8 (January 1952): 4.

54. Conrad Hilton, "We Are the Innkeepers" (speech, Junior Chamber of Commerce, Kansas City, January 11, 1962), box 16, file 3, speeches—1957–1962, CNH. The badge of the city of Istanbul, which was conferred on Hilton by the municipality of Istanbul on June 1, 1955, is now among the prized possessions of the Hospitality Industry Archives at the University of Houston, decorating its walls.

55. Hilton, *Be My Guest*, pp. 265–66.

56. On Gökay's career as a eugenicist psychiatrist, see Aslı Iğsız, *Humanism in Ruins: Biopolitics, Culture and the Entangled Legacies of the 1923 Greek-Turkish Population Exchange*, forthcoming.

57. Houser to Hilton, August 27, 1950, and January 27, 1952, box 1, general correspondence: 1952, HHI.

58. "Turizm Sanayine Hız Verilecek" [Speed to the tourism industry], *Vatan*, May 7, 1953; "İstanbul'da Yapılacak Büyük Otel" [Large hotel to be built in Istanbul], *Ulus*, December 16, 1950.

59. Murat Gül, *The Emergence of Modern Istanbul: Transformation and Modernization of a City* (New York: IB Tauris, 2009), p. 152; Sibel Bozdoğan and Esra Akcan, *Turkey: Modern Architectures in History* (London: Reaktion, 2012), pp. 108–9.

60. *Karayolları Bülteni* 5, no. 54 (April 1955).

61. Henry Russell Hitchcock, introduction to *Architecture of Skidmore, Owings & Merrill, 1950–62*, by Ernst Danz (New York: Frederick A. Praeger, 1963), p. 10.

62. "Istanbul Hilton," *SOM News*, no. 8, October 15, 1954.

63. Wharton, *Building the Cold War*, p. 22.

64. "Istanbul Hilton," *The Hotel Monthly*, November 1955, p. 27.

65. De Grazia, *Irresistible Empire*, p. 353.

66. "Istanbul Hilton," *The Hotel Monthly*, November 1955, p. 27.

67. "Turistik Hotel" [Touristic hotel], *Arkitekt*, no. 243–44 (1952): 62. It should be noted, of course, that the Istanbul Hilton was not novel in its provision of these facilities. As Yavuz Yıldırım and Suha Özkan point out, "When it was opened in 1927, the Ankara Palas was popularly acclaimed as the symbol of modernity and civilization, with its pressurized water and central heating systems, its Western type toilets and bathtubs and its powerful electric generator, a unique feature in this rural Anatolian town accustomed to dim kerosene lamps." "Finding a National Idiom: The First National Style," in *Modern Turkish Architecture*, eds. Ahmet Evin and Renata Holod (Philadelphia: University of Pennsylvania Press, 1984), p. 56.

68. "Gala Opening in Istanbul," *Hilton Items* 19, no. 2 (July 1955).

69. "Expansion in Turkey," *Hilton Items* 15, no. 8 (January 1952): 4.

70. "Istanbul Hilton," *The Hotel Monthly*, November 1955, pp. 24–27.

71. "Hotel in Istanbul," *Architectural Review* 118, no. 11 (1955); "Gala Opening in Istanbul," *Hilton Items* 19 no. 2 (July 1955).

72. "Istanbul Hilton," *The Hotel Monthly*, November 1955, pp. 24–27.

73. Hilton, *Be My Guest*, p. 265.

74. On "staged authenticity," see Dean MacCannell, *The Tourist: A New Theory of the Leisure Class* (New York: Schocken, 1976).

75. Nathaniel Owings, *The Spaces in Between: An Architect's Journey* (Boston: Houghton Mifflin, 1973), p. 104.

76. Carol Krinsky, *Gordon Bunshaft of Skidmore, Owings & Merrill* (New York: Architectural History Foundation, 1988), p. 54.

77. Sibel Bozdoğan, "Modernity in Tradition: Works of Sedad Hakkı Eldem," in

Sedad Eldem: Architect in Turkey, eds. Sibel Bozdoğan, Suha Őzkan, and Engin Yenal (New York: Aperture, 1987), pp. 50, 61.

78. Bunshaft to Blackall, September 16, 1936, box 1, folder 16, Gordon Bunshaft Architectural Drawings and Papers, Avery Architectural and Fine Arts Library, Columbia University, New York (hereafter cited as GBP).

79. Mete Tapan, "International Style: Liberalism in Architecture," in Evin and Holod, *Modern Turkish Architecture*, p. 110; Enis Kortan, *Türkiye'de Mimarlık Hareketleri ve Eleştirisi (1950–60)* [Architectural movements and their critique in Turkey] (Ankara: ODTÜ Mimarlık Fakültesi, 1971), pp. 33 and 53.

80. Sibel Bozdoğan, "The Predicament of Modernism in Turkish Architectural Culture: An Overview," in *Rethinking Modernity and National Identity in Turkey*, eds. Sibel Bozdoğan and Reşat Kasaba (Seattle: University of Washington Press, 1997).

81. Suha Őzkan, "Echoes of Sedad Eldem," in Bozdoğan, Őzkan, and Yenal, *Sedad Eldem*, p. 16

82. Wharton, *Building the Cold War*, p. 37.

83. Sibel Bozdoğan, "Democracy, Development, and the Americanization of Turkish Architectural Culture in the 1950s," in *Modernism and the Middle East: Architecture and Politics in the Twentieth Century*, eds. Sandy Isenstadt and Kishwar Rizvi (Seattle: University of Washington Press, 2008).

84. Bozdoğan and Akcan, *Turkey*, pp. 66, 70, 98–99. On amnesia and memory, see Carel Bertram, *Imagining the Turkish House: Collective Visions of Home* (Austin: University of Texas Press, 2008), pp. 99–100.

85. Ela Kaçel, "Intellectualism and Consumerism: Ideologies, Practices and Criticisms of Common Sense Modernism in Postwar Turkey," PhD diss., Cornell University, 2009, chap. 2.

86. The Directorate supervised many of the construction's works and supplied the machinery, and the army also supplied the equipment and manpower for many of the demolitions and works. Gül, *The Emergence of Modern Istanbul*, pp. 124, 150.

87. "Olmayan Otelin İşletilmesi" [The management of a nonexistent hotel], *Akşam*, December 23, 1950.

88. Şevki Vanlı, "Hiltonculuk," *Kim*, November 28, 1958. Vanlı's coined phrase can be translated as "Hiltonism" with pejorative undertones. See Kaçel, "Intellectualism and Consumerism."

89. "Turkey 1951," box 5, folder 4, GBP.

90. Skidmore, Owings and Merrill, *Construction and Town Planning in Turkey*, pp. 4, 25, 28.

91. Bunshaft, interview by Marion L. Vanderbilt, September 1979 (as part of the oral autobiographies of the partners of SOM), box 8, GBP.

92. Despite these frustrations, Bunshaft's and Eldem's friendship seems to have persevered well into the 1970s, with Eldem asking to find work for young protégés at SOM (with no success) and Bunshaft visiting him in Istanbul. See Eldem to Bunshaft, June 19, 1973, box 1, folder 4, GBP; Bunshaft to Eldem, July 10, 1973, box 1, folder 4, GBP; and Bunshaft to Eldem, December 10, 1971, box 1, folder 4, GBP.

93. Hilton, *Be My Guest*, p. 264.

94. Carl Hilton to Conrad Hilton, August 8, 1952, and January 27, 1952, box 1, general correspondence: 1952, HHI.

95. Dean Carpenter to Conrad Hilton, April 28, 1954, box 1, general correspondence: 1953–54, HHI.

96. Cohn, "Some Propositions Concerning the Role of Human Factors in Economic Development," October 14, 1957, box 164, folder 4, CFR Records; "Time, the Future and Economic Development," November 12, 1957, box 164, folder 4, CFR Records.

97. Ahmet Emin Yalman, "Yeni Fahri Hemşerimiz" [Our new honorary citizen], *Vatan*, June 10, 1955.

98. "Thornburg Müşkülleri Yeneceksiniz Dedi" [Thornburg said you will overcome the difficulties], *Vatan*, January 17, 1954; Ahmet Emin Yalman, "Korkunç bir Baltalama Hareketi" [A terrible act of sabotage], *Vatan*, February 12, 1954; Lerner, *Passing*, p. 42.

99. "Turistik Otel İnşası İçin" [For the building of a touristic hotel], *TBMM Meclis Tutanakları*, Dönem 9, Cilt 12, January 30, 1952.

100. Ayşe Parla and Ceren Özgül, "Property, Dispossession, and Citizenship in Turkey; or, The History of the Gezi Uprising Starts in the Surp Hagop Armenian Cemetery," *Public Culture* 28, no. 3 (2016): 627.

101. Clause 30 involved the Hilton, wherein the tourism credit deposited at the Iller Bankasi (Provinces Bank) in the amount of $2 million each year (beginning with the budget year of 1953, until reaching $50 million) could be used towards the completion of this particular hotel. The exemptions provided for the project of a private firm were heatedly questioned, with Burhanettin Onat insisting that this clause expressed the spirit of this law. *TBMM Meclis Tutanakları*, Dönem 9, Cilt 21, April 30, 1953.

102. *TBMM Meclis Tutanakları*, Dönem 9, Cilt 21, April 20, 1953.

103. *TBMM Meclis Tutanakları*, Dönem 9, Cilt 21, April 27, 1953.

104. Asım Karaömerlioğlu, "Turkey's 'Return' to Multi-Party Politics: A Social Interpretation," *East European Quarterly* 40, no. 1 (2006): 97. Those who could not pay the taxes were sent to labor camps in eastern Turkey.

105. Rifat Bali, ed. *Anti-Greek Riots of September 6–7, 1955, Documents from the American National Archives* (Istanbul: Libra, 2015), pp. 17, 27, 121, 196, 223. See also Bali, ed., *6–7 Eylül 1955 Olayları: Tanıklar-Hatıralar* [The events of September 6–7, 1955: Witnesses, memories] (Istanbul: Libra 2010); Dilek Güven, *Cumhuriyet Dönemi Azınlık Politikalari ve Stratejileri Bağlamında 6–7 Eylül Olayları* [The events of September 6–7 in the context of Republican era minority policies and strategies] (Istanbul: Tarih Vakfı Yurt Yayınları, 2005).

106. *TBMM Meclis Tutanakları*, Dönem 9, Cilt 21, April 30, 1953.

107. Ibid.

108. Mübeccel Kıray, *Yedi Yerleşme Noktasında Turizmle Ilgili Sosyal Yapı Analizi* [Social-structure analysis in seven settlement units] (Ankara: Turizm ve Tanıtma Bakanlığı, 1964), pp. 11, 38–39, 41, 88–89.

109. Anne McClintock, *Imperial Leather: Race, Gender, and Sexuality in the Colonial Contest* (New York: Routledge, 1995); Ross, *Fast Cars, Clean Bodies*.

110. "Obtaining Private Investment Capital from the United States for Turkey for Hotel Building and Tourism," enclosed in memorandum, Mitchell to Dorr, June 22, 1950, entry 1399, box 35, projects: Private H–I, folder: Hotels—Intercontinental, RG 469.

111. Moore to Wadsworth, November 11, 1949, entry 1399, box 35, projects: Private H–I, folder: Hotels—Intercontinental, RG 469.

112. On the history of Pan Am's role in foreign aviation development projects, such as its collaboration with the US military in Latin America during World War II, see Van Vleck, *Empire of the Air.*

113. Moore was born on December 1, 1908, in Washington, DC, where his father, having fought in Cuba and the Philippines during the Spanish-American War, served as military aide to President Theodore Roosevelt. Moore Jr. became an investment banker after studying physics at Yale, and he drafted Ohio's securities act in 1938.

114. Moore to Francis Green, September 15, 1950, enclosed in Green to Paul Hoffman, October 11, 1950, entry 1399, box 35, folder: Hotels—Intercontinental (1 of 2), RG 469. Moore also wrote to Robert Taft, Claude Pepper, and Mike Mansfield.

115. Moore got his brother-in-law, the Washington pundit Drew Pearson, to attack both the ECA and Ambassador Wadsworth in the *Washington Post.* "ECA Snarls Pan Am Hotel Plan," December 28, 1949; "Ambassador May Be on Way Out," December 29, 1949.

116. Pepper to Dorr, March 15, 1950, entry 1399, box 35, folder: Hotels—Intercontinental, RG 469; Mansfield to Hoffman, March 14, 1950, entry 1399, box 35, folder: Hotels—Intercontinental, RG 469; Dorr to Pepper, March 29, 1950, entry 1399, box 35, folder: Hotels—Intercontinental, RG 469.

117. Mansfield to Hoffman, September 19, 1950, entry 1399, box 35, folder: Hotels—Intercontinental, RG 469 (emphasis in original).

118. Dorr to Pepper, March 29, 1950, entry 1399, box 35, folder: Hotels—Intercontinental (1 of 2), RG 469; Hochstetter to Dorr, November 25, 1949, entry 1399, box 35, folder: Hotels—Intercontinental (1 of 2), RG 469. It should be noted that Hilton also had difficulties with the administration in Rome and London, with John Houser initially describing interactions with the ECA as the "darnedest struggle" up to the moment they secured the Istanbul deal. Houser to Hilton, August 13, 1950, box 1, general correspondence: 1950, HHI.

119. Memorandum, meeting at the Ministry of State between Fevzi Lütfü Karaosmanoğlu, minister of state, and Russell Dorr, October 18, 1950, entry 1399, box 18, 1948–53 meetings, Istanbul Hotel Project, RG 469).

120. Memorandum, conference with George Asp of Intercontinental Hotels with Dorr and McJunkins, October 24, 1950, entry 1399, box 35, folder: Hotels—Intercontinental, RG 469. Moore went on to become a public speaker and novelist. His *Terrible Game*, published a few years after his taxing stay in Turkey, revolves around an atomic howitzer base in the TransBaikal region, which is populated with a Turkish-speaking, oil-wrestling community (New York: Berkley Publishing, 1958).

121. Ali Nuri Okday to McJunkins, August 20, 1951, entry 1399, box 35, folder: Hotels—Intercontinental, RG 469; McJunkins to Okday, August 31, 1951, entry 1399, box 35, folder: Intercontinental Hotel, RG 469.

Conclusion

1. Frederick Frey, "Niçin Türkiye?" [Why Turkey?, Part 1], *Forum* 11, no. 128 (July 15, 1959).

2. Frey, "Niçin Türkiye?" [Why Turkey?, Part 2], *Forum* 11, no. 129 (July 31, 1959).

3. Tsing, *Friction*, p. 5. On contact zones, see Mary Louise Pratt, *Imperial Eyes: Travel Writing and Transculturation* (New York: Routledge, 1992).

4. Gabriel Almond, *A Discipline Divided: Schools and Sects in Political Science* (Newbury Park: Sage, 1990), p. 227.

5. Oren, *Our Enemies and US*, p. 147.

6. Rohde, *Armed with Expertise*, p. 19. Rohde's account draws on "Remarks of Leonard W. Doob," in *Proceedings of the Symposium: The US Army's Limited-War Mission and Social Science Research*, ed. William A. Lybrand (Washington, DC: SORO, 1962), p. 236.

7. Rohde, *Armed with Expertise*, pp. 140–41.

8. Immerwahr, *Thinking Small*, p. 135. See also Sackley, "Village Models."

9. "Commander's Guide to Money as a Weapons System Handbook: Tactics, Techniques, and Procedures," prepared by the Center for Army Lessons Learned, April 2009, http://www.usma.edu/cnrcd/SiteAssets/SitePages/Government%20Publications/CALL%20MAAWS%20Handbook%2009-27%20%28APRIL%2009%29.pdf. The handbook credits General David Petraeus with the concept, saying, "In fact, depending on the situation, money can be more important than real ammunition—and that has often been the case in Iraq since early April 2003." David Petraeus, "Learning Counterinsurgency: Observations from Soldiering in Iraq," *Military Review* (January–February 2006): 4.

10. See "Iraq's Investment Climate 2012," prepared by the World Bank, http://documents.worldbank.org/curated/en/224621468261277147/pdf/770960ICA020120IRACoB0x377289B00PUBLIC0.pdf; "Doing Business in Iraq: 2013 Country Commercial Guide for US Companies," prepared by US & Foreign Commercial Service and US Department of State, photos.state.gov/libraries/iraq/216651/. . ./Doing_Business_in_Iraq_CCG_2012.pdf; and "Kurdish Investment Guide 2011," prepared by the Kurdish Regional Government, http://cabinet.gov.krd/uploads/documents/Kurdistan_Investment_Guide_2011.pdf.

11. "Hard Lessons: The Iraq Reconstruction Experience," January 2009, https://usiraq.procon.org/sourcefiles/hard_lessons12-08.pdf; "Commander's Emergency Response Program: Hotel Construction Completed, but Project Management Issues Remain," July 2009, https://permanent.access.gpo.gov/gpo4713/09-026.pdf; "Learning from Iraq: A Final Report from the Special Inspector General for Iraq Reconstruction," March 2013, pdf.usaid.gov/pdf_docs/pcaac502.pdf.

12. Toby Dodge, "Coming Face to Face with Bloody Reality: Liberal Common Sense and the Ideological Failure of the Bush Doctrine in Iraq," *International Politics* 46, no. 2/3 (2009): 253–75.

13. Larry Diamond, "What Went Wrong in Iraq?," *Foreign Affairs* (September/October 2004).

14. Larry Diamond, *Squandered Victory: The American Occupation and the Bungled Effort to Bring Democracy to Iraq* (New York: Henry Holt, 2006), p. 294.

15. Rohde, *Armed with Expertise*, p. 3.

16. Diamond, *Squandered Victory*, p. 305.

17. Citino, *Envisioning the Arab Future*, chap. 6.

18. Nilüfer Göle, "Engineers: 'Technocratic Democracy'" in *Turkey and the West: Changing Political and Cultural Identities*, eds. Metin Heper, Ayşe Öncü, and Heinz Kramer (New York: IB Tauris, 1993).

19. Landon Thomas Jr., "In Turkey's Example, Some See Map for Egypt," *New York Times*, February 5, 2011; Tariq Ramadan, "Democratic Turkey Is the Template for Egypt's Muslim Brotherhood," *Huffington Post*, 2011, http://www.huffingtonpost.com/tariq-ramadan/post_1690_b_820366.html; Benjamin Harvey, Gregory Viscusi, and Massoud A. Derhally, "Arabs Battling Regimes See Erdogan's Muslim Democracy as Model," *Bloomberg*, February 4, 2011, http://www.bloomberg.com/news/articles/2011-02-04/arabs-battling-regimes-see-erdogan-s-muslim-democracy-in-turkey-as-model.

20. Tuğal, *Fall of the Turkish Model*, p. 11.

21. Jerry Bowyer, "As the Arab Spring Fades and the Turkish Model Collapses, Can Islam Foster Prosperity?," *Forbes*, June 25, 2013, http://www.forbes.com/sites/jerrybowyer/2013/06/25/as-the-arab-spring-fades-and-the-turkish-model-collapses-can-islam-foster-prosperity/.

22. Nicholas Glastonbury and Defne Kadıoğlu, "'Cleaning out the Ghettos': Urban Governance and the Remaking of Kurdistan," *Jadaliyya*, March 18, 2016, http://www.jadaliyya.com/pages/index/24097/"cleaning-out-the-ghettos"_-urban-governance-and-t.

Bibliography

Government Archives and Private Collections

Avery Architectural and Fine Arts Library, Columbia University, New York
 Gordon Bunshaft Architectural Drawings and Papers
DRP, Dankwart Rustow Private Papers, New York
Grand National Assembly Archives, Ankara, Turkey
 Parliamentary Records
Hospitality Industry Archives, Massad Family Library Research Center, University of Houston, Conrad N. Hilton College of Hotel and Restaurant Management, Houston, Texas
 CNH, Conrad N. Hilton Papers
 HHI, Records of the Hilton Hotels International
MIT Institute Archives and Special Collections, Cambridge, Massachusetts
 DLP, Daniel Lerner Papers
National Archives and Record Administration, College Park, MD
 Record Group 30, Bureau of Public Roads Classified Central Files
 Record Group 59, Records of the Department of State
 Record Group 306, Records of the US Information Agency
 Record Group 469, Records of US Foreign Assistance Agencies, 1948–1961
Rare Book & Manuscript Library, Columbia University, New York City, New York
 (HHP) Herbert H. Hyman Papers
Records of the General Directorate of Highways, Ankara, Turkey
 KGM Records, Records of the General Directorate of Highways, Ankara, Turkey
Seely G. Mudd Library, Princeton University, Princeton, New Jersey
 (CFR) Records of the Council on Foreign Relations

Newspapers and Magazines

Akşam
Arkitekt

Forum
Hilton Items
Hürriyet
Karayolları Bülteni [Highway Bulletin]
Milliyet
SOM News
Ulus
Vatan

Secondary Sources

A Committee of the Ankara University Faculty of Political Science. *Economic and Social Aspects of Farm Mechanization in Turkey*. Ankara: Ankara Üniversitesi SBF, 1953.

A Committee of the Ankara University Faculty of Political Science and New York University Graduate School of Public Administration and Social Service. *Kaza ve Vilayet İdaresi Üzerinde Bir Araştırma*. Ankara: Ankara Üniversitesi SBF Yayınları, 1957.

Abadan, Nermin. *Batı Almanya'daki Türk İşçileri ve Sorunları*. Ankara: T. C. Başbakanlık Devlet Planlama Teşkilatı, 1964.

———. "Devlet İdaresinde Menfaat Gruplarının Rolü." *Ankara Üniversitesi SBF Dergisi* 14, no. 1 (1959).

———. *Halk Efkarı*. Ankara: Ankara Üniversitesi SBF Yayınları, 1956.

———. "Siyasi İlimlerde Gelişim Eğilimleri: Birleşik Amerika, İngiltere, Batı Almanya ve Fransa'daki Çalışmaların Mukayeseli İncelenmesi." *Ankara Üniversitesi SBF Dergisi* 17, no. 3 (1962).

———. *Üniversite Öğrencilerinin Serbest Zaman Faaliyetleri: Ankara Yüksek Öğrenim Gençliği Üzerinde Bir Araştırma*. Ankara: Ankara Üniversitesi SBF Yayınları, 1962.

Abadan, Yavuz. "Mukayeseli Devlet İdaresinin Ana Konuları ve Ortadoğu." *Ankara Üniversitesi SBF Dergisi* 17, no. 3 (1962).

Abadan-Unat, Nermin. *Kum Saatini Izlerken*. Istanbul: İletişim, 1996.

Abrams, Charles. *The Need for Training and Education for Housing and Planning*, TAA 173/57/018, Report No: TAA/TUR/13. New York: United Nations Technical Assistance Program, 1955.

Abu El-Haj, Nadia. *Facts on the Ground: Archaeological Practice and Territorial Self-Fashioning in Israeli Society*. Chicago: University of Chicago Press, 2001.

Adalet, Begüm. "Questions of Modernization: Coding Speech, Regulating Attitude in Survey Research." *Comparative Studies in Society and History* 57, no. 4 (October 2015).

Adams, Walter, and John A. Garraty. *Is the World Our Campus?* Michigan: Michigan State University Press, 1960.

Adas, Michael. *Dominance by Design: Technological Imperatives and America's Civilizing Mission*. Cambridge, MA: The Belknap Press of Harvard University Press, 2006.

———. *Machines as the Measure of Men: Science, Technology, and Ideologies of Western Dominance*. Ithaca, NY: Cornell University Press, 1989.

Ahmad, Feroz. *The Turkish Experiment in Democracy, 1950–1975*. Boulder, CO: Westview Press, 1977.

Ahmad, Feroz, and Bedia Turgay Ahmad. *Türkiye'de Çok Partili Politikanın Açıklamalı Kronolojisi (1945–1971)*. Ankara: Bilgi, 1976.

Akça, Ismet, Ahmet Bekmen, and Barış Ozden, eds. *Turkey Reframed: Constituting Neoliberal Hegemony*. London: Pluto Press, 2014.

Aksel, Keith. "The Engineering Generation: The Story of the Technicians Who Enabled American Cold War Foreign Policy, 1945–1961." PhD diss., University of Colorado, 2016.

Aktüre, Sevgi, Sevin Osmay, and Ayşen Savaş. *1956'dan 2006'ya ODTU Mimarlık Fakültesinin 50 Yılı*. Ankara: ODTU Mimarlık Fakültesi, 2007.

Almond, Gabriel. "Comparative Political Systems." *The Journal of Politics* 18, no. 3 (August 1956): 391–409.

———. *A Discipline Divided: Schools and Sects in Political Science*. Newbury Park: Sage, 1990.

———. "Political Theory and Political Science." *The American Political Science Review* 60, no. 4 (December 1966): 869–79.

———. "Research in Comparative Politics: Plans of a New Council Committee." *Items* 8, no. 1 (March 1954).

Almond, Gabriel, and James Coleman, eds. *The Politics of the Developing Areas*. Princeton, NJ: Princeton University Press, 1960.

Almond, Gabriel, Cole Taylor, and Roy Macridis. "A Suggested Research Strategy in Western European Government and Politics." *The American Political Science Review* 49, no. 4 (December 1955): 1042–49.

Almond, Gabriel, and Sidney Verba. *The Civic Culture: Political Attitudes and Democracy in Five Nations*. Princeton, NJ: Princeton University Press, 1963.

Amadae, S. M. *Rationalizing Capitalist Democracy: The Cold War Origins of Rational Choice Liberalism*. Chicago: University of Chicago Press, 2003.

American Association for Public Opinion Research Conference Proceedings. "Contributions of Opinion Research to Psychological Warfare." In Simpson, *Science of Coercion*.

Anderson, Benedict. *Imagined Communities*. London: Verso, 1983.

Anılarla Karayolları Tarihi. Ankara: Karayolları Genel Müdürlüğü, 2007.

Appadurai, Arjun. *The Social Life of Things*. Cambridge, UK: Cambridge University Press, 1986.

Araştırma Şubesi Toplum Yapısı Araştırma Grubu. *Türk Köyünde Modernleşme Eğilimleri Araştırması*. Ankara: Devlet Planlama Teşkilatı, 1970.

Armaoğlu, Fahir H., and Guthrie G. Birkhead. *Siyasal Bilgiler Fakültesi 1946–55 Mezunları Hakkında Bir Araştırma*. Ankara: TODAIE, 1956.

Asad, Talal. *Anthropology and the Colonial Encounter*. London: Ithaca Press, 1973.

Aydemir, Şevket Süreyya. *Menderes' in Dramı, 1899–1960*. Istanbul: Remzi Kitabevi, 1969.

Babur, Mustafa, İsmet İlter, and Nevzat Erdoğdu, eds. *Karayolları Genel Müdürlüğü 25 Yaşında*. Ankara: Karayolları Genel Müdürlüğü, 1975.

Bakhtin, M. M. *The Dialogic Imagination: Four Essays*. Translated by Emerson, Caryl, and Holquist, Michael. Austin: University of Texas Press, 2008.

Bali, Rifat, ed. *Anti-Greek Riots of September 6–7, 1955, Documents from the American National Archives*. Istanbul: Libra, 2015.

———, ed. *6–7 Eylül 1955 Olalylari: Taniklar-Hatiralar*. Istanbul: Libra 2010.

Balta, Ecehan. "1945 Çiftçiyi Topraklandırma Kanunu: Reform Mu Karşı Reform Mu?" *Praksis* 5 (2002): 277–98.

Bamba, Abou. "Triangulating a Modernization Experiment: The United States, France, and the Making of the Kossou Project in Central Ivory Coast." *Journal of Modern European History* 8, no. 1 (2010): 66–84.

Barak, On. *On Time: Technology and Temporality in Modern Egypt*. Berkeley: University of California Press, 2013.

Barker, James, and the Economic Mission to Turkey. *The Economy of Turkey: An Analysis and Recommendations for a Development Program*. Washington, DC: IBRD, 1951.

Barry, Andrew. "Lines of Communication and Spaces of Rule." In Barry, Osborne, and Rose, *Foucault and Political Reason*.

Barry, Andrew, Thomas Osborne, and Nikolas Rose. *Foucault and Political Reason: Liberalism, Neo-Liberalism, and Rationalities of Government*. Chicago: University of Chicago Press, 1996.

Barthes, Roland. "The Eiffel Tower." In *A Barthes Reader*, edited by Susan Sontag. New York: Hill and Wang, 2001.

Belge, Burhan. "Bizdeki Azliklar." *Kadro* 16 (1933).

Bell, Duncan. "Writing the World: Disciplinary History and Beyond." *International Affairs* 85, no. 10 (2009).

Berkes, Niyazi. *Bazı Ankara Köyleri Üzerinde Bir Araştırma*. Ankara: Uzluk Basımevi, 1942.

———. *The Development of Secularism in Turkey*. Montreal: McGill University Press, 1964.

———. "Review Essay: Political Modernization in Japan and Turkey." *International Journal* 20, no. 2: 1965.

———. *Türkiye'de Çağdaşlaşma*. Ankara: Bilgi Yayınevi, 1973.

———. *Unutulan Yıllar*. Istanbul: Iletişim, 1997.

Bertram, Carel. *Imagining the Turkish House: Collective Visions of Home*. Austin: University of Texas Press, 2008.

Beşikçi, İsmail. *Doğuda Değişim ve Yapısal Sorunlar*. Ankara: Sevinç, 1969.

———. *Doğu Mitingleri'nin Analizi*. Istanbul: Yurt, 1967.

Binschof, Gunter. "Conquering the Foreigner: The Marshall Plan and the Revival of Postwar Austrian Tourism." In *The Marshall Plan in Austria*, edited by Gunter Binschof, Anton Pelinka, and Dieter Stiefel. Livingston, NJ: Transaction Publishers, 2000.

Birtek, Faruk. "The Rise and Fall of Etatism in Turkey, 1932–1950: The Uncertain Road in the Restructuring of a Semiperipheral Economy." *Review (Fernand Braudel Center)* 8, no. 3 (1985): 407–38.

Birtek, Faruk, and Çağlar Keyder. ""Agriculture and the State: An Inquiry into Agricultural Differentiation and Political Alliances: The Case of Turkey." *Journal of Peasant Studies* 2, no. 4 (July 1975).

Bisbee, Eleanor. *The New Turks: Pioneers of the Republic, 1920–1950*. Philadelphia: University of Pennsylvania Press, 1951.

Blatt, Jessica. "'To Bring Out the Best That Is in Their Blood': Race, Reform, and Civilization in the *Journal of Race Development* (1910–1919)." *Ethnic and Racial Studies* 27, no. 5 (2004): 691–709.

Bockman, Johanna, and Gil Eyal. "Eastern Europe as a Laboratory for Economic Knowledge: The Transnational Roots of Neoliberalism." *American Journal of Sociology* 108, no. 2 (September 2002): 310–52.

Bonilla, Frank. "Survey Techniques." In Ward, *Studying Politics Abroad*.

Bora, Tanıl. "Türkiye'de Siyasi İdeolojilerde ABD/Amerika İmgesi." In *Modern Türkiye'de Siyasi Düşünce Cilt 3/Modernleşme ve Batıcılık*, edited by Tanil Bora and Murat Gültekingil. Istanbul: İletişim Yayinlari, 2002.

Boran, Behice. *Toplumsal Yapı Araştırmaları: İki Köy Çeşidinin Mukayeseli Tetkiki*. Ankara: Türk Tarih Kurumu Basımevi, 1945.

Bozdoğan, Sibel. "Democracy, Development, and the Americanization of Turkish Architectural Culture in the 1950s." In *Modernism and the Middle East: Architecture and Politics in the Twentieth Century*, edited by Sandy Isenstadt and Kishwar Rizvi. Seattle: University of Washington Press, 2008.

———. *Modernism and Nation Building: Turkish Architectural Culture in the Early Republic*. Studies in Modernity and National Identity. Seattle: University of Washington Press, 2001.

———. "Modernity in Tradition: Works of Sedad Hakkı Eldem." In Bozdoğan, Őzkan, and Yenal, *Sedad Eldem*.

———. "The Predicament of Modernism in Turkish Architectural Culture: An Overview." In Bozdoğan and Kasaba, *Rethinking Modernity and National Identity in Turkey*.

Bozdoğan, Sibel, and Esra Akcan. *Turkey: Modern Architectures in History*. London: Reaktion, 2012.

Bozdoğan, Sibel, and Reşat Kasaba, eds. *Rethinking Modernity and National Identity in Turkey*. Seattle: University of Washington Press, 1997.

Bozdoğan, Sibel, Suha Özkan, and Engin Yenal. *Sedad Eldem: Architect in Turkey*. New York: Aperture, 1987.

Byrne, Jeffrey James. "Our Own Special Brand of Socialism: Algeria and the Contest of Modernities in the 1960s." *Diplomatic History* 33, no. 3 (2009).

Çağaptay, Soner. "Reconfiguring the Turkish Nation in the 1930s." *Nationalism and Ethnic Politics* 8, no. 2 (2002): 68.

Callon, Michel. "Some Elements of a Sociology of Translation: Domestication of the

Scallops and the Fishermen of St. Brieuc Bay." In *Power, Action, Belief: A New Sociology of Knowledge?*, edited by John Law. New York: Routledge, 1986.
———. "What Does It Mean to Say That Economics Is Performative?" Working Papers Series 5, Centre de Sociologie de l'Innovation, 2006.
Callon, Michel, Pierre Lascoumes, and Yannick Barthe. *Acting in an Uncertain World: An Essay on Technical Democracy.* Translated by Graham Burchell. Cambridge, MA: MIT Press, 2009.
Cammack, Paul. *Capitalism and Democracy in the Third World: The Doctrine for Political Development.* London: Leicester University Press, 1997.
Carroll-Burke, Patrick. *Science, Culture, and Modern State Formation.* Berkeley: University of California Press, 2006.
———. "Tools, Instruments and Engines: Getting a Handle on the Specificity of Engine Science." *Social Studies of Science* 31, no. 4 (August 2001): 593–625.
Çelik, Zeynep. *The Remaking of Istanbul: Portrait of an Ottoman City in the Nineteenth Century.* Berkeley: University of California Press, 1986.
Cengizkan, Ali. *Modernin Saati: 20. Yüzyılda Mondernleşme ve Demokratikleşme Pratiğinde Mimarlar, Kamusal Mekan ve Konut Mimarlığı.* Istanbul: Boyut Yayın Grubu, 2002.
Citino, Nathan. "The 'Crush' of Ideologies: The United States, the Arab World, and Cold War Modernization." *Cold War History* 12, no. 1 (2012): 89–110.
———. *Envisioning the Arab Future: Modernization in US-Arab Relations, 1945–1967.* Cambridge, UK: Cambridge University Press, 2017.
———. "The Ottoman Legacy in Cold War Modernization." *International Journal of Middle East Studies* 40, no. 4 (2008): 579–97.
Clapp, Gordon. *The TVA: An Approach to the Development of a Region.* Chicago: University of Chicago Press, 1955.
Clifford, James. *Routes: Travel and Translation in the Late Twentieth Century.* Cambridge, MA: Harvard University Press, 1997.
———. *Writing Culture: The Poetics and Politics of Ethnography.* Berkeley: University of California Press, 1986.
Cody, Jeffrey. *Exporting American Architecture, 1870–2000.* New York: Routledge, 2003.
Cohn, Edwin. "The Climate for Research in the Social Sciences in Turkey." *Middle East Journal* 22, no. 2 (Spring 1968): 205.
———. "Social and Cultural Factors Affecting the Emergence and Functioning of Innovators." In *Social Aspects of Economic Development: A Report of the International Conference on Social Aspects of Economic Development*, Istanbul, August 4–24, 1963, sponsored by the Economic and Social Studies Conference Board. Istanbul: Conference Board, 1964.
———. *Turkish Economic, Social, and Political Change: The Development of a More Prosperous and Open Society.* New York: Praeger Publishers, 1970.
Coleman, James. *Education and Political Development.* Princeton, NJ: Princeton University Press, 1965.

Converse, Jean. *Survey Research in the United States: Roots and Emergence*. Berkeley: University of California Press, 1987.

Cooper, Frederick. *Colonialism in Question: Theory, Knowledge, History*. Berkeley: University of California Press, 2005.

———. "Writing the History of Development." *Journal of Modern European History* 8 (2010).

Cooper, Frederick, and Randall Packard, eds. *International Development and the Social Sciences: Essays on the History and Politics of Knowledge*. Berkeley: University of California Press, 1997.

Çoruh, Selahattin . *Herkes İçin Turizm Bilgisi*. Ankara: Turing Yayınları, 1954.

———. *Turizm Bilgi ve Terbiyesi: Turizm Öğretimi*. Ankara: Turing Yayınları, 1958.

———. *Turizm ve Propaganda*. Ankara: Turing Yayinlari, 1958.

Crick, Malcolm. "Representations of International Tourism in the Social Sciences: Sun, Sex, Sights, Savings, and Servility." *Annual Review of Anthropology* 18 (1989).

Cullather, Nick. "Damming Afghanistan: Modernization in a Buffer State." *The Journal of American History* 89, no. 9 (2002): 512–37.

———. "Development? It's History." *Diplomatic History* 24, no. 4 (2000): 641–53.

———. *The Hungry World: America's Cold War Battle Against Poverty in Asia*. Cambridge, MA: Harvard University Press, 2010.

Cummings, Bruce. "Boundary Displacement: Area Studies and International Studies During and After the Cold War." In Simpson, *Universities and Empire*.

Cummings, Herbert. "Turkish Highway Program—An Interim Economic Appraisal." *Foreign Commerce Weekly* 45, no. 8 (November 19, 1951).

Danz, Ernst. *Architecture of Skidmore, Owings & Merrill, 1950–1962*. New York: Frederick A. Praeger, 1963.

Daston, Lorraine, and Peter Galison. "The Image of Objectivity." *Representations* 40 (Autumn 1992).

De Grazia, Victoria. *Irresistible Empire: America's Advance Through Twentieth-Century Europe*. Cambridge, MA: Harvard University Press, 2005.

De Long, Bradford, and Barry Eichengreen. "The Marshall Plan: History's Most Successful Structural Adjustment Program." Working Paper No. 3899, National Bureau of Economic Research, 1991.

Derrida, Jacques. "Archive Fever: A Freudian Impression." *Diacritics* 25, no. 2 (1995).

———. *Dissemination*. Translated by Barbara Johnson. Chicago: University of Chicago Press, 1981.

Desroiseres, Alain. *The Politics of Large Numbers: A History of Statistical Reasoning*. Cambridge, MA: Harvard University Press, 2002.

Deutsch, Karl. "Social Mobilization and Political Development." *The American Political Science Review* 55, no. 3 (1961): 493–514.

Diamond, Larry. *Squandered Victory: The American Occupation and the Bungled Effort to Bring Democracy to Iraq*. New York: Henry Holt, 2006.

———. "What Went Wrong in Iraq?," *Foreign Affairs* (September/October 2004).

Diker, Vecdi. "Amerika'da Yol Sistemi ve Türkiye'de Tatbiki İktisadi Olabilecek Yol Tipleri." In Yollar Türk Milli Komitesi, *Vecdi Diker'in Ardından*, p. 16.

Dodge, Toby. "Coming Face to Face with Bloody Reality: Liberal Common Sense and the Ideological Failure of the Bush Doctrine in Iraq." *International Politics* 46, no. 2/3 (2009): 253–75.

Dündar, Fuat. *Ittihat ve Terakki'nin Müslümanları Iskan Politikası 1913–1919*. Istanbul: İletişim, 2001.

———. *Modern Türkiye'nin Şifresi: Ittihat ve Terakki'nin Etnitiste Mühendisliği (1913–1918)*. Istanbul: İletişim, 2008.

Eco, Umberto. "Function and Sign." In *Rethinking Architecture: A Reader in Cultural Theory*, edited by Neil Leach. New York: Routledge, 1997.

Ekbladh, David. *The Great American Mission: Modernization and the Construction of an American World Order*. Princeton, NJ: Princeton University Press, 2010.

———. "Mr. TVA": Grass-Roots Development, David Lilienthal, and the Rise and Fall of the Tennessee Valley Authority as a Symbol for US Overseas Development, 1933–1973." *Diplomatic History* 26, no. 3 (2002): 335–374.

Elshakry, Marwa. *Reading Darwin in Arabic, 1860–1950*. Chicago: University of Chicago Press, 2013.

El Shakry, Omnia. *The Great Social Laboratory: Subjects of Knowledge in Colonial and Postcolonial Egypt*. Stanford, CA: Stanford University Press, 2007.

Elyachar, Julia. "Upending Infrastructure: *Tamarod,* Resistance, and Agency after the January 25th Revolution in Egypt." *History and Anthropology* 25, no. 4 (2014): 452–71.

Endy, Christopher. *Cold War Holidays: American Tourism in France*. Chapel Hill: University of North Carolina Press, 2004.

Engerman, David. "Bernath Lecture: American Knowledge and Global Power." *Diplomatic History* 31, no. 4 (2007): 599–622.

———. *Modernization from the Other Shore: American Intellectuals and the Romance of Russian Development*. Cambridge, MA: Harvard University Press, 2003.

———. "The Second World's Third World." *Kritika: Explorations in Russian and Eurasian History* 12, no. 1 (2011): 183–211.

———. "Social Science in the Cold War." *Isis* 101, no. 2 (June 2010): 393–400.

Engerman, David, Nils Gilman, Mark Haefele, and Michael Latham, eds. *Staging Growth: Modernization, Development, and the Global Cold War*. Culture, Politics, and the Cold War. Amherst: University of Massachusetts Press, 2003.

Engerman, David, and Corinna Unger. "Introduction: Towards a Global History of Modernization." *Diplomatic History* 33, no. 3 (June 2009): 375–85.

Ergün, Süreyya. *Milli Kalkınma Vasıtalarından Otelcilik ve Turizm Milli Kredisi*. Ankara: Başvekalet Basın Yayın ve Umum Müdürlüğü Turizm Dairesi Yayınları, 1944.

Erten, Oğuz. *Sıradışı Bir Hayattan Sıradışı Bir Sanata: Tosun Bayrak*. Istanbul: Galeri Baraz Yayınları, 2014.

Escobar, Arturo. *Encountering Development: The Making and Unmaking of the Third World*. Princeton, NJ: Princeton University Press, 1995.

Esen, Berk, and Sebnem Gümüşçü. "Rising Competitive Authoritarianism in Turkey." *Third World Quarterly* 37, no. 9 (2016): 1581–606.

Evin, Ahmet, and Renata Holod, ed. *Modern Turkish Architecture.* Philadelphia: University of Pennsylvania Press, 1984.

Eyal, Gil, and Larissa Buchholz. "From the Sociology of Intellectuals to the Sociology of Interventions." *The Annual Review of Sociology* 36 (2010): 117–37.

Fabian, Johannes. *Time and the Other: How Anthropology Makes Its Object.* New York: Columbia University Press, 1983.

Farr, James, John Dryzek, and Leonard Stephen, eds. *Political Science in History: Research Programs and Political Traditions.* Cambridge, UK: Cambridge University Press, 1995.

Feldman, Ilana. *Governing Gaza: Bureaucracy, Authority, and the Work of Rule, 1917–1967.* Durham, NC: Duke University Press, 2008.

Feldman, Keith. *A Shadow Over Palestine: The Imperial Life of Race in America.* Minneapolis: University of Minnesota Press, 2015.

Ferguson, James. *The Anti-Politics Machine: "Development," Depoliticization and Bureaucratic Power in Lesotho.* Cambridge, UK: Cambridge University Press, 1990.

Ferguson, James. *Expectations of Modernity: Myths and Meanings of Urban Life on the Zambian Copperbelt.* Perspectives on Southern Africa 57. Berkeley: University of California Press, 1999.

———. *Global Shadows: Africa in the Neoliberal World Order.* Durham, NC: Duke University Press, 2006.

Flink, James. *The Car Culture.* Cambridge, MA: MIT Press, 1975.

Foucault, Michel. *The Archaeology of Knowledge and the Discourse on Language.* Translated by A. M. Sheridan Smith. New York: Pantheon Books, 1982.

———. *Madness and Civilization: A History of Insanity in the Age of Reason.* New York: Vintage, 1988.

———. *Security, Territory, Population: Lectures at the College de France 1977-1978.* Translated by Graham Burchell. New York: Palgrave, 2007.

Frey, Frederick. "Cross-Cultural Survey Research in Political Science." In Holt and Turner, *The Methodology of Comparative Research.*

———. "Education." In Ward and Rustow, *Political Modernization in Japan and Turkey.*

———. "Political Development, Power, and Communications in Turkey." In Pye, *Communications and Political Development.*

———. "Political Leadership in Turkey: The Social Backgrounds of Deputies to the Grand National Assembly, 1920–1957." PhD diss., Princeton University, 1962.

———. *Rural Development Research Project Report No. 3: The Mass Media and Rural Development in Turkey.* Cambridge, MA: CENIS, 1966.

———. *Rural Development Research Project Report No. 4: Regional Variations in Rural Turkey. Cambridge: CENIS*, 1966.

———. "Surveying Peasant Attitudes in Turkey." *The Public Opinion Quarterly* 27, no. 3 (Autumn 1963): 335–55.

———, ed. *Survey Research on Comparative Social Change: A Bibliography*. Cambridge, MA: MIT Press, 1969.

———. *The Turkish Political Elite*. Cambridge, MA: MIT Press, 1965.

Frey, Frederick, George Angell, and Abdurrahman Sanay. *Lise Seviyesindeki Öğrencilerin Değer Sistemleri: Öğrencilerin Meslek Gruplarına Bağladıkları Değerler*. Ankara: MEB Talim ve Terbiye Dairesi Eğitim Araştırmaları ve Değerlendirme Merkezi, 1962.

Frey, Frederick, and Herbert Hyman. *Rural Development Research Project Report 1: General Description and Evaluation*. Cambridge, MA: MIT, 1967.

Frey, Frederick, Allan Kessler, and Joan Rothchild. *Rural Development Research Project Report No. 2: Index Construction and Validation*. Cambridge, MA: CENIS, 1967.

Frey, Frederick, and Noralou Roos. *Rural Development Research Project Report No. 7: The Propensity to Innovate among Turkish Peasants*. Cambridge, MA: CENIS, 1967.

Frey, Frederick, and Ayşe Sertel. *Rural Development Research Project Report No. 6: Land Ownership and Peasant Orientations in Rural Turkey*. Cambridge, MA: CENIS, 1967.

Frye, Richard, ed. *Islam and the West*. Gravenhage: Mouton, 1957.

Fujimura, Joan. "Crafting Science: Standardized Packages, Boundary Objects, and 'Translation.'" In Pickering, *Science as Practice and Culture*.

Gambetti, Zeynep, and Joost Jongerden, eds. *The Kurdish Issue in Turkey: A Spatial Perspective*. New York: Routledge, 2015.

Gencer, Mustafa. *Jön Türk Modernizmi ve "Alman Ruhu."* Istanbul: Iletisim, 2003.

Gendzier, Irene. *Managing Political Change: Social Scientists and the Third World*. Boulder, CO: Westview Press, 1985.

Ghannam, Farha. *Remaking the Modern: Space, Relocation, and the Politics of Identity in a Global Cairo*. Berkeley: University of California Press, 2002.

Gillespie, James, and Gordon Allport. *Youth's Outlook on the Future*. Garden City, NJ: Doubleday, 1955.

Gilman, Nils. *Mandarins of the Future: Modernization Theory in Cold War America*. Baltimore: Johns Hopkins University Press, 2003.

———. "Modernization Theory, the Highest Stage of American Intellectual History." In *Staging Growth: Modernization, Development and the Global Cold War*, edited by David Engerman, Nils Gilman, Mark Haefele, and Michael Latham. Amherst: University of Massachusetts Press, 2003.

Glock, Charles Young. *Survey Research in the Social Sciences*. New York: Russell Sage Foundation, 1967.

Göle, Nilüfer. "Engineers: 'Technocratic Democracy.'" In *Turkey and the West: Changing Political and Cultural Identities*, edited by Metin Heper, Ayşe Öncü, and Heinz Kramer. New York: IB Tauris, 1993.

Goswami, Manu. *Producing India: From Colonial Economy to National Space*. Chicago Studies in Practices of Meaning. Chicago: University of Chicago Press, 2004.

Grathwol, Robert, and Donita Moorhus. *Bricks, Sand, and Marble: US Army Corps of Engineers Construction in the Mediterranean and Middle East, 1947–1991*. Washington, DC: Center of Military History and Corps of Engineers, United States Army, 2009.

Greenberg, Udi. *The Weimar Century: German Emigres and the Ideological Foundations of the Cold War*. Princeton, NJ: Princeton University Press, 2014.

Gül, Murat. *The Emergence of Modern Istanbul: Transformation and Modernization of a City*. New York: IB Tauris, 2009.

Guldi, Jo. *Roads to Power: Britain Invents the Infrastructure State*. Cambridge, MA: Harvard University Press, 2012.

Gündoğan, Azat Zana. "Space, State-Making and Contentious Kurdish Politics in the East of Turkey: The Case of Eastern Meetings, 1967," *Journal of Balkan and Near Eastern Studies* 13, no. 4 (2011).

Gunnell, John. *The Descent of Political Theory: The Genealogy of an American Vocation*. Chicago: University of Chicago Press, 1993.

Gürel, Meltem Ö. "Seashore Readings: The Road from Sea Baths to Summerhouses in Mid-Twentieth Century Izmir." In *Mid-Century Modernism in Turkey: Architecture Across Cultures in the 1950s and 1960s*, edited by Meltem Ö. Gürel. New York: Routledge, 2016.

Gűven, Dilek. *Cumhuriyet Dőnemi Azınlık Politikalari ve Stratejileri Bağlamında 6–7 Eylül Olayları*. Istanbul: Tarih Vakfı Yurt Yayınları, 2005.

Hacking, Ian. *The Taming of Chance*. Cambridge, UK: Cambridge University Press, 1990.

Harris, George. *Troubled Alliance; Turkish-American Problems in Historical Perspective, 1945–1971*. AEI-Hoover Policy Studies 2. Washington, DC: American Enterprise Institute for Public Policy Research, 1972.

Hartmann, Robert. *Uncle Sam in Turkey*. New York: Turkish Information Office, 1951.

Harvey, David. *The Condition of Postmodernity: An Enquiry into the Origins of Cultural Change*. Cambridge, MA: Blackwell, 1990.

Harvey, Penny, and Hannah Knox. *Roads: An Anthropology of Infrastructure and Expertise*. Ithaca, NY: Cornell University Press, 2015.

Hazbun, Waleed. *Beaches, Ruins, Resorts: The Politics of Tourism in the Arab World*. Minneapolis: University of Minnesota Press, 2008.

Helling, Barbara, and George Helling. *Rural Turkey: A New Socio-Statistical Approach*. Istanbul: Istanbul Üniversitesi İktisat Fakültesi, 1958.

Herring, Pendleton. "The Social Sciences in Modern Society." *Items* 1, no. 1 (March 1947).

Highway Transportation in Turkey. Ankara: Turkish General Directorate of Highways, 1957.

Hilton, Conrad. *Be My Guest*. New York: Simon & Schuster, 1994.

"Hilton's Newest Hotel." *Architectural Forum*, December 1955.

Hitchcock, Henry Russell. Introduction to *Architecture of Skidmore, Owings & Merill, 1950–1962*, by Ernst Danz. New York: Frederick A. Praeger, 1963.

Hitchcock, William. "The Marshall Plan and the Creation of the West." In Leffler and Westad, *Cambridge History of the Cold War*.

Hodge, Joseph Morgan. *Triumph of the Expert: Agrarian Doctrines of Development and the Legacies of British Colonialism*. Athens: Ohio University Press, 2007.

———. "Writing the History of Development (Part 2: Longer, Deeper, Wider)." *Humanity* 7, no. 1 (2016).

Hogan, Michael. *The Marshall Plan: America, Britain, and the Construction of Western Europe, 1947–1952*. Cambridge, UK: Cambridge University Press, 1987.

Holt, Robert T., and John E. Turner, eds. *The Methodology of Comparative Research*. New York: The Free Press, 1970.

Huber, Matthew. *Lifeblood: Oil, Freedom, and the Forces of Capital*. Minneapolis: University of Minnesota Press, 2013.

Hull, Matthew. "Democratic Technologies of Speech: From World War II America to Postcolonial Delhi." *Journal of Linguistic Anthropology* 20, no. 2 (2010): 257–82.

———. "Documents and Bureaucracy." *Annual Review of Anthropology* 41 (2012): 251–67.

———. *Government of Paper: The Materiality of Bureaucracy in Urban Pakistan*. Berkeley: University of California Press, 2012.

Huntington, Samuel. "Change to Change: Modernization, Development and Politics." *Comparative Politics* 3 (1971).

———. "Political Development and Political Decay." *World Politics* 17, no. 3 (1965): 386–430.

———. *Political Order in Changing Societies*. New Haven, CT: Yale University Press, 1968.

Hyman, Herbert. *Interviewing in Social Research*. Chicago: University of Chicago Press, 1954.

———. "Mass Media and Political Socialization: The Role of Patterns of Communication." In Pye, *Communications and Political Development*, p. 145.

———. "Research Design." In Ward, *Studying Politics Abroad*, 182.

———. "Studying Expert Informants by Survey Methods: A Cross-National Inquiry." *The Public Opinion Quarterly* 31, no. 1 (Spring 1967): 9–26.

———. *Taking Society's Measure: A Personal History of Survey Research*. New York: Russell Sage Foundation, 1991.

Hyman, Herbert, Arif Payaslıoğlu, and Frederick Frey. "The Values of Turkish College Youth." *The Public Opinion Quarterly* 22, no. 3 (Autumn 1958): 275–91.

Igo, Sarah. *The Averaged American: Surveys, Citizens, and the Making of a Mass Public*. Cambridge, MA: Harvard University Press, 2007.

Iğsız, Aslı. *Humanism in Ruins: Biopolitics, Culture and the Entangled Legacies of the 1923 Greek-Turkish Population Exchange*, forthcoming.

Immerwahr, Daniel. *Thinking Small: The United States and the Lure of Community Development*. Cambridge, MA: Harvard University Press, 2015.

İnalcık, Halil. "Türkiye ve Japonya'nın Siyasi Modernleşmesi Üzerine Bir Konferans." *Türk Kültürü* 1 (November 1962): 50.

Inkeles, Alex, and David Smith. *Becoming Modern: Individual Change in Six Developing Countries*. Cambridge, MA: Harvard University Press, 1974.

Ireland, Geoffrey. *Türkiye'de Karayolları Nakliyat İdaresi*. Ankara: Karayolları Genel Müdürlüğü, 1961.

"Istanbul Hilton." *The Hotel Monthly*, November 1955.

Jameson, Frederic. *A Singular Modernity: Essay on the Ontology of the Present*. London: Verso, 2002.

Joint Committee on the Economic Report. *Highways and the Nation's Economy*, prepared with BPR representatives. Washington, DC: US Government Printing Office, 1950.

Jones, Toby. *Desert Kingdom: How Oil and Water Forged Modern Saudi Arabia*. Cambridge, MA: Harvard University Press, 2011.

Jongerden, Joost. *The Settlement Issue in Turkey and the Kurds: An Analysis of Spatial Policies, Modernity and War*. Leiden: Brill, 2007.

Joyce, Patrick. *The Rule of Freedom: Liberalism and the Modern City*. London: Verso, 2003.

Kaçel, Ela. "Intellectualism and Consumerism: Ideologies, Practices and Criticisms of Common Sense Modernism in Postwar Turkey." PhD diss., Cornell University, 2009.

Kağıtçıbaşı, Çiğdem. "Sosyal İlim Metodolojisi." In *Türkiye'de Sosyal Araştırmaların Gelişmesi: Hacettepe Nüfus Etütleri Enstitüsü ve Türk Sosyal Bilimler Derneği Seminerinde Sunulan Bildiriler*. Ankara: Hacettepe Üniversitesi Yayınları, 1971.

Kahin, George McT., Guy Pauker, and Lucian Pye. "Comparative Politics of Non-Western Countries." *The American Political Science Review* 49, no. 4 (December 1955): 1022–41.

Karaömerlioğlu, Asım. "Elite Perceptions of Land Reform in Early Republican Turkey." *Journal of Peasant Studies* 27, no. 3 (2000): 115–41.

———. "Turkey's 'Return' to Multi-Party Politics: A Social Interpretation." *East European Quarterly* 40, no. 1 (2006): 97.

———. "The Village Institutes Experience in Turkey." *British Journal of Middle Eastern Studies* 25, no. 1 (1998): 47–73.

Karpat, Kemal, ed. *Social Change and Politics in Turkey: A Structural-Historical Analysis*. Leiden: E. J. Brill, 1973.

———. "Social Effects of Farm Mechanization in Turkish Villages." *Social Research* 27, no. 1 (1960).

———. *Turkey's Foreign Policy in Transition, 1950–1974*. Vol. 17, Social, Economic, and Political Studies of the Middle East. Leiden: E. J. Brill, 1975.

———. *Turkey's Politics: The Transition to a Multi-Party System*. Princeton, NJ: Princeton University Press, 1959.

Kasaba, Reşat, ed. *The Cambridge History of Turkey, Volume 4*. Cambridge: Cambridge University Press, 2006.

———. *A Moveable Empire: Ottoman Nomads, Migrants and Refugees*. Seattle: University of Washington Press, 2009.

———. "Populism and Democracy in Turkey, 1946–1961." In *Rules and Rights in the Middle East: Democracy, Law, and Society*, edited by Ellis Goldberg, Reşat Kasaba, and Joel Migdal. Seattle: University of Washington Press, 1993.

Kaynar, Mete Kaan, ed. *Türkiye'nin 1950'li Yılları*. Istanbul: Iletisim, 2015.

Kerwin, Robert. "Etatism in Turkey, 1933–50." In *The State and Economic Growth*, edited by Hugh G. J. Aitken. New York: Social Science Research Council, 1959.

———. "The Turkish Roads Program." *Middle East Journal* 4, no. 2 (April 1950): 196–208.

Keyder, Çağlar. "The Political Economy of Turkish Democracy." *New Left Review* 115 (1979): 3–44.

———. *State and Class in Turkey: A Study in Capitalist Development*. London: Verso, 1987.

Keyder, Çağlar, and Şevket Pamuk. "1945 Çiftçiyi Topraklandırma Kanunu Üzerine Tezler." *Yapıt* (Ocak 1984): 52–64.

Khalil, Osamah. *America's Dream Palace: Middle East Expertise and the Rise of the National Security State*. Cambridge. MA: Harvard University Press, 2016.

Khuri-Makdisi, Ilham. *The Eastern Mediterranean and the Making of Global Radicalism, 1860–1914*. Oakland: University of California Press, 2010.

Kıray, Mübeccel. *Ereğli: Ağır Sanayiden Önce Bir Sahil Kasabası*. Ankara: TC Başbakanlık Devlet Planlama Teşkilatı, 1964.

———. *Hayatımda Hiç Arkaya Bakmadım*. Istanbul: Bağlam, 2001.

———. *Yedi Yerleşme Noktasında Turizmle Ilgili Sosyal Yapı Analizi*. Ankara: Turizm ve Tanıtma Bakanlığı, 1964.

Kırbaşlı, Faik. *1920–1972 Döneminde Kalkınmada Öncelikli Yörelere İlişkin Hükümet Programları*. Ankara: TC Başbakanlık Devlet Planlama Teşkilatı, 1973.

Klein, Christina. *Cold War Orientalism: Asia in the Middlebrow Imagination, 1945–1961*. Berkeley: University of California Press, 2003.

Klingensmith, Daniel. *"One Valley and a Thousand": Dams, Nationalism, and Development*. New Delhi: Oxford University Press, 2007.

Kolars, John. *Tradition, Season, and Change in a Turkish Village*. Chicago: University of Chicago Press, 1963.

Kortan, Enis. *Türkiye'de Mimarlık Hareketleri ve Eleştirisi (1950–60)*. Ankara: ODTÜ Mimarlık Fakültesi, 1971.

Koselleck, Reinhart. *Futures Past: On the Semantics of Historical Time*. Translated by Keith Tribe. New York: Columbia University Press, 2004.

Kotef, Hagar. *Movement and the Ordering of Freedom: On Liberal Governances of Mobility*. Durham, NC: Duke University Press, 2015.

Kozat, Burçak Keskin. "Negotiating Modernization through US Foreign Assistance: Turkey's Marshall Plan (1948–1952) Reinterpreted." PhD diss., University of Michigan, 2007.

Kramer, Paul. *The Blood of Government: Race, Empire, the United States, and the Philippines*. Chapel Hill: The University of North Carolina Press, 2006.

Krinsky, Carol. *Gordon Bunshaft of Skidmore, Owings & Merrill*. New York: Architectural History Foundation, 1988.

Kuniholm, Bruce Robellet. *The Origins of the Cold War in the Near East: Great Power Conflict and Diplomacy in Iran, Turkey, and Greece*. Princeton, NJ: Princeton University Press, 1980.

Kuruç, Bilsay. *Belgelerle Türkiye İktisat Politikası, 1929–1932*. Ankara: Ankara Üniversitesi Siyasal Bilgiler Fakültesi, 1988.

———. *Belgelerle Türkiye İktisat Politikası, 1933–1935*. Ankara: Ankara Űniversitesi Siyasal Bilgiler Fakültesi, 1993.

LaPalombara, Joseph, ed. *Bureaucracy and Political Development*. Princeton, NJ: Princeton University Press, 1963.

Larkin, Brian. "The Politics and Poetics of Infrastructure." *Annual Review of Anthropology* 42 (2013): 327–43.

———. *Signal and Noise: Media, Infrastructure, and Urban Culture in Nigeria*. Durham, NC: Duke University Press, 2008.

Laron, Guy. *Origins of the Suez Crisis: Postwar Development Diplomacy and the Struggle over Third World Industrialization, 1945–56*. Baltimore: Johns Hopkins University Press, 2013.

Latham, Michael. "Modernization." In *The Cambridge History of Social Science Vol. 7: The Modern Social Sciences*, edited by Theodore Porter and Dorothy Ross. Cambridge, UK: Cambridge University Press, 2008.

———. *Modernization as Ideology: American Social Science and "Nation Building" in the Kennedy Era*. Chapel Hill: The University of North Carolina Press, 2000.

Latour, Bruno. *The Pasteurization of France*. Cambridge, MA: Harvard University Press, 1988.

———. *Reassembling the Social: An Introduction to Actor-Network-Theory*. Oxford, UK: Oxford University Press, 2005.

———. *Science in Action: How to Follow Scientists and Engineers through Society*. Cambridge, MA: Harvard University Press, 1987.

Law, John. *After Method: Mess in Social Science Research*. New York: Routledge, 2004.

———. "Seeing like a Survey." *Cultural Sociology* 3, no. 2 (2009): 239–56.

Leffler, Melvyn, and Odd Arne Westad, eds. *Cambridge History of the Cold War*. Cambridge, UK: Cambridge University Press, 2012.

Lehman, Robert. "Building Roads and a Highway Administration in Turkey." In *Hands Across Frontiers: Case Studies in Technical Cooperation*, edited by Howard M. Teaf and Peter G. Franck. Ithaca, NY: Publications of the Netherlands Universities Foundation for International Cooperation, 1955.

Lerner, Daniel. "The Grocer and the Chief." *Harper's Magazine*, September 1955.

———. "Interviewing Frenchmen." *American Journal of Sociology* 62, no. 2 (1956): 187–94.

———. Introduction to "Attitude Research in Modernizing Areas." *The Public Opinion Quarterly* 22, no. 3 (Autumn 1958): 217–22.

———. *The Passing of Traditional Society: Modernizing the Middle East*. Glencoe, IL: Free Press, 1958.

———. "A Scale Pattern of Opinion Correlates: Communication Networks, Media Exposure, and Concomitant Responses." *Sociometry* 16, no. 3 (August 1953): 266–71.

———. "Towards a Communication Theory of Modernization: A Set of Considerations." In *Communications and Political Development*. Princeton, NJ: Princeton University Press, 1963.

Lerner, Daniel, and David Riesman. "Self and Society: Reflections on Some Turks in Transition." *Explorations* 5 (June 1955): 67–80.

Lerner, Daniel, and Richard Robinson. "Swords and Ploughshares: The Turkish Army as a Modernizing Force." *World Politics* 13, no. 1 (October 1960): 19–44.

Lewis, Bernard. *The Emergence of Modern Turkey*. Oxford, UK: Oxford University Press, 1961.

Li, Tania. *The Will to Improve: Governmentality, Development, and the Practice of Politics*. Durham, NC: Duke University Press, 2007.

Lilienthal, David. *TVA: Democracy on the March*. New York: Harper and Brothers, 1944.

Lockman, Zachary. *Contending Visions of the Middle East: The History and Politics of Orientalism*. The Contemporary Middle East 3. Cambridge, UK: Cambridge University Press, 2004.

———. *Field Notes: The Making of Middle East Studies in the United States*. Stanford, CA: Stanford University Press, 2016.

Loewenstein, Karl. "Report on the Research Panel on Comparative Government." *The American Political Science Review* 38, no. 3 (June 1944): 540–48.

Long, David, and Brian Schmidt, eds. *Imperialism and Internationalism in the Discipline of International Relations*. Albany: State University of New York Press, 2005.

Lubin, Alex. *Geographies of Liberation: The Making of an Afro-Arab Imaginary*. Chapel Hill: University of North Carolina Press, 2014.

Lybrand, William A., ed. *Proceedings of the Symposium: The US Army's Limited-War Mission and Social Science Research* (Washington, DC: SORO, 1962).

MacCannell, Dean. *The Tourist: A New Theory of the Leisure Class*. New York: Schocken, 1976.

Mackenzie, Donald, Fabian Muniesa, and Lucia Siu, eds. *Do Economists Make Markets? On the Performativity of Economics*. Princeton, NJ: Princeton University Press, 2007.

Macridis, Roy, and Richard Cox. "Seminar Report." *The American Political Science Review* 47, no. 3 (September 1953): 641–57.

Makal, Mahmut. *Kalkinma Masali*. Istanbul: Varlik, 1960.

———. *A Village in Anatolia*. Edited by Paul Stirling. Translated by Wyndham Deedes. London: Vallentine, Mitchell, 1954.

Makdisi, Ussama. *Artillery of Heaven: American Missionaries and the Failed Conversion of the Middle East*. Ithaca, NY: Cornell University Press, 2009.

Mardin, Şerif. *Din ve Ideoloji*. Istanbul: Iletişim, 1983.

———. *Türk Modernleşmesi*. Istanbul: İletişim Yayinlari, 1991.

Markovitz, Irving Leonard. "In Memoriam: Dankwart A. Rustow: Personal Remembrances." *Comparative Politics* 29, no. 3 (1996).

Matthews, A. T. J. *Emergent Turkish Administrators: A Study of the Vocational and Social Attitudes of Junior and Potential Administrators*. Ankara: Turk Tarih Kurumu Basimevi, 1955.

Matthews, Gail. "Modern-Day Role Explored: The Political Scientist and Society." *The Christian Science Monitor*, July 11, 1964.

Matthews, Weldon. "The Kennedy Administration, Counterinsurgency, and Iraq's First Ba'thist Regime." *International Journal of Middle East Studies* 43 (2011): 635–53.

Maxfield, Sylvia, and James H. Nolt. "Protectionism and the Internationalization of Capital: US Sponsorship of Import Substitution Industrialization in the Philippines, Turkey and Argentina." *International Studies Quarterly* 34, no. 1 (March 1990): 49–81.

McAlister, Melani. *Epic Encounters: Culture, Media, and US Interests in the Middle East since 1945*. Berkeley: University of California Press, 2005.

McClintock, Anne. *Imperial Leather: Race, Gender, and Sexuality in the Colonial Contest.* New York: Routledge, 1995.

———. "Paranoid Empire: Specters from Guantánamo and Abu Ghraib." *Small Axe* 13, no. 1 (2009): 50–74.

McClosky, Herbert. *Political Inquiry: The Nature and Uses of Survey Research.* New York: Macmillan, 1969.

McGhee, George. *On the Frontline in the Cold War: An Ambassador Reports.* Westport, CT: Praeger, 1997.

———. "Turkey Joins the West." *Foreign Affairs* 32, no. 4 (July 1954): 617–30.

———. *The US-Turkish-NATO-Middle East Connection: How the Truman Doctrine Contained the Soviets in the Middle East.* New York: St. Martin's Press, 1990.

McKenzie, Brian Angus. *Remaking France: Americanization, Public Diplomacy, and the Marshall Plan.* New York: Berghahn Books, 2005.

Mehta, Uday. *Liberalism and Empire: A Study in Nineteenth-Century British Liberal Thought.* Chicago: University of Chicago Press, 1999.

Merritt, Richard L. *Political Science Enters the 1970s: Abstracts of Papers Presented at the 66th Annual Meeting of the American Political Science Association, September 8–12, 1970, Los Angeles, California.* Washington, DC: American Political Science Association, 1971.

Milne, David. *America's Rasputin: Walt Rostow and the Vietnam War.* New York: Hill and Wang, 2008.

Mitchell, Robert. "Survey Materials Collected in the Developing Countries." In *Comparative Research Across Cultures and Nations*, edited by Stein Rokkan. Publications of the International Social Science Council, no. 8. The Hague: Mouton, 1968.

Mitchell, Timothy. *Carbon Democracy: Political Power in the Age of Oil.* New York: Verso, 2013.

———. *Colonizing Egypt.* Berkeley: University of California Press, 1988.

———. "The Middle East in the Past and Future of Social Science." In Szanton, *The Politics of Knowledge.*

———, ed. *Questions of Modernity.* Minneapolis: University of Minnesota Press, 2000.

———. *Rule of Experts: Egypt, Technopolitics, Modernity.* Berkeley: University of California Press, 2002.

Miyoshi, Masao, and Harry Harootunian, eds. *Learning Places: The Afterlives of Area Studies.* Durham, NC: Duke University Press, 2002.

Monroe, Kristin. "Automobility and Citizenship in Interwar Lebanon." *Comparative Studies of South Asia, Africa, and the Middle East* 34, no. 3 (2014): 518–31.

Moore, Dan Tyler, Jr. *Terrible Game.* New York: Berkley Publishing, 1958.
Morgan, Mary. "Making Measuring Instruments." *History of Political Economy* 33 (2001): 235–51.
———. "'On a Mission' with Mutable Mobiles." *Working Papers on the Nature of Evidence: How Well Do "Facts" Travel?* 34/08 (2008).
Morrison, John. *Alisar: A Unit of Land Occupance in the Kanak Su Basin of Central Anatolia.* Chicago: University of Chicago Press, 1939.
Mrázek, Rudolf. *Engineers of Happy Land: Technology and Nationalism in a Colony.* Princeton, NJ: Princeton University Press, 2002.
Mühendis Nazir. "Demiryollarımızda Nakil Ücretleri." *Kadro* 18 (June 1933).
Mutlu, Yücel. *Bayındırlık Bakanlığı Tarihi.* Ankara: Bayındırlık ve İskan Bakanlığı, 2005.
Naff, Thomas, ed. *Paths to the Middle East: Ten Scholars Look Back.* Albany: State University of New York Press, 1993.
Nedim, Vedat. "Demiryolu Tarife Siyasetimizde İnkılap." *Kadro* 32 (August 1934).
Neumann, Sigmund. "Comparative Politics: A Half-Century Appraisal." *The Journal of Politics* 19, no. 3 (August 1957): 369–90.
———. "The Comparative Study of Politics." *Comparative Studies in Society and History* 1, no. 2 (January 1959): 105–112.
Norris, Jacob. *Land of Progress: Palestine in the Age of Colonial Development, 1905–1948.* Oxford, UK: Oxford University Press, 2013.
Norton, Anne. "Political Science as a Vocation." In *Problems and Methods in the Study of Politics,* edited by Ian Shapiro, Rogers Smith, and Tarek Masoud. Cambridge, UK: Cambridge University Press, 2004.
———. *Reflections on Political Identity.* Baltimore: Johns Hopkins University Press, 1988.
Novick, Peter. *That Noble Dream: The "Objectivity Question" and the American Historical Profession.* Cambridge, UK: Cambridge University Press, 1988.
Nucho, Joanne. *Everyday Sectarianism in Urban Lebanon: Infrastructures, Public Services, and Power.* Princeton, NJ: Princeton University Press, 2016.
Ogborn, Miles. *Indian Ink: Script and Print in the Making of the English East India Company.* Chicago: The University of Chicago Press, 2007.
Oran, Baskın, ed. *Türk Dış Politikası: Kurtuluş Savaşından Bugüne Olgular, Belgeler, Yorumlar. Cilt 1: 1919–1980.* Istanbul: İletişim Yayinlari, 2001.
Oren, Ido. *Our Enemies and US: America's Rivalries and the Making of Political Science.* Ithaca, NY: Cornell University Press, 2003.
Örnek, Cangül. "1950li Yıllarda Amerikan Sosyal Bilim Anlayışının Türkiye'de Disiplinler Üzerinde Yarattığı Metodolojik ve Tematik Etkiler." *Birikim* 123: 2012.
Osborne, Thomas, and Nikolas Rose. "Do the Social Sciences Create Phenomena: The Case of Public Opinion Research." *British Journal of Sociology* 50, no. 3 (1999): 367–96.
Owen, Roger, and Sevket Pamuk. *A History of Middle East Economies in the Twentieth Century.* Cambridge, MA: Harvard University Press, 1998.

Owings, Nathaniel. *The Spaces in Between: An Architect's Journey*. Boston: Houghton Mifflin, 1973.

Ozankaya, Özer. "Japonya'nın Modernleşme Denemesi." *Ankara Üniversitesi SBF Dergisi* 20, no. 1 (1965).

———. "The Stages of Economic Growth." *Ankara Üniversitesi SBF Dergisi* 20, no. 2 (1965).

———. "Toplumsal Değişme Olarak İktisadi Gelişme." *Ankara Üniversitesi SBF Dergisi* 20, no. 1 (1965).

Özdil, İlhan. "A Causative-Diagnostic Analysis of Turkey's Major Problems and a Communicative Approach to Their Solution." PhD diss., Ohio State University, 1954.

Özkan, Suha. "Echoes of Sedad Eldem." In Bozdoğan, Özkan, and Yenal, *Sedad Eldem*.

Packenham, Robert. *Liberal America and the Third World: Political Development Ideas in Foreign Aid and Social Science*. Princeton, NJ: Princeton University Press, 1973.

Parla, Ayşe, and Ceren Özgül. "Property, Dispossession, and Citizenship in Turkey; or, The History of the Gezi Uprising Starts in the Surp Hagop Armenian Cemetery." *Public Culture* 28, no. 3 (2016).

Parmar, Inderjeet. *Foundations of the American Century: The Ford, Carnegie, and Rockefeller Foundations in the Rise of American Power*. New York: Columbia University Press, 2012.

Payaslıoğlu, Arif, and Frederick Frey. "Babalarının Mensup Olduğu Meslekler Bakımından Siyasal Bilgiler Fakültesi Öğrencileri Üzerinde Bir İnceleme." *Ankara Universitesi SBF Dergisi* 13, no. 3 (1958).

Petraeus, David. "Learning Counterinsurgency: Observations from Soldiering in Iraq." *Military Review*, January–February 2006.

Phillips, Sarah. *This Land, This Nation: Conservation, Rural America and the New Deal*. Cambridge, UK: Cambridge University Press, 2007.

Pickering, Andrew, ed. *Science as Practice and Culture*. Chicago: University of Chicago Press, 1992.

Pitts, Jennifer. *A Turn to Empire: The Rise of Imperial Liberalism in Britain and France*. Princeton, NJ: Princeton University Press, 2005.

Poiger, Uta. *Jazz, Rock, and Rebels: Cold War Politics and American Culture in a Divided Germany*. Berkeley: University of California Press, 2000.

Poovey, Mary. *A History of the Modern Fact: Problems of Knowledge in the Sciences of Wealth and Society*. Chicago: University of Chicago Press, 1998.

Popp, Roland. "An Application of Modernization Theory during the Cold War? The Case of Pahlavi Iran." *The International History Review* 30, no. 1 (2008): 76–98.

Porter, Theodore. *Trust in Numbers: The Pursuit of Objectivity in Science and Public Life*. Princeton, NJ: Princeton University Press, 1996.

Porter, Theodore M., and Dorothy Ross, eds. *The Cambridge History of Science Volume 7: The Modern Social Sciences*. Cambridge, UK: Cambridge University Press, 2008.

Prashad, Vijay. *The Darker Nations: A People's History of the Third World*. New York: New Press, 2007.

Pratt, Mary Louise. *Imperial Eyes: Travel Writing and Transculturation*. New York: Routledge, 1992.

Pye, Lucian, ed. *Communications and Political Development*. Princeton, NJ: Princeton University Press, 1963.

———. "The Developing Areas: Field Research in the Developing Areas." In Ward, *Studying Politics Abroad*.

———. "The Non-Western Political Process." *The Journal of Politics* 20, no. 3 (August 1958): 468–86.

Pye, Lucian, and Sidney Verba, eds. *Political Culture and Political Development*. Princeton, NJ: Princeton University Press, 1965.

Qaimmaqami, Linda Williams. "The Catalyst of Nationalization: Max Thornburg and the Failure of Private Sector Developmentalism in Iran, 1947–1951." *Diplomatic History* 19, no. 1 (1995): 1–31.

Quarterly Report on the Marshall Plan in Turkey. Number 7 (4/1/1951–6/30/1951) and number 13 (10/1/1952–12/31/1952). Ankara: Günes, 1964.

Rabinow, Paul. *Reflections on Fieldwork in Morocco*. Berkeley: University of California Press, 1977.

Reed, Howard. "Hacettepe and Middle East Technical Universities: New Universities in Turkey." *Minerva* 13, no. 2 (Summer 1975): 200–235.

———. "A New Force at Work in Democratic Turkey." *Middle East Journal* 7, no. 1 (Winter 1953): 33–44.

"Remarks of Leonard W. Doob." In Lybrand, *Proceedings of the Symposium*.

Ricci, David. *The Tragedy of Political Science: Politics, Scholarship, and Democracy*. New Haven, CT: Yale University Press, 1984.

Riesman, David. Introduction to *The Passing of Traditional Society: Modernizing the Middle East*, by Daniel Lerner. Glencoe, IL: Free Press, 1958.

———. *The Lonely Crowd: A Study of the Changing American Character*. New Haven, CT: Yale University Press, 1950.

Riles, Annelise. "Collateral Expertise: Legal Knowledge in the Global Financial Markets." *Current Anthropology* 51, no. 6 (December 2010): 795–818.

———, ed. *Documents: Artifacts of Modern Knowledge*. Ann Arbor: The University of Michigan Press, 2006.

Robinson, Richard. *The First Turkish Republic: A Case Study in National Development*. Cambridge, MA: Harvard University Press, 1963.

———. "The Lessons of Turkey." *Middle East Journal* 5, no. 4 (1951).

———. *Letters from Turkey*. Reprinted for the Peace Corps by permission of the Institute for Current World Affairs. Istanbul: Robert College, 1965.

———. "A Personal Journey through Time and Space." *Journal of International Business Studies* 25, no. 3 (1994): 435–65.

———. "Tractors in the Village: A Study in Turkey." *Journal of Farm Economics* 34, no. 4 (November 1952): 451–62.

———. "Turkey's Agrarian Revolution and the Problem of Urbanization." *The Public Opinion Quarterly* 22, no. 3 (Autumn 1958): 397–405.

Rodgers, Daniel. "American Exceptionalism Revisited." *Raritan* 24, no. 2 (Fall 2004).

Rohde, Joy. *Armed with Expertise: The Militarization of American Social Research during the Cold War*. Ithaca: Cornell University Press, 2013.

———. "Social Science and Foreign Affairs." In *The Oxford Research Encyclopedia of American History*, edited by Jon Butler. New York: Oxford University Press, 2015.

Rokkan, Stein, ed. *Comparative Research Across Cultures and Nations*. Publications of the International Social Science Council, no. 8. The Hague: Mouton, 1968.

———. "Comparative Survey Analysis: Trends, Issues, Strategies," in *Comparative Survey Analysis*. Vol. 12, Confluence; Surveys of Research in the Social Sciences. The Hague: Mouton, 1969.

Roos, Leslie. "Development versus Distribution: An Attitudinal Study of Turkish Local Administration." *Economic Development and Cultural Change* 17, no. 4 (July 1969): 552–66.

Roos, Leslie, and Noralou Roos. "Secondary Analysis in the Developing Areas." *Public Opinion Quarterly* 31, no. 2 (1967).

Ross, Kristin. *Fast Cars, Clean Bodies: Decolonization and the Reordering of French Culture*. Cambridge, MA: MIT Press, 1995.

Rostow, W. W. *The Stages of Economic Growth: A Non-Communist Manifesto*. Cambridge, UK: Cambridge University Press, 1960.

Rottenburg, Richard. *Far-Fetched Facts: A Parable of Development Aid*. Translated by Allison Brown and Tom Lampert. Cambridge, MA: MIT Press, 2009.

Rudolph, Lloyd, and Susanne Rudolph. "Surveys in India: Field Experience in Madras State." *The Public Opinion Quarterly* 22, no. 3 (Autumn 1958): 235–44.

Ruppert, Evelyn, John Law, and Mike Savage. "Reassembling Social Science Methods: The Challenge of Digital Devices." *Theory, Culture and Society* 30, no. 3 (2013): 22–46.

Rustow, Dankwart. "The Army and the Founding of the Turkish Republic." *World Politics* 11, no. 4 (July 1959): 513–52.

———. "Ataturk as Founder of a State." *Daedalus* 97, no. 3 (Summer 1968): 793–828.

———. "Connections." In Naff, *Paths to the Middle East*.

———. "The Development of Parties in Turkey." In Weiner and LaPalombara, *Political Parties and Political Development*.

———. "Modernization and Comparative Politics: Prospects in Research and Theory." *Comparative Politics* 1, no. 1 (October 1968): 37–51.

———. "Mukayeseli Devlet İdaresi ve Türkiye Üzerine Bir Seminer." *Ankara Universitesi SBF Dergisi* 16, no. 4 (1961): 189–203.

———. "New Horizons for Comparative Politics." *World Politics* 9, no. 4 (July 1957): 530–49.

———. "Politics and Islam in Turkey, 1920–1955." In *Islam and the West*, edited by Richard N. Frye. Gravenhage: Mouton, 1957.

———. *Politics of Modernization and Westernization in the Near East*. Princeton, NJ: Center for International Studies, 1956.

———. "The Politics of the Near East: Southwest Asia and Northern Africa." In Almond and Coleman, *The Politics of the Developing Areas*.

———. "Relevance in Social Science, or the Proper Study of Mankind." *American Scholar* 40, no. 3 (1971).

———. "Transitions to Democracy: Toward a Dynamic Model." *Comparative Politics* 2, no. 3 (April 1970): 337–63.

———. "Transitions to Democracy: Turkey's Experience in Historical and Comparative Perspective." In *State, Democracy, and the Military: Turkey in the 1980s*, edited by Metin Heper and Ahmet Evin. New York: Walter de Gruyter, 1988.

———. *Turkey: America's Forgotten Ally*. New York: Council on Foreign Relations, 1987.

———. "Turkey: The Modernity of Tradition." In Pye and Verba, *Political Culture and Political Development*.

———. *A World of Nations: Problems of Political Modernization*. Washington, DC: The Brookings Institution, 1967.

Sackley, Nicole. "Village Models: Etawah, India, and the Making and Remaking of Development in the Early Cold War." *Diplomatic History* 37, no. 4 (2013): 749–78.

———. "The Village as Cold War Site: Experts, Development, and the History of Rural Reconstruction." *Journal of Global History* 6, no. 3 (2011): 481–504.

Said, Edward. *Orientalism*. New York: Vintage, 1979.

———. *The World, the Text, and the Critic*. Cambridge, MA: Harvard University Press, 1983.

Saunders, Frances Stonor. *The Cultural Cold War: The CIA and the World of Arts and Letters*. New York: New Press, 1999.

Savage, Michael. *Identities and Social Change in Britain since 1940: The Politics of Method*. Oxford, UK: Oxford University Press, 2010.

———. "The 'Social Life of Methods': A Critical Introduction." *Theory, Culture and Society* 30, no. 3 (2013): 3–21.

Schayegh, Cyrus. "Iran's Karaj Dam Affair: Emerging Mass Consumerism, the Politics of Promise, and the Cold War in the Third World." *Comparative Studies in Society and History* 54, no. 3 (2012): 612–43.

Schipper, Frank. "Changing the Face of Europe: European Road Mobility during the Marshall Plan Years." *Journal of Transport History* 28, no. 2 (2007): 211–28.

Schmidt, Brian. *The Political Discourse of Anarchy: A Disciplinary History of International Relations*. Albany: State University of New York Press, 1998.

Scott, James. *Seeing like a State: How Certain Schemes to Improve the Human Condition Have Failed*. New Haven, CT: Yale University Press, 1998.

Secord, James. "Knowledge in Transit." *Isis* 95, no. 4 (December 2004): 654–72.

Seely, Bruce. *Building the American Highway System: Engineers as Policy Makers*. Philadelphia: Temple University Press, 1987.

Seely, Bruce, Donald Klinger, and Gary Klein. "'Push' and 'Pull' Factors in Technology Transfer Moving American-Style Highway Engineering to Europe, 1945–1965." *Comparative Technology Transfer and Society* 2, no. 3 (December 2004): 229–46.

Seikaly, Sherene. *Men of Capital: Scarcity and Economy in Mandate Palestine*. Stanford, CA: Stanford University Press, 2015.

Seiler, Cotten. *Republic of Drivers: A Cultural History of Automobility in America*. Chicago: University of Chicago Press, 2008.

Şen, Leyla. *Türkiye'de Demiryolları ve Karayollarının Gelişim Süreci*. Ankara: Tesav Yayınları, 2003.

Şerif, Muzaffer. *An Outline of Social Psychology*. Rev. ed. New York: Harper, 1956.

Shah, Hemant. *The Production of Modernization: Daniel Lerner, Mass Media, and the Passing of Traditional Society*. Philadelphia: Temple University Press, 2011.

Shapin, Steven, and Simon Schaffer. *Leviathan and the Air-Pump: Hobbes, Boyle, and the Experimental Life*. Princeton, NJ: Princeton University Press, 1985.

Sheller, Mimi, and John Urry. "Places to Play, Places in Play." In *Tourism Mobilities: Places to Play, Places in Play*, edited by Mimi Sheller, and John Urry. London: Routledge, 2004.

Shissler, Holly. "'If You Ask Me': Sabiha Sertel's Advice Column, Gender Equity, and Social Engineering in the Early Turkish Republic." *Journal of Middle East Women's Studies* 3, no. 2 (Spring 2007): 1–30.

Simpson, Bradley. *Economists with Guns: Authoritarian Development and US-Indonesian Relations, 1960–1968*. Stanford, CA: Stanford University Press, 2008.

Simpson, Christopher. *Science of Coercion: Communication Research and Psychological Warfare, 1945–1960*. New York: Oxford University Press, 1994.

———, ed. *Universities and Empire: Money and Politics in the Social Sciences During the Cold War*. New York: New Press, 1998.

Sketches from Turkish Life: The Road Comes to the Village. New York: Turkish Information Office, 1950.

Skidmore, Owings and Merrill. *Construction, Town Planning and Housing in Turkey*. New York: Skidmore, Owings and Merrill, 1951.

Social Aspects of Economic Development: A Report of the International Conference on Social Aspects of Economic Development, Istanbul, August 4–24, 1963, sponsored by the Economic and Social Studies Conference Board. Istanbul: Istanbul Matbaasi, 1964.

Smith, Benjamin. "Some Notes on the Social Science Research Council and the Governing Class Theory of American Politics." In Merritt, *Political Science Enters the 1970s*.

Smith, Jason Scott. *Building New Deal Liberalism: The Political Economy of Public Works, 1933–1956*. Cambridge, UK: Cambridge University Press, 2006.

Star, Susan Leigh, and James Griesemer. "Institutional Ecology, 'Translations' and Boundary Objects: Amateurs and Professionals in Berkeley's Museum of Vertebrate Zoology, 1907–39." *Social Studies of Science* 19, no. 3 (August 1989): 387–420.

Steinmetz, George, ed. *Sociology and Empire: The Imperial Entanglements of a Discipline*. Durham, NC: Duke University Press, 2013.

Stoler, Ann. *Along the Archival Grain: Epistemic Anxieties and Colonial Common Sense*. Princeton, NJ: Princeton University Press, 2009.

Stravrianos, L. S. *Global Rift: The Third World Comes of Age*. New York: William Morrow, 1981.

Suleiman, Ezra. "Dankwart A. Rustow." *Comparative Politics* 29, no. 3 (1996).

Sunar, Lütfi. "Türkiye'de Sosyal Bilimlerde Toplumsal Değişim." *Sosyoloji Dergisi* 29, no. 3 (2014): 83–116.

Szanton, David, ed. *The Politics of Knowledge: Area Studies and the Disciplines*. Berkeley: University of California Press, 2004.

Tanrıyar, Emin. *Dağı Delen Irmak: Kemal H. Karpat Söyleşi Kitabı*. Ankara: Imge, 2008.

Tapan, Mete. "International Style: Liberalism in Architecture." In Evin and Holod, *Modern Turkish Architecture*.

Teaf, Howard M., and Peter G. Franck, eds. *Hands Across Frontiers: Case Studies in Technical Cooperation*. Ithaca: Publications of the Netherlands Universities Foundation for International Cooperation, 1955.

Tekeli, Ilhan. "Involuntary Displacement and the Problem of Resettlement in Turkey from the Ottoman Empire to the Present." *Center for Migration Studies* 11, no. 4 (2012): 202–26.

———. *Modernizm, Modernite ve Türkiye'nin Kent Planlama Tarihi*. Istanbul: Tarih Vakfi Yurt Yayinlari, 2009.

Tekeli, Ilhan, and Selim Ilkin. *Cumhuriyetin Harcı: Modernin Altyapısı Oluşurken*. Istanbul: Bilgi Üniversitesi Yayınları, 2004.

———. *Savaş Sonrası Ortamında 1947 Türkiye İktisadi Kalkınma Planı*. Ankara: ODTÜ, 1974.

Tezel, Yahya. *Cumhuriyet Döneminin İktisadi Tarihi*. Ankara: Yurt Yayıncılık, 1982.

Thomas, Lewis. Foreword to *A Village in Anatolia*, by Mahmut Makal. Edited by Paul Stirling. Translated by Wyndham Deedes. London: Vallentine, Mitchell, 1954.

Thomas, Lewis, and Richard Frye. *The United States and Turkey and Iran*. Cambridge, MA: Harvard University Press, 1951.

Thompson, E. P. "Time, Work-Discipline, and Industrial Capitalism." *Past and Present* 38 (December 1967): 56–97.

Thornburg, Max. "The Middle East and the American Engineer." *Journal of Engineering Education* 39 (March 1949).

———. *People and Policy in the Middle East: A Study of Political Change as a Basis for United States Policy*. New York: Norton, 1964.

———. *Turkey: An Economic Appraisal*. New York: The Twentieth Century Fund, 1949.

Tilley, Helen. *Africa as a Living Laboratory: Empire, Development, and the Problem of Scientific Knowledge, 1870–1950*. Chicago: University of Chicago Press, 2011.

Timur, Taner. *Türkiye'de Çok Partili Hayata Geçiş*. Istanbul: Iletişim, 1991.

Tipps, Dean. "Modernization Theory and the Comparative Study of Societies: A Critical Perspective." *Comparative Studies in Society and History* 15, no. 2 (March 1973): 199–226.

Tőren, Tolga. *Yeniden Yapılanan Dünya Ekonomisinde Marshall Planı ve Türkiye Uygulaması*. Istanbul: Sosyal Araştırmalar Vakfı, 2007.

"Tourist Hotel for Istanbul, Turkey." *Architectural Record* 113 (1953).

Trentin, Massimiliano. "Modernization as State-Building: The Two Germanies in Syria, 1962–1972." *Diplomatic History* 33, no. 3 (2009): 487–505.

Truman, Harry S. "Inaugural Speech." January 20, 1949, https://www.trumanlibrary.org/whistlestop/50yr_archive/inagural20jan1949.htm.

Tsing, Anna. *Friction: An Ethnography of Global Connection*. Princeton, NJ: Princeton University Press, 2005.

Tuğal, Cihan. *The Fall of the Turkish Model: How the Arab Uprisings Brought Down Islamic Liberalism*. New York: Verso, 2016.

"Turistik Otel." *Arkitekt* V, no. 243–44 (1952).

Turkish Roads and Highways. New York: Turkish Information Office, 1950.

Türkiye'de Sosyal Araştırmaların Gelişmesi: Hacettepe Nüfus Etütleri Enstitüsü ve Türk Sosyal Bilimler Derneği Seminerinde Sunulan Bildiriler. Ankara: Hacettepe Üniversitesi Yayınları, 1971.

Turner, Louis, and John Ash. *The Golden Hordes: International Tourism and the Pleasure Periphery*. New York: St. Martin's Press, 1975.

Tütengil, Cavit Orhan. *İçtimai ve İktisadi Bakımdan Türkiye'nin Karayolları*. Istanbul: Elif Kitabevi, 1961.

Űlgener, Sabri. "Value Patterns of Traditional Societies: Turkish Experience." In *Social Aspects of Economic Development*.

Ülman, Haluk, and Frank Tachau. "Turkish Politics: The Attempt to Reconcile Rapid Modernization with Democracy." *Middle East Journal* 19, no. 2 (Spring 1965): 153–68.

Ünalın, Çetin. *Cumhuriyet Mimarlığının Kuruluşu ve Kurumlaşması Sürecinde Türk Mimarlar*. Ankara: Mimarlar Derneği, 2002.

Űngőr, Uğur Űmit. *The Making of Modern Turkey: Nation and State in Eastern Anatolia, 1913–1950*. Oxford, UK: Oxford University Press, 2011.

United States Department of State. *Aid to Turkey: Agreement between the United States of America and Turkey*. Washington, DC: Government Printing Office, 1947.

Uysal, Şefik. "Türkiye'de Yapılan Sosyolojik Araştırmalar." In *Türkiye'de Sosyal Araştırmaların Gelişmesi: Hacettepe Nüfus Etütleri Enstitüsü ve Türk Sosyal Bilimler Derneği Seminerinde Sunulan Bildiriler*. Ankara: Hacettepe Üniversitesi Yayınları, 1971.

Vanderlippe, John. *The Politics of Turkish Democracy: Ismet Inönü and the Formation of the Multi-Party System, 1938–1950*. Albany: State University of New York Press, 2005.

Vanlı, Şevki. "Hiltonculuk." *Kim*, November 28, 1958.

Van Vleck, Jenifer. "An Airline at the Crossroads of the World: Ariana Afghan Airlines, Modernization, and the Global Cold War." *History and Technology* 25, no. 1 (2009): 3–24.

———. *Empire of the Air: Aviation and the American Ascendancy*. Cambridge, MA: Harvard University Press, 2013.

Verba, Sidney. "The Uses of Survey Research in the Study of Comparative Politics: Issues and Strategies." *Historical Social Research* 18, no. 2 (1993): 55–103.

Vitalis, Robert. *America's Kingdom: Mythmaking on the Saudi Oil Frontier*. Stanford, CA: Stanford University Press, 2006.

———. "The Midnight Ride of Kwame Nkrumah and Other Fables of Bandung (Ban-Doong)." *Humanity* 4, no. 2 (2013).

———. *White World Order, Black Power Politics*. Ithaca, NY: Cornell University Press, 2015.

Von Eschen, Penny. *Satchmo Blows Up the World: Jazz Ambassadors Play the Cold War*. Cambridge, MA: Harvard University Press, 2006.

Ward, Robert, ed. *Studying Politics Abroad: Field Research in the Developing Areas*. Boston: Little, Brown, 1964.

Ward, Robert, and Dankwart Rustow, eds. *Political Modernization in Japan and Turkey*. Studies in Political Development 3. Princeton, NJ: Princeton University Press, 1964.

Watenpaugh, Keith David. *Being Modern in the Middle East: Revolution, Nationalism, Colonialism, and the Arab Middle Class*. Princeton, NJ: Princeton University Press, 2012.

Wedeen, Lisa. "Scientific Knowledge, Liberalism, and Empire: American Political Science in the Modern Middle East." In *Middle East Studies for the New Millennium: Infrastructures of Knowledge*, edited by Shami Seteney and Cynthia Miller-Idris. New York: Social Science Research Council, 2016.

Weiker, Walter. *The Turkish Revolution, 1960–1961: Aspects of Military Politics*. Washington, DC: Brookings Institution, 1963.

Weiner, Myron. "Political Interviewing." In Ward, *Studying Politics Abroad*.

Weiner, Myron, and Joseph LaPalombara, eds. *Political Parties and Political Development*. Studies in Political Development 6. Princeton, NJ: Princeton University Press, 1966.

Westad, Odd Arne. *The Global Cold War: Third World Interventions and the Making of Our Times*. Cambridge, UK: Cambridge University Press, 2009.

Wharton, Annabel Jane. *Building the Cold War: Hilton International Hotels and Modern Architecture*. Chicago: University of Chicago Press, 2001.

Yasa, İbrahim. *Hasanoğlan: Socio-Economic Structure of a Turkish Village*. Ankara: TODAIE, 1957.

Yavaşça, Kerem. "'Sark Meselesi'nden 'Doğu Sorunu'na: Ellili Yıllarda Kürt Sorunu." In Kaynar, *Türkiye'nin 1950'li Yılları*.

Yeğen, Mesut. "Turkish Nationalism and the Kurdish Question." *Ethnic and Racial Studies* 30, no. 1 (2007).

Yıldırım, Kadir, and Marc Lynch. "Is There Still Hope for Turkish Democracy?" *POMEPS Studies 22: Contemporary Turkish Politics* (December 7, 2016).

Yıldırım, Yavuz, and Suha Özkan. "Finding a National Idiom: The First National Style." In Evin and Holod, *Modern Turkish Architecture*.

Yıldırmaz, Sinan. *From "Imaginary" to "Real": A Social History of the Peasantry in Turkey (1945–1960)*, PhD Diss., Boğaziçi University, 2009.

Yol Davamız: 9 Yılda 23000 Kilometre. Ankara: Bayındırlık Bakanlığı, 1948.

Yollar Türk Milli Komitesi. *Karayolları Genel Müdürlüğü'nün Kurucusu Vecdi Diker'in Ardından* (Ankara: YTKM, 1998).

Yörük, Erdem. "Welfare Provision as Political Containment: The Politics of Social Assistance and the Kurdish Conflict in Turkey." *Politics & Society* 40, no. 517 (2012): 517–47.

Zeydanlıoğlu, Welat. "The White Turkish Man's Burden: Orientalism, Kemalism and the Kurds in Turkey." In *Neo-Colonial Mentalities in Contemporary Europe? Language and Discourse in the Construction of Identities*, edited by Guido Rings and Anne Ife, 155–74. Newcastle upon Tyne: Cambridge Scholars Publishing, 2008.

Zimmerman, Andrew. *Alabama in Africa: Booker T. Washington, the German Empire, and the Globalization of the New South.* Princeton, NJ: Princeton University Press, 2012.

Zürcher, Erik Jan. *Turkey: A Modern History.* London: IB Tauris, 1998.

Index

Stanford Studies in Middle Eastern and Islamic Societies and Cultures

---

Elif M. Babül, *Bureaucratic Intimacies: Translating Human Rights in Turkey*
2017

Maha Nassar, *Brothers Apart: Palestinian Citizens of Israel and the Arab World*
2017

Orit Bashkin, *Impossible Exodus: Iraqi Jews in Israel*
2017

Asef Bayat, *Revolution without Revolutionaries: Making Sense of the Arab Spring*
2017

Nahid Siamdoust, *Soundtrack of the Revolution: The Politics of Music in Iran*
2017

Laure Guirguis, *Copts and the Security State: Violence, Coercion, and Sectarianism in Contemporary Egypt*
2016

Michael Farquhar, *Circuits of Faith: Migration, Education, and the Wahhabi Mission*
2016

Gilbert Achcar, *Morbid Symptoms: Relapse in the Arab Uprising*
2016

Jacob Mundy, *Imaginative Geographies of Algerian Violence: Conflict Science, Conflict Management, Antipolitics*
2015

Ilana Feldman, *Police Encounters: Security and Surveillance in Gaza under Egyptian Rule*
2015

Tamir Sorek, *Palestinian Commemoration in Israel: Calendars, Monuments, and Martyrs*
2015

Adi Kuntsman and Rebecca L. Stein, *Digital Militarism: Israel's Occupation in the Social Media Age*
2015

Laurie A. Brand, *Official Stories: Politics and National Narratives in Egypt and Algeria*
2014

Kabir Tambar, *The Reckonings of Pluralism: Citizenship and the Demands of History in Turkey*
2014

Diana Allan, *Refugees of the Revolution: Experiences of Palestinian Exile*
2013

Shira Robinson, *Citizen Strangers: Palestinians and the Birth of Israel's Liberal Settler State*
2013

Joel Beinin and Frédéric Vairel, editors, *Social Movements, Mobilization, and Contestation in the Middle East and North Africa*
2013 (Second Edition), 2011

Ariella Azoulay and Adi Ophir, *The One-State Condition: Occupation and Democracy in Israel/Palestine*
2012

Steven Heydemann and Reinoud Leenders, editors, *Middle East Authoritarianisms: Governance, Contestation, and Regime Resilience in Syria and Iran*
2012

Jonathan Marshall, *The Lebanese Connection: Corruption, Civil War, and the International Drug Traffic*
2012

Joshua Stacher, *Adaptable Autocrats: Regime Power in Egypt and Syria*
2012

Bassam Haddad, *Business Networks in Syria: The Political Economy of Authoritarian Resilience*
2011

Noah Coburn, *Bazaar Politics: Power and Pottery in an Afghan Market Town*
2011

The authorized representative in the EU for product safety and compliance is:
Mare Nostrum Group
B.V Doelen 72
4831 GR Breda
The Netherlands

www.ingramcontent.com/pod-product-compliance
Lightning Source LLC
Chambersburg PA
CBHW020502270326
41926CB00008B/713

* 9 7 8 1 5 0 3 6 0 5 5 4 1 *